Information Systems Reengineering, Integration and Normalization

Joseph S. P. Fong • Kenneth Wong Ting Yan

Information Systems Reengineering, Integration and Normalization

Heterogeneous Database Connectivity

4th edition

Springer

Joseph S. P. Fong
Department of Computer Science,
Rm AC1- Y6418
City University of Hong Kong
Kowloon, Kowloon, Hong Kong

Kenneth Wong Ting Yan
International Hybrid Learning Society
Lantau Island, Hong Kong

ISBN 978-3-030-79583-2 ISBN 978-3-030-79584-9 (eBook)
https://doi.org/10.1007/978-3-030-79584-9

This Springer imprint is published by the registered company Springer Nature Switzerland AG
The registered company address is: Gewerbestrasse 11, 6330 Cham, Switzerland

To the memory of my parents Fong Chung Lung and Sun Oil Yuk

Preface

Over the past three decades, there has been a tremendous investment made in information systems. Such systems have evolved from file systems through database systems, and we are now seeing the emergence of management information systems (MIS) and executive information systems (EIS). With the advent of each new form of technology, there has been a need to redesign and re-implement existing information systems.

In recent years, a great deal of resources has been put into the area of reengineering. Reengineering involves the redesign of existing information systems, while using as much of the existing systems as possible. That is, the approach taken is to transform the existing information systems into the format needed for the new technology, rather than to throw away the old systems. Such an approach has obvious benefits, particularly if it can be automated and/or supported by methods and tools.

Very often, a large company has multiple heterogeneous databases for MIS operations. The company needs to integrate them into a corporate database for its decision support systems. Subsequently, schemas integration must be performed to resolve the conflicts between two databases with respect to data name, data type, and data semantics. Schemas integration must be done before data integration, which is mainly concerned with the automation of loading data from source databases into an integrated database. Furthermore, in reality, user demands are changing daily. It is essential for companies to enhance and evolve the existing database schemas to meet the new data requirements.

Database normalization aims to remove irregularity and abnormality of update. In un-normal database, it is difficult to maintain the correctness of database after update. Relational data normalization is to eliminate data redundancy and update irregularity of relational schema. Irregularity of database design must be normalized in order to ensure user friendliness of updating data. Similarly, we need to normalize nonrelational database such as XML document to get rid of their repeating redundant data, and also to normalize their XML schema design to ensure good performance in accessing data.

This book will focus upon practical approaches to information systems reengineering and integration, including:

- The conversion of hierarchical or network database systems into relational database technology, or from a relational to an object-oriented database and XML database.
- The schemas integration includes the integration of relational schemas, and the integration of XML schemas according to the relevance of the schemas.
- The integration of multiple databases, and also between a database system and an expert system to produce MIS (management information systems) and EIS (executive information systems).

The book will summarize the concepts, the approach to be taken, and the benefits to be gained in the above crucial technological areas. It will focus upon proven methods and tools for:

- Converting hierarchical and network databases to relational technology, or from relational to object-oriented databases, or from relational to XML databases.
- Reengineering existing systems to produce MIS and EIS.
- Normalizing relational database and XML schema design.

The book will describe in detail:

- Database conversion techniques
- Reverse engineering and forward engineering for data modeling
- A reengineering methodology for information systems
- Techniques of schemas and data integration
- Normalize database to eliminate redundant data

From a professional point of view, this book proposes a general solution for the problem of system migration to new database technology. It offers a systematic software engineering approach for reusing existing database systems built with "old" technology by converting them into the "new" database technology. As a result, investment in the existing information systems can be protected by upgrading database systems and expert systems, rather than phasing them out.

This book focuses on methodologies for information systems reengineering, integration, and normalization for the interoperability of their database systems. It applies many examples, illustrations, and case studies of procedures for reusing existing database systems and information systems. The objective is to make the methodologies very practical for readers to follow. Even though there are many technical terminologies used in the book, the techniques proposed are simple enough for students or computer professionals to follow. The content of the book is divided into ten chapters.

Chapter 1 gives an overview of information systems, and deals with its past history, its evolution to management information systems, its problems encountered in file systems, its solution found in database systems and expert systems, and the need for the reengineering of existing database systems and information systems. It also describes database conversion, the merger of multiple databases, and the integration of the expert systems and the database systems into an expert database system. It shows how to apply data transformation for electronic data interchange on the Internet.

Chapter 2 describes basic theories and data structures of various data models, including hierarchical, network, relational, object-oriented, and XML. Their pros and cons are discussed. Expert systems technology is explained. The advanced expert database systems are introduced. The basic concepts discussed include data definition language, data manipulation language, forward chaining, backward chaining, procedural language and non-procedural language, data type definition, and XML schema definition.

Chapter 3 covers various techniques in schema translation from nonrelational to relational, and from relational to object-oriented and XML databases. Reverse engineering is adopted to recover original schema's semantics into the conceptual model of the Extended Entity Relationship (EER) model. Forward engineering is used to map the EER model into relational or Unified Model Language (UML), a conceptual model for an object-oriented database.

Chapter 4 shows a methodology of converting data from nonrelational database to relational database, and from relational database to object-oriented database, and also from relational database into XML database. Download and upload processing in a logical level approach is adopted to do the task.

Chapter 5 explains a methodology of emulating SQL by using a hierarchical or network database data manipulation language. The methodology can be used in program translation from relational database programs to nonrelational database programs. The objective is to provide a relational interface to the nonrelational database so that the users can use SQL to access a hierarchical or network database. It also presents a methodology of translating SQL query into OSQL (Object SQL or Object Query Language) and XQL (XML Query Language).

Chapter 6 offers a state-of-the-art methodology for integrating two relational or XML database schemas by resolving their name, data type, and data semantics conflicts with user supervision. The relational, object-relational, or XML data integration can only be done after relational, object-relational, or XML schemas integration for the loading of data into the integrated databases is performed. The rational of schemas integration is based on the application relevance of the schemas. A Frame model metadata is introduced to store data operation for encapsulation in the object-oriented database.

Chapter 7 lays out the rules in integrating expert systems and database systems for the purpose of reengineering. The technique is to transform both expert systems rules and database systems relations into a common Frame model metadata. This Frame model metadata offers object-oriented-like database functions by treating each frame as an object and a collection of objects as a class. Coupling classes, active classes, static classes, and integrated classes are introduced to implement an expert database system (EDS). The users can then apply EDS to develop new applications.

Chapter 8 shows how to normalize un-normal form relational schema into first, second, third, Boyce Codd, fourth, and fifth normal form. On the other hand, the denormalization is the inverse of normalization. It transforms the normalized database design into un-normal form for better performance. As XML document has become a data standard on the Internet, XSD Graph is a conceptual schema to represent the data semantics of XML document. We need to detect and normalize XML schema and document by factorizing their redundant elements into a single unique element in XML Schema Definition.

Chapter 9 shows how to transform legacy database into flattened XML documents back into any other legacy database. The flattened XML document is a mixture of relational and XML data model. The future research of this book is to explore using NoSQL as common data model as a replacement for HDBC.

Chapter 10 summarizes the methodologies proposed by the book. The main theme is that knowledge engineering is a requirement for information systems reengineering, integration, and normalization. We need users' knowledge to assist system developers in reusing existing database systems and expert systems in order to develop new applications. The final result is database systems upgrade, multiple databases integration, and expert systems enhancement to knowledge-based systems. As knowledge engineering becomes important in data processing, the resultant knowledge-based system, that is, the expert database system, will become a very important asset to companies. Heterogeneous Database Connectivity (HDBC) aims to change proprietary data of heterogeneous database into common data model of XML documents and distribute them to the users. If necessary, it also converts the common XML documents into a target database data format to meet user requirements. In fact, it extends the functions of ODBC (open database connectivity) by including databases in different data models.

Kowloon, Kowloon, Hong Kong Joseph S. P. Fong

Lantau Island, Hong Kong Kenneth Wong Ting Yan

Acknowledgments

This book is a tribute to the University of Sunderland in the United Kingdom since the author developed most of the methodologies there.

The author thanks Professor Shi-Ming Huang as the original inventor of Frame model metadata used in the book, and also Dr. Chuk Yau for his joint articles with the author, which contribute the MIS overview in the book. The author appreciates the word-processing work by Shing-han Li in formatting and drawing the diagrams for the book. Special thanks go to Dr. Reggie Kwan and Frances Fong for their review and proofreading of the book. This book is the result of the combined research of the author and his project students such as Chan Kam Lam and others over more than a decade.

Kenneth Wong is an MPhil student of Dr. Joseph Fong, and he helps him with his research in Heterogeneous database connectivity in Chapter 9, which is part of his MPhil thesis at City University of Hong Kong.

Since the topics cover a wide range, the authors provide a forum for readers to ask questions and display their answers, also those by other readers, on the Internet.

Forum: https://hdbc2021.webboard.org/

Kowloon, Kowloon, Hong Kong — Joseph S. P. Fong

Lantau Island, Hong Kong — Kenneth Wong Ting Yan

Contents

Chapter 1
Information Systems Reengineering, Integration, and Normalization

1.1 History of Information Systems

The primary goal of electronic data processing (EDP) in the 1960s and 1970s was the automation of existing business operations in organizations. However, except for the quicker availability of more accurate management reporting information, such operations were automated without fundamental changes. During these two decades, data were stored in flat file formats that could be classified into two different forms, namely, batch files and online files.

Batch Files
Computer applications were initially developed for batch processing where programs would process a specific type of data regularly. Each suite of programs was associated with its own data files. Generally, magnetic tapes were used to hold these files. The sequential nature of the storage medium required the reading and writing of the entire file to reflect any changes to the data stored. Sequential access was simple and effective for batch applications. As more applications were computerized, it became obvious that some of the required data already existed in the data files used by other computer applications.

Online Files
With the advent of direct access storage devices (DASD) and advances in telecommunications, many batch applications were redesigned for online processing. The random sequence of data input by online applications requires a monitor that examines each input transaction and then passes its transaction to the appropriate computer program.

DASD such as magnetic discs made possible the direct retrieval of the required data record for immediate processing. However, the application program had to first calculate the physical location of the data record on disc using an algorithm that

J. S. P. Fong, K. Wong Ting Yan, *Information Systems Reengineering, Integration and Normalization*, https://doi.org/10.1007/978-3-030-79584-9_1

operated on an identifying key. When it became necessary to move the data file to another location on the disc, the program that accessed the file had to be modified.

Indexed sequential access method (ISAM) was developed to help isolate the application programs from changes made to the location of the files on the DASD. ISAM uses the record key to reference an intermediate index stored on the DASD to locate the physical location of the record on the DASD; ISAM then retrieves this record from the data file for presentation to the program. In many cases, application programs needed to access the data record by some identifying key other than the existing indexed sequential key. To reduce some of this data file housekeeping by the application program, generalized routines were written for accessing interrelated records via appropriate record pointers, and updating these pointers to reflect changes in the associated record relationships (e.g., insertion or deletion of records). These generalized routines were the precursors of today's database management systems (DBMS).

Problems in Maintaining File Systems

The structures of conventional files restrict the efficiency and effectiveness of information system applications. For example, changes in the types of information recorded in the files, such as the addition of attributes to its record structure would, at the very least, necessitate the recompilation of all applications accessing the data. The application programs that reference the changed record format may be completely rewritten if modifying the program becomes more complex than completely rewriting it.

As more complex applications are developed, the number of data files referenced by these applications increases. Such proliferation of files means that a minor change in either a data file or a program may snowball into a series of major program modifications, and a maintenance nightmare.

Since the same data exists in several different files, programmers must also maintain the data by updating all the files to ensure the accuracy and consistency of the stored data. In the event of master file corruption or incomplete processing due to system or operational human errors, data processing practitioners must reprocess the various batches of input data against an earlier version of the corrupted master file for data recovery. Further complexity is added to the system to ensure that sensitive data is accessed only by authorized personnel.

Lastly, such file-based systems do not support the requirements of management. Very often, management needs ad hoc reports for decision-making, which requires processing on multiple files in a very short time and adds the burden to file processing systems.

Solution in Converting File Systems to Database Systems

As the requirements of the users increased, a more powerful and flexible data processing system was required. This was achieved by abstracting the routines for the management of data and combining the data files into a large corpus of structured information solutions, known as the database management system (DBMS) or database. With a database system, data can be shared, and data redundancy can be more easily supported. Security and recovery are also more easily implemented by maintaining a database instead of a set of various files. Even database programming can be easier to support because of the standard utilization of a database among all the production application programs. Once the problems of file management are solved through the introduction of database systems, practitioners are able to consider the information needs of the organization in a new light.

Management Information System

Traditionally, an organization is seen as a three-tiered pyramid, where there is strategic planning and policy-making at the top, management planning and control activities in the middle, and routine operational activities at the bottom. The corporate database is composed of data pertaining to the organization, its operations, its plans, and its environment. Figure 1.1 shows all internal and external components and their relationships in a computerized management information system (MIS) (Yau and Fong 1989).

Generally, decisions are executed based on information generated from the corporate database and managerial expertise. Higher-level managers set goals to direct operational-level activities and produce plans that form part of the corporate database. Business transactions reflect actual results of operational activities, and the database is updated by these transactions to reflect the current state of the business. Operational-level managers query the database to perform daily operations. Tactical level managers receive reports derived from the transaction data stored in the database. They compare the actual results shown in these reports with planned results. For managers at the strategic level, they need information for modeling and forecasting. The corporate database supports all levels of information needs for operations, decision-making, and the management process.

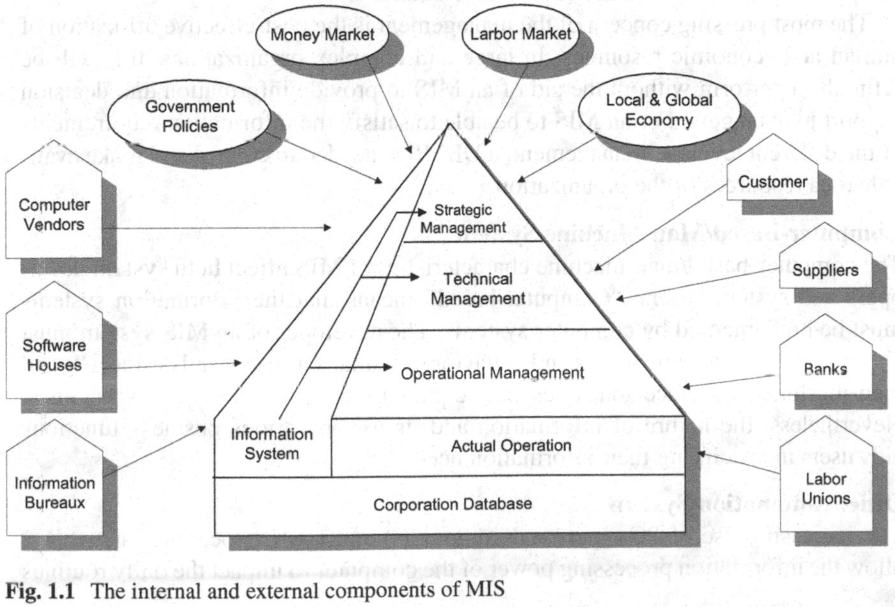

Fig. 1.1 The internal and external components of MIS

When the concept of MIS was first introduced, its supporters envisaged a single system that would integrate all organizational functions. Others doubted the possibility of designing computer-based information systems to support management planning and decision-making functions, particularly at the strategic level. Over the years the concept of a total system proved to be too complex to implement. Now MIS consists of a federation of subsystems, engineered as needed but conforming to the overall organizational plan, standards, and procedures. MIS continues to evolve.

Knowledge and Information Needs

The most fundamental element of MIS and the management process is knowledge/information about the objectives of the organization, as well as its policies, resources, operations, and environment. In today's complex management environment, no individual manager can have sufficient personal knowledge to serve the diverse needs of the organization. Knowledge and information relating to the organization's management and operations must be stored on the computer file system.

The gathering of data and dissemination of information are complex. Data/information is voluminous, scattered, and often difficult and costly to obtain. The costs and complexities of producing various types of management reports usually cause data duplication and uncoordinated efforts within the organization. Often people and departments prefer to duplicate information rather than share, which results in considerable redundancy within the organization.

Departments fail to recognize the importance of interaction within the company. For example, the production department is concerned with maximizing its production capacity, assuming that goods produced can all be sold by the sales department. In order to achieve good organizational congruence, it is essential that activities of these departments be synchronized via an effective information system that enables the various departments to act on the same database.

The most pressing concern of the management is the cost-effective utilization of human and economic resources. In large and complex organizations, this will be difficult to perform without the aid of an MIS to provide information and decision support to managers. For an MIS to be able to satisfy the information requirements of the different levels of management, a DBMS is needed to control and make available data resources of the organization.

Computer-Based/Man-Machine System

The computer-based/man-machine characteristics of MIS affect both system developers and systems users. "Computer-based" means that the information systems must be implemented by computer systems. The developer of an MIS system must also understand the capabilities and behavior of humans as users and define a "good man-machine" interface that does not require users to be computer specialists. Nevertheless, the nature of information and its use in various business functions aids users in specifying their information needs.

Office Automation System

The increasing use of PCs (personal computers) and LANs (local area networks) allow the information processing power of the computer to impact the daily routines and functions of all office workers, including the managers. Intelligent terminals can offer time management, project management, and message management facilities.

Personal terminals aid in project management. A budget and time schedule can be established for each project to allow automatic tracking and status monitoring. Information from monthly status reports on each project can be abstracted, classified, and stored in the database as they are produced, forming a research database. Researchers in the company can interactively search the database by keywords or categories, construct personal databases of relevant research information, and exchange ideas and references with other researchers in the network.

Decision Support Systems

Data ought to be processed and presented so that the result is directed towards the decision at hand. To do this, the processing of data items must be based on a decision model. Models are simplified representations of reality. The models of many business problems are widespread and complex, involving operational research and statistical techniques. A decision support system (DSS) provides information through computer-based modeling facilities to help managers make decisions for relatively unstructured problems.

Traditional information systems have essentially been operational in nature, and attempts to structure these systems to provide management information have had little success because of the ill-defined nature of problems at a strategic level of management. The emergence of the database, PC, 4GL (fourth-generation language), and modeling tools have enabled DSS to partially support management planning and decision-making. Figure 1.2 shows a fundamental structure of DSS.

Expert Systems

Expert systems (ES) have been widely used in our society from technical and medical to financial, teaching, and administrative applications. They are a general term for special software systems that preserve the knowledge of human experts and reason with it. The basic differences between ESs and conventional software systems are:

- Conventional software systems are algorithmic. They produce unique and certain answers, e.g., yes or no.
- ESs, by their nature, are heuristic. The results that they produce are not always unique, nor are they necessarily certain and correct, e.g., yes, no, or unknown.

In recent years, ESs have played an important role in information systems. Their technologies have been used in the more advanced information systems, such as executive information systems (EIS) and executive support systems (ESS). The purpose of the EISs is to assist high-level managers with either information or knowledge relating to an organization's decision processing. Most current EISs generate decision knowledge for an organization by integrating expert systems with databases. The technical term for this type of system is called *expert database systems* (EDS). The ESS often combines DSS and MIS capabilities. ESs usually are the kernel of these types of systems.

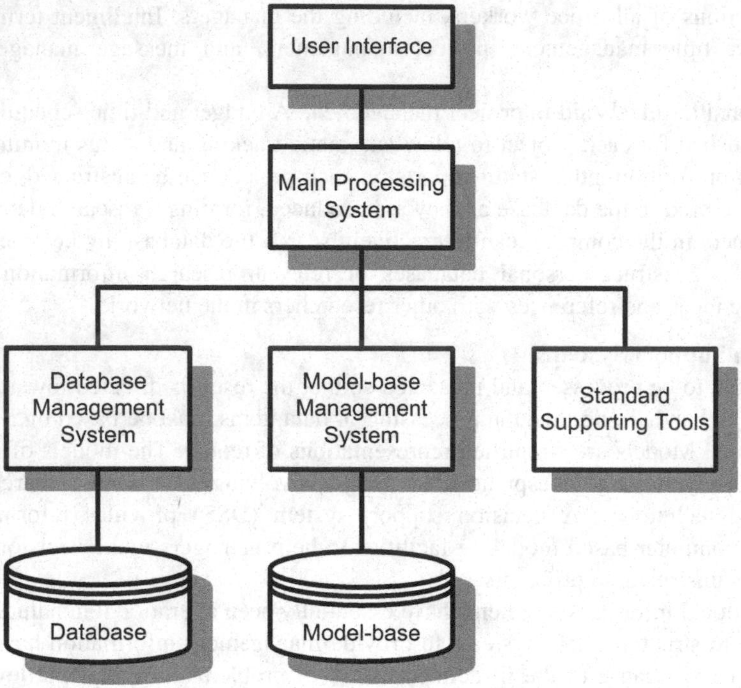

Fig. 1.2 Fundamental structure of decision support system

1.2 The Need

The recent rapid growth in database technology has actually encouraged more installations of database management systems in different kinds of organizations. In addition to new database system installations, there is considerable interest in converting conventional file-oriented systems to database systems and upgrading outdated database systems to newer database technology. The need to compete, reduce costs, and standardize operational procedures make conversions to a new technology a necessity for many organizations. The fact that many large companies still have a large number of sequential file systems indicates a strong need to convert such systems to a database system for better management. The introduction of Internet computing makes the XML model a necessity for most companies.

The concept of a relational database was proposed by E.F. Codd in the 70s. It is recognized as a more user-friendly model than nonrelational (e.g., hierarchical or network) models. However, it was not adopted by the industry until the 80s because of its poor performance. Thanks to the improvements in their performance, relational databases have gained wider industry acceptance. These improvements have created a need to convert data from a nonrelational to a relational structure.

The object-orientated approach to software engineering has recently become popular, with many manufacturers claiming to have object-oriented systems.

Object-oriented modeling is a new way of representing static and dynamic data semantics in the form of objects, links, associations, and methods. Traditional record-based databases (e.g., hierarchical, network, and relational) have been generally used over the past two decades. Organizations with such record-based databases could reengineer their databases into object-oriented databases to capture more semantics of the application domain.

Any medium to a large organization that has an independent EDP department typically has a number of databases. Over the last four decades, a number of database systems have come onto the market using these predominant data models: hierarchical, network, relational, object-oriented, and XML. As a result of this proliferation of systems, many large organizations have found that they must support various types of database systems at the same time. However, as the performance of the relational database systems has improved, they have been accepted by the industry and consequently, created the need to convert a company's nonrelational database systems to relational.

The hierarchical and network database systems use the concept of currency and require users to navigate through the database from one point to the next. This makes them difficult to use for both end users and programmers because of the level of skill and experience required to perform this navigation. On the other hand, a relational database is simpler, as it presents to users relations that resemble files in a manual cabinet file system.

In the hierarchical and network models, the connections between sets of data are hard-coded into the data structure and the addition of a new relationship requires a new access path to be added. In relational databases, access paths are not pre-established but are based upon the matching of values in separate tables using a join operation. This makes a relational database a more flexible system for inquiries required. The predefined relationships of the hierarchical or network structures require a complex data definition language (DDL) and data manipulation language (DML). Maintenance of this predefined relationship is difficult. In the relational model, the DDL and DML are simpler and user-oriented, both having relatively simple maintenance and physical storage conditions. Relational databases can provide better flexibility and data independence. Since an organization's need for information changes over time, and because having a relational database encourages new uses, this flexibility of the relational model is highly desirable. Furthermore, with the increasing use of SQL (Structured Query Language), the portability of application programs using SQL as the DML is improved.

As database technologies evolve from hierarchical and network to relational and object-oriented models, companies need guidelines on how to select a new database system, and what to do with their old and obsolete systems. The database approach to information systems is a long-term investment. It requires a large-scale commitment of an organization's resources in compatible hardware and software, skilled personnel, and management support. Accompanying costs are the education and training of the personnel, conversion of existing applications, and the creation of new documentation. It is essential for an organization to fully appreciate, if not understand, the problems of converting an existing, file-based system to a database system, or upgrading an obsolete database system to a more user-friendly one, and to accept the implications of this operation before they initiate such projects.

Before anything else, the management must decide whether or not the project is a feasible one and if it matches the users' requirements. Costs, timetables, are performance considerations, as well as the availability of expertise are also major concerns.

Management is concerned with a long-term corporate strategy. The database selected must be consistent with the commitments of that corporate strategy. But if the organization does not have a corporate database, then one must be developed before conversion is to take place. Selecting a database must be from the top-down. Data flow diagrams, representing the organization's business functions, processes, and activities should be drawn up first. This should be followed by an Entity-Relationship (ER) model (Chan 1976) detailing the relationships of different business information, and then finally by data modeling. If the ER model has a tree-like structure, then a hierarchical model should be adopted; if the ER model shows a network structure, a network model should be chosen. Otherwise, a relational model should be chosen for a more user-friendly structure, or an object-oriented model should be chosen for a universal structure. For Internet applications, an XML model is needed for e-commerce because XML has become the data standard of Internet computing.

Although there are many theories of database design, many databases are found to be unreliable, difficult to modify, and poor in performance. Database designers face a complicated problem: how to arrange the data and programs on different computers to obtain the intended performance, reliability, and availability. Leaving this problem unsolved will restrict the success of database system reengineering. There is a need for a framework for measuring the quality of converted databases. The following criteria are derived from the requirements of software engineering and database technology:

- Integrity – Only syntactically and semantically correct data should be stored in databases to enforce domain integrity. Referential integrity is another type of semantic integrity such that data cannot exist or be modified unless some precursor data values exist or some actions are taken.
- Traceability – A good database design should support traceability from the requirements down to the physical design stage back through documentation. So traceability is necessary for different phases of database development. Simplification and overload errors can occur in any phase and will affect the degree of traceability.
- Consistency – In distributed database systems, data are often replicated to improve performance and availability. All copies of the same logical data item must agree on exactly one "current value" for the data item. All users within the environment should have a uniform view of the system. If the data are inconsistent, the users cannot share the same information. It is particularly important for parallel applications that partition data into different parts to increase their processing speed. If the partitions are stored in different sites, consistency is a key factor to ensure the correctness of the application.

- Correctness – A database is correct if it correctly describes the external objects and processes that it is intended to model. They use a set of static constraints on objects and their attributes, and a set of dynamic constraints on how objects can interact and evolve. A database is said to be syntactically correct if the concepts are properly defined in the schema at each stage; it is said to be semantically correct if the concepts are used according to their definition at each stage.
- Completeness – A database schema can be defined as complete when the schema represents all relevant features of the application domain. Two major principles can be used to check the completeness of the design: (a) checking all the requirements of the application domain and ensuring that each of them is represented somewhere in the final system; (b) checking to see whether each concept is mentioned in the requirements.
- Efficiency – A database schema can be regarded as an efficient design if the schema (a) can support any processes on the component schema; (b) provides both timely and accurate data access for a given set of queries and transactions.

Information technologists have moved from data processing to information processing and are now moving into the field of knowledge processing. The new term expert database system (EDS) has emerged to refer to an important area in this field. An EDS is a system that results from the integration of expert systems and database management system technology.

Consider the following problem taken from a real application: A personnel manager must find the best person for a particular job, or the best group of people for a particular project (i.e., a project that includes different types of jobs) by considering the total departmental manpower. A common way to solve this problem is to send the employee information and the job vacancy information to a human resource management consultant agency. The experts in this agency will then use their expertise to produce a human resource plan and hence give the manager some suggestions. Figure 1.3 shows the relationship between these components. Taking a system view, the manager is the end user, the human resource consultant is the expert system, and the personnel information and job vacancy information are stored in the database (for detailed information, see Sec. 8.4, which contains a description of a human resource management expert database system).

An easy way to model this application situation is to view each component as an independent module. The system's performance will depend on the performance of each module and communication (i.e., message passing). The normal way for information passing is as follows: The manager (end user) asks the consultant (expert system (ES)) to do a job, then the consultant (ES) analyses this particular job and asks the company (database (DB)) to supply the necessary information that is needed for this particular job. The company (DB) then sends this information to the consultant (ES) and the consultant (ES) uses his/her expertise to generate a result that is sent back to the manager (end user). The consultant may be a foreigner and may not know the local language. Thus sometimes an interpreter (interface) is needed at the same time. It is also necessary to support an open structure to allow any new subsystem to join the system.

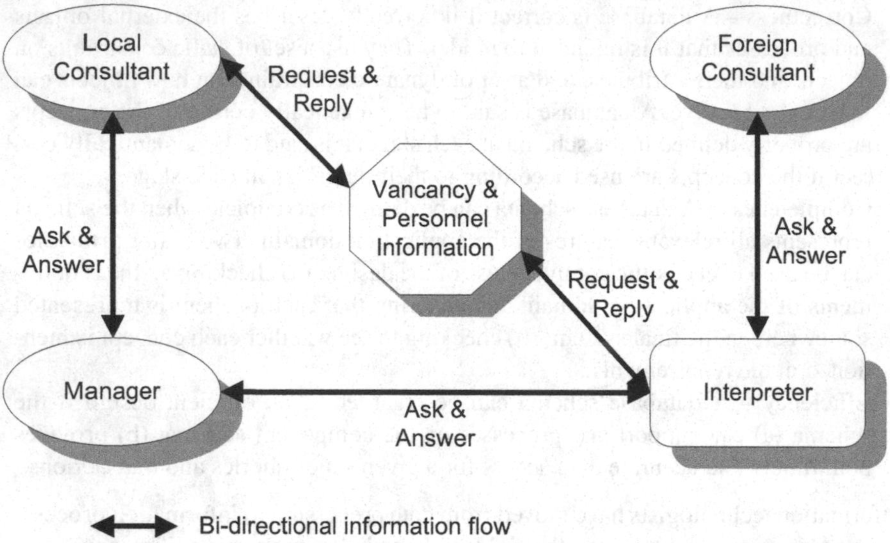

Fig. 1.3 A job vacancy problem application model

EDSs are widely used in the current information systems. Further examples can be found in the areas of business, industry, banking, and retail. For example, a business plan is necessary when planning for future events. A planning manager (end user) asks experts (ES) to analyze the plan and give suggestions by using the company information, market information (DB), and so on.

Current EDS technology still has a long way to go in order to achieve the full requirements of EDSs from the two different viewpoints, i.e. DB users and ES users. The main reasons are that those information systems are complex systems that require multiple environments to deal with different situations. In general, there are four different situations that system developers will meet when designing an EDS.

- Case 1: Building a new EDS. The system developer must create a new database(s) and expert system(s) for the EDS. No usable systems exist.
- Case 2: Reusing expert system(s). The system developer reuses existing expert system(s) and builds new database(s) for the EDS.
- Case 3: Reusing database(s). The system developer reuses existing database(s) and builds new expert system(s) for the EDS.
- Case 4: Reusing both database(s) and expert system(s). The system developer reuses both existing database(s) and expert system(s) in the EDS.

The last three cases use the concept of reengineering to save the cost of implementation. A recent EDS empirical survey conducted in the United Kingdom has shown that a large number (59%) of the respondents thought that enhancing existing systems to couple both technologies is the most feasible approach. The main reason behind this result is the concept of reengineering.

1.3 The Problems

Database system reengineering is not an easy task. The acquisition and running of a new system is both a long-term commitment and a long-term investment for an organization. This being the case, it is important that the top management understand the objectives of committing to a new environment, as well as some of the problems that may lead to the collapse of such a project.

The following are the major strategic issues that must be considered in the early stage of the reengineering process.

Selecting a Database Model

Advocates of network and hierarchical models argue that the two models correspond more closely to the real world and that there is less redundancy of data. Since the connections among the data are built into the database structure, access time is shorter, therefore making the two systems very suitable for fairly stable databases with uses that can be precisely predetermined.

Supporters of the relational model argue that the relational concept is simple and that the model can provide flexibility and data independence. Since an organization's need for information changes over time, and because having a database encourages new uses, this flexibility is highly desirable.

One might wonder with these comparative advantages why all databases are not relational in nature. The answer is that for many applications the relational model is simply unsuitable. The pointer approach is much more efficient than general table operations if relationships between sets of data can be predetermined. So, if the database contains a large number of records or performance requirements or both, or if the transaction volume is high and the ad hoc queries are not common, then the hierarchical or network models are more efficient than the relational model.

Relational databases have over the last decade become an accepted solution to the issue of storing and retrieving data. Based upon the mathematical concept of a relation, these systems use tables (relations) and fixed size fields (domains) to represent the information and its interrelationships. The mathematical rigor and simplicity of these systems have been their major attraction. However, there are many drawbacks to such database systems. For one thing, the semantics of relational databases are often hidden within the many relationships and cannot be extracted without users' help. Also, relations stored in the database must first at least be in normal form, preventing the representation of multiple or set attributes. Furthermore, relational data models accept entities in a certain form, and structural changes to an entity require changes to all the instances of that entity in the database. Thus, it is not possible to change a single instance without affecting the whole database.

Object-oriented databases offer solutions to many of these problems. Based on the notions of abstraction and generalization, object-oriented models capture the semantics and complexity of the data. Fundamentals to the object-oriented approach are the concepts of class, instance, and inheritance. An instance is an occurrence of a class, where a class is a description of an entity. Classes may inherit the attributes of one or more superclass(es) and thus capture some of the semantics of an entity.

Also, an object-oriented database supports complex data types. An object-oriented model is thus more reusable and flexible in schema evolution and data storage.

Database Conversion

The complexity of converting an existing system to a new database system may cause a project to become unmanageable. Most people assume that there is an application system ready to be converted to the new environment. The assumption presumes that most application systems are technically up to date, logically sound, and properly organized. A careful review of the majority of application systems, however, will prove otherwise. A successful system conversion depends on a good understanding of management requirements and technical requirements.

A systems manager should consider redesigning the application system if it becomes unmaintainable. The redesign should be based on the database concept rather than wasting precious resources by wandering around a conversion process. There is no absolute certainty about planning and controlling reengineering projects because there are no foolproof methods to abide by. However, there are three conventional approaches to system conversion (Yau and Fong 1989).

- Parallel Conversion: This approach converts application programs and other data for the new system while the existing system is still in operation. This is a very safe approach permitting the old system to return to operation when problems crop up in the new system. However, handling two systems at the same time requires extra effort.
- Direct Cutover: This approach converts application programs and other data to replace the old one in a specified period of time. It is less costly than the parallel approach and is well suited to conversion projects involving a small system.
- Phase In: This approach is employed when the system is a very large one and one cannot be completely converted in one go. It divides the whole conversion process into several phases.

To successfully convert an information system, people such as software engineers, users, managers, and operations personnel must have a common ground to discuss with one another their individual needs, goals, expectations and constraints, and the goals of the organization. Common ground can be established by holding regular meetings for the related parties. The result of the meetings should be management commitment, transportable documentation that is understandable by appropriate parties, and a jointly owned, user-oriented set of structured models of the systems' design. These models should contain why, what, where, and how the conversion will affect the organization. In brief, users' involvement is an essential factor in all phases of the conversion: planning, requirements, design, construction, implementation, and operations.

On the technical side, system conversion can be separated into two main parts: program conversion and data conversion. Converting programs will be less of a problem if the installation has good software quality standards. Problems arise when such quality standards do not exist or when they are loosely enforced.

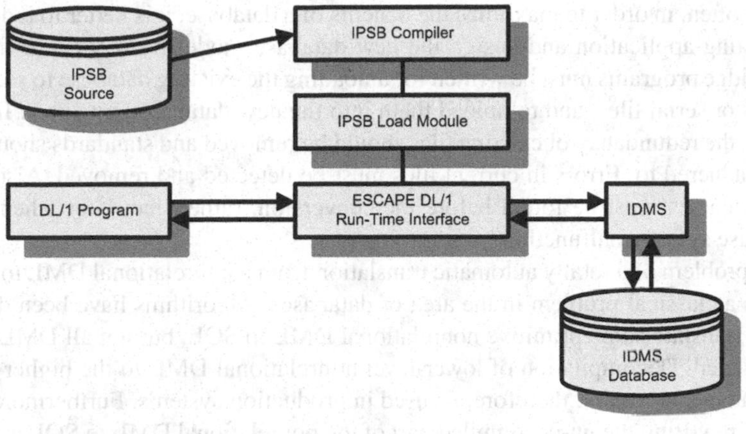

Fig. 1.4 A practical database conversion approach

Many software vendors supply software utility tools to help clients convert their databases. For example, Computer Associates International Ltd. has a software tool called ESCAPE DL/1, which translates the input-output statements in IMS to that in IDMS so that IMS programs can access IDMS databases without converting the data. (IMS and IDMS are database management systems supplied by IBM Corp.) Computer Associates also supplies programs to convert specification blocks in IMS into corresponding IDMS schemas and subschemas, including those that help unload IMS databases to sequential files and reload them into IDMS databases. Figure 1.4 describes the function of ESCAPE DL/1 (CA 1992).

Data conversion can be very complicated if the existing data organization is very different from the new database model. Similar to program conversion, some software vendors also provide utilities for data conversion. One example is converting sequential files to a database system called ADABAS.

The use of customer-made programs is the more common approach to converting existing files, but this has several serious shortcomings. Each translation required is handled by a specially written program that is used only once, hence, a costly solution. Such programs may be unreliable for restructuring complex databases because of possible program errors or data misinterpretation. This process becomes even more complex if the conversions of software and hardware are going on at the same time. Although the use of the generalized program can overcome such problems, the disadvantage is that it may not be able to be executed efficiently (because the program is generalized), meaning it cannot convert all the data from the source to the target. Reconstructing data files is time-consuming, and some data files may not be reconstructed because of drastic changes to the database semantics. Furthermore, this approach depends on one language to describe the data structure (at both the source and the target) and another to describe the restructuring specifications; these languages may be cumbersome to use. With the Bridge Program Technique, some redundant data may have to be retained in the database so that the files needed by the existing programs can be created again.

Very often, in order to maximize the benefits of a database, it is better to redesign the existing application and design the new database model from scratch. In this case, bridge programs must be written for unloading the existing database to sequential files or serial files, and to upload them into the new database structures. In this process, the redundancy of existing files should be removed and standards should be strictly adhered to. Errors in current files must be detected and removed. Also, file inconsistencies must be found before the conversion, rather than later when they may cause system malfunction.

The problem of a totally automatic translation from a nonrelational DML to SQL remains a classical problem in the area of databases. Algorithms have been developed to translate some primitive nonrelational DML to SQL, but not all DMLs can be translated. Decompilation of lower-level nonrelational DML to the higher-level SQL statements cannot, therefore, be used in production systems. Furthermore, the effort of rewriting the un-decompiled part of the nonrelational DML to SQL is similar to a rewrite of the whole nonrelational database program, as the time for program analysis in both approaches is about the same.

Integration of Multiple Databases

There has been a proliferation of databases in most organizations. These databases are created and managed by the various units of the organization for their own localized applications. Thus, the global view of all the data that is being stored and managed by the organization is missing. Schema integration is a technique to present such a global view of an organization's databases. There has been a lot of work done on schema integration. Özsu and Valduriez (1991) presented surveys of work in this area. But all these techniques concentrate on integrating database schemas without taking into consideration new database applications. We need a practical approach to schema integration to support new database applications by comparing the existing databases against the data requirements of the new applications. If the existing databases are inadequate to support new applications, they must then be evolved to support them.

Since relational databases emerged, they have been widely used in commercial organizations. However, in an organization, different departments or sections would have probably developed their own relational database systems according to their own requirements at various times. Thus, large quantities of data are fragmented across a variety of databases. Data could then be redundant and inconsistent. A global view of all data is not there. This will affect the effectiveness of decision-making in an organization, as these disparate data do not adequately support the information needs of an organization operating in a dynamic business environment. It is vital that a data resource should provide current data for the development of up-to-date information to support just-in-time decision-making in an organization. There is a great need to create a global view of all existing disparate data by integrating them in a global database so as to support dynamic and complex business activities.

Data integration is to implement a global database by integrating various *source* databases into a global *target* database. To accomplish the task of data integration,

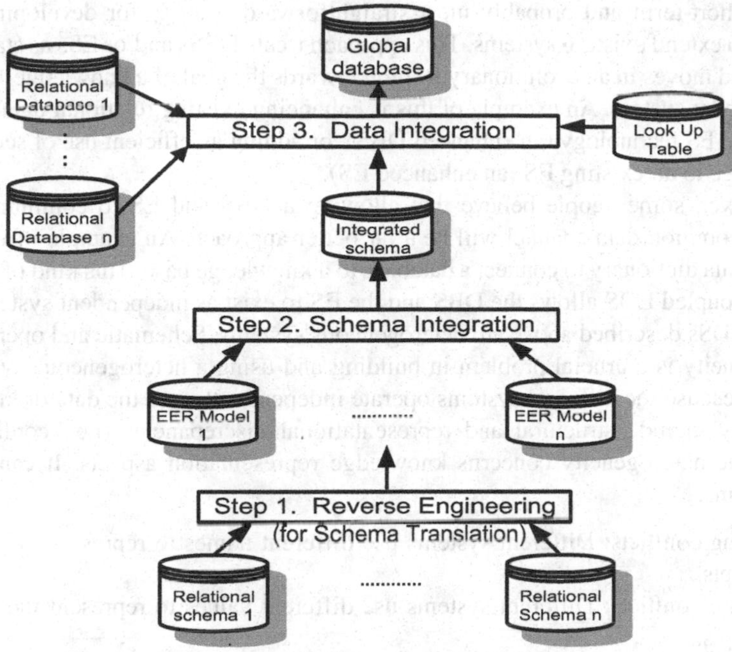

Fig. 1.5 Architecture of multiple databases integration

the first step is schema integration. This process involves many steps including solving conflicts between source databases, capturing the semantics of entity, weak entity, cardinality, isa, generalization, categorization, and aggregation of the relations, and merging to a new integrated schema for each pair of the existing relational schemas in the source databases.

The next process is data integration. Its objective is to merge data from source databases to the new global database without any loss of information. It must transform the data structure from the sources to the target integrated global database whilst preserving its semantics. It also uses the data structure of the integrated schema derived from schema integration.

The integrated global database can be verified by confirming the recaptured semantics from examining its data occurrence. If the recovered semantics matches the semantics of the integrated schema, then the original semantics have been preserved in the integrated databases and there is no loss of information after integration. Figure 1.5 shows the data flow of data integration after schema integration of source relational schemas.

Integration of Database and Expert Systems

Integration of existing databases with new updated computing technology is another issue of database reengineering. The integration will update the existing systems to meet a new requirement. Our main theme, in this subsection, is to describe the problem of integrating expert systems (ES) with database systems (DBS), i.e., EDS.

The short-term and probably most straightforward strategy for developing an EDS is to extend existing systems. This approach treats DBSs and/or ESs as starting points and moves in an evolutionary fashion towards the goal of a knowledge-based management system. An example of this is enhancing existing relational databases to include ES technology (an enhanced DBS), or adding an efficient use of secondary storage to an existing ES (an enhanced ES).

However, some people believe that allowing a DBS and ES to communicate down a common data channel will be a far better approach. An example of this is using a data dictionary to connect a database to a knowledge base. This kind of peer-to-peer coupled EDS allows the DBS and the ES to exist as independent systems.

The EDSs described above are heterogeneous systems. Schematic and operation heterogeneity is a crucial problem in building and using a heterogeneous system. This is because the different systems operate independently and the data or knowledge may include structural and representational discrepancies (i.e., conflicts). Schematic heterogeneity concerns knowledge representation aspects. It can take these forms:

- Naming conflicts: Different systems use different names to represent the same concepts.
- Domain conflicts: Different systems use different values to represent the same concepts.
- Metadata conflicts: The same concepts are represented at the schema level in one system and the instance level in another.
- Structural conflicts: Different data models of hierarchical, network, relational, object-oriented, and XML are used together, representing different structures for the same concepts.

In most ESs, facts are realized according to the constraints imposed by the characteristics of the inference engine and by the properties of the problem at hand. Most of these systems mention nothing of the ad hoc ways of structuring a database of facts. That is why this type of problem becomes a major task in enhanced ESs. On the other hand, the relational model is not really compatible with logic, rules, frames, and semantic networks, which are typical of ES systems. Several performance problems arise from this mismatch, especially those requiring data to be exchanged by using redundant data descriptions to form the interface between the coupled systems.

An ES reasoning mechanism makes use of data through its variables instantly; therefore, it requires some data during each inference and in an atomic form (individual tuples of data values). However, a relational DBMS answers a query by returning results as sets of tuples. Accordingly, when the front-end breaks down a query into a sequence of queries on tuples, each of them incurs a heavy back-end performance overhead. We lose, therefore, the benefits of the set-oriented optimization that is characteristic of the back-end relational database.

The third criticism concerns the limited functionality and general information provided by the integrating system. Ideally, the integrated system should support the full functionality of both systems plus some additional functionality arising from the integration. Unfortunately, most current systems either do not support all of the functions of both systems or support only a very limited set of additional functions. Also, the general resource information (i.e., the data dictionary), is poor in current EDSs. Most systems do not support this resource information. This makes programming expert database systems extremely difficult.

The fourth criticism concerns the development lifecycle of re-using the existing systems to create a new information system. Currently, there are no formal methodologies to implement this type of system. How can the developer know the existing data is sufficient for the new system requirements? If it is not sufficient, what will be the remedial action? How can the existing system join the system analysis and design phase? How do we test this type of system during the development lifecycle?

1.4 Approaches to Reengineering

Reengineering information systems involves reusing the existing outdated database systems and expert systems by upgrading or integrating them to new technology systems to meet the new users' requirements. Database upgrading, in a logical sense, is to upgrade old database technologies, i.e., one using a hierarchical or network model, to new database technology, i.e., a relational, object-oriented, or XML model. Reusing an expert system can be accomplished by integrating it with a database system.

Database Reengineering

Database reengineering consists of three parts: schema translation, data conversion, and program translation. It can be described as follows:

In schema translation, there are two approaches:

- Direct translation – One can directly translate a nonrelational schema to a relational schema. However, such translations may result in the loss of information because of their primitive mode of operation that cannot recover or identify all the original nonrelational schema's semantics. Certain advanced semantics are lost once they are mapped from a conceptual schema (e.g., ER model) to a logical schema (e.g., Hierarchical or Network schema). Thus, users' input is needed to recover the lost semantics.
- Indirect translation – Indirect translations can be accomplished by mapping a logical hierarchical or network schema into a conceptual ER model schema in reverse engineering. The translated conceptual schema must have all the original logical schema's semantics. User input can be used to recapture the semantics of the conceptual schema. A knowledge base can be used to support the process of recovering such semantics. Then the conceptual schema can be automatically mapped to a relational schema. Similarly, in order to translate a relational schema to an object-oriented schema, we can map the relational schema first into the ER model, then into a UML (Unified Modeling Language) (Booch et al 1999), a conceptual model for object-oriented model, and finally translate the UML

model onto the object-oriented model of the target database. Similarly, we can map relational to XML model through DTD graph and XSD graph.

Chapter 3 will describe in detail methods for schema translation.

In data conversion, there are three approaches:

- Physical conversion – The physical data of the nonrelational database is directly converted to the physical data of the relational database. This can be done using an interpreter approach or a generator approach. The former is a direct translation from one data item to another. The latter is to provide a generator that generates a program to accomplish the physical data conversion.
- Logical conversion – The logical approach is to unload the nonrelational database to sequential files in the logical sequence, similar to the relational model. The sequential files can then be uploaded back to a target relational database. This approach is concerned with the logical sequence of the data rather than the physical attributes of each data item.
- Bridge program – Each nonrelational file requires a bridge program to convert it to the relational model.

Chapter 4 will describe in detail the methods for data conversion.

In program conversion, the five approaches to translating nonrelational database programs to relational database programs are as follows:

- Rewrite – One can translate the nonrelational schema into a relational schema, map a nonrelational database into a relational database, and rewrite all the application programs to run on the relational database.
- Bridge program – One can map the nonrelational schema into a relational schema, then add a relational interface software layer on the top of the nonrelational DBMS. The relational interface layer translates the relational program DML into nonrelational program DML statements to access the existing nonrelational database. The user can then view the nonrelational database as a relational database, and use relational DML commands to extract and manipulate the underlying nonrelational database system.
- Emulation – This is the technique of providing software or firmware in the target system that maps source program commands into functionally equivalent commands in the target system. Each nonrelational DML is substituted by relational DML statements to access the converted relational database.
- Decompilation – Decompilation is the process of transforming a program written in a low-level language into an equivalent but more abstract version and the implementation of the new programs to meet the new environment, database files, and DBMS requirements.
- Coexistence – One can continue to support a nonrelational database while developing an information capacity equivalent relational database for the same application.

Chapter 5 will describe in detail the methods for program translation.

Adding a Relational Interface to Nonrelational Database

Even though a lot of problems have been resolved in database conversion, the difficulty arises in the translation of semantics. Not only do we not know whether there is a 1:1 or a 1:n relationship between the parent (owner) and the child (member) segments (records) in the hierarchical (network) schema, but we also cannot obtain unique key transformation. The complication in semantic analysis appears not only in the DDL of the schema but also in the database programs. The automation of the direct translation from procedural (with database navigation) nonrelational DML statement to non-procedural (without database navigation) relational DML statement is still a challenge to database researchers.

In order to resolve the above problems, an alternative approach for database reengineering is endorsed in a methodology of RELIKEDB (Relational-like-database) (Fong 1993), which is similar to the relational interface approach in that both provide a relational interface to make the hierarchical or network DBMS a relational-like DBMS.

RELIKEDB provides schema translation in which user input contributes to the process. Direct schema translation from a hierarchical model or network model into a relational cannot guarantee the capture of all the original conceptual schema semantics. With user input, we can at least provide a relational schema that is closer to the user's expectations and which preserves the existing schema's constraints such as record key, relationships, and attributes.

As to data conversion, RELIKEDB provides algorithms to unload a hierarchical or a network database into sequential files directly and efficiently, which can then be uploaded into a relational database.

In program translation, RELIKEDB provides an "open" data structure by adding secondary indices in the existing hierarchical or network database. This eliminates the navigation access path required to retrieve a target record from a system record. Instead, each target record type can be accessed directly without database navigation. The database access time is thus reduced and the program conversion effort simplified. RELIKEDB provides algorithms to translate SQL statements into hierarchical or network DML statements. These are sound solutions to the program conversion problem.

Schemas Integration

Chapter 6 describes schemas integration of heterogeneous databases, including relational schemas, object-oriented schemas, and XML schemas. The integration is to locate the relevance of the schemas such as their data semantic relevance of cardinality, is a generalization, and categorization, etc.

Very often, a global view of multiple XML schemas is necessary for data warehousing in a company. Therefore, we need to integrate their correspondent XML documents for information retrieval.

Integrated Expert Systems and Database Systems

Chapter 7 describes in detail EDS technology. It presents a case study that illustrates one EDS scenario, where existing DBs and ESs have been used to build an EDS application. The consequent lessons are then addressed and some problems of current techniques for the integration of ESs and DBs are explored. The "ideal" future for EDSs using object-oriented technology is also discussed.

There are fundamentally different opinions coming from the current ES and DB communities for EDS. The use of ES functions in DB products is to achieve "deductive data", retrieve the semantics of data, and create an intelligent interface, integrity constraints, etc. The use of DB functions in ES products is to represent factual knowledge in the original knowledge base. These differences mean that current EDSs have very different working environments.

Different approaches have been taken by various research projects and commercial products to achieve the requirements of an EDS. They can be classified into two different groups (see Fig. 1.6):

- Based on existing systems: There are four different architectures in this area, i.e., enhancing existing database systems, enhancing existing expert systems, master-slave coupling of ES-DB, and peer-to-peer coupling of ES-DB. Most current products can be categorized into one of these four architectures.
- A new knowledge base management system: This architecture involves searching for a new model to represent knowledge. One example of this type of system is Generis (Deductive System Ltd. 1988).

Reengineering functions and a high-level synthesis model are two main requirements for the future EDS (Huang 1994). These two functions cannot be traded off against one another. They can combine together to become a very powerful and sophisticated EDS. Another interesting result is that both ES and DB researchers are using object-oriented technology. It seems that most people currently believe that object-oriented technology will become the future for EDS.

Chapter 8 is to normalize a relational database and XML database. In general, an information system is not user-friendly if its database is unnormalized. Data normalization is to eliminate data irregularity for data update, and also for removing data redundancy.

Chapter 9 describes using XML document as a common data model for heterogeneous databases information highway on the Internet by converting current database into XML document which is then converted into a target database upon user request.

In XML documents, elements with the same key values can be factorized into a primary element under the root element. The result replaces repeating data by pointers and removes the data redundancy between these elements, and make them easier to be updated.

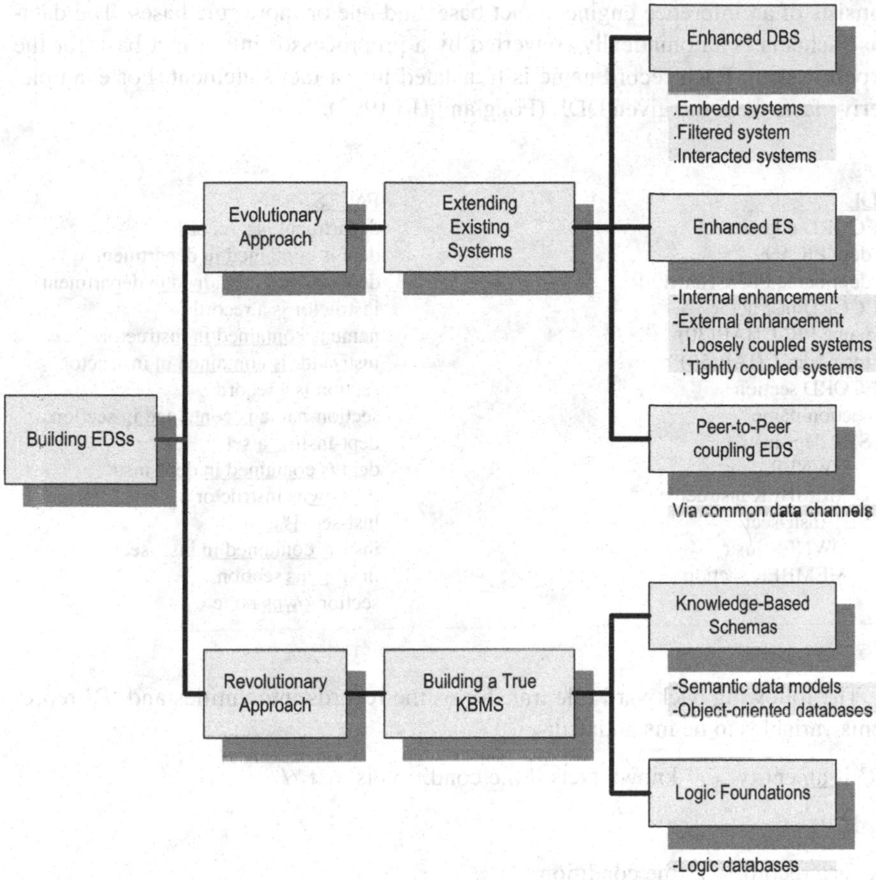

Fig. 1.6 EDS typology

1.5 Conclusion

Chapter 10 concludes with a discussion of a suggested overarching framework for future information system reengineering. It first discusses the application of database conversion methodologies. It then describes the concepts of the multiple databases integration, and also the database system and expert system integration application, and data normalization. The final part of this chapter explores the issues of the future trends for information systems reengineering, integration and normalization.

User Interface to Knowledge-Based Systems

To recover the advanced semantics such as generalization, categorization, and n-ary relationship from the relational schema, user input is needed during the process of reverse engineering. To support this process we need an expert system shell. This consists of an inference engine, a fact base, and one or more rule bases. The database schema is automatically converted by a preprocessor into a fact base for the expert system. Each record name is translated into a fact statement. For example, derive facts from the given DDL (Fong and Ho 1993).

DDL	FACTS
RECORD department	department is a record
dept PIC 999	dept is contained in department
dept-name PIC CHAR(30)	dept-name is contained in department
RECORD instructor	instructor is a record
name PIC CHAR(30)	name is contained in instructor
instr-addr CHAR(50)	instr-addr is contained in instructor
RECORD section	section is a record
section-name	section-name is contained in section
SET dept-instr	dept-instr is a set
OWNER dept	dept is contained in dept-instr
MEMBER instructor	dept owns instructor
SET instr-sect	inst-sect is a set
OWNER instr	instr is contained in instr-sect
MEMBER section	instr owns section
	section owns none

The following backward rule transforms the records into entities and 'R' represents variables to be instantiated:

'R' is an entity /* known facts if the condition is met */

If

'R' is a record /* the condition */

The expert system shell provides a mechanism to obtain facts from users in the form of "askable facts", such as 'E' identified fully? When 'E' is bound to a department, for example, will generate

Is the statement: department identified fully, true? Please enter (Y)es, (N)o, or (W)hy.

Typing "why" will generate an explanation of why the system asked the question, by showing the rules that may help the user to respond better. If the answer is "yes," the entity is tagged as fully internally identified and the premise succeeds. If the answer is "No," this premise fails. In order for the conclusion to fire, the premises must succeed, otherwise, the system will try the next rule.

The whole rule base is shown below, illustrating how the "askable fact" is used within a rule:

Read key-attribute 'K'

IF

'E' is an entity and

'E' identified fully?

Read partial-key-attribute 'K'

IF

'E' is an entity and
NOT 'E' identified partially?

Introduce sequence 'K'

IF

'E' is an entity and
NOT 'E' identified fully and
NOT 'E' identified partially

There are three kinds of record identifiers as follows:

- Fully internally identified – The existing record key can uniquely identify the record as an entity. For example, 'a dept' can be a record identifier that uniquely identifies a department in the same record.
- Partial internally identified – The concatenation of owner record keys with the existing record keys can uniquely identify the record as an entity. For example, the record identifier of instructor record is the concatenation of its parent record department identifier: dept with its own record key: instructor-name. That is, dept, instructor-name can uniquely identify instructor-address of the instructor working in the department.
- Internally unidentified – The concatenation of owner record keys with a sequence# can uniquely identify the record as an entity. For example, the record identifier of the bookshelf is the concatenation of the identifier of its parent record instructor (instructor-name) with a sequence#. That is, instructor-name, sequence# can uniquely identify bookshelf records. A computer-generated sequence# is necessary because there is no unique identifier in the book-shelf record (i.e. an instructor may have n bookshelves where n varies from 1 to many).

1.6 The Applications

The Internet has opened up a multitude of opportunities for many businesses to improve customer relationships and operations efficiency. The Internet is adopted by most companies because the cost of having Internet access via an Internet Services Provider can be as low as less than one hundred Hong Kong dollars per month.

Electronic Data Interchange (EDI) is the electronic transfer of structured business information between trading partners. The idea behind it is simple: Companies have to exchange an enormous amount of paperwork to conduct business. We replace the paperwork with electronic files. EDI reduces administrative costs and

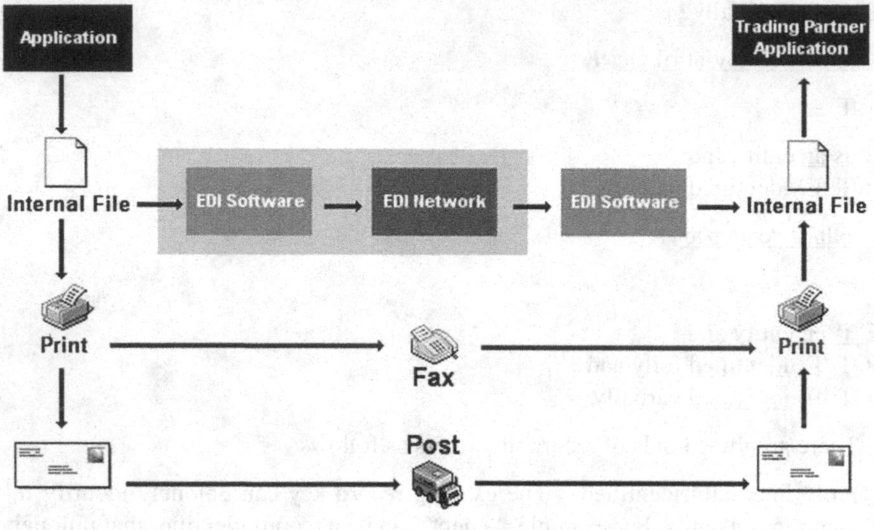

Fig. 1.7 Traditional EDI exchange

improves relationships between trading partners. Figure 1.7 shows the data flow diagram of a traditional EDI operation on the Internet.

However, EDI systems are very expensive and time-consuming to implement and maintain; they are inflexible and limited to integration between trading partners. The traditional EDI systems are seven to ten times more expensive than Internet-based options. Besides, the Internet offers broad connectivity that links networks around the world and offers a platform-independent means of exchanging information. Internet technology can extend the capabilities of existing EDI systems. It is easier to implement and maintain. This has led a growing number of companies to look for an alternative to the EDI formats. XML (Extensible Markup Language) (W3C 2004) is the most attractive alternative because it offers superior conversion features.

XML is defined as EXtensible Markup Language as developed by the World Wide Web Consortium (W3C) recommendation Version 1.0 as of 10/02/1998 as a Meta-Markup Language with a set of rules for creating semantic tags used to describe data.

To apply XML in EDI on the Internet, in Fig. 1.8, an XML Receiver Transmitter (XMLRT) system can automate the translation of relational schema and data into the topological XML documents based on their data semantics. They are integrated into an XML document. The translated XML document is mapped and stored into the receiver's relational database for computing. The contribution of XMLRT architecture is to automate the translation of schema and data through the topological data structures of an XML document.

Using an XMLRT system with an XML document, we can enrich data portability and application access on the Internet more efficiently than ever before. XMLRT

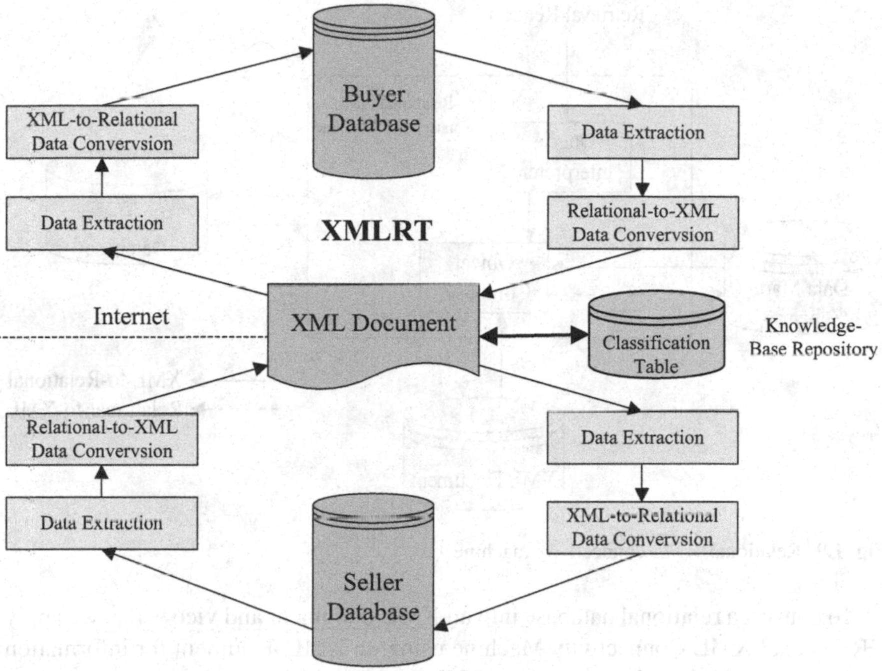

Fig. 1.8 Architecture of XML receiver transmitter

and XML documents allow a company to realize long-term benefits via improved feasibility in the market. We also bring information into any Web browser anywhere in the world. By providing an information highway on the Internet, an XML document is made to suit a company's inter-company and self-defined requirements for data exchange The tasks involved are: (1) Select and map a view of the sender's relational database into different topological XML documents. (2) Integrate the translated topological XML documents into one. (3) Translate the XML document to the receiver's relational database for storage.

To make relational tables compatible with the XML document, we join the former into a single relation and transfer the joined relational schema into XML schema. We load tuples of the joined relation into object instances of elements or attributes in the XML document according to the XML schema and preserve their data dependencies.

To receive an XML document from the Internet, we need an XML-to-Relational Connectivity Machine. This machine maps an XML schema into a relational schema. By traversing the XML document from Root to all element instances, it loads XML instances into tuples in relation to *OID* (object identity). The Data Map schemas consist of relational schemas and their corresponding XML schemas. The company relational database consists of seller and buyer databases (Fong and Wong 2004).

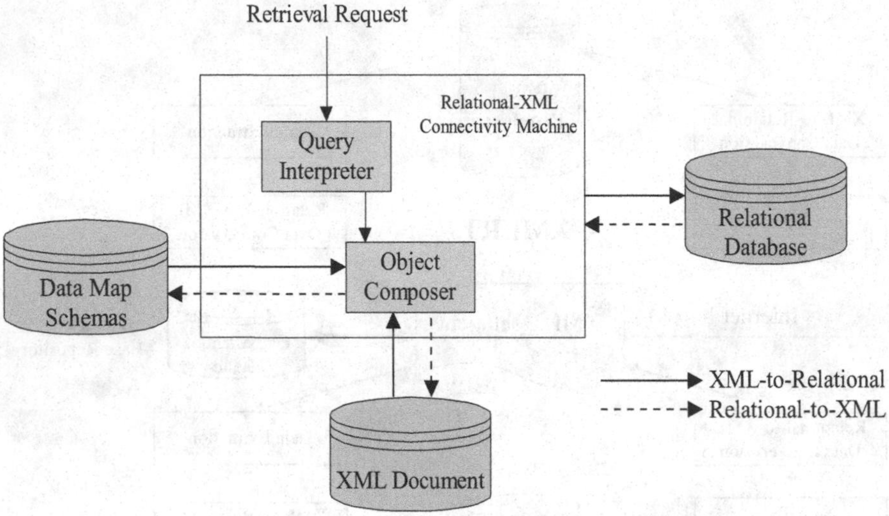

Fig. 1.9 Relational-XML connectivity machine

To convert a relational database into an XML document and vice versa, we apply a Relational XML Connectivity Machine using an XML document for information exchange standard on the Internet for B2B (business-to-business) applications. The Data Map schema files consist of relational schema and corresponding XML schema. The company relational database consists of seller/buyer databases. The XML document is for the information exchange on the Internet in Fig. 1.9.

1.7 Summary

The evolution of information system technologies started with file systems in the 60s, database systems in the 70s, and expert systems in the 80s. The need to upgrade a company's information system is vital to its success. Database technologies offer a solution for a company's organization to share information efficiently and effectively. Expert systems provide important information for management decision-making. To protect a company's huge investment in the information system, reengineering rather than rewriting seems to be more cost-effective. Information engineering includes database reengineering and expert system reengineering. The former can be accomplished by upgrading an obsolete record-based hierarchical or network database into a relation-based relational or reengineering a relational database into an object-based object-oriented, or Internet-based XML. The upgrade (conversion) process includes schema translation, data conversion, and program translation. The aspect of reengineering an existing database system into an object-oriented or XML system is also very attractive due to the increase of productivity and user-friendliness of object-oriented systems, and the importance of Internet application of XML systems. Data integration must be done after schema integration and schema translation. An expert system can be reused by integrating it with a new or existing database system. The resultant expert database system is the core information resource system for a company for future reengineering purposes. The problems in database reengineering are in the handling of different data structures of various data models. Also, the existing expert systems can become obsolete due to changes in user requirements and production databases. The suggested solution is to upgrade record-based data models of hierarchical or network databases to table-oriented relational databases, object-oriented databases, and XML databases. We can also reuse expert systems by integrating them with the database into an expert database system. An example of the application of reengineering can be seen in the electronic data interchange on the Internet. The EDI system can help trading companies exchange information for their business. However, EDI needs programming solutions that are too expensive and not promptly developed. The alternative is to use XMLRT and XML documents as a medium for data transmission on the Internet. Since XML is the default data standard on the Internet, which can be browsed through Internet Explorer without programming, the XMLRT and XML document solution can perform better with less cost than EDI. We will show how to perform data transformation between relational data and an XML document in the later chapters.

Questions

Question 1.1

How can one validate and measure the quality of a converted database?

Answer

A database is a collection of data organized by a DBMS. To validate a database is to prove that there is no loss of information, that is, preserving the meaning and the function of data. After converting from an old database to a new database, testing must be done to ensure that the user can extract the same data from both the old and the new databases. Another testing can also be done to recover the old database from the new database. In this case, there is no loss of information. It is not an easy job because a database conversion involves both schema and data, and they have to work together to form a database.

Question 1.2

What operation steps are needed for data conversion in a database for a company to follow?

Answer

In general, data conversion in a database involves steps as follows:

Step 1: Planning – Management must communicate with all database users to why, what, where, and how the database conversion to be done in a company. For example, a bank wants to enlarge a user account number from 12 digits to 16 digits, the current account record size must be enlarged, which involves data conversion in a database.

Step 2: Requirements – For data conversion, which physical files with the account record are to be converted, and which programs accessing the account record are to be edited.
Step 3: Design – After data conversion, which application programs accessing the account record are to be redesigned to accommodate the new changes.
Step 4: Construction – Write a data conversion program to update the current database into a new database with the enlarged record. Edit application programs to access the to-be-updated new database for trial testing.
Step 5: Implementation – Both the updated new database and edited programs must be fully tested together with the correct result.
Step 6: Operation – Parallel conversion means the old database and programs must be run in parallel with the new database and the edited programs until the results are correct. Then discard the old database and program as a cutoff point, and start running the new database and edited programs in production operation.
Step 7: The above steps can be done in phases as a project.

Bibliography

Booch G, Rumbaugh J, Jacobson I (1999) The unified modeling language user guide. Addison Wesley

CA (1992) Escape DL/1 user's guide. Computer Associates International Limited

Chen P (1976) The entity relationship model – toward a unified view of data. ACM Trans Database Syst 1(1):9–36

Deductive Systems Ltd. (1988) Generis: user menu. Deductive Systems Ltd, Brunel Science Park, Uxbridge, Middlesex UB8 3 PQ, U.K

Fong J (1993) A methodology for providing a relational interface to access hierarchical or network database. University of Sunderland, Ph.D. thesis

Fong J, Ho M (1993) Knowledge-based approach for abstracting hierarchical and network schema semantics. Lecture Notes in Computer Science, ER '93. Springer

Fong J, Wong HK (2004) XTOPO: an XML-based topology for information highway on the Internet. J Database Manage 15(3):18–44

Huang SM (1994) An integrated expert database system. Phd thesis, University of Sunderland, UK

Özsu M, Valdariez P (1991) Principles of distributed database systems. Prentice Hall International Edition

Yau C, Fong J (1989) Considerations for converting conventional file-oriented systems to database systems. Proceedings of Hong Kong Computer Society Database Workshop, March 1988

Chapter 2
Database and Expert System Technology

2.1 Hierarchical Model

The hierarchical data model is a logical schema and can be viewed as a subset of a network model because it imposes a further restriction on the relationship types in the form of an inverted tree structure. The linkage between record types is in an automatically fixed set membership. The database access path of a hierarchical database follows the hierarchical path from a parent-child record. The default path is a hierarchical sequence of top-to-bottom, left-to-right, and front-to-back.

It is common that many real-life data can be structured in hierarchical form. For example, enrollment in a university can be ordered according to the department organizations. Because hierarchies are so familiar in nature and in human society, it seems natural to represent data in a hierarchical structure. Data represent ideas about the real world that people conceive in terms of entities. Based on the characteristics of entities, entity type can be defined. Figure 2.1 shows a generic hierarchical tree that represents entity types where entities refer to record types and records. In the tree, the record type at the top is usually known as the "root." Record types are groups of entities or records that can be described by the same set of attributes. In general, the root may have any number of dependents, each of these may have any number of lower-level dependents, and so on, to any number of levels. Individual records are the actual occurrences of data. The righthand side is the hierarchical sequence.

There are some important properties of the hierarchical database model.

There is a set of record types (R_1, R_2,…. R_N). It is possible to designate a field of record type as an identifier of a record occurrence of this type. This may provide either a unique or a nonunique identification. This identifier is called a key.

- There is a set of relationships connecting all record types in one data structure diagram.

J. S. P. Fong, K. Wong Ting Yan, *Information Systems Reengineering, Integration and Normalization*, https://doi.org/10.1007/978-3-030-79584-9_2

- There is no more than one relationship between any two record types R_i and R_j. Hence, relationships need not be labeled.
- The relationships expressed in the data structure diagram form a tree with all edges pointing towards the leaves.
- Each relationship is 1:n and it is total. That is, if R_i is the parent of R_j in the hierarchy, then for every record occurrence of R_j there is exactly one R_i record connected to it.

To construct a hierarchical model, it is natural to build an ER model and map it to a hierarchical model because an ER model carries more semantics. Once an ER model is built, if relationships are all binary, we can map a 1:n or 1:1 relationship from A to B as a binary tree. To map an m:n relationship from A to B, we can use virtual record types (pointer to actual records) which are distinguished by an ID field in a physical address as shown in Fig. 2.2 (McElreath 1981).

2.1.1 *Hierarchical Data Definition Language*

Two types of structures are used to implement the inverted tree structure of a hierarchical model: namely data definition trees and data occurrence trees. The role of a data definition tree is to describe the data types and their relationships. For example, Fig. 2.1 shows seven data types, in a parent (the top one)-child (the bottom one) relationship with respect to each other. The data occurrence tree represents the

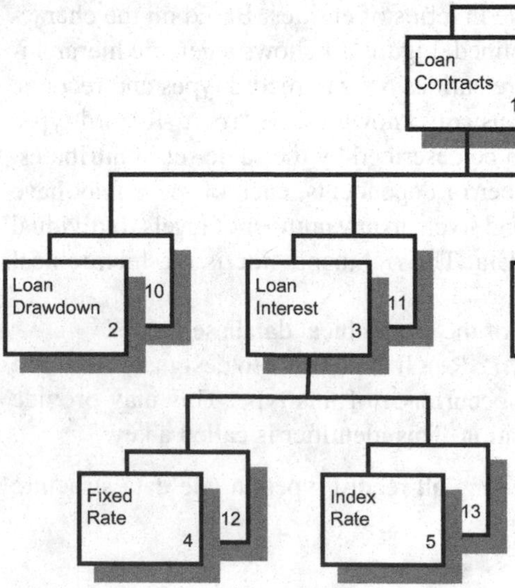

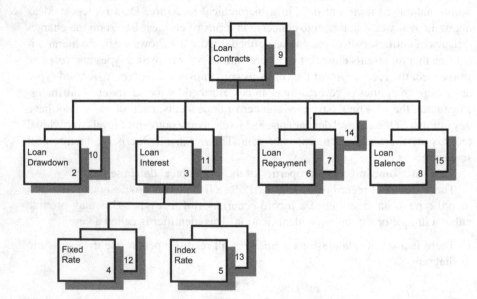

Fig. 2.1 Hierarchical database of a loan system

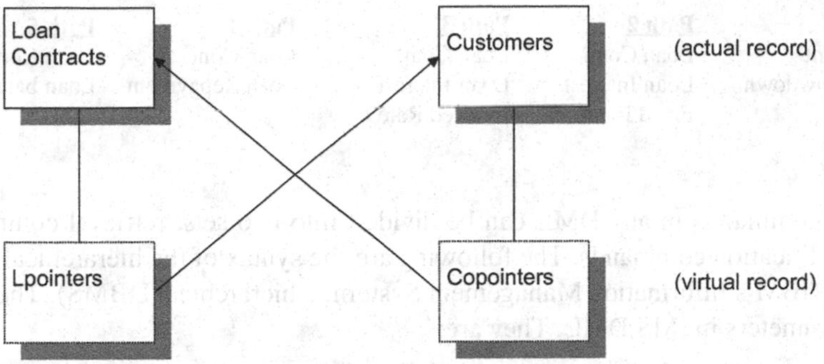

Fig. 2.2 m:n relationship of a hierarchical model in a loan system

actual data in the database. Figure 2.1 shows 15 data occurrences in a hierarchical sequence, the default read sequence in a hierarchical model.

Due to the limitation of an inverted tree structure, the hierarchical model cannot be used to implement the following:

- m:n relationship between two record types
- A child record type with more than one parent record type
- n-ary relationships with more than two participating record types

But with virtual pointers architecture, each record type can be in an m:n relationship with another record type through the pointers. The record type with the source pointers is called the logical child. Its target record type is called the logical parent. For example, Fig. 2.2 shows that the record types of Cpointers and Lpointers are logical child record types. Their corresponding logical parent record types are Customers and Loan Contracts. As a result of these pointers, Record type Customers and Loan Contracts are in an m:n relationship such that each customer can sign many loan contracts, and each loan contract can be signed by many customers.

2.1.2 Hierarchical Data Manipulation Language

Hierarchical data manipulation language (HDML) is a record-at-a-time language for manipulating hierarchical databases. The commands of an HDML must be embedded in a general-purpose programming language, called a host language. Following each HDML command, the last record accessed by the command is called the current database record. The system maintains a pointer to the current record. Subsequent database commands proceed from the current record and move to a new current record depending on the operation of the command. The traversal of the database access follows the inverted tree structure, i.e., each database navigation path according to the hierarchical sequence. For example, Fig. 2.1 has five access paths as follows:

Path 1	Path 2	Path 3	Path 4	Path 5
Loan Cont	Loan Cont.	Loan Cont.	Loan Cont.	Loan Cont.
Loan Drawdown	Loan Interest	Loan Interest	Loan Repayment	Loan balance
	Fixed Rate	Indexed Rate		

The commands in any DML can be divided into two sets: retrieval commands and modification commands. The following are the syntax of the hierarchical DML of IMS (IBM's Information Management System, a hierarchical DBMS). There are four parameters in IMS DML. They are:

- Function Code, which defines the database access function
- Program Control Block, which defines the external subschema access path
- I-O-Area, which is a target segment address
- Segment Search Argument, which defines the target segment selection criteria as follows:

```
CALL "CBLTDLI" USING FUNCTION-CODE
        PCB-MASK
        I-O-AREA
        SSA-1
        ...
        SSA-n.
```

Note: CBLTDLI is a call by a Cobol program to access the DL/1 database.

Retrieval Command:

- Get Unique (GU)

This command retrieves the leftmost segment that satisfies the specified condition. For example, the following Get unique command is to retrieve a Loan Balance segment of a loan with the loan contract number 277988 and loan balance date of July 22, 1996.

```
CALL "CBLTDLI" USING GU
        PCB-MASK
  I-O-AREA
        LOAN_CONTRACT# = 277988
      BALANCE_DATE = '960722'
```

- Get Next (GN)

This command retrieves the next segment based on the pre-order traversal algorithm from the current location. The clause for the record identifier and retrieval conditions is optional. If the clause is not given, GET NEXT would retrieve the next sequential segment from the current location. For example, the following command is to retrieve the next Loan Contract record after the current Loan Contract record occurrence.

```
CALL "CBLTDLI" USING GN
   PCB-MASK
   LOAN_CONTRACT
```

- Get Next WITHIN PARENT(GNP)

This command retrieves segments from the set of children sharing the same parent as the current segment of the given type. The parent segment is visited by a previous GET command, i.e., it establishes the parentage of a segment type according to the current pointer of its parent segment type. For example, the following command retrieves the next in a hierarchical sequence of a Loan_interest segment under the loan_contract segment type with a loan_contract# of "277988".

```
CALL "CBLTDLI" USING GNP
   PCB-MASK
   LOAN_INTEREST
   LOAN_CONTRACT# = 277988
```

Hierarchical Modification Commands:

- INSERT(ISRT)

This command stores a new segment and connects it to a parent segment. The parent segment must be selected by the previous GET command. For example, the following commands are to insert a balance segment of $1,000,000 under the Loan_contract number 277988 on July 22, 1996.

```
CALL "CBLTDLI" USING GU
   PCB-MASK
   I-O-AREA
   LOAN_CONTRACT# = 277988.
MOVE "19960722" TO BALANCE_DATE.
MOVE 1000000 TO BALANCE_AMOUNT.
CALL "CBLTDLI" USING ISRT
   PCB-MASK
   LOAN_BALANCE.
```

- REPLACE(REPL)

This command replaces the current segment with the new segment. It can be used to alter the detail of the current segment. For example, the following commands are to update the loan balance of loan contract# 277988 from 1,000,000 to 2,000,000 on July 22, 1996. The GHU function is a get hold a unique call to apply a record lock on a segment before an update.

```
CALL "CBLTDLI" USING GHU
   PCB-MASK
   I-O-AREA
   LOAN_CONTRACT# = 277988
   BALANCE_DATE = '960722'
MOVE 2000000 TO BALANCE_AMOUNT.
CALL "CBLTDLI" USING REPL.
```

- DELETE (DELT)

This command physically deletes the current segment and all of its child segments. For example, the following command deletes a balance segment of loan contract# 277988 on July 22, 1996.

```
CALL "CBLTDLI" USING GHU
   PCB-MASK
   I-O-AREA
   LOAN_CONTRACT# = 277988
BALANCE_DATE = '960722'
CALL "CBLTDLI" USING DELT.
```

2.2 Network (CODASYL) Model

The Network model is a logical schema and is based on tables and graphs (CODASYL 1971). The nodes of a graph (segment types) usually correspond to the entity types, which are represented as connections (sets) between tables in the form of a network. The insertion and retention of segment types depend on the set membership constraints that exist between the owner and member segments, with automatic or manual insertion, and fixed, mandatory, or optional retention.

A network database model is similar to a hierarchical database model that represents data and a data relationship in a graphical form. The network model differs from the hierarchical model as:

- There can be more than one edge between a given pair of entities
- There is no concept of root and
- A segment can have more than one parent segment

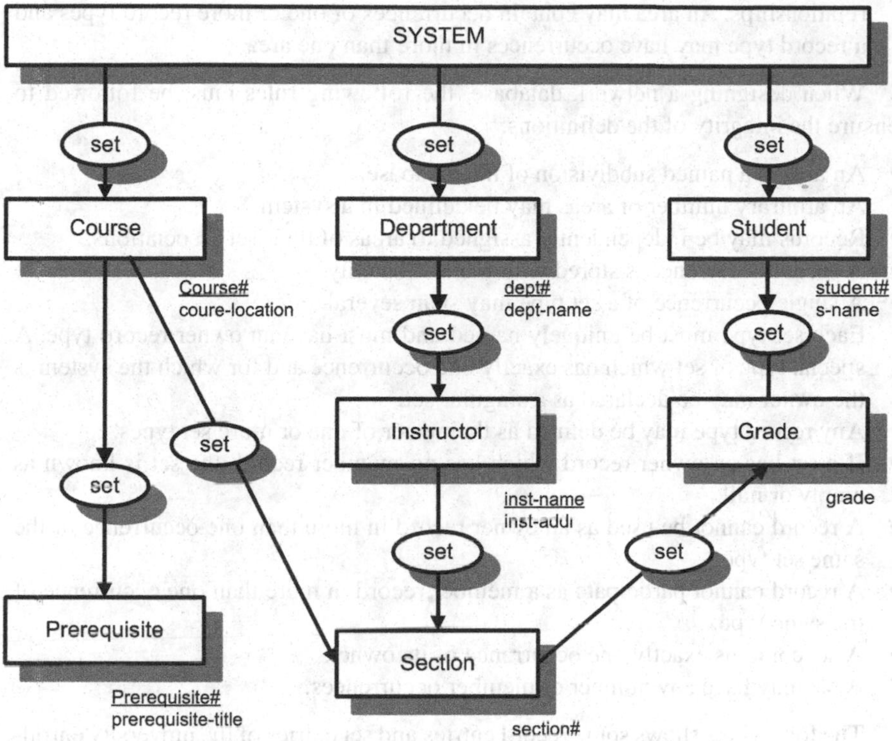

Fig. 2.3 A Network model for university enrollment

For example, Fig. 2.3 is a network model for the university enrollment system.

The CODASYL (Network) model is composed of two basic data constructs: the record and the set respectively. These two data constructs are built up from simpler data elements which are discussed in the following:

- Data Item – An occurrence of the smallest unit of named data. It is represented in the database by a value. A data item may be used to build other more complicated data constructs. This corresponds to an attribute in the ER data model.
- Data Aggregation – An occurrence of a named collection of data items within a record.
- Record – An occurrence of a named collection of data items or data aggregates. This collection is in conformity with the record type definition specified in the database schema.
- Set – An occurrence of a named collection of records. A set occurrence is in direct correspondence with the set type definition specified in the database schema. Each set type consists of one owner record type and at least one member record type.
- Area – The notion of an area used to identify the partition of record occurrences. An area is a named collection of records that need not preserve owner-member

relationships. An area may contain occurrences of one or more record types and a record type may have occurrences in more than one area.

When designing a network database, the following rules must be followed to ensure the integrity of the definitions:

- An area is a named subdivision of the database.
- An arbitrary number of areas may be defined in a system.
- Records may be independently assigned to areas of their set associations.
- A record occurrence is stored within one area only.
- A single occurrence of a set type may span several areas.
- Each set type must be uniquely named and must have an owner record type. A special type of set which has exactly one occurrence and for which the system is the owner may be declared as a singular set.
- Any record type may be defined as the owner of one or more set types.
- If a set has an owner record which has no member record, the set is known as empty or null.
- A record cannot be used as an owner record in more than one occurrence of the same set type.
- A record cannot participate as a member record in more than one occurrence of the same type.
- A set contains exactly one occurrence of its owner.
- A set may have any number of member occurrences.

The followings shows some record entries and set entries of the university enrollment system.

```
RECORD NAME IS DEPARTMENT WITHIN ANY AREA
  KEY DEPARTMENTID IS DEPARTMENT#
  DUPLICATES ARE NOT ALLOWED
  CALL CHECK-AUTHORIZATION BEFORE DELETE
  DEPARTMENT# TYPE IS NUMERIC INTEGER
  DEPARTMENT-NAME TYPE IS CHARACTER 30
```

```
RECORD NAME IS INSTRUCTOR WITHIN ANY AREA
  KEY INSTRUCTORID IS INSTRUCTOR-NAME
  DUPLICATES ARE ALLOWED
  CALL CHECK-AUTHORIZATION BEFORE DELETE.
  INSTRUCTOR-NAME TYPE IS CHARACTER 30
  INSTRUCTOR-ADDRESS TYPE IS CHARACTER 40
```

```
SET NAME IS HIRE
  OWNER IS DEPARTMENT
  ORDER IS PERMANENT INSERTION IS FIRST
```

```
MEMBER IS INSTRUCTOR
INSERTION IS AUTOMATIC RETENTION IS MANDATORY
SET SELECTION IS THRU HIRE OWNER IS IDENTIFIED
  BY APPLICATION
```

The INSERTION clause specifies the class of membership of a member record in a set type. There are two options in this clause: AUTOMATIC and MANUAL. For the AUTOMATIC option, the system ensures the status of the member record in the occurrences of the set type. For the MANUAL option, the application must handle the record as a member of some set occurrence in the database. The RETENTION is concerned with the ways in which records retain their membership in the database. There are three ways: FIXED, MANDATORY and OPTIONAL, for handling set membership. For the FIXED option, if a record occurrence is made a member in a set, then that record must exist as a member of the set in which it associates. For MANDATORY, if a record is made a member in some set, then it must exist as a member of some occurrence of this set type. Therefore, it is possible to transfer the record from one set occurrence to another. For OPTIONAL, a record is allowed to be moved from a set occurrence without requiring that the record be placed in a different occurrence.

2.2.1 Network Data Definition Language

As shown in Fig. 2.4, the DBTG (database task group) specification proposeS three levels of data organization. There are two pairs of DDL and DML for the schema level and sub-schema level respectively. The four languages are:

- The schema Data Definition Language, schema DDL
- The sub-schema Data Definition Language, sub-schema DDL
- The Data Manipulation Language, DML and
- The Data Storage Description Language, DSDL
- The schema is the logical description of the global database and is made up of a description of all the areas, set types, and record types as well as associated data items and data aggregates. A database is defined as consisting of all areas, records, and sets that are controlled by a specific schema. A schema definition consists of the following elements:
- A schema entry
- One or more area entries
- One or more record entities and
- One or more set entries

The schema must be mapped to the physical storage device. This transformation is achieved by declaring the physical properties of the schema in the DSDL. The use of the DDL and DSDL provide the DBMS with a certain degree of data

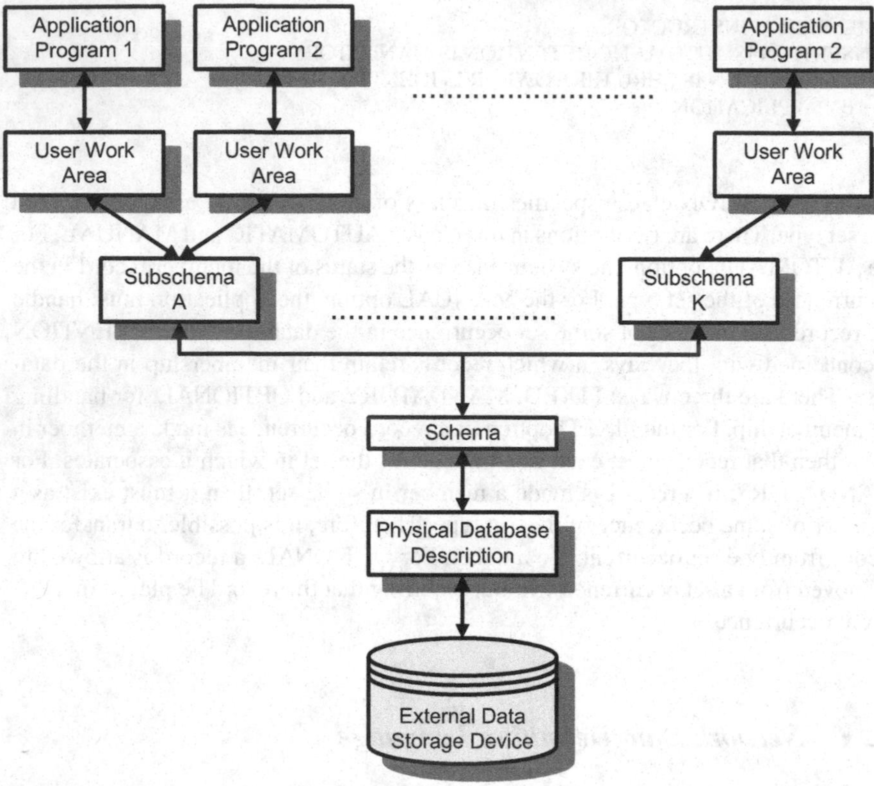

Fig. 2.4 Architecture of a CODASYL DBTG system

independence. In the DDL, the schema and area entries are more simple than the record and set entries. When declaring records and sets, database procedures must be defined by the database designer. Database procedures are specific to a particular database and are stored in the system. These procedures include validation of access, computation of data items values, and sorting sequence.

2.2.2 *Network Data Manipulation Language*

The language for operating a network database is called the network data DML. These DML commands can be embedded in a third-generation programming language called a host language. The DML commands can be divided into three groups: Navigation, Retrieval, and Updating. Navigation commands are used to set the currency indicators to specific records and set occurrences in the database. Retrieval commands extract the current record of the run unit. Updating commands are used to update, store, and delete records and set occurrences.

Several currency indicators are maintained by the database network system to enable the programmer to navigate through the database. The following currency indicators are useful when a DML is used.

- Current of run unit – A run unit currency indicator refers to the record most recently accessed by the run unit; there is only one currency indicator of this kind.
- Current of a set type – A set type currency indicator refers to the record within a given set type that was most recently accessed. There are as many currency indicators of this kind as the number of set types defined in the sub-schema referenced by this run unit.
- Current of record type – A record currency indicator refers to the record within a given type that was most recently accessed.

The following are the major network DML statements:

(a) OBTAIN First/Next record-name-i [USING {identifier-j}]
The OBTAIN statement is used to establish a specific record occurrence in the database. The target record of the OBTAIN statement becomes the current record. A number of different record selection expressions can be used in the OBTAIN statement. For example, the following statements are to obtain an occurrence of STUDENT record with student# = 1234 (Martin 1990).

```
MOVE            1234 TO STUDENT#.
OBTAIN ANY STUDENT USING STUDENT#.
```

(b) CONNECT record-name-i to set-name-j/all
The CONNECT statement makes a record of members of one or more set types. If these set types are enumerated, then the type of the current record must be either an OPTIONAL AUTOMATIC or a MANUAL member of these types. If ALL is selected, then this record type must be specified as an OPTIONAL AUTOMATIC or a MANUAL member in at least one set type declared in the sub-schema. For example, the following commands are to assign the student with student# = 1234 to the Computer Science Department.

```
MOVE        "Computer Science" TO name.
OBTAIN      Department USING name.
MOVE        1234 TO student#.
OBTAIN      Student USING student#
CONNECT     Student TO Department.
```

(c) DISCONNECT [record-name-i] from set-name-j/all
The DISCONNECT statement removes the current member record from all specified set types. If set types are enumerated, then the record type of the

current record must be an OPTIONAL member in each of the enumerated types. In the case when ALL is selected, the record type must be an OPTIONAL member in at least one set type of the subschema. For example, the following commands disconnect a student record from the department of computer science.

```
MOVE          "Computer Science" TO name.
OBTAIN        Department USING name.
MOVE          1234 TO student#.
OBTAIN        Student USING student#.
DISCONNECT    Student FROM Department.
```

(d) STORE record-name-i

The STORE statement actually writes the record created in the record area of the UWA (user working area) to the database. For example, the following commands store a student record of John Doe with student# = 1234.

```
MOVE          "John Doe" TO Name.
MOVE          1234 TO student#.
STORE         Student.
```

(e) MODIFY record-name-i

The modify statement is issued to change the contents of one or more data items in a record. It can also change the set membership of a record. For example, the following command changes a student's name from John Doe to John W. Doe.

```
MOVE          1234 TO student#.
OBTAIN        Student USING student#.
MOVE          "John W. Doe" TO Name.
MODIFY        Student.
```

(f) ERASE [ALL] [record-name-i].

To delete a record by the ERASE statement, the record must be located as the current record of the run unit. The current record of the run unit is removed provided that all affected sets are null sets. If ALL is specified and the current of the run unit is the owner of a non-null set, then all members of the set are removed. If the ALL option is not specified, then an affected set with member records can be removed only if its member records have FIXED or OPTIONAL membership in the set. For example, the following is the command to erase the student record with student# of 1234.

```
MOVE        1234 TO student#.
ERASE Student.
```

2.3 Relational Model

The relational model is a logical schema in the form of tables (relations) corresponding to the representation of an entity type. A column (attribute) of the tables represents the extension of attributes in the entity. The row (tuple) of the tables represents instances of the entity. Such tables are commonly called record types and consist of a non-null primary key that can uniquely identify a tuple. The parent-child relationship of relations is represented in the foreign key residing in the child relation referencing the primary key of parent relation.

The following are fundamental properties of a relational database:

- Column Homogeneous: For any given column of a relation, all items must be of the same kind whereas items in different columns may not be of the same kind.
- Indivisible Items: Each item is a simple number or a character string. It should represent a data element with the simplest form.
- Uniqueness of Records: All rows (records) of a relation are distinct. This implies that there must be a primary key for each record.
- Row Ordering: The ordering of rows within a relation is immaterial.
- Column Ordering: The columns of a relation are assigned distinct names and the ordering of the columns is immaterial.

For example, the following represents a relational model for university enrollment, where each table is a relation.

Relation Course

Course	Course-title	Location
CS101	Introduction to Computer Science	Lecture theater 1
IS201	System Analysis	Lecture theater 2
IS301	Decision Support System	Room P7818

Relation Prerequisite

*Course#	Prerequisite	Prereq-title
IS301	IS201	System Analysis

Relation Instructor

Inst-name	<u>SS#</u>	Inst-addr
A.B. Adams	415223614	White Plains
J.S. Fink	613557642	Brooklyn
A.M. Jones	452113641	Long Island

Relation Section

<u>SS#</u>	*<u>Course</u>	<u>Section#</u>	Lecture-hour
415,223,614	CS101	1	30
613,557,642	CS101	2	30

Relation Graduate Student

<u>Student#</u>	Degree-to-be
012888	M.Sc.
120,008	Ph.D.

Relation Student

<u>Student</u>	Student-name	Sex
012888	Paul Chitson	M
120008	Irene Kwan	F
117402	John Lee	M

Relation Enrollment

*<u>Student#</u>	*<u>Course</u>	<u>SS#</u>	<u>Section#</u>	<u>Year</u>	Grade
012888	CS101	415223614	1	1995	A
120008	CS101	613557642	2	1996	B

2.3.1 Normalization

The primary problem of relational database design is how the data item types should be combined to form record types that naturally and completely describe entities and the relationships between entities. E.F. Codd developed the theory of normalization in the 1970s to overcome this problem. The purpose of normalization is to reduce complex user views to a set of manageable and stable data structures.

Normalization theory is built around the concept of normal forms. A relation is said to be a particular normal form if it satisfies a certain specified set of constraints. Numerous normal forms have been defined. All normalized relations are in first normal form (1NF). Some 1NF relations are also in second normal form (2NF). Some 2NF are also in third normal form (3NF) (Elmasri and Navathe 1989).

A 1NF relates to the structure of relations such that the field of a relation should have simple and atomic values, and relations should have no repeating groups.

A 2NF is one where all partial dependencies have been removed from its 1NF. That is, no non-key field depends on a subset of a composite key.

A 3NF is one where all transitive dependencies have been removed from its 2NF. That is, no non-key field depends on another non-key field.

The normalization applies functional dependencies in its normal forms. Functional dependency is a relationship that exists between any two fields. We say that field A determines field B if each value of A has precisely one value of B. In other words, field B is functionally dependent on field A. This can be written as.

FD:A $\rightarrow$ B where A is a determinant and B is a dependent field.

The following is an example to illustrate normalization where student details form a repeating group.

Class#__________

Begin_date______________

Lecturer_name_______________

End_date______________

Lecturer_address______________

Student#	Student_name	Grade
…..	…..	….

The data in the above table is in unnormalized form because there are repeating groups of Student#, Student_name, and Grade. To normalize it into 1NF, we must eliminate the repeating groups by making them single data items in each tuple as follows:

Class (<u>Class#</u>, Lecturer_name, Lecturer_address,Begin_date, End_date)
Enrolled_Student (<u>Class#</u>, <u>Student#</u>, Student_name, Grade)

To normalize it into 2NF, we must eliminate the partial dependencies by making dependent field Student_name fully functionally dependent on Student# as follows:

Class (<u>Class#</u>, Lecturer_name, Lecturer_address, Begin_date, End_date)
Enrolled_Student (<u>Class#</u>, <u>Student#</u>, Grade)
Student (<u>Student#</u>, Student_name)

Finally, to normalize the relations into 3NF, we eliminate the transitive dependencies by making Lecturer_address dependent on Lecturer_name, not transitively dependent on class# as follows:

Class (Class#, Lecturer_name, Begin_date, End_date)
Lecturer (Lecturer_name, Lecturer_address)
Enrolled_Student (Class#, Student#, Grade)
Student (Student#, Student_name)

2.3.2 *Structured Query Language (SQL)*

SQL was introduced as the standard query language for relational DBMS. The basic structure of an SQL retrieval command, a Select statement, is as follows:

Select A_1, A_2, … A_n
from r^1, r^2…. r^n.
[where P].
[order by O]
[group by G]
[having H]

All classes contained within the square brackets are optional. The A_i represents attributes, the r_i represents relations, and P is a predicate and is default to be true. The attribute A_is may be replaced with a star (*) to select all attributes of all relations appearing in the form clause. O is the sort order of the target tuples based upon attribute values. G is the display group of the target attributes. H is the selection criteria of the display groups.

2.4 Relational Model Example

For example, if we use the normalized relations as the source, we can issue the following select statements:

- To retrieve the student# of all students

  Select Student# from Student

- To retrieve the student# of all students who are taking CS101

  Select Student# from Enroled-Student

  where Class# = CS101

- To retrieve the student# of all students who are taking CS101 and whose grade is A.

  Select Student# from Enroled-Student

  where Class# = CS101 and Grade = A

- To retrieve the address of all lecturers who teach CS101

  Select Lecturer_address from Enroled_Student, Lecturer

  where Enroled_Student.Lecturer_name =
  Lecturer.Lecturer_name
  and Class# = CS101

- List all student_name and student# of all students ordered by student_name. The default ordering is ascending lexiographic.

  Select Student# from Student

  order by Student_name

- List the class#, student#, and student_name of all students for each class.

  Select Class#, Student#, Student_name from

  Student,Enroled_Student
  where Student.Student# = Enroled_student.Student#
  group by Class#

- List all class#, student#, and student_name of all students for each class and whose grade is A.

  Select Class#, Student#, Student_name from

  Student,Enrolled_Student
  where Student.Student# = Enrolled_student.Student#
  group by Class#
  having Grade = 'A'

The database modification statements of SQL are as follows:

- Insertion

- The syntax of Insert statement of SQL is:

  Insert into R
  attributes (A1, A2… An)
  values (V_1, V_2 ,….V_n)

For example, insert a student with student# = 1234 and student name ="John Doe".

Insert into Student
attributes (Student#, Student_name)
values (1234, "John Doe")

- Updating
- The syntax of the update statement of SQL is:

  Update R
  Set $A_i = V_i$
  [where P]

For example, modify the grade of all students enrolled into CS101 to 'B'.

- Update Enrolled_Student
- Set Grade = 'B'
- where class# = 'CS101'
- Delete
- The syntax of delete statement of SQL is:
- Delete R
- [where P]

For example, delete the grade of student whose student# is 1234 and who is taking CS101.

Delete Enrolled_student
where Student# = 1234 and Class# = 'CS101'

2.5 Extended Entity Relationship Model

The Entity-Relationship (ER) Model (Chen 1976) is a special diagram technique used as a tool for logical database design. It serves as an informal representation to model the real world by adopting the more natural view such that the real world consists of entities and relationships; it also incorporates some important semantic information into the model. The model can achieve a high degree of data independence and is based on set theory and relation theory. It can be used as a basis for a unified view of data and a prelude to designing a conceptual database.

The components of an ER model are:

1. Entity set – An entity set (i.e. entity type) or an entity (i.e., entity instance) is an important, distinguishable object for an application, e.g., a regular entity, a weak entity.
2. Entity key – An entity attribute that can uniquely identify an entity instance.
3. Entity attribute – Fields that describe an entity (i.e., properties of an entity).
4. Degree of relationship – The number of entity sets that are related to each other. For example, unary means one entity, binary means two entities, ternary means three entities, and n-ary means n entities related to each other.
5. Cardinality – The connectivity of two entities, that is, one-to-one, one-to-many, and many-to-many.
6. Relationship membership – The insertion rules of relationship.

For example, mandatory means compulsory relationship; optional means not compulsory relationship.

7. (Minimum, maximum) occurrence – The minimum and maximum instances of cardinality. (For example, zero minimum occurrence means partial participation in an optional relationship.)

The Entity-Relationship (ER) model has been widely used but does have some shortcomings. It is difficult to represent cases where an entity may have varying attributes depending upon some property. For example, one might want to store different information for different employees dependent upon their role, although there will still be certain data such as name, job title, and department that remain common to all employees. Employees who are engineers may require professional qualifications to be stored. We may need to know the typing speed of typist employees and would need to store the language spoken by each translator employee.

Because of these limitations, the Extended Entity-Relationship Model (EER) has been proposed by several authors (Kozaczynski and Lilien 1988), although there is no general agreement on what constitutes such a model. Here, we will include in our model the following additions to the ER model:

- Generalization (Elmasri and Navathe 1989) – More than one isa relationship can form data abstraction (superclass/subclass) among entities. A subclass entity is a subset of its superclass entity. There are two kinds of generalization. The first is disjoint generalization such that subclass entities are mutually exclusive, which can be differentiated by a field in the superclass entity. The second is overlap generalization in which subclass entities can overlap each other and can be differentiated by fields in the superclass entity.
- Categorization – More than one isa relationship form data abstraction among entities such that the union of entities form a superclass entity to a subclass entity.
- Aggregation – The relationship between entities and relationships can be aggregated (grouped) as an entity.

In summary, an Extended Entity Relationship model consists of eight data semantics as shown in Fig. 2.5 (Teroey et al. 1986).

Figure 2.5 illustrates different data semantics including:

(a) One-to-many cardinality between entities E_a and E_b.
(b) Weak entity E_b concatenates the key of A1 from E_a
(c) Subclass entity E_b is a subset of entity E_a with the same key A_b A_c
(d) Entity E_b is in total participation with Entity E_a
(e) Binary relationship R_b of entity E_{b1} relating with entity E_{b2} is an aggregate entity
(f) Subclass entity E^a and E^b can be generalized into superclass entity $E^{x.}$
(g) Subclass E_a is a subset of the union of superclass entity E_{x1} and E_{x2}.
(h) Entities E_a, E_b and E_c are in many-to-many ternary relationship

A sample of an Extended Entity-Relationship model for a hospital patient record system is in Fig. 2.6. A patient is insured by many insurance coverage. A patient belongs to many record folders. Each record folder contains many medical records. An AE record, a ward record, and an outpatient record can be generalized as medical records.

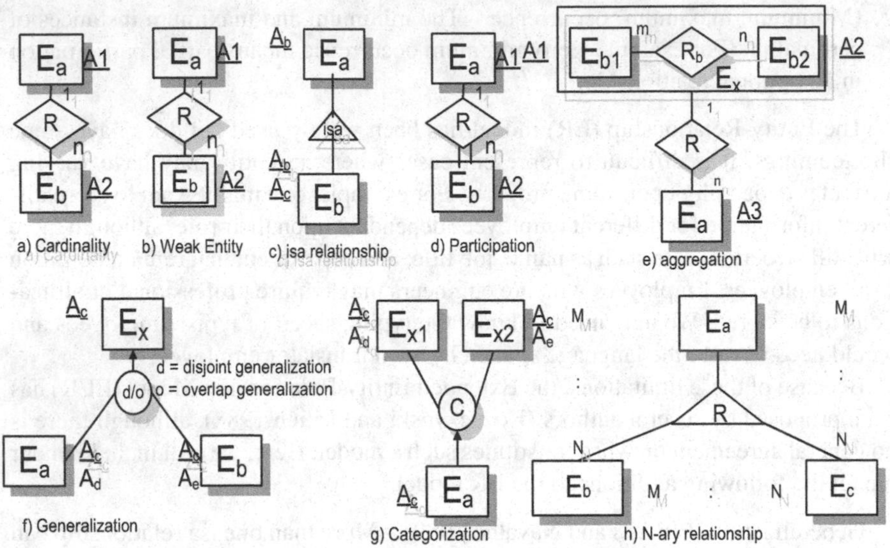

Fig. 2.5 Eight data semantics in Extended Entity Relationship model

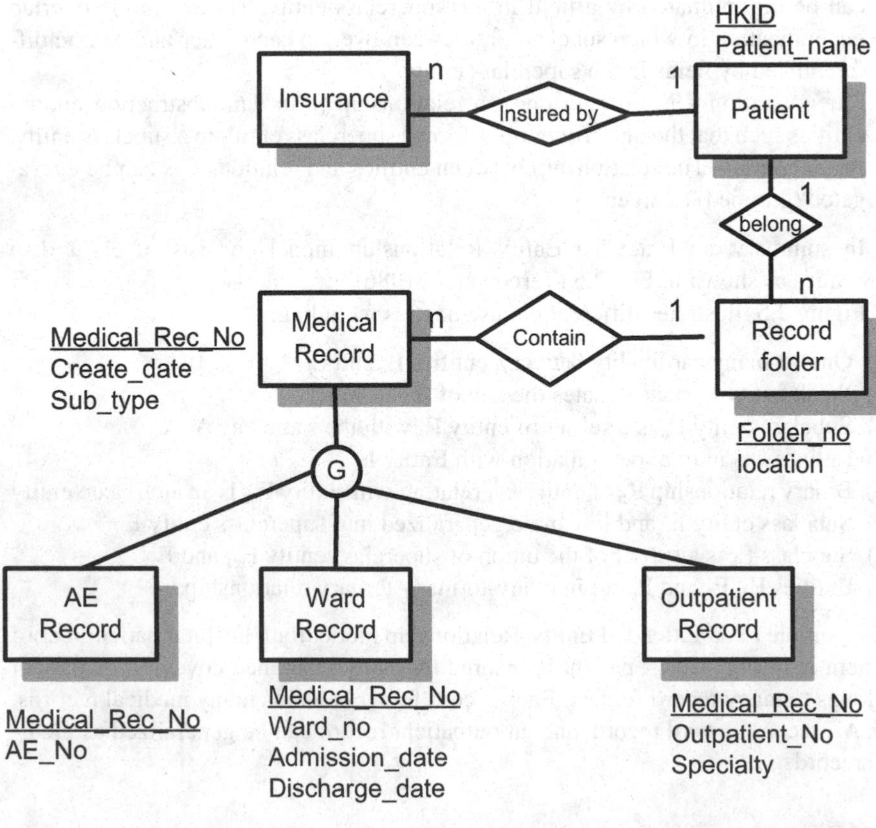

Fig. 2.6 An Extended Entity Relationship model for hospital patient record

2.6 Object-Oriented Model

To date, numerous object-oriented data models have been proposed. In an object-oriented data model (Hughes 1991), the world is viewed as a set of objects that communicate with each other by exchanging messages and can be described as follows.

Object-oriented model is a logical schema in the form of objects with names, properties, and behavior. An object represents "a thing" that is important to users in the portion of reality that the users want to model. Each object belongs to a family, or class, of similar objects. A class is a template (containing code and data) that describes the common characteristics of a set of objects. Object-oriented database systems simplify programming database updates and provide faster access to stored data by blurring the distinction between programming language and database.

Objects that have similar properties are grouped together into a class. Each class has an ID that is called the object ID (i.e., OID). The object IDs are unique. The IDs need not necessarily be the same as the primary key values used to identify the tuples in the relational model.

A class has properties that describe the objects of the class. These properties are called instance variables (i.e., attributes). A link is a physical or conceptual connection between object instances (i.e., classes). A link is an instance of an association.

Classes have methods associated with them. Methods are procedures that are executed when they are invoked. Methods are invoked when appropriate messages are received. An instance variable (i.e., attribute) could be either a non-composite instance variable or it could be a composite variable. Non-composite instance variables are divided further into simple instance variables and complex instance variables. Simple instance variables take individual objects as their values. An individual object could be a basic system object such as integer, string, or Boolean, or a user-defined object. Complex instance variables (i.e., complex objects) take a set or a list of individual objects as their values. For example, a complex instance variable HOBBY can have multiple values (SWIMMING, TENNIS, MUSIC).

Any class that has a composite instance variable is a composite class. The instances belonging to such a class are composite objects. A composite object together with its components forms an IS-PART-OF hierarchy. The link from a composite object to its component is called a composite link. For example, a composite class CAR can have attributes (BODY, ENGINE, TIER) and each one of them is a class itself.

A second hierarchy that may be formed is the ISA hierarchy, where subclasses are associated with a class. The subclasses inherit all the methods and instance variables defined for the class. A subclass could also have some additional instance variables and methods. For example, a subclass GRADUATE_STUDENT can inherit all the attributes and methods of its superclass STUDENT.

An object-oriented data model has the following properties:

- An object is an instance value of a class. A class can have many instances. A class has attributes and methods. The attributes of a class describe its properties. The methods of a class describe its operations.

- A class must support encapsulation (i.e., hiding operations from the users) such that.

  object = data + program
  data = values of attributes
  program = methods that operates on the state

- Object attributes can be either simple or complex. The value of a complex attribute is a reference to the instance of another class. In other words, an object can be a nested object such that the value of an object is another object.
- Polymorphism allows a program entity to refer at run-time to instances of a variety of types.
- Object attributes can be single-valued or multi-valued.
- Objects are uniquely identified by an object identifier (OID) that are assigned by the system.
- In a class hierarchy, a subclass inherits attributes and methods from one or more superclasses.

An example of a class Department and a class Instructor is shown below:

```
Class Department
   attribute Dept#: integer
   attribute Dept-name: string
   association attribute hire ref set(Instructor)
   Method
   Create Department
end Department
Class Instructor
   attribute Inst-name: string
   attribute Inst-addr: string
   association attribute hired-by ref Department
   Method
   Create Instructor
 end Instructor.
```

In this example, the class Department has a complex attribute Instructor such that the attributes and the methods of an independent class Instructor is contained in the class Department. The data structure of the Object-oriented schema can be illustrated in Fig. 2.7 where the class defining and object is used to find the code for the method that is applied to the object (Date 1995).

In an object-oriented schema, a special relationship between an instance of a subclass and the instances of the deep extent of a class exists. Such a relationship can be represented by a "class instance inclusion dependence" indicating that the class instances of a subclass are a subset of the class instances of its superclass. In other words, every instance value of a subclass is also an instance value of its superclass. However, for every instance value of a superclass, there may not be any subclass object. Thus, the isa relationship can be described as an ID (inclusion dependency) in an object-oriented schema as follows:

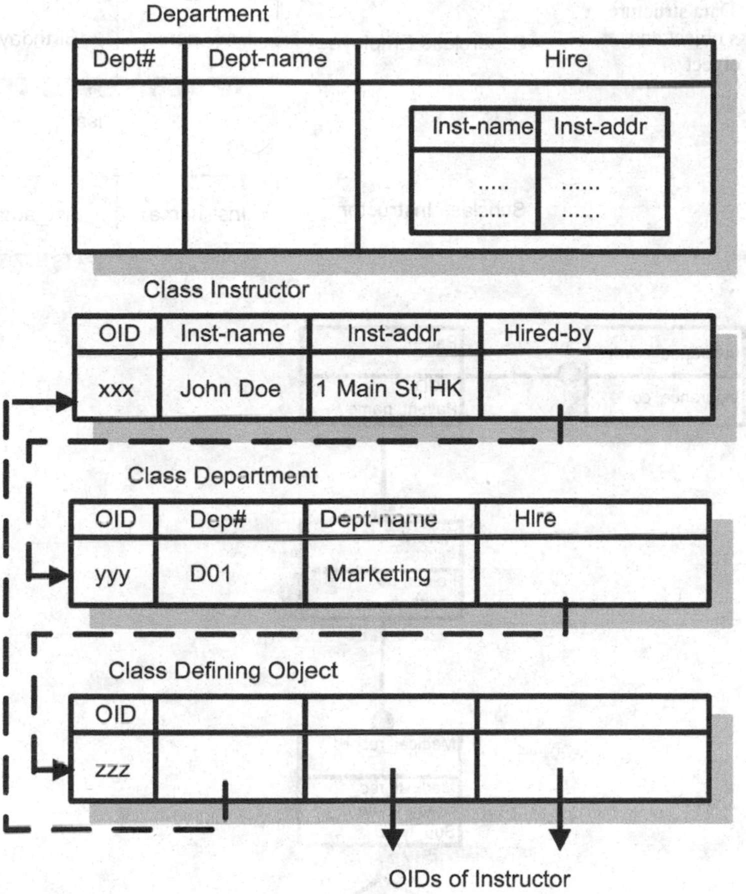

Fig. 2.7 A containment hierarchy data structure in object-oriented schema

ID: subclass object OID ⊆ All superclass object OID.
(Note: "All" refers to the deep extent of the class.)

This can be illustrated in Fig. 2.8.

2.6.1 Unified Model Language

To describe the semantic of the object-oriented database, we use an object-oriented conceptual model such as Unified Model Language, which is popular in object-oriented system design. In general, UML is more powerful than the EER model because UML includes not only static data but also dynamic data behavior in its method. The syntax of Unified Model Language can be described as follows (Booch 1994):

Fig. 2.8 Data structure of superclass object and subclass object

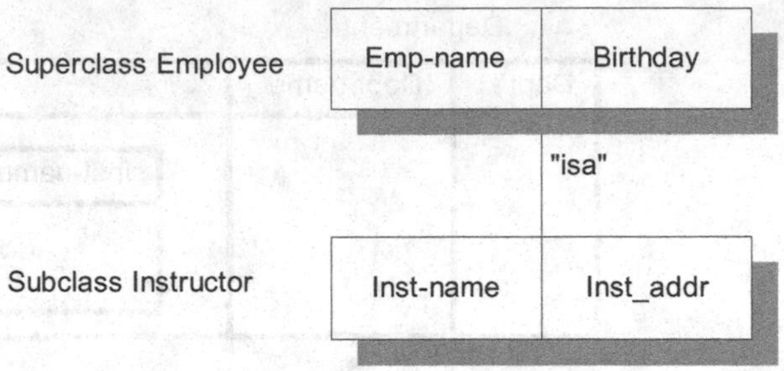

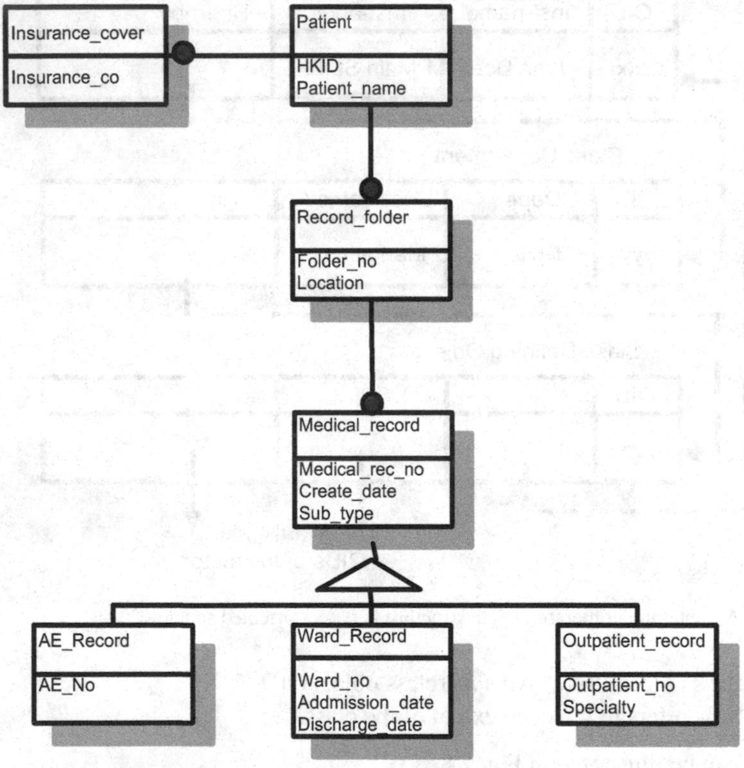

Fig. 2.9 An object-oriented model for hospital patient record

- Class – Each rectangular box is a class. For example, in Fig. 2.9 Patient is a class.
- Each class consists of three components: class name, attributes, and methods. For example, Class Patient has attributes HKID and Patient_name, and a method Create Patient.
- Links – The association between two classes are called links. The dot sign at the end of the link indicates the cardinality of the association. A dot sign means that more than one occurrence of the entity exist at that end. A straight line without a dot sign means one occurrence of the entity exists at that end. For example, in Fig. 2.9, there is a link between class Patient and class Insurance. The solid dot sign where the link attaches to the class Insurance side means each Patient can link with more than one Insurance.

- Aggregation – A diamond sign that links classes is called aggregation. Aggregation represents "part-of" semantics. The bottom part(s) is the component(s) of the top part (the aggregated class). The existence of the component(s) part depends on its aggregated class. If the aggregated class is deleted, then the component parts are also deleted. The components of aggregation must exist before the aggregate can be created.
- Inheritance – An triangular symbol that links classes is called the inheritance symbol. The apex of the triangle is linked to the superclass with the subclasses being linked to the base of the triangle. Figure 2.9 shows that class AE_Record is a subclass that inherits the attributes and methods of its superclass Medical_Record.
- Navigation – Given an association between two classes, it is possible to navigate from objects of one kind to objects of the other kind. Unless otherwise specified, navigation across an association is bidirectional.

In Unified Model Language, a class diagram is a collection of declarative model elements, such as classes, their contents and relationships. It is a graphical view of the static structural model. It shows the relationship between classes and the attributes and operations of a class.

A class is a description of a set of objects that share the same data structure (attributes), behaviors (operations), methods, and relationships. Objects are instances of classes. An attribute is a class property that specifies the data structure that instances of the class may contain. An operation is a class interface that is invoked on an object to manipulate attributes. A method is the implementation of an operation. It specifies a program or procedure associated with an operation. The relationship is a connection among model elements.

Association and generalization are useful relationships specified in Unified Model Language. Association is the semantic relationship between two or more classes that specifies connections among their instances. It consists of at least two ends, each specifying a connected class and a set of properties such as navigability and multiplicity that must be fulfilled for the relationship to be valid. Association class is a model element that has both association and class properties. It allows the addition of attributes and operations to an association.

In summary, there are basically five major data semantics in the Unified Model Language class diagram as shown in Fig. 2.9 in the following semantics:

(a) One-to-many association between classes Patient and class Record folder
(b) Subclass AE record, subclass Ward record, and subclass Outpatient record is a subset of superclass Medical record.

2.6.2 Object-Oriented Data Definition Language

There are many commercial object-object databases in the industry. In this book, we choose UniSQL (UniSQL 1992) as a representative for illustration purposes. In order to implement the abstract data type, we must first define each class. A class is a collection of many objects with similar properties. Each object is an instance of a class. A class consists of a class name, attributes,

and methods, and can be defined as follows:

```
Class <class-name>
Attributes
   [inherit    <class-name>]
   <attribute-name>: [set] <primitive data type>/<class>
Method
   [operations]
```

A class must have a unique name and can inherit from any other class that is not a descendant of itself. The attribute describes the properties of a class. Its data type can be a primitive one such as integer, numeric, and character. It can be another class. If it is another class, it is called a complex object, which means a class is within another class or a nested class. If an object associates many other objects, then we must use Set in describing the associated attributes. This is similar to 1:m cardinality in the ER model and in a relational model.

The inherit statement is to indicate that the subclass inherits attributes and methods from its superclass. The class with the inherit statement is the subclass. The target class after the inherit keyword is the superclass. The methods are the defined/stored operation(s) of a class.

The object-oriented data definition language of UniSQL consists of Create class statement, as follows:

Create – Use a create statement to define a class. For example,

```
Create class Department
  (Dept#: integer,
  Dept-name: char(30),
  Hire: set-of Instructors)
Procedure
  Display Department.
```

```
Create class Instructor
  (Inst-name: char(30),
  Inst-addr: char(50),
  Hired-by: Department)
Procedure
  Display Instructor.
```

2.7 Extensible Markup Language

XML is defined as EXtensible Markup Language (XML). Its development can be traced up to World Wide Web Consortium (W3C 2004) recommendation Version 1.0 as of 10/02/1998. It describes data, rather than instructing a system on how to process it, and provides powerful capabilities for data integration and data-driven styling, introduces new processing paradigms, and requires new ways of thinking about Web development. It is a Meta-Markup Language with a set of rules for creating semantic tags used to describe data.

XML is a supplement to HTML such that it is not a replacement for HTML. It will be used to structure and describe the Web data while HTML will be used to format and display the same data. XML can keep data separated from an HTML document. XML can also store data inside HTML documents (Data Islands). XML can be used to exchange and store data.

With the development of the Internet, the third generation of post-relational database may be an XML database, which uses an XML document as its fundamental unit, defines a model such as elements, attributes, PCDATA, etc. for an XML instance, and is stored as either binary code or text file. XML has been widely used on the Internet for business transactions in both B2B and B2C. We can expect a strong need to migrate relational databases into XML documents for the reengineering and the interoperability of the relational and XML databases.

The XML schema can be described in the form of Data Type Declaration (DTD) which is a mechanism (set of rules) to describe the structure, syntax, and vocabulary of XML documents. DTD defines the legal building blocks of an XML document. It has a set of rules to define document structure with a list of legal elements, and declared inline in the XML document or as an external reference. All names are user-defined. One DTD can be used for multiple documents.

An XML element is made up of a *start tag*, an *end tag*, and data in between. The name of the element is enclosed by the less than and greater than characters, and these are called tags. The start and end tags describe the data within the tags, which is considered the *value* of the element. For example, the following XML element is a < Hospital> element with the value "Queen's".

<Hospital>Queen's</Hospital>.

XML has three kinds of tags as follows:

- **Start-Tag**
- In the example <Patient> is the start tag. It defines type of the element and possible *attribute specifications*

<Patient HKID="E376684" Patient_name="John Doe"></Patient>

All XML documents must have a root (start) tag.
Documents must contain a single tag pair to define the root element.
All other elements must be nested within the root element.
All elements can have sub (children) elements.
Sub-elements must be in pairs and correctly nested within their parent element:

```
<root>
   <child>
      <subchild>
      </subchild>
   </child>
</root>
```

- **End-Tag**
- In the example </Patient> is the end tag. It identifies the type of element that tag is ending. Unlike start tag, an end tag cannot contain *attribute specifications.*
- All XML elements must have a closing tag. In XML, all elements must have a closing tag like this:

<p > This is a paragraph</p>
<p > This is another paragraph</p>

- **Empty Element Tag.**
- Like start tag, this has *attribute specifications* but it does not need an end tag. It denotes that the element is empty (does not have any other elements). Note that the symbol is for ending tag '/' before '>'

<Patient HKID = "E376684" Patient_name="John Doe"/>

Attributes are always contained within the start tag of an element. Here is an example:

<Patient HKID="E376684" patient_name="John Doe" />

Patient	- Element Name
HKID	- Attribute Name
E376684	- Attribute Value

Attribute values must always be quoted. XML elements can have attributes in name/value pairs just like in HTML. An element can optionally contain one or more *attributes*. In XML, the attribute value must always be quoted. An attribute is a name-value pair separated by an equal sign (=). An example of an XML document is:

```
<?xml version="1.0"?>
<note>
<to>Tan Siew Teng</to>
<from>Lee Sim Wee</from>
<heading>Reminder</heading>
<body>Don't forget the Golf Championship this weekend!</body>
</note>
```

The first line in the document: *The XML declaration* must be included. It defines the XML version of the document. In this case the document conforms to the 1.0 specification of XML. <?xml version = "1.0"? > The next line defines the first element of the document (the root element): <note>.

The next lines defines four child elements of the root (to, from, heading, and body):

```
<to>Tan Siew Teng</to>
<from>Lee Sim Wee</from>
<heading>Reminder</heading>
<body>Don't forget the Golf Championship this weekend!
</body>
```

The last line defines the end of the root element:

```
</note>
```

A typical XML system is as shown in Fig. 2.10.

1. XML Document (content)
2. XML Document Type Definition – DTD (structure definition; this is an operational part)
3. XML Parser (conformity checker)
4. XML Application (uses the output of the Parser to achieve your unique objectives)

A sample XML DTD schema for Hospital patient record in DTD is:

```
<?xml version-“1.0”
<!ELEMENT Patient_Records (Patient+)>
<!ELEMENT Patient (Record_Folder+)>
<!ATTLIST Patient

    HKID CDATA #REQUIRED
    Patient_Name CDATA #REQUIRED
    Country_Code CDATA #REQUIRED>

<!ELEMENT Record_Folder (Medical_Record+, Borrow*)>
<!ATTLIST Record_Folder

    Folder_No ID #REQUIRED
    Location CDATA #REQUIRED>

<!ELEMENT Medical_Record (AE | Ward | Outpatient)>
<!ATTLIST Medical_Record

    Medical_Rec_No CDATA #REQUIRED
    Create_Date CDATA #REQUIRED
    Sub_Type CDATA #REQUIRED>
```

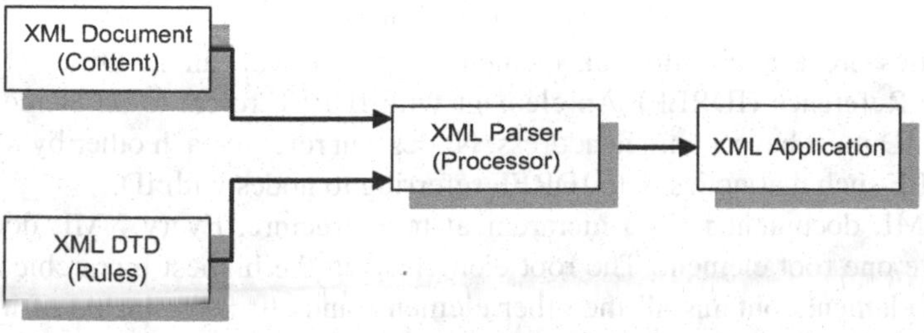

Fig. 2.10 Architecture of XML database system

```
<!ELEMENT AE EMPTY>
<!ATTLIST AE
      AE_No CDATA #REQUIRED>
<!ELEMENT Ward EMPTY>
<!ATTLIST Ward
      Ward_No CDATA #REQUIRED
      Admission_Date CDATA #REQUIRED
      Discharge_Date CDATA #REQUIRED>
<!ELEMENT Outpatient EMPTY>
<!ATTLIST Outpatient
      Outpatient_No CDATA #REQUIRED
      Specialty CDATA #REQUIRED>
,!ELEMENT Borrow(Loan_History)>
<!ATTLIST Borrow Borrow_no CDATA #REQUIRED>
<!ELEMENT Loan_History EMPTY>
<!ATTLIST Loan_History Loan_date CDATA REQUIRED>
```

2.7.1 Data Type Definition Graph

XML started in 1998 as a new data standard on the Internet. XML documents can be stored in a native XML database or an XML enabled database. The former is an XML-oriented database management system. The latter is a relational database with an XML Application Program Interface (API).

To design an XML database, one needs to construct an XSD Graph in the form of a hierarchical containment, starting with a root element on top of other elements. An XML schema can be stored in a Data Type Definition (DTD) or an XML schema Definition Language (XSD).

Given the DTD information of the XML to be stored, we can create a structure called the Data Type Definition Graph (Funderburk et al. 2002) that mirrors the structure of the DTD. Each node in the Data Type Definition graph represents an XML element in rectangle, an XML attribute in semi-cycle, and an operator in the cycle. They are put together in a hierarchical containment under a root element node, with element nodes under a parent element node.

Facilities are available to link elements together with an Identifier (ID) and Identifier Reference (IDREF). An element with IDREF refers to an element with ID. Each ID must have a unique address. Nodes can refer to each other by using ID and IDREF such that nodes with IDREF referring to nodes with ID.

An XML document is in a hierarchical tree structure. Every XML document must have one root element. The root element is in the highest hierarchical level. The root element contains all the other elements and attributes inside of it. Other elements are in hierarchical order such that they are in relative parent or child nodes.

That is, the relative higher level is the parent node and the relative lower level is the child node.

An element is the basic building block of an XML document. An element name must start with a letter or underscore character. An element can have a sub-element under it. An empty element does not have a sub-element. Between element and sub-element, there are declarations that control the occurrences of sub-elements. For example, one can define element instances in a Document Type Definition (DTD) with an Occurrence indicator. For example, the "*" operator identifies "set" sub-elements that can occur from zero to many times under a parent element. The "+" occurrence indicator specifies one to many times occurrence under a parent element. The "?" occurrence indicator specifies zero to one time occurrence under a parent element.

Attributes give more information about an element and reside inside of the element. Attributes can further define the behavior of an element and allow it to have extended links by giving it an identifier.

For example, the following is a Data Type Definition Graph with the root element Patient_Record. In Fig. 2.11, the Data Type Definition Graph has a root element Patient record. Under the root element Patient Record, there is an element of Patient. Element Patient has a sub-element Record folder. The Element Record folder has one sub-element, Medical record. Element Medical record has the sub-element AE record, sub-element Ward record, or sub-element Outpatient record.

2.7.2 *XML Schema Definition and XSD Graph*

XML Schema Definition (XSD) (Fong and Cheung 2005) is at the logical level of the XML model and is used in most Web applications. At present, there is no standard format for the conceptual level of the XML model. Therefore, we introduce an XSD Graph as an XML conceptual schema for representing and confirming the data semantics according to the user requirements in a diagram. The XSD Graph consists of nodes representing all elements within the XSD and can capture the data semantics of root elements, weak elements, participation, cardinality, aggregation, generalization, categorization, and n-ary association. These data semantics can be implemented by the structural constraints of XSD such as key, keyref, minOccurs, maxOccurs, Choice, Sequence, and extension. They can be shown as follows:

Element

Element are tags with texts between them

– Proper nesting

<account> … <balance> …. </balance> </account>

– Improper nesting

<account> … <balance> …. </account> </balance>

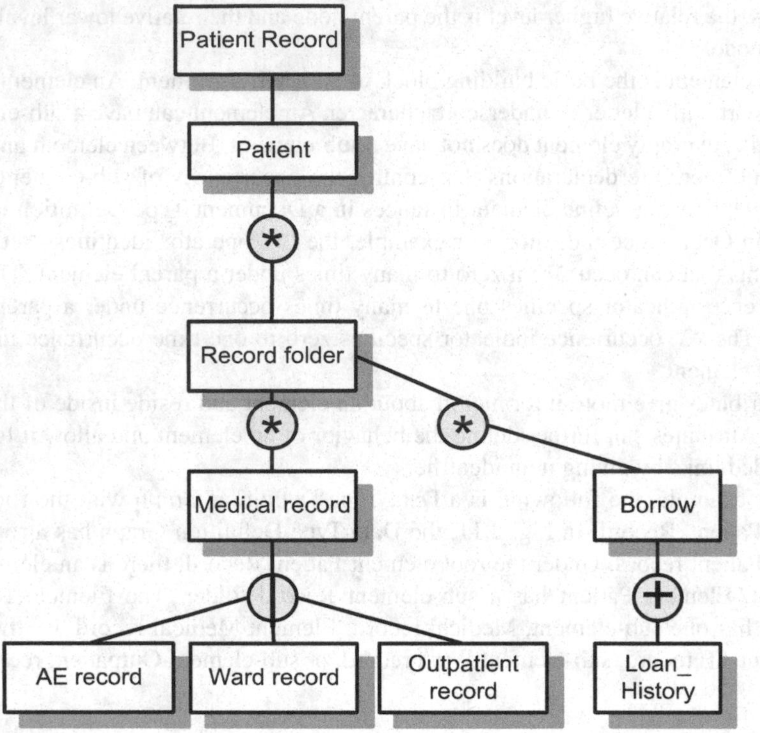

Fig. 2.11 A data type definition graph for patient record

Sub-element
Sub-element is an element inside another element.

– <account> <balance>…. </balance> </account>
– <balance>…</balance> is a sub-element of <account>…</account>

Attribute
An element may have several attributes, but each attribute name can only occur once

<account type = "checking" charge = "5">

Name Space
XML data is to be exchanged and appended by regions
Same tags may be used by multiple regions.

– Can't avoid using the same names

Solution: "name_space : element_name"

<bank xmlns:FB='http://www.HKBank.com'>

Complex Element

- A complex element is an XML element that contains other elements and/or attributes.

There are four kinds of complex elements:

- Empty elements
- Elements that contain only other elements
- Elements that contain only text
- Elements that contain both other elements and text

Element Groups
Element groups are defined with the group declaration, like this:

```
<xs:group name="persongroup">
<xs:sequence>

    <xs:element name="firstname" type="xs:string"/>
    <xs:element name="lastname" type="xs:string"/>
    <xs:element name="birthday" type="xs:date"/>

</xs:sequence>
</xs:group>
```

User-defined Data Type
User can define their own data type by definion <type: "xxx">; xxx is not a primitive data type. The following is an example.

```
<xs:element name="staff">
<xs:complexType>
    <xs:sequence>
    <xs:element name="staff_name" type="name"/>
    <xs:element name="post" type="xs:string"/>
    </xs:sequence>
</xs:complexType>
</xs:element>
<xs:complexType name="name">
<xs:sequence>
    <xs:element name="firstname" type="xs:string"/>
    <xs:element name="lastname" type="xs:string"/>

</xs:sequence>
</xs:complexType>
```

Extension
Extension can be used for defining Generalization or Isa constraint.
The following is an example.

```
<xs:element name="b" type="b_type"/>
<xs:complexType name="b_type">
<xs:complexContent>

    <xs:extension base="a"/>
```

```
</xs:complexContent>
</xs:complexType>
<xs:complexType name="a">
<xs:sequence>

    <xs:element name="a_name" type="xs:string"/>

</xs:sequence>
</xs:complexType>
```

Choice

The <choice> indicator specifies that either one child element or another can occur:

```
<xs:element name="person">
<xs:complexType>

    <xs:choice>

        <xs:element name="employee“ type="employee"/>
        <xs:element name="member" type="member"/>

    </xs:choice>

</xs:complexType>
</xs:element>
```

We can also apply an XML Schema Definition Graph (XSD Graph) (Fong and Cheung 2005), as shown in Fig. 2.12, as an XML conceptual schema to model and analyze the structure of an XML database. The benefit of using the XSD Graph is being able to visualize, specify, and document structural constraints in a visible diagram, and also to construct executable systems. The model can be used to represent the inter-relationship of elements inside a logical schema, such as XSD, DTD, Schematron, XDR. SOX, DSD, and so on, together with various data semantics specifications.

In general, an XSD Graph can be used to represent the structural constraints of an XML schema and an XML document with the following specifications:

Rule 1: Root element – An XML schema must be in a hierarchical tree structure starting with a root element. Other relevant elements must be under the root element.

Fig. 2.12 (continued) (m) E_b with "min = 1" keyword that is a sub-element links up with an element E_a for showing total participation relationship.
(n) E_a links up with an element E_b by a concrete line with an arrow for showing partial participation relationship.
(o) Three elements named E_a, E_b, and E_c are pointed by a group named G_{abc} with "m:n:n" keyword pointed by an element E_r for showing "m:n:n" ternary relationship.
(p) Broken line with an arrow represents a "ref" keyword within a group declaration.
(q) Concrete Line with arrow represents a "ref" keyword within an element declaration.
(r) Hierarchy path shows one top element with two sub-elements

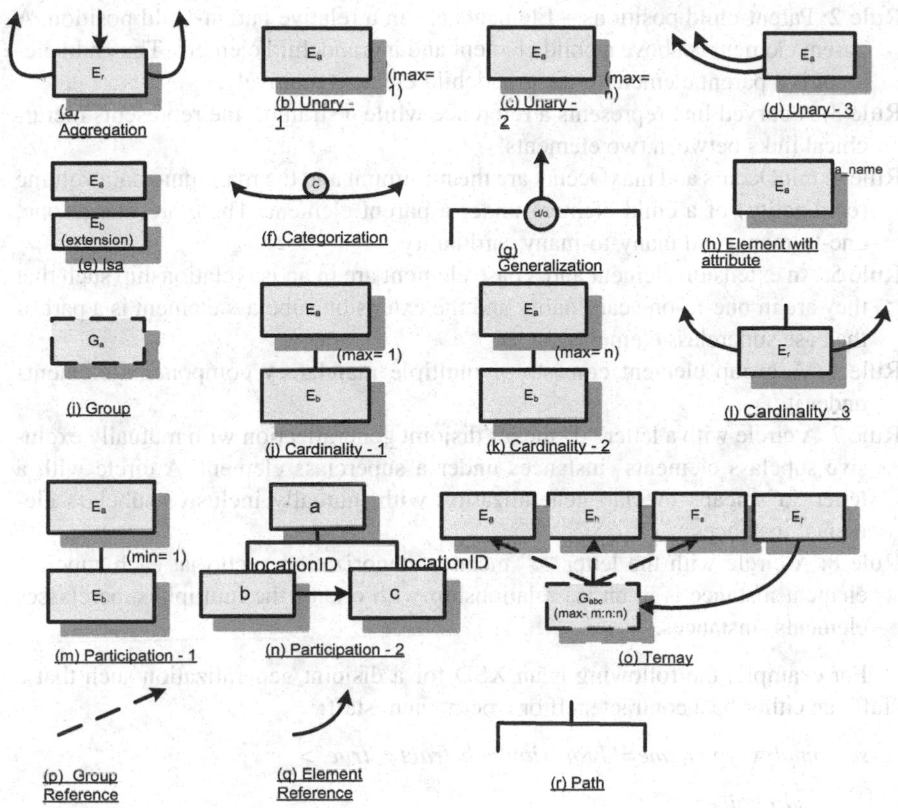

Fig. 2.12 Legends for XSD graph
where

(a) Sub-element E_r that is an aggregate element addresses to two elements for creating a binary relationship in "m:n" cardinality.
(b) E_a that is in "1:1" cardinality addresses to itself for creating u-ary relationship.
(c) E_a that is in "1:n" cardinality addresses to itself for creating u-ary relationship.
(d) E_a that is in "m:n" cardinality constructs two links addressing to the same element for creating u-ary relationship.
(e) E_b with the "extension" keyword inherits all properties of E_a for showing the "isa" relationship.
(e) Sub-element with "c" circle that is a subset in union operation of relational algebra links up with two group elements by using "choice" keyword.
(f) Two or more sub-elements with "d" or "o" circle can be generalized from element for showing disjoint or overlap generalization.
(h) E_a represents an element with an attribute declaration.
(i) G_a represents a group declaration.
(j) E_b is a sub-element belonging to an element E_a. E_b is in a "1:1" cardinality relationship in connection with E_a.
(k) E_b is a sub-element belonging to an element E_a. E_b is in a "1:n" cardinality relationship in connection with E_a.
(l) E_r that is a sub-element addresses to two elements for creating a "m:n" cardinality relationship.

(continued)

Rule 2: Parent-child positions – Elements are in a relative parent-child position. A parent element is above a child element and a grandchild element. The child element is a parent element to the grandchild element relatively.

Rule 3: A curved line represents a reference while a straight line represents hierarchical links between two elements.

Rule 4: minOccurs and maxOccurs are the minimum and the maximum data volume (cardinality) of a child element under a parent element. There are one-to-one, one-to-many, and many-to-many cardinality.

Rule 5: An extension element and a base element are in an isa relationship such that they are in one-to-one cardinality and the extension subclass element is a part of the base superclass element.

Rule 6: A group element consists of multiple mandatory components elements under it.

Rule 7: A circle with a letter "d" means disjoint generalization with mutually exclusive subclass elements' instances under a superclass element. A circle with a letter "o" means overlap generalization with mutually inclusive subclass elements' instances.

Rule 8: A circle with the letter "c" means categorization such that each subclass element instance is in an isa relationship with one of the multiple superclasses elements' instances.

For example, the following is an XSD for a disjoint generalization such that a staff can either be a contract staff or a permanent staff:

```
<xsd:complexType name="Librarian" abstract="true">

    <xsd:choice>
    <xsd:element name="contract" type="lib:ContractStaff"/>

<xsd:element name="permanent" type="lib:PermanentStaff"/>
</xsd:choice>
</xsd:complexType>
```

Its corresponding XSD graph is shown in Fig. 2.13.

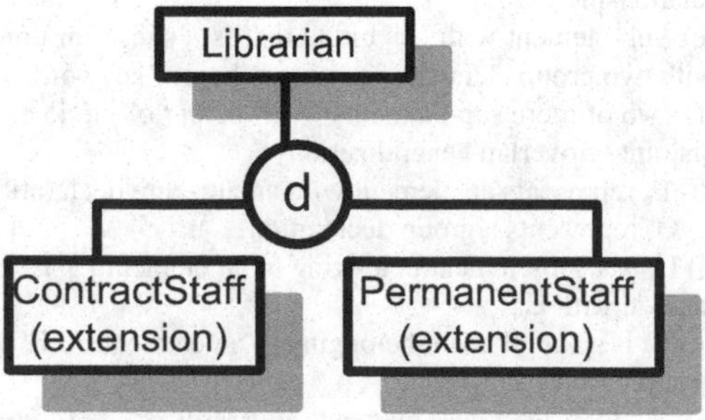

Fig. 2.13 An XSD graph for a disjoint generalization

2.8 Expert System

An expert system (ES) has been seen as an important information system for organizations in recent years. It is a piece of software that seeks to model the expertise of a human expert within a specific narrow problem domain. It has a comparatively short history under the aegis of Artificial Intelligence (AI). The early period of AI was dominated by the brief that a few general problem-solving strategies implemented on a computer could produce expert-level performance in a particular domain. As AI was developed, it was soon realized that such general-purpose mechanisms were too weak to solve the most complex problems. In reaction to these limitations, users began to concentrate on more narrowly defined problems, and expert systems were developed.

An ES generally consists of five parts (see Fig. 2.14):

- Inference engine: The component of the system that uses the knowledge base to respond to queries posed by users.
- Knowledge base: The repository of domain-specific knowledge.
- Working memory: A data area used for storing the intermediate or partial results of problem solving.
- User interface: An interface that allows end-users to interact with the ES.
- Explanation subsystem: A set of facilities that enable the user to ask questions of the system, about how, for instance, the system came to a particular conclusion.

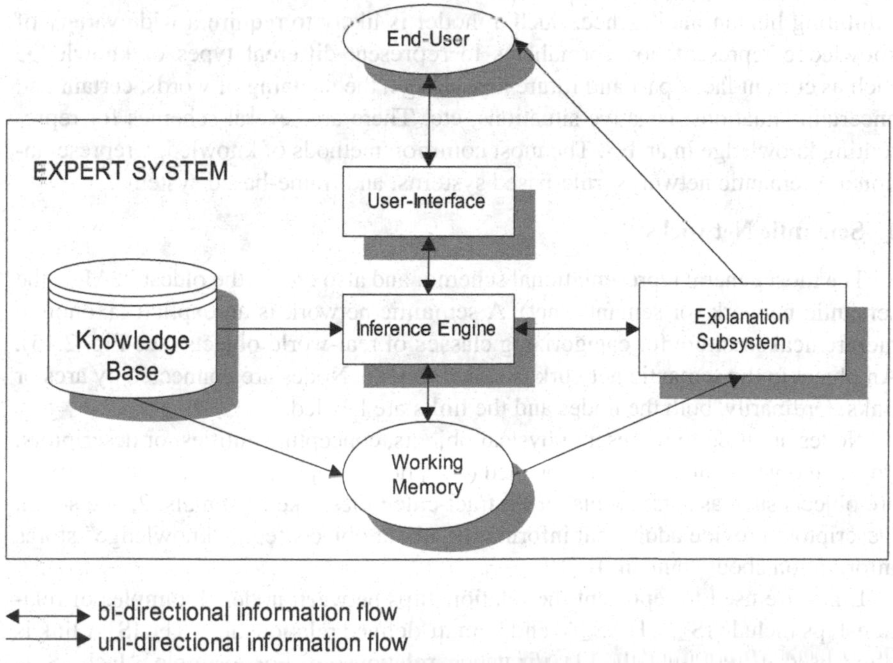

Fig. 2.14 An expert system architecture

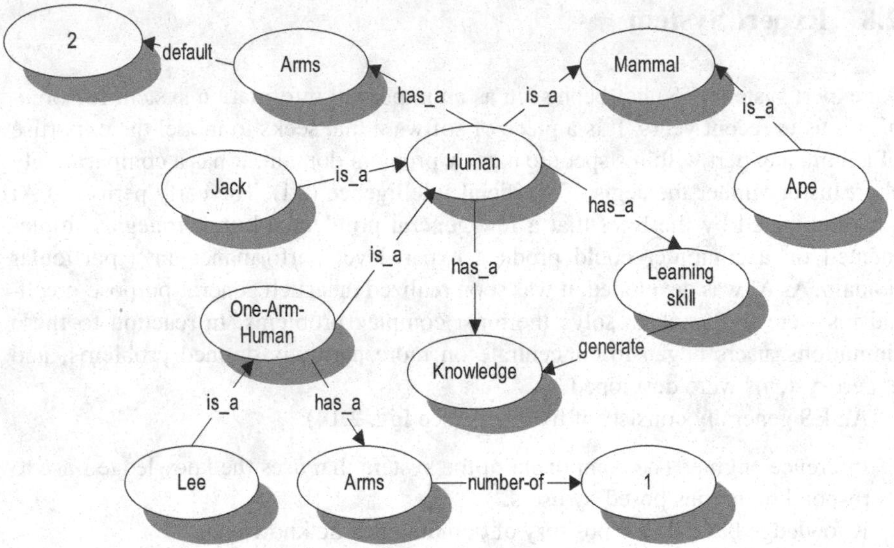

Fig. 2.15 A semantic network

2.8.1 *Knowledge Representation*

A general model for knowledge representation is to form the basis of a system exhibiting human intelligence. Such a model is likely to require a wide variety of knowledge representation formalisms to represent different types of knowledge such as current facts, past and future knowledge, the meaning of words, certain and uncertain situations, negative situations, etc. There are several schemes for representing knowledge in an ES. The most common methods of knowledge representation are semantic networks, rule-based systems, and frame-based systems.

1. **Semantic Networks**

The most general representational scheme, and also one of the oldest in AI, is the semantic network (or semantic net). A semantic network is an explicit taxonomic hierarchical structure for categorizing classes of real-world objects (see Fig. 2.15). An object in the semantic network is called a node. Nodes are connected by arcs or links. Ordinarily, both the nodes and the links are labeled.

Nodes are used to represent physical objects, conceptual entities, or descriptors. Physical objects can be seen or touched (e.g., human, ape, etc.). Conceptual entities are objects such as acts, events, or abstract categories, like mammals, 2, and so on. Descriptors provide additional information about objects (e.g., "knowledge" stores information about "human").

Links are used to represent the relationships between nodes. Examples of relationships include IS_A, HAS_A, and human-defined relationships. The IS_A link is often used to represent the class/instance relationship. For example, 'Jack IS_A

Human' or 'Human IS_A Mammal'. The IS_A link is, also, used for the purpose of generalization. It is used to provide inference using property inheritance deduction and organization in a generalization hierarchy. Inheritance has become an important feature of semantic networks. It refers to the ability of one node to "inherit" characteristics from other related nodes. Property inheritance means that instances of a class are assumed to have all of the properties of the more general classes of which they are members.

HAS_A links identify nodes that are properties of other nodes. For example, 'Human HAS_A Knowledge.' or 'Human HAS_A two Legs.' The HAS_A link has thus often been used for aggregation. It is the same as the A_PART_OF relationship that represents a situation where one class is an assembly (or aggregate) of component objects in a database application. Aggregation is one important feature of the semantic network by which the relevant facts about objects or concepts can be inferred from the nodes to which they are directly linked, without the need for a search through a large database.

Human-defined links are used to capture heuristic knowledge such as 'Learning Skill GENERATEs Knowledge' (see Fig. 2.13). Relationships like these enrich the network by providing additional paths.

Flexibility is a major advantage of this representational scheme. New nodes and links can be defined as needed. The lack of any formal semantics and difficulties handling exceptions are the major disadvantages. A system that was built using semantic networks cannot generally distinguish between instances and classes. For example, 'Jack is a human' represents an instance, while 'Human is a Mammal' represents a class. This disadvantage has meant that semantic networks have limited success for large knowledge representation systems.

2. **Production Rule Systems**

Production rules were previously used in automata theory, formal grammars, and the design of programming languages, before being used in psychological modeling and expert systems. In the expert system literature, they are sometimes called 'condition-action rules', 'situation-action rules', 'premise-conclusion rules', or 'if-then rules'. The syntax of production rules includes two parts: the IF-part and the THEN-part. For example:

Production Rule:

condition situation premise if	If C1 and ..... and Cn	Then A1 and ..... and Cn	actions conclusion then

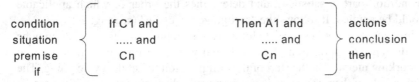

When the IF-part is true (i.e., conditions C1 and ... and Cn are true), the THEN-part (i.e., perform actions A1 and .... and An) is executed.

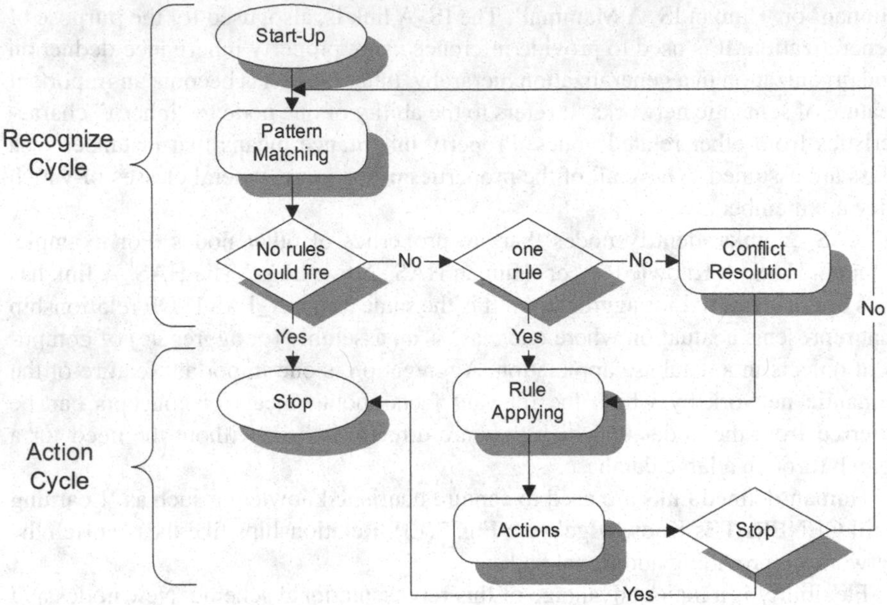

Fig. 2.16 Recognize-act cycle

A production rule system is a system to effectively manage production rules. Roughly speaking, a production rule system consists of:

- A set of rules called production rules.
- A working memory that can hold data, goals, or intermediate results.
- A rule interpreter that decides how and when to apply the rules, and which rules to apply.

The working memory holds a number of facts relevant to the particular problem to which the production system is being applied. These facts are used by the interpreter to drive the production rules, in the sense that the presence or absence of data elements in the working memory will "trigger" some rules, by satisfying their activation patterns.

The "rule interpreter" is a program that identifies applicable rules (i.e., rules whose condition part is satisfied), and determines the order in which applicable rules should be applied. It follows the "recognize-act cycle" (see Fig. 2.16).

Working memory supplies the data for pattern matching and its structure may be modified during the application of rules. Usually, a 'start-up' element is inserted into the working memory at the start of the computation to get the cycle going. The computation halts if there is a cycle in which no rules become active, or if the action of a fired rule contains an explicit command to stop.

Pattern matching identifies which rules could be fired. The interpreter matches the calling patterns of rules against elements in working memory. Two major control strategies used for pattern matching are forward chaining and backward chaining. We can chain forward from those conditions that we know to be true, towards conclusions that the facts allow us to establish, by matching data in working memory against the IF-part of rules. However, we can also chain backward from a conclusion that we wish to establish, towards the conditions necessary for its truth, to see if they are supported by the facts.

Conflict resolution determines which rule to fire. There is no conflict resolution problem in deterministic rule sets because we can always determine the right rule to fire at any point in the computation. The problem we need to solve is in the case of non-deterministic rules. Good performance conflict resolution is dependent on both sensitivity and stability from an expert system point of view. Sensitivity means responding quickly to changes in the environment reflected in the working memory, while stability means showing some kind of continuity in the line of reasoning (Jackson 1990).

Finally, we summarize the advantages and disadvantages of using production rules through the work of Reichgelt (1991). The advantages are:

- Naturalness of expression: Production rules have proved particularly successful in building expert systems. One of the main reasons for this has been the naturalness with which expert knowledge can be expressed in the terms of production rules.
- Modularity: The architecture of a production system supports a very structured knowledge base. First, "permanent" knowledge is separated from "temporary" knowledge. Production rule systems contain both a rule base, in which the more permanent knowledge resides and a working memory, which contains the temporary knowledge describing the problem the system is currently working on. Second, the different rules are structurally independent. Third, the interpreter is independent of the knowledge that is encoded in the rule base and working memory. The advantages gained from this modularity are that it is easy to construct, maintain, and debug the knowledge base.
- Restricted syntax: Production rules have a very restricted syntax. The main advantage is that it becomes feasible to write a program that can read and/or modify a set of production rules. It is also useful in generating natural language explanations.
- The problem-solving process: Production rules determine what to do next by examining the representation of the present state of the problem-solving process in working memory. This particular feature gives important advantages for the overall problem-solving process. The system can quickly focus on a hypothesis that looks particularly promising without being forced to do so at a premature stage.
- Explanation: Production rules have been claimed to facilitate the construction of programs that can explain their reasoning.
- The disadvantages of the production system are:
- Inefficiency in the case of large rule bases: There are two possible sources of inefficiency for large rule bases. First, determining the conflict set for a large rule base might become a very time-consuming process. Second, once the conflict set is determined, and turns out to contain a lot of rules, conflict resolution can require a lot of computational power. Some work has been done in this area, such

as the RETE matching algorithm (Forgy 1982), and the use of meta-rules (Davis 1980).

- Limited express ability: The expression of negative and disjunctive knowledge is difficult in the THEN-part of rules.
- Lack of formality: There is a lack of formality in the descriptions of production rules and of the reasoning processes that they use. It is not, therefore, clear whether one can sustain the claim that rule bases can be constructed incrementally. Without this capability, a lot of the attractive features of production rules would disappear.

3. **Frame-Based Systems**

The main idea of a frame is to collect all information related to one concept in one place. It attempts to reason about classes of objects by using "prototypical" representations of knowledge that hold for the majority of cases. The intuition behind the theory was that conceptual encoding in the human brain is less concerned with defining strictly and exhaustively the properties that entities must possess in order to be considered exemplars of some category, and more concerned with the salient properties associated with objects that are somehow typical of their class (Jackson 1990). Figure 2.17 shows an example of a frame-based system based on the KAPPA system (IntelliCorp 1994).

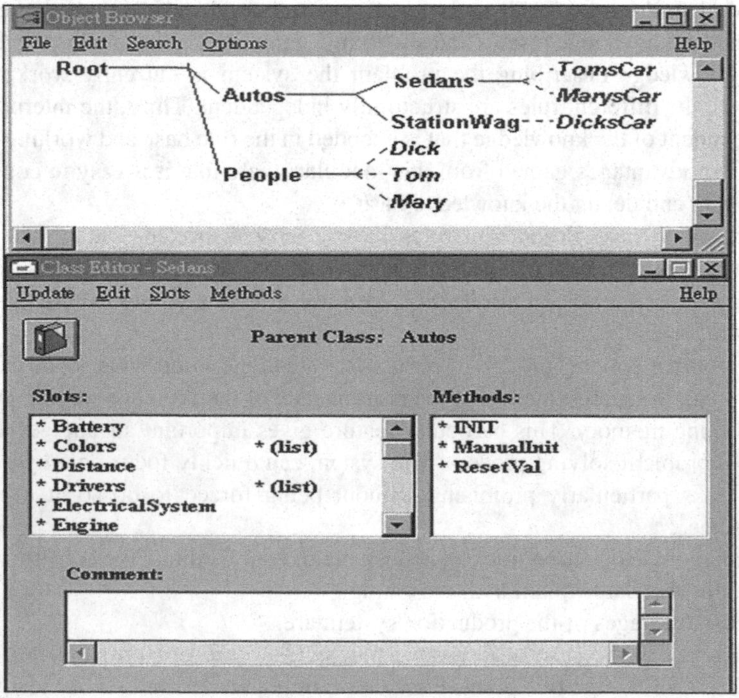

Fig. 2.17 An example of frame-based system: Kappa

A frame is a complex structure that can store and represent knowledge by using the 'Slot and Filler'formalisms, as termed in (Frost 1987). A slot is an attribute that describes a frame. A frame usually consists of a number of slots. A filler describes the values of a slot. A slot has only one filler. There are two types of frames in most frame systems: a class frame and an instance frame. A class frame is a description of a class of entities in the world. An instance frame is an intention description of an individual entity in the world. For example, "Jack is a Human". In this knowledge, "Human" is generic knowledge and can be a class frame. "Jack" is an individual object and can be an instance frame.

Frames are always linked into taxonomies by using two types of links: subclass links and member links. A subclass link represents the generalization relationship between class frames. Class frames can have subclass links to one or more other class frames. For example (see Fig. 2.17), Sedans is a subclass of Autos. The member link represents the class membership between the instance frame and class frame. Any instance frame can have a member link to one or more class frames. For example, Tomscar is a member of Sedans. These links provide two standard interpretations of the meaning of 'is-a' links, such as 'Jack is a Human' and 'Human is a Mammal' (see Fig. 2.15. The 'is_a' link supports inheritance for frame-based systems. Most current frame-based systems support multiple inheritances. There are two main problems that must be solved here. First, there is a need for the system to distinguish between its own slots and those it has inherited and to decide the priority of the two types of slots. The systems own slots will usually get higher priority than inherited slots. For example (see Fig. 2.15): A human has two arms, but one arm-human is a human who only has one arm. The own slot property will overwrite the inheritable property. Another example is 'Bird is an animal'. 'The locomotion mode of animal is walking' but 'Bird can not only walk but also fly'. The own slot property and inheritable property must exist together. The second is a need to solve any conflict problems between inherited slots. If inherited slots from different frames have the same slot name there is a conflict. The general solution for this problem is to keep only one slot from the highest priority inheritance frame or to keep these slots at different levels. The situation is similar to the first problem.

An important source of the expressive power of frame-based languages are the facilities that they provide for describing object attributes, called slots (Minsky 1975). These facilities allow frames to include partial descriptions of attribute values and help preserve the semantic integrity of a system's knowledge base by constraining the number and range of allowable attribute values. A slot usually consists of two parts: a slot name, which describes an attribute, and a slot-filler, which describes the character of the slot values. The slot-filler supports very powerful features (see Fig. 2.18). It allows the filler to be represented as single/multiple values, instance frames, or procedures. The single or multiple value situation is dependent on the "cardinality". A slot-filler usually has an attribute type, such as Text, Number, or Boolean, to represent the values. Frame-based systems also allow users to define the object type in their slot-filler. This creates a new relationship called aggregation, i.e., the 'a_part_of'link. Aggregation is an abstraction in which a relationship between objects is represented by a higher level, aggregate object. Most

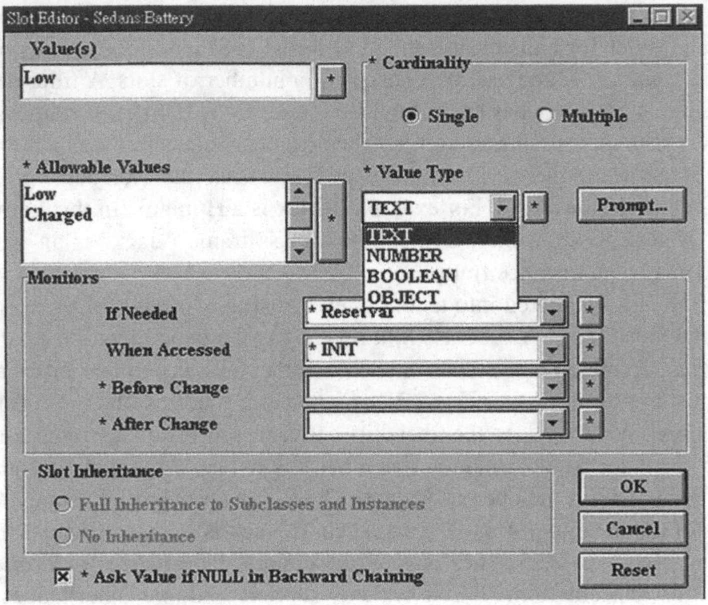

Fig. 2.18 A slot-filler in KAPPA frame based system

current systems only allow a single instance frame. Procedural attachment is also found in most frame-based systems. This allows users to define the attribute type as a procedure so as to represent procedural information. The procedure is a normal routine that is called whenever a value for a slot is required.

Restriction and Default functions are also important features of frame-based systems. Many frame-based systems allow the use of the logical connectives NOT, OR, and AND in the formulation of restrictions on slots. For example, you can put the following restriction on the gender slot associated with the member frame to represent a school for girls. Members of the school are students and staff. Most of them are female.

(gender (default female) (restrict (OR male female)))

Procedural attachment may also be used here for constraints or monitors. There is one type of procedure called a 'demon' which is a restriction (constraint) or integrity function that is called whenever the slot in question receives a value or is updated.

Implementing reasoning is a complex process in frame-based systems. Most frame-based inference mechanisms are based on the structural properties of frames and taxonomies. There are five major mechanisms that can be used for reasoning in frame-based systems (Reichgelt 1991).

- Matching
- This mechanism concerns taking a decision as to which of the many frames in the knowledge base is applicable to the current situation. The system must compare descriptions of incoming stimuli with frames in the knowledge base, and retrieve the class frame that best matches the situation.
- Inheritance
- The matching retrieves the relevant frame that contains general information for the reasoning process and applies inherited information to specific information. The basic inheritance mechanism uses member links, sub-class links, and prototype descriptions of class members to assert and retrieve the specific information.
- Instance Frame Reasoning
- The inheritance reasoning infers the frame by using the 'is_a' link and the instance frame reasoning infers the frame through their 'a_part_of'link. It is a mechanism to retrieve specific information for a slot with instance frame values.
- Procedural Reasoning
- This is a mechanism to retrieve specific information for a slot with procedure values or to perform constraint and integrity checking by the use of demons. The technique includes sending a message to an object-oriented method or performing an external call in order to run a normal routine (e.g., calling standard functions in LISP).
- Cardinality and Constraint Checking.
- A frame-based system considers cardinality, default, and restriction specifications as constraints on the legal values of a slot. The system provides constraint checking procedures for determining whether a slot's value is valid.
- Currently, most frame-based representation facilities also provide a convenient rule-based management facility. There are usually two ways to combine rules and frames. One is to attach a production rule language to the frame-based system, such as in GoldWorks (Casey 1989), The frame facility supplies an expressively powerful language for describing the objects being reasoned about and automatically performs a useful set of inferences on those descriptions. The other involves representing a rule as a frame, such as in KEE (Fikes and Kehler 1985). KEE allows production rules to be represented by frames so that they can easily be classified into taxonomies, created, analyzed, and modified as necessary.
- Several advantages have been claimed for frame-based knowledge representation schemes. Many of these advantages involve the representation of stereotypes and assertion clustering, which improves access to knowledge by storing associated representations together. It is expected that this technique will become common in the future, particularly in large and sophisticated expert systems.

2.9 Summary

Database systems and expert systems are the major components of information systems. The legacy data models include hierarchical, network, relational, object-oriented, and XML. The hierarchical model has an inverted tree structure data structure, which makes it most suitable for top-down applications. Its main DBMS is IMS by IBM Corp. It is a record-based database and the users follow a hierarchical sequence to access the database by default. However, the users can also access the database directly by specifying the segment keys along the access paths. Its main disadvantage is its implementation of m:n relationships in the conceptual model. Data redundancy occurs as a result of the implementation.

The network database has a graphic data structure (i.e., a record can have multiple input and multiple-output). It has Set data structure that is used as pointer to link the owner record and member records. It has the best performance among the other data models but is also the less user-friendly model. Its main advantage is to implement an m:n relationship among the records. IDMS is a main legacy network DBMS by Computer Associates International Ltd.

The relational database is the most popular data model in the industry now. It is very user-friendly among all the other models. Its data structure is tables that link to each other through foreign keys or composite keys. However, these keys may cause data redundancy. Normalization is needed to eliminate anormalies. At present, SQL is the standard DDL and DML for relational databases and is also the most used database language.

The object-oriented database is based on grouping related instances (i.e., objects) into classes. Its data structure is based on OID, an object identity that is generated as a unique number by the system. OID is used as a pointer to link class objects together. Its major advantages are increased productivity by inheritance and encapsulation. Its major attraction is its ability in reengineering existing object-oriented database systems for future enhancements, i.e., it is more flexible than the other data models. It seems to take a more important role in the future to replace relational as the dominant model. An example of an object-oriented data model can be found in UniSQL.

As Internet computing becomes part of everyday life, the Extensible Markup Language defined by the W3C committee has also been adopted as the data standard on the Internet. The XML is an extension to HTML, and is programmable with XML schema and XML document. The XML schema can be in the form of Document Type Definition (DTD) or XML Schema Definition (XSD). It has a hierarchical tree structure that focuses on the root element with other elements under it. The DTD can also be visualized in the form of a DTD Graph. Each element represents a node in the graph, and the attributes describe the properties of the element. The ID and IDREF must exist in pair with IDREF addressing to ID in the XML document. The DTD Graph and XSD Graph can be used as an XML conceptual schema for the design of an XML database.

The expert system is the core software for a decision support system and information systems. It plays the role of the experts by transferring expert knowledge into a computer system. Technically, it can perform forward and backward chaining to derive condition to conclusion, or conclusion from condition. As the information age evolves to the knowledge age, so do information systems evolve to knowledge-based systems. The role of expert systems becomes more important since knowledge-based systems and knowledge engineering becomes more popular in the industry.

Questions

Question 2.1

What is data modeling? What are the relationships between conceptual schema, logical schema, and internal schema in the Anxi-X3 database?

Answer:

Data modeling is a way to design a database for data to be stored and extracted from a database. An Anxi-X3 architecture is a data modeling technique describing data from a higher level of conceptual schema data structure to middle level of logical schema data structure, and then to low level internal schema physical data structure. The conceptual schema is a paper design such as Entity-Relationship Model describing data relationships in a meaningful concept understood by the users in their minds and meet users' data requirements. The logical schema is a data structure map such as relational schema tables for DBMS to follow and access data in a database. The internal schema describes the data structure such as records, indexing and pointers physical files that stores data in a database.

Question 2.2

How can one show the process of reengineering in terms of the process of forward engineering and reverse engineering?

Answer:

Reengineering is to reuse an existing computer system to create a new computer system for the benefit of updating old existing databases without discarding it. For example, a system developer creates a new database from scratch, which is called system development. In case the developer only wants to update an existing database to a new platform or to a new data model, for example, from relational model to XML document, which is called reengineering. A database system can be implemented in a higher level of concepts of conceptual schema only, or in a logical level of data structure map of a database of logical level. Forward engineering is to implement from a high-level system to a low-level system, for example, from conceptual schema to logical schema. Reverse engineering is to recover a high-level system from a low-level system, for example, from logical schema to conceptual schema. The steps involve is to analyze the low-level data structure, and summarizes them into simplified high-level data structure.

Bibliography

Booch G (1994) Object-Oriented Analysis Design with Application. The Bensamin/Cummings Publishing Co, Inc, p 15

Casey JS (1989) GoldWorks II for the SUN-3 or SUN386i. Gold Hills Computers Inc, Cambridge, MA

Chen, P. (1976) The entity relationship model – toward a unified view of data, ACM Trans Database Syst, Volume 1, Number 1, p9–36

CODASYL (1971) CODASYL Data Base task group report. Conferenc on data system languages. ACM, New York

Date C (1995) Introduction to database systems, 6th edn. Addison-Wesley Systems Programming Series, pp 669–685

Davis R (1980) Meta-rules: reasoning about control. Artif Intell 15:179–222

Elmasri R, Navathe S (1989) Fundamentals of database systems. The Benjamin/Cummings Publishing Company

Fikes R, Kehler T (1985) The role of frame-based representation in reasoning. Commun ACM 28(9):904–920

Fong J, Cheung SK (2005) Translating relational schema into XML schema definition with data semantic preservation and XSD graph. Inf Softw Technol 47(7):437–462

Forgy C (1982) RETE: a fast algorithm for the many pattern/many object pattern match problem. Artif Intell 19:17–37

Frost RA (1987) Introduction to knowledge-base systems. William Collins, New York. ISBN 0-00-383114-0

Funderburk JE, Kierman G, Shanmugasundaram J, Shekita E, Wei C (2002) XTABLES: bridging relational technology and XML. IBM Syst J 41(4):616–641

Hughes J (1991) Object-oriented databases. Prentice Hall Inc.

IntelliCorp (1994) Kappa User Menu. IntelliCorp Inc.

Jackson P (1990) Introduction to expert systems, 2nd edn. Addison-Wesley Publishing Company, New York. ISBN 0-201-17578-9

Kozaczynski W, Lilien L (1988) An extended entity-relationship (E2R) Database Specification and its automatic verification and transformation into the logical relational design. Entity-Relationship Approach:533–549

Martin J (1990) IDMS/R concepts, design and programming, Prentice Hall Inc

McElreath J (1981) IMS design and implementation techniques Q.E.D. Information Sciences, Inc

Minsky M (1975) A framework for representing knowledge. In: Winston P (ed) The psychology of computer vision. McGraw-Hill, New-York

Reichgelt H (1991) Kowledge representation – an AI perspective. Ablex Publishing Corporation, London. ISBN 0-89391-590-4

Teroey T, Yang D, Fry J (1986) A logical design methodology for relational databases using the extended entity-relationship model. Comput Survey 18(2):197–220

UniSQL (1992) UniSQL/X user's manual. UniSQL Inc

W3C (2004). www.w3c.org

Chapter 3
Schema Translation

A database system consists of three components: schemas, data, and programs. Database reengineering starts with the schema, which defines the meaning of data and their relationship in different models. Only after a schema has been redefined can data and programs then be reengineered into a new database system, which makes use of the translated schema. Schema translation is the process of changing a schema expressed in one data model into an equivalent schema expressed in a different data model.

This chapter describes the techniques of translating the hierarchical model or the network model into the relational model. It also outlines a methodology for transforming a relational schema into an object-oriented database schema, and an XML database schema.

Some work has been done to translate directly from a hierarchical model or network model to a relational model. Others translate a logical hierarchical schema or a logical network schema into a conceptual schema based on the extended entity-relationship (EER) model. The EER model is then translated into a logical relational schema (Elmasri and Navathe 1989).

The object-oriented model is becoming very popular; however, there is no such thing as a standard object-oriented model. Nevertheless, many conceptual models for object-oriented database systems exist and have been adopted by the industry. For example, UML, Booch (Booch 1994), and Yourdon are some of the conceptual object-oriented models used to design object-oriented databases. We consider it premature to address direct translation from a relational to the object-oriented database. Instead, we present a method to translate a relational model to a UML model. We choose the UML model because of its similarity with the EER model. One can translate from a relational model to a EER model in a reverse engineering step and then from the EER model to a UML model in forward engineering step, which can then be mapped to a proprietary object-oriented schema.

J. S. P. Fong, K. Wong Ting Yan, *Information Systems Reengineering, Integration and Normalization*, https://doi.org/10.1007/978-3-030-79584-9_3

Record-based relational databases built by using top-down modeling techniques such as the EER model have been generally used over the past two decades. Organizations with such record-based databases could seek to reengineer their databases into object-oriented databases to capture more of the semantics of the application domain. The UML model can be regarded as an extension of the EER model with complete object-oriented features, a comprehensive object-oriented database model enhanced with advanced semantic features. UML model improves the EER model in the areas of expressiveness and readability. It is thus reasonable to follow the traditional method to design a database starting with the EER model for its richness in static semantic data modeling techniques, and then map it to a UML model as part of an object-oriented database design.

3.1 Direct Translating a Network Model to a Relational Model

Translation from a network schema to a relational schema involves a one-to-one mapping between the record type and the relation. The set structure of the network schema is translated into the referential relationship between parent and child relations. For example, Zaniolo (1979) designed a set of relations that recast the logical network schema in terms of a relational model as shown in the following procedure:

Step 1 – Derive relations.

Map each network record type to a relation in a one-to-one manner.

Step 2 – Derive relation keys.

Map each record key of a network schema to a primary key in a relational table. However, if the existing network record key is not unique, then it is concatenated with its owner record key in order to create a unique primary key. The owner record key is also mapped to a foreign key in the relational table to link the parent and child records. If the set membership in the logical network schema is manual, then the record key of the member record will be mapped as a candidate key in the relational table. For instance, Fig. 3.1 is the network schema for a US President.

Applying the above steps, we can map the network schema in Fig. 3.1 to the following relations:

PRESIDENT (<u>Plname</u>, <u>Pfname</u>, Party, Collg, *Sname)
ADMINISTRATION (<u>Adm#</u>, Iny, Inm, Ind, *Plname, *Pfname)
STATE (<u>Sname</u>, Cap, *Pln, Pfn, Adm#, Yad*)
ELECTION (<u>Eyear</u>, Winvotes, *Plname, *Pfname)
LINK (*<u>Plname</u>, *<u>Pfname</u>, <u>Cngr#</u>)
CONGRESS (<u>Cngr#</u>, Hd, Hr, Sd, Sr)

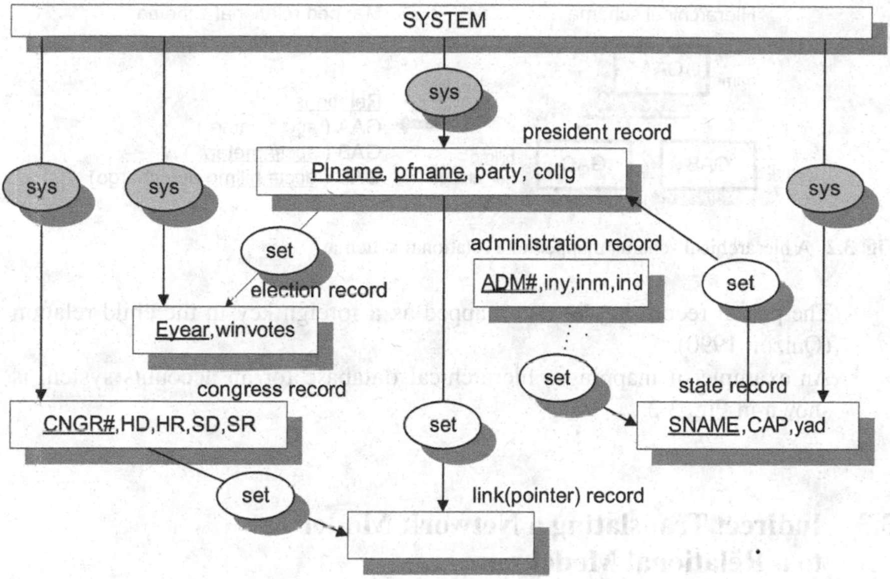

Fig. 3.1 Network schema on US president

Note: Italic are candidate keys, underlined words are primary keys, and words with '*' prefixes are foreign keys.

3.2 Direct Translating a Hierarchical Model to a Relational Model

Mapping between hierarchical and relational schema is similar to the one between network and relational. It can be considered as a subset of a network schema because the inverted tree structure of its data structure can be modeled directly in a network data model. However, it does not have as many set memberships types and constraints as in the network schema. All parent-child relationships in the hierarchical schema are "fixed", i.e., not changeable once it is inserted. A relational schema can be derived using the following steps:

Step 1 – Derive relations.

Map each record type into a relation.

Step 2 – Derive relation keys.

The record key of a hierarchical schema is mapped as a primary key of a relation. However, if the record type of the hierarchical schema is a child record, then the primary key is derived by concatenating it with its parent record key.

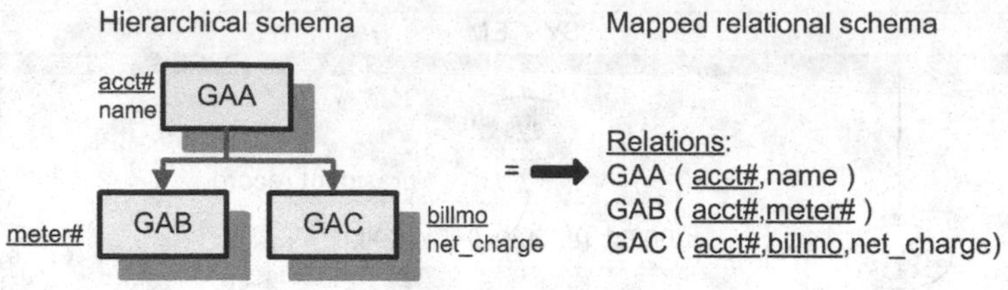

Fig. 3.2 A hierarchical schema mapped to a relational schema

The parent record key is also mapped as a foreign key in the child relation (Quizon 1990).

An example of mapping a hierarchical database for an accounts system is shown in Fig. 3.2.

3.3 Indirect Translating a Network Model to a Relational Model

In much of the published literature on schema translation by direct translation, assumptions have generally been made on the semantics of the database. There is always the chance that the translated schema may not encapsulate the original designer's idea. This problem occurs because there is so many possible relational schemas that can be derived from a known hierarchical schema or a network schema and the translation analyst makes many very primitive assumptions (for example, the direct translation hierarchical schema or a network schema into a composite key of a hierarchical schema or a network schema into a composite key of the relational model by concatenating its parent record key with its own key). However, there are exceptions such that the child record is fully internally identified, which can be transformed directly to a primary key of a logical relational schema. As a result, the translated relational model may be incorrect.

When a company's existing database system needs to be upgraded into a new model such as relational, object-oriented, or XML, the current nonrelational data models must be translated into the new models. To translate from one model to another involves not just data structure transformation, but also the transfer of semantics. Very often, semantics are lost once a conceptual model has been mapped into a logical model because the former is richer in semantics than the latter. Thus, schema translations between logical schema such as hierarchical, network, relational, object-oriented, and XML are done by mapping them back to a higher semantic model of the EER model.

To solve the problem in a logical manner, we need users as the domain and relation integrity experts for the nonrelational schema. They can provide information on the semantics of the data; that is, their domain values and constraints in the database. A knowledge acquisition system can assist the user to confirm the translated

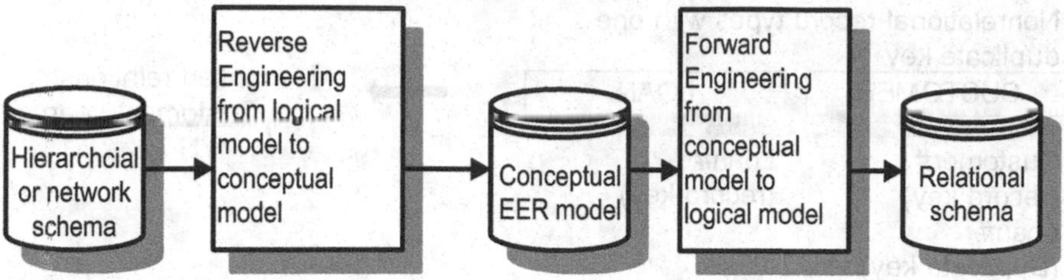

Fig. 3.3 Indirect schema translation data flow diagram

EER model by enforcing the database integrity heuristic rules such as FDs (functional dependencies) and IDs (inclusion dependencies) in the translation. The resultant conceptual model can meet the heuristic rule requirements in the existing nonrelational schema. Even though there are many possible EER models that can be constructed from a known logical schema, the translated EER model should be the one closest to the user's expectation.

A conceptual schema based on the EER model carries richer semantics than a hierarchical schema or a network schema. Since it is dangerous to make assumptions on how to recover the semantics lost in the logical schema, our strategy is to capture these semantics from the users' knowledge of the database and rebuild the conceptual schema in an EER model. We can then map directly from the EER model to a logical relational schema; refer to Fig. 3.3 (Fong 1992).

This section describes the step-by-step mapping process.

Step 1 – Reverse engineering from network schema to conceptual EER model.

Since the EER structure is built upon other lower-level structures, we must normalize existing network schema, followed by translating the primitive semantics such as existence and navigational semantics into cardinalities, entity keys and relationships, and lastly we need to add the higher level semantics of aggregation, generalization, and categorization.

Substep 1 – Derive implied relationships.

The network schema to be translated may not be normalized. Modifications may have been made to the schema for performance or other reasons. Generally, modifications are made to improve performance. The explicit semantic implies a 1:n relationship if there is one duplicate key in one record type, or 1:1 if there is a duplicate key found in the record on both sides of the relationships. User input is sought to confirm the existence of such semantics.

For example, in the loan system in Fig. 3.4, one duplicate key of Loan# implies a 1:n relationship between Loan and Customer records such that a loan can be participated by many customers whose records can be found by matching the loan#. In some cases, you may have two duplicate keys imply a 1:1 relationship between Customer and Loan records such that a customer books a particular loan.

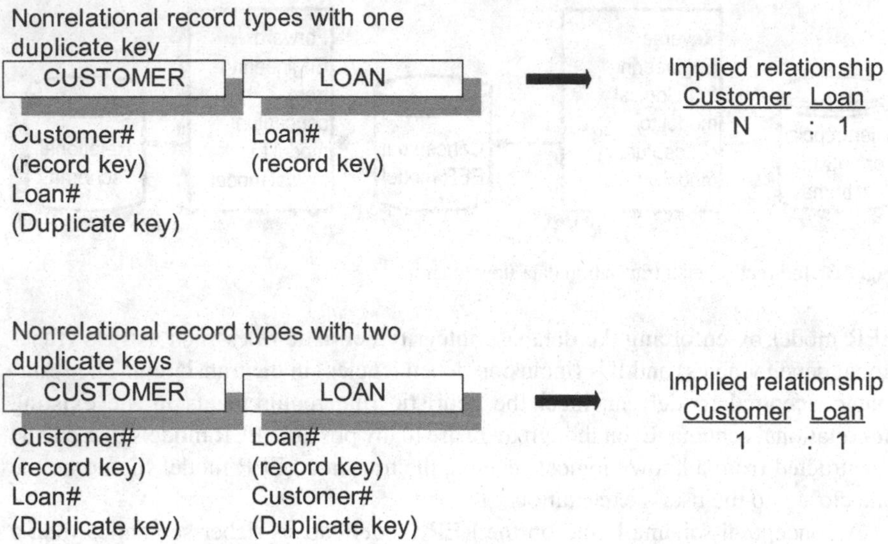

Fig. 3.4 Derive implied relationship

Substep 2 – Derive multiple (alternative) relationships.

In a network schema, a circuit of record types may carry different navigational semantics. For example, Fig. 3.5 is a circuit or loopy network schema:

Here the relationship between Cities and Items is in a loop because the same relationship can be derived by joining the relationship between Cities and Stores and between Stores and Items. The former may carry the semantics of manufactured items in cities and the latter may carry the semantics of available items in stores under cities. They thus carry different semantics.

On the other hand, the default assumption is that the alternative access path may be for better performance because it takes a shorter access path by alternative path from record Cities to record Items directly.

It is up to the user to confirm the original database designer's idea on the function of the alternative path. If the user confirms the existence of a navigational semantic, then the record types and Sets in the alternative path are mapped to different network subschema (one subschema for each path) before translating to the relational schema.

Substep 3 – Derive unary relationships.

We map link (dummy) records of network schema into unary relationships. These dummy records are either without any attributes or contain key attributes only as shown in Fig. 3.6. The default is a 1:n relationship between owner and member for each Set record type, but user input is sought to confirm or modify this relationship into a 1:1 or an isa relationship.

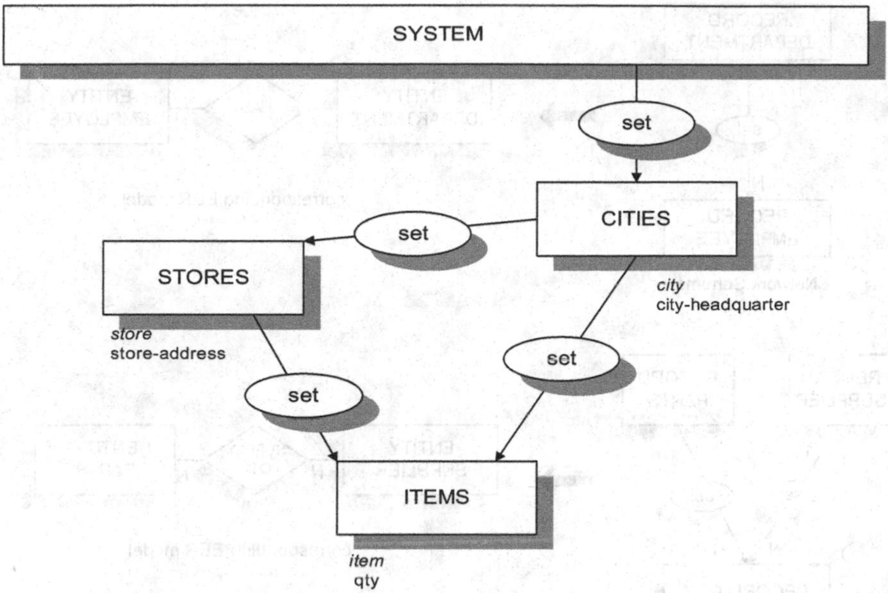

Fig. 3.5 A circuit loop network schema

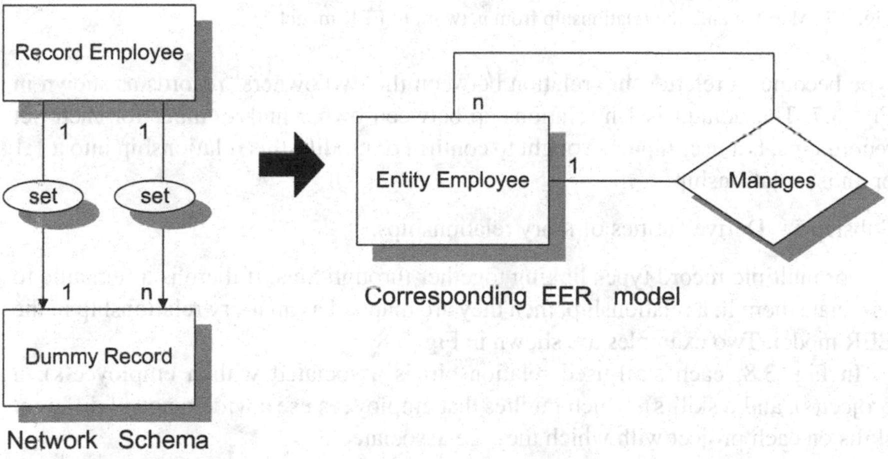

Fig. 3.6 Map unary 1:n relationship from network to EER model

Substep 4 – Derive binary relationships.

Next, we map each SET into a relationship between the owner and member records, assuming a default 1:n cardinality. However, one record type can be a member of more than one SET. Multiple memberships logically intersects the owner records of two (or more) SETs. A member record type with two owner record types implies a m:n relationship between the two owner record types. The member record

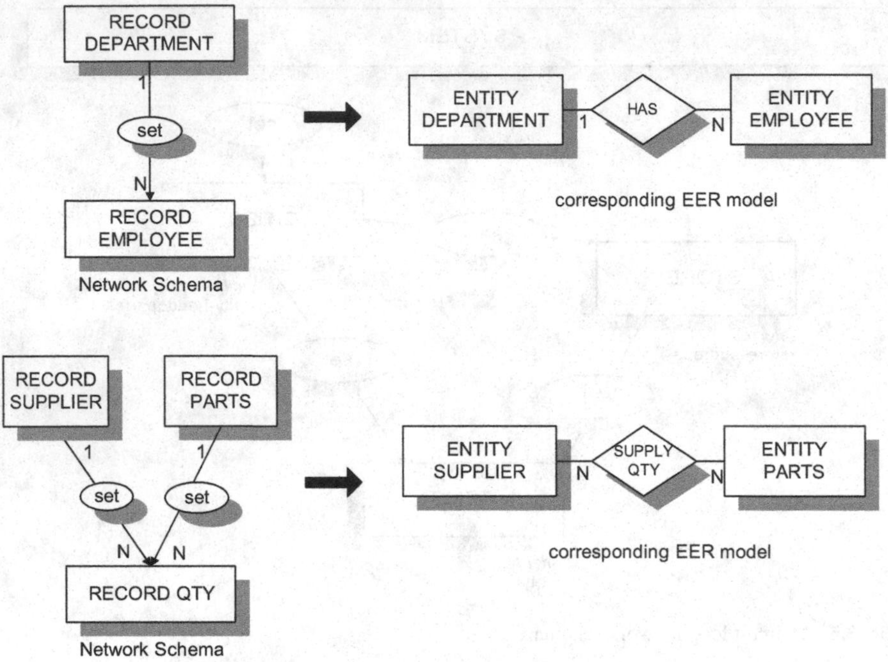

Fig. 3.7 Map 1:n and m:n relationship from network to EER model

type becomes a relationship relation between the two owners' records as shown in Fig. 3.7. The default is 1:n relationship between owner and member for each Set record type, but user input is sought to confirm or modify this relationship into a 1:1 or an isa relationship.

Substep 5 – Derive entities of n-ary relationships.

For multiple record types linking together through Sets, if there is a semantic to associate them in a relationship, then they are mapped as an n-ary relationship in the EER model. Two examples are shown in Fig. 3.8.

In Fig. 3.8, each skill-used relationship is associated with n employee(s), n project(s), and n skill(s), which implies that employees use a wide range of different skills on each project with which they are associated.

The default is a binary relationship as described in step 3. A knowledge acquisition system should be able to detect a possible n-ary relationship from the DDL of the network schema. Again, user input is sought to confirm or modify this relationship. The user must be aware that a mandatory binary relationship can be grouped as an m:n or n-ary relationship depending on the semantics. Above all, any optional relationship must stay as a binary relationship.

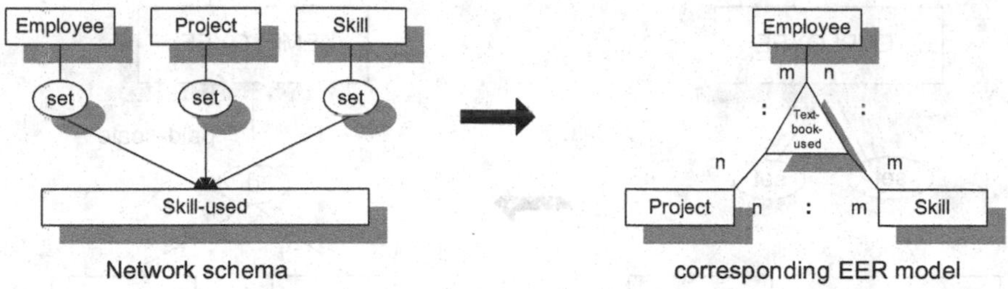

Fig. 3.8 Map n-ary relationship to EER model

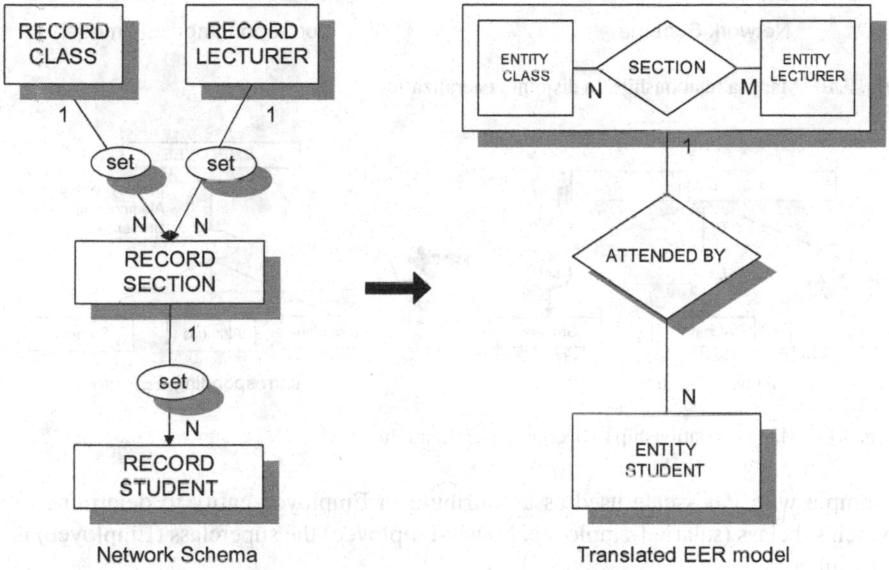

Fig. 3.9 Map set of relationships to aggregation in EER model

Substep 6 – Derive aggregation, generalization, and categorization.

An aggregation is derived if an m:n relationship from step 4 further relates to another entity. The knowledge acquisition system should be able to detect a possible aggregation if there is a potential m:n relationship relation record type that is further linked to another record type. In the network schema, such a relationship can be represented by the record type shown in Fig. 3.9.

A disjoint generalization is derived by mapping isa relationships and their record types to a superclass/subclass entities relationship such that a superclass entity (mapped from an owner record type) is a generalized class for the subclass entities (mapped from member record types) which are mutually exclusive. Again, the knowledge acquisition system should be able to detect such potential generalization by locating isa relationship linkages with one owner and more than one member record type. However, user input is needed to confirm this. Figure 3.10 is an

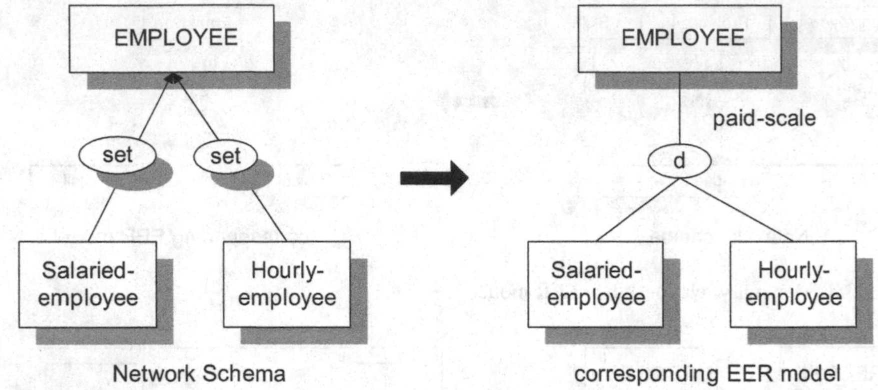

Fig. 3.10 Map isa relationships to disjoint generalization

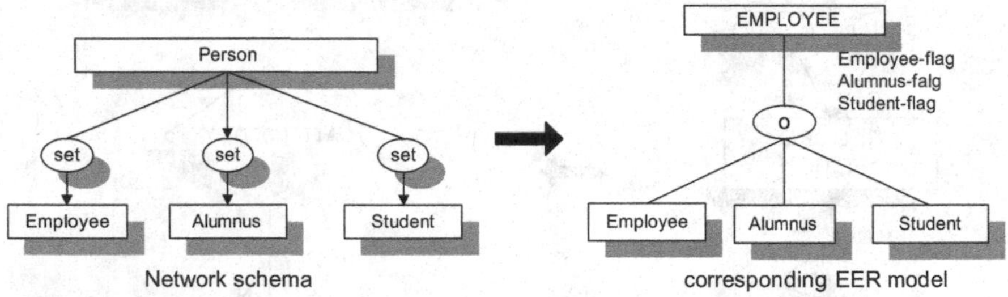

Fig. 3.11 Map isa relationship to overlap generalization

example with Paid-scale used as an attribute in Employee entity to determine of which subclass (salaried-employee, hourly-employee) the superclass (Employee) is a member.

An overlap generalization is derived by mapping isa relationships and their record types to a superclass/subclass relationship such that a superclass entity (mapped from an owner record type) is a generalized class for the subclass entities (mapped from member record types) that overlap each other. Again, the knowledge acquisition system should be able to detect such a potential generalization by locating isa relationships with one owner and more than one member record type. However, user input is needed to confirm these semantics. Figure 3.11 is an example with Employee-flag, Alumnus-flag, and Student-flag being used to indicate the membership of the subclass entities (Employee, Alumnus, Student). An employee can be both a student and a person. The difference between disjoint and overlap generalization is that the former needs only one predicate field while the latter needs one predicate field for each subclass entity.

A categorization is derived by mapping isa relationships and their record types to superclass/subclass entities relationships such that a set of class entities (mapped from a set of owner record types) can be united to form the superclass entity of a subclass entity (mapped from a member record type). Again, the knowledge

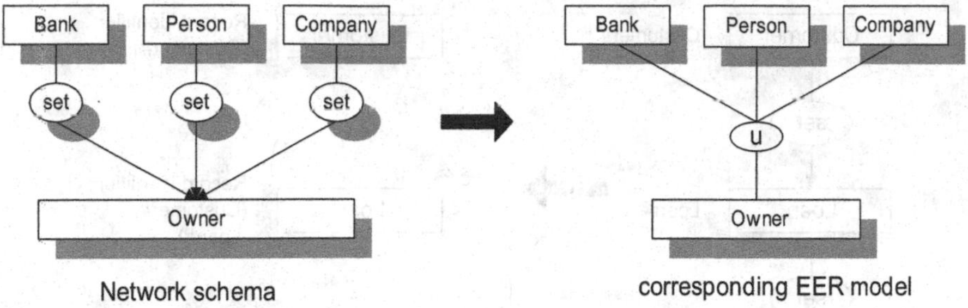

Fig. 3.12 Map isa relationships to categorization in EER model

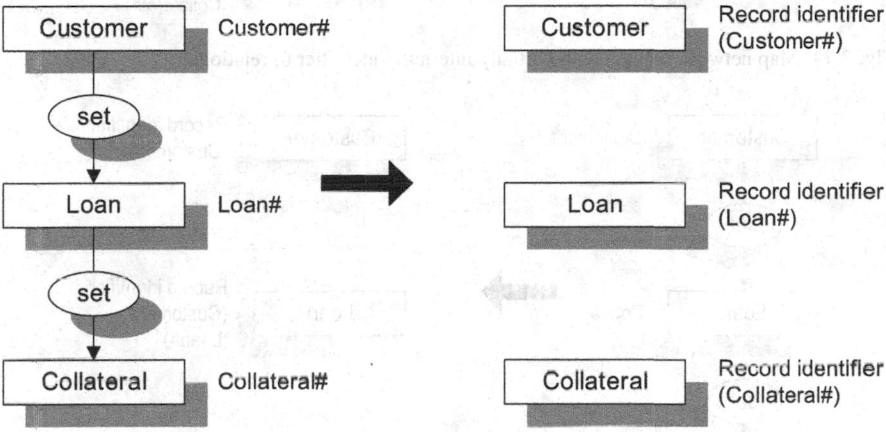

Fig. 3.13 Map network schema with fully internally identifier to relational

acquisition system should be able to detect a potential categorization by locating isa relationships with more than one owner and one member record type. However, user input is needed to confirm such a semantic. Figure 3.12 is an example.

Substep 7 – Derive entity keys and other constraints.

There are three forms of identifiers. They can be described as follows:

- Fully internally identified – The record key uniquely identifies the record. For example, in a loan system records can be identified as in Fig. 3.13. Here Loan# and Collateral# are unique in the whole loan system.
- Partially internally identified – Concatenation of owner record(s) key(s) with the member record key can uniquely identify the member record (i.e., identifier dependency). For example, the same loan system records could be identified as in Fig. 3.14. Here Loan# is only unique within a customer and Collateral# is only unique within a loan.
- Internally Unidentified – The record key does not exist. Some other properties (such as ordering) may be used to impart an implicit internal identifier. This is an

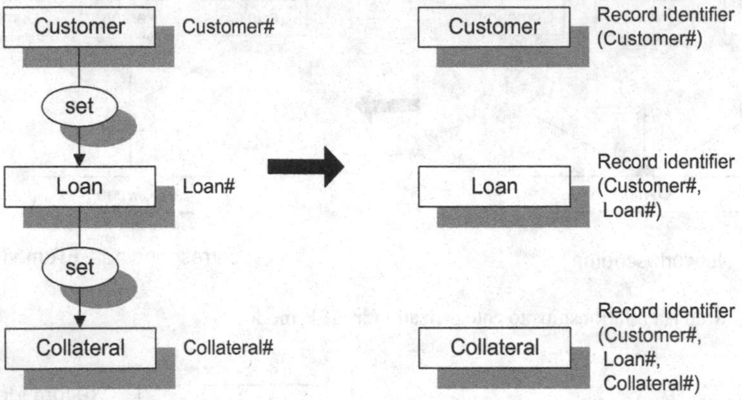

Fig. 3.14 Map network schema with partially internally identifier to relational

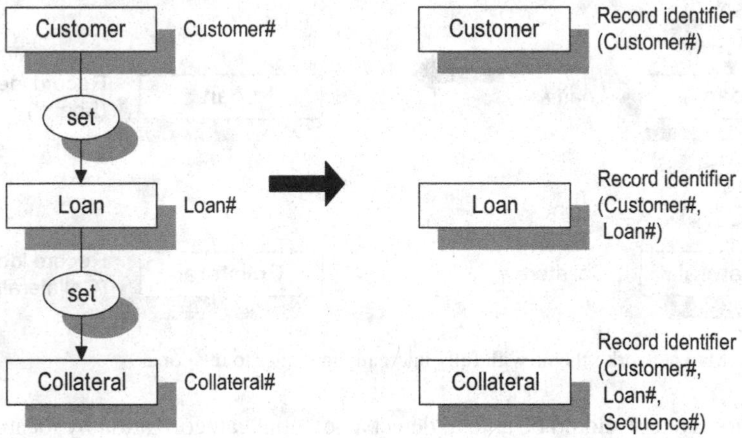

Fig. 3.15 Map network schema with internally unidentified to relational

extreme case of a partially internally identified group for which an augmented identifier consists solely of external identifiers. For example, in the same loan system, the Collateral record may not have a key. Its record identifiers must then be derived as in Fig. 3.15. Here Sequence# is added as an additional field for the identifier.

These identifiers are mapped into entity keys. Partial internally identified is taken as the default, and the user confirms this or specifies the entity key for the other two cases.

Note that the record identifier for the partially internally identified is the concatenation of the owner record identifier with the target record identifier. The record identifier for the internally unidentified record type is the concatenation of the owner record identifier with a unique sequence#.

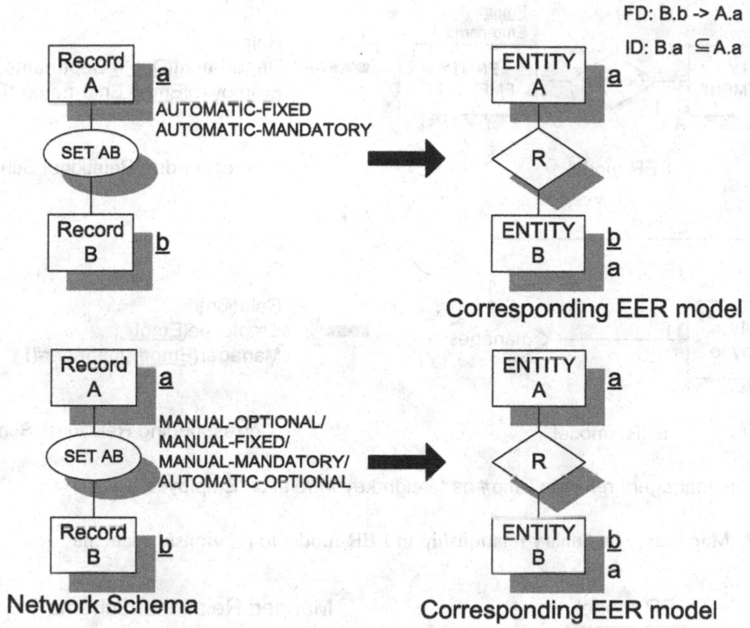

Fig. 3.16 Network schema dependency relationship translation

The member record types with the SET membership clause fixed-automatic or mandatory-automatic must be connected to their owner record. For the SET membership clause of fixed-manual, mandatory-manual, optional-manual, the member may be disconnected from the owner record. If they are connected to owner records, their FDs and IDs can be derived. If they are disconnected with owner records, there is only an FD as illustrated in Fig. 3.16.

Substep 8 – Draw EER model.

Draw a derived EER model as a result of the previous steps. This is provided to enable the users to review the translated semantics of the original network schema. The above steps can be assisted by a knowledge-based system as described in Chap. 1.

Step 2 – Forward engineering from conceptual EER model to relational schema.

This section describes the procedure to map EER model to relational schema:

Substep 1 – Map entities into relations.

Translate each entity into a relation containing the key and non-key attributes of the entity. If there is an n:1 relationship between an entity and another entity, add the key of the entity on the '1' side into the relation as shown in Fig. 3.17. If there is a 1:1 relationship between an entity and another entity, then add the key of one of the entities into the relation for the other entity (i.e., the addition of a foreign key due to

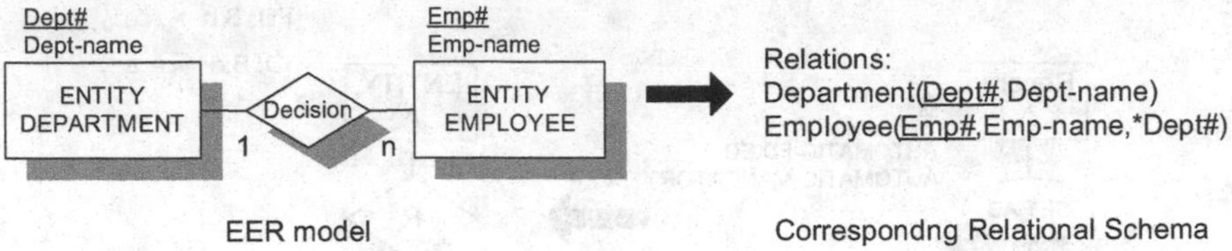

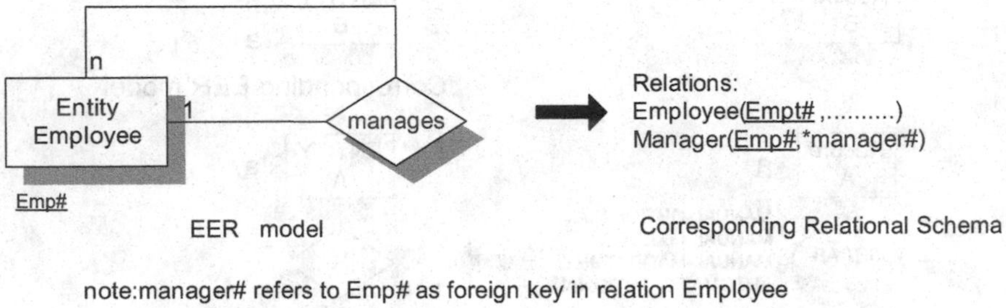

Fig. 3.17 Map binary and unary relationship in EER model to relationship schema

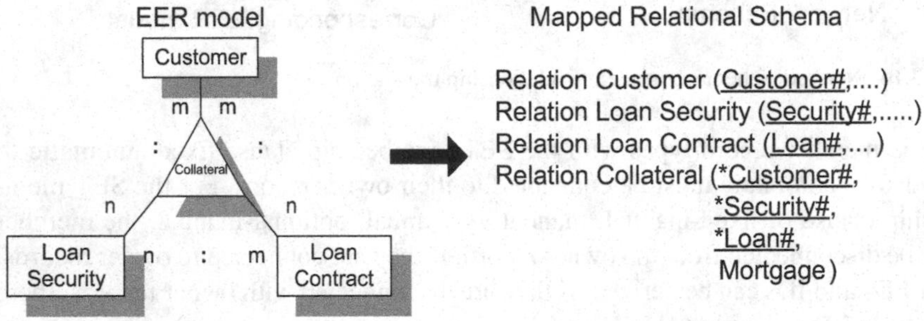

Fig. 3.18 Map ternary relationship of all n:m relationship from EER model to relational schema

a 1:1 relationship can be made in either direction). For a unary relationship, the foreign key of 1:1 and a 1:n relationship can be mapped in the same or different relation(s). For a unary m:n relationship, a relationship relation must be mapped into the relational schema.

Substep 2 – Map an n-ary relationship into relationship relation.

An n-ary relationship has n + 1 possible varieties of connectivity: all n sides with connected "1", n−1 sides with connected "1" and one side with connectivity "n", n−2 sides with connectivity "1" and two sides with "n" and so on until all sides are "n." As an example, consider a Collateral system where customers provide loan security for various loan contracts. Four of the possible ternary relationships are illustrated in Cases 1 to 4.

Case 1: Many customers may participate in any one collateral for many loan contracts secured by many loan securities as shown in Fig. 3.18.

Case 2: A customer may participate in any one collateral for one contract secured by one loan security as shown in Fig. 3.19.
Case 3: Many customers may participate in any one collateral for many loan contracts secured by one loan security as shown in Fig. 3.20.
Case 4: Many customers may participate in any one collateral for one loan contract secured by one loan security as shown in Fig. 3.21.

Substep 3 – Map aggregation, generalization, and categorization into relations.

An aggregation is derived when a relationship relation is further related to another entity. This is treated as an entity to be related to the third entity in a relationship. The mapping of such a relationship follows steps 1 and 2.

For disjoint generalization, superclass and subclass entities are mapped into relations on a one-to-one basis. The superclass entity key will be mapped as the primary key for all the mapped relations. The "predicate" attribute will be mapped as an attribute of the "generalized" relation. As an example, the disjoint generalization of Fig. 3.10 can be mapped to the following relations:

Relations

Employee	(Employee#, Employee-name, paid-scale)
Salaried-employee	(*Employee#, month-salary, bonus)
Hourly-employee	(*Employee#, hourly-salary, overtime-paid)

where paid-scale ("predicate" attribute) must be either "salaried" or "hourly".

For an overlap generalization, the superclass and subclass entities are mapped into relations on a one-to-one basis. The superclass entity key will be mapped as the primary key for all the mapped relations. The "subclass predicate" attributes (one for each subclass entity) will be mapped as attributes of the "generalized" relation. As an example, the overlap generalization of Fig. 3.11 can be mapped to the following relations:

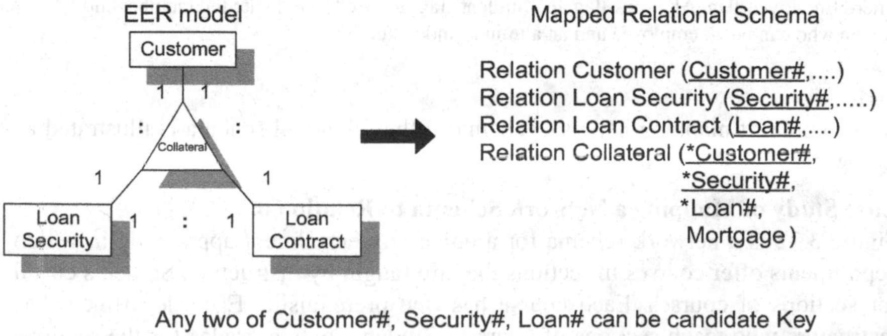

Fig. 3.19 Map ternary relationship of all 1:1 relationship from EER model to relational schema

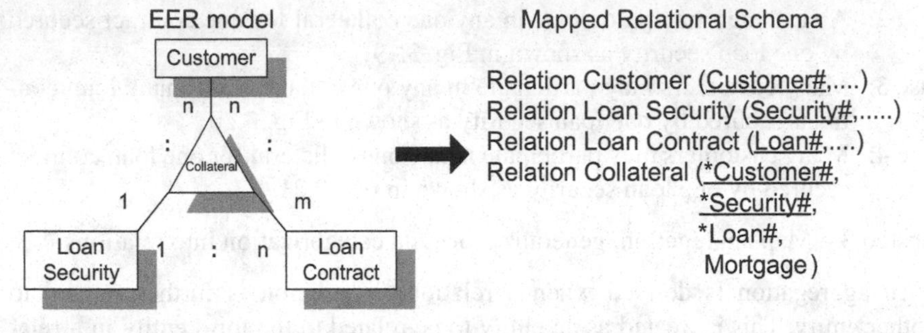

Fig. 3.20 Map ternary relationship of 2 m:n relationship from EER model to relational schema

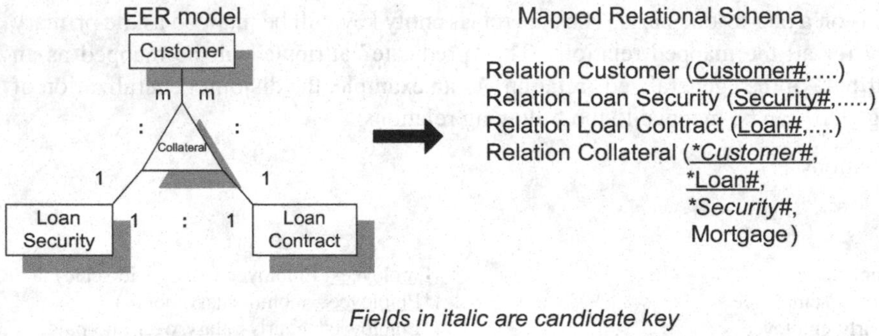

Fig. 3.21 Map ternary relationship of two 1:1 relationships from EER model to relational schema

Relations

Person	(Name, Address, Phone#, Age, Sex, Employee-flag, Alumnus-flag, Student-flag)
Employee	(*Name, Start-date, Salary)
Alumnus	(*Name, Graduation-date, degree)
Student	(*Name, Supervisor, department)

where Employee-flag, Alumnus-flag and Student-flag are used to indicate the membership of a person who can be an employee and an alumnus and a student.

An example of mapping network schema to the relational schema is illustrated as follows:

Case Study of Mapping a Network Schema to Relational

Figure 3.22 is a network schema for a university enrollment application in which departments offer courses in sections that are taught by instructors. Students enroll for sections of courses. Each course has one prerequisite. Each department has instructors who teach sections of courses. Students obtain grades for the sections they take. The following steps illustrate the different stages in the translation process.

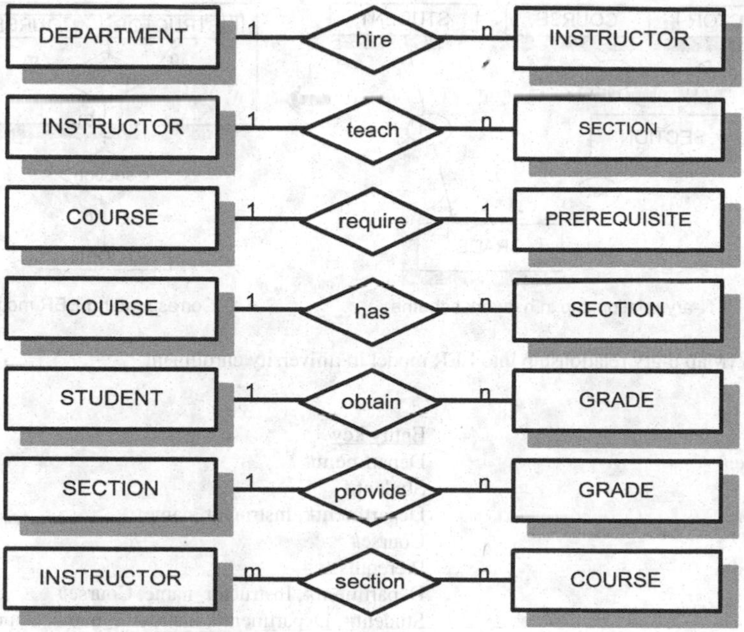

Fig. 3.22 Derive binary relationships in university enrollment

Preprocess step 1 (implied relationship), preprocess step 2 (alternative paths), step 1 (derive unary relationship), and step 3 (derive n-ary relationship) are not applied since there are no implied relationships (i.e., no duplicate key fields), no multiple access paths (i.e., no alternative paths), no unary relationships (i.e., no member records consisting of pointers only and referring back to its owner record occurrences), and no n-ary relationships (i.e., more than two owners or member record types linked to each other through sets).

Step 2 – Derive binary relationships.

The user specifies a 1:1 relationship between Course and Prerequisite. The relationships between the entities are shown in Fig. 3.22.

Step 4 – Derive aggregation entities.

The m:n relationship derived in step 2 is in aggregation because its relationship relation Section also relates to the entity Student in another m:n relationship as shown in Fig. 3.23.

Step 5 – Derive entities keys.

Entities are partial internally identified by default. In this case, the identifier type of record Prerequisite has been changed from partially internally identified to fully internally identified through user interrogation. Thus, we have its key changed as follows:

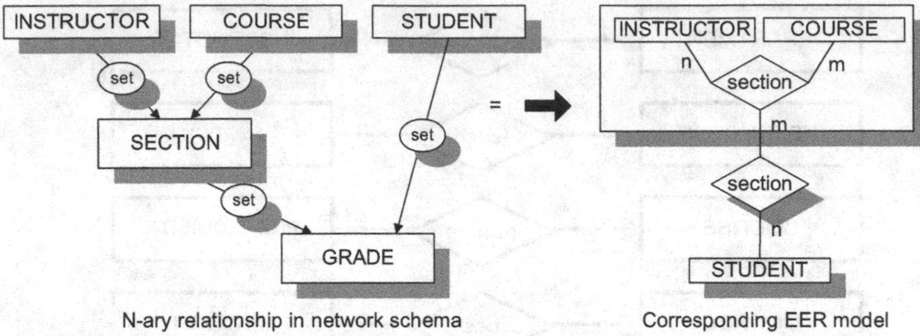

Fig. 3.23 Map n-ary relationship into EER model in university enrollment

<u>Entity</u>	<u>Entity key</u>
Department	Department#
Student	Student#
Instructor	Department#, Instructor_name
Course	Course#
Prerequisite	Prerequisite#
Section	Department#, Instructor_name, Course#
Grade	Student#, Department#, Instructor_name, Course#

Step 6 – Draw EER model.

As a result of the previous steps, an EER model can be drawn, as shown in Fig. 3.24.

The following steps map the derived EER model into a relational schema:

Step 1 – Map entities into relations.

Each entity can be translated into a relation as shown below:

Relation Department	(<u>Department#</u>, Department_name)
Relation Instructor	(*<u>Department#</u>, <u>Instructor_name</u>, Instructor_address)
Relation Course	(<u>Course#</u>, Course_location)
Relation Prerequisite	(<u>Prerequisite#</u>, Prerequisite_title, *Course#)
Relation Student	(<u>Student#</u>, Student_name)

Step 2 – Map m:n relationships into relationship relation.

In this example, the relation Section is derived as follows:

Relation Section (*<u>Department#</u>, *<u>Course#</u>, *<u>Instructor_name</u>, Section#)

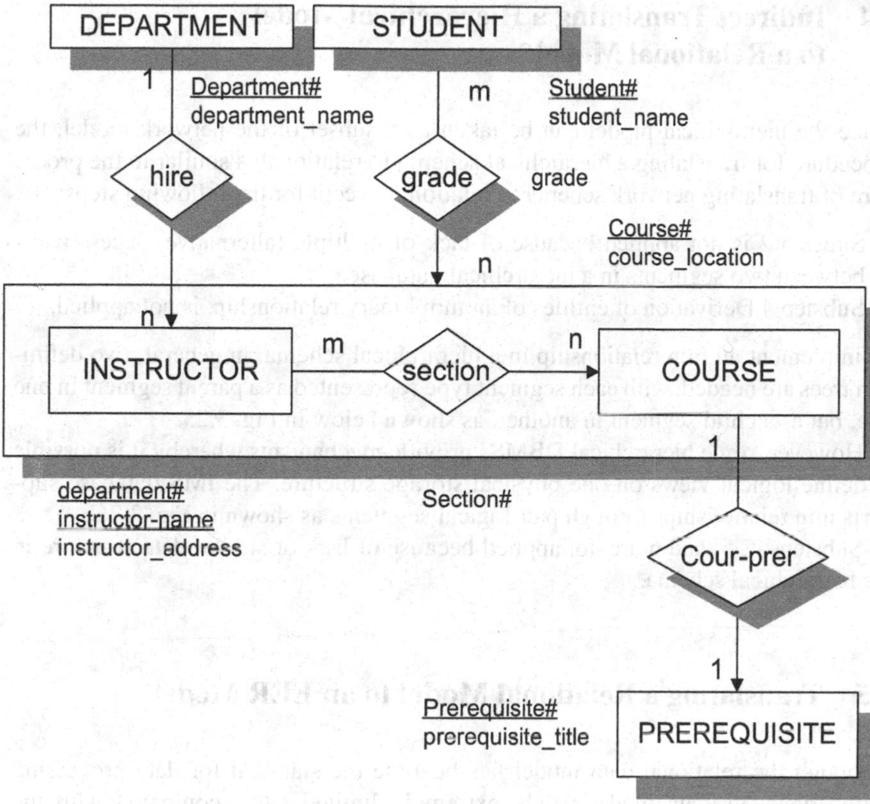

Fig. 3.24 Mapped EER model for university enrollment

Step 3 – Map aggregation into relation.

As relationship relation Section is related to entity Student in an m:n relationship, there is an aggregation relation as follows:

Relation Grade (*<u>Department#</u>, *<u>Instructor_name</u>, *<u>Course#</u>, *<u>Student#</u>, Grade)

As a result of the previous steps, the derived relations can be merged as follows:

Relation Department	(<u>Department#</u>, Department_name)
Relation Instructor	(*<u>Department#</u>, <u>Instructor_name</u>, Instructor_address)
Relation Course	(<u>Course#</u>, Course_location)
Relation Prerequisite	(<u>Prerequisite#</u>, Prerequisite_title, *Course#)
Relation Student	(<u>Student#</u>, Student_name)
Relation Section	(*<u>Department#</u>, *<u>Course#</u>, *<u>Instructor_name</u>, Section#)
Relation Grade	(*<u>Department#</u>, *<u>Instructor_name</u>, *<u>Course#</u>, *<u>Student#</u>, Grade)

3.4 Indirect Translating a Hierarchical Model to a Relational Model

Since the hierarchical model can be taken as a subset of the network model, the procedure for translating a hierarchical schema to relational is similar to the procedure of translating network schema to relational except for the following steps:

- Substep 2 is not applied because of lack of multiple (alternative) access paths between two segments in a hierarchical database.
- Substep 4 Derivation of entities of an m:n binary relationship, is not applied.

To implement an m:n relationship in a hierarchical schema, in general, two definition trees are needed, with each segment type represented as a parent segment in one tree, but as a child segment in another, as shown below in Fig. 3.25.

However, some hierarchical DBMSs provide mechanisms whereby it is possible to define logical views on one physical storage structure. The IMS database supports m:n relationships through pair logical segments as shown in Fig. 3.26.

Substeps 4, 5, and 6 are not applied because of lack of similar data structure in the hierarchical schema.

3.5 Translating a Relational Model to an EER Model

Although the relational data model has become the standard for data processing applications, its data modeling are extremely limited when compared with the object-oriented data model. For object-oriented data models, however, at present, there are no formal standards describing the exact format and syntax for representing an object-oriented database. Therefore, in the work described below, we define a methodology to reengineer existing relational model schemas into the UML model. The relational model is the first reverse-engineered into an EER model with users' input to recover some lost semantics. The EER model is then mapped into a UML model. This latter transformation is prescribed by a set of transformation rules devised by the author. Such reengineering practices can not only provide us with significant insight into the "interoperability" between the object-oriented and the

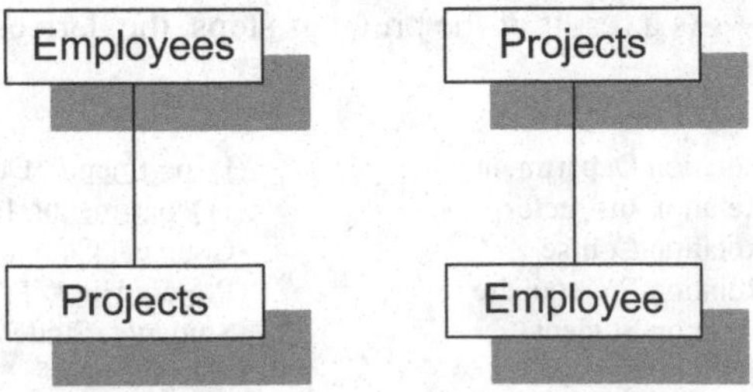

Fig. 3.25 m:n relationship with redundant hierarchical segments.

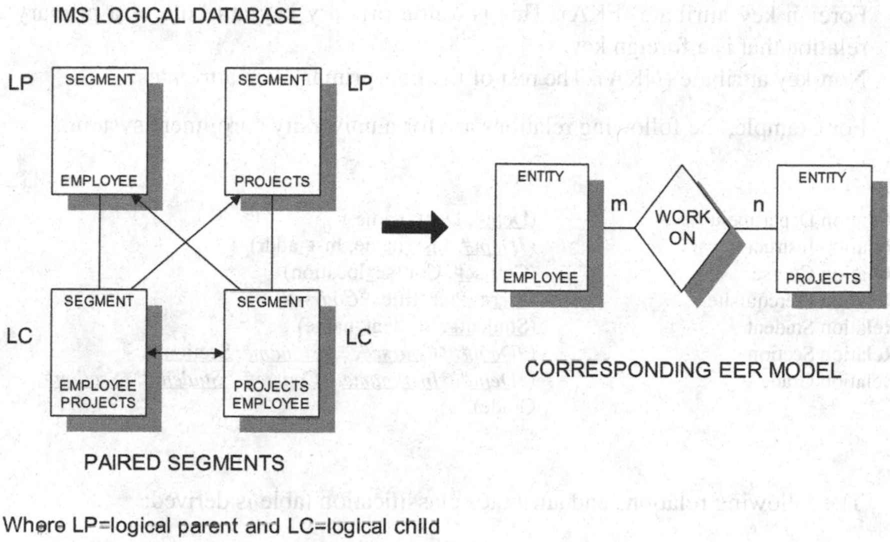

Fig. 3.26 Map IMS logical database into EER model

traditional semantic model techniques but also can lead us to the development of a practical design methodology for the object-oriented databases.

Step 1 – Reverse engineering from relational model to conceptual EER model (Navathe and Awong 1988).

The translation process can be described as follows:

Substep 1 – Define each relation, key, and field.

The relations are preprocessed by making any necessary candidate key substitutions as follows:

- Primary relation. These relations describe entities.
- Primary relation – Type 1 (PR_1). This is a relation whose primary key does not contain a key of another relation.
- Primary relation – Type 2 (PR_2). This is a relation whose primary key does contain a key of another relation.
- Secondary relation. This is a relation whose primary key is full or partially formed by the concatenation of primary keys of other relations.
- Secondary relation – Type 1 (SR_1). If the key of the secondary relation is formed fully by concatenation of primary keys of primary relations, it is of Type 1 or SR_1.
- Secondary relation – Type 2 (SR_2). Secondary relations that are not of Type 1.
- Key attribute – Primary (KAP). This is an attribute in the primary key of a secondary relation that is also a key of some primary relation.
- Key attribute – General (KAG). These are all the other primary key attributes in a secondary relation that are not of the KAP type.

- Foreign key attribute (FKA). This is a non-primary key attribute of a primary relation that is a foreign key.
- Non-key attribute (NKA). The rest of the non-primary-key attributes.

For example, the following relations are for a university enrollment system:

Relation Department	(Dept#, Dept_name,)
Relation Instructor	(**Dept#*, Inst_name, Inst_addr)
Relation Course	(Course#, Course_location)
Relation Prerequisite	(Prer#, Prer_title, **Course#*)
Relation Student	(Student#, Student_name)
Relation Section	(**Dept#*, **Course#*, **Inst_name*, Section#)
Relation Grade	(**Dept#*, **Inst_name*, **Course#*, **Student#*, **Section#*, Grade)

The following relations and attributes classification table is derived:

Relation Name	Rel Type	Primary-Key	KAP	KAG	FKA	NKA
DEPT	PR_1	Dept#				Dept_name
INST	PR_2	Dept#	Dept#	Inst_name	Inst_name	Inst_addre
COUR	PR_1	Course#				Course_location
STUD	PR_1	Student#		Stud_name		
PREP	PR_1	Prer			Course#	Prer_title
SECT	SR_2	Course#	Course#	Inst_name	Inst_name	
		Dept#	Dept#			
		Section#		Section#		
GRADE	SR_1	Inst_name	Inst_name			Grade
		Course#	Course#			
		Student#	Student#			
		Dept#	Dept#			
		Section#	Section#			

Substep 2 – Map each PR_1 into an entity.

For each Type 1 primary relation (PR_1), define a corresponding entity type and identify it by the primary key. Its non-key attributes map to the attributes of the entity type with the corresponding domains. For example, the PR_1 relational types in the classification table can be mapped to the following entities in Fig. 3.27.

Substep 3 – Map each PR_2 into a weak entity.

For each Type 2 primary relation (PR_2), define a weak entity with its primary key being the key of the PR_2 relation. The entity on which it is ID-dependent will be that entity identified by the primary key on which the PR_2 primary key is dependent. Define a relationship between the owner and the weak entities. All NKA type

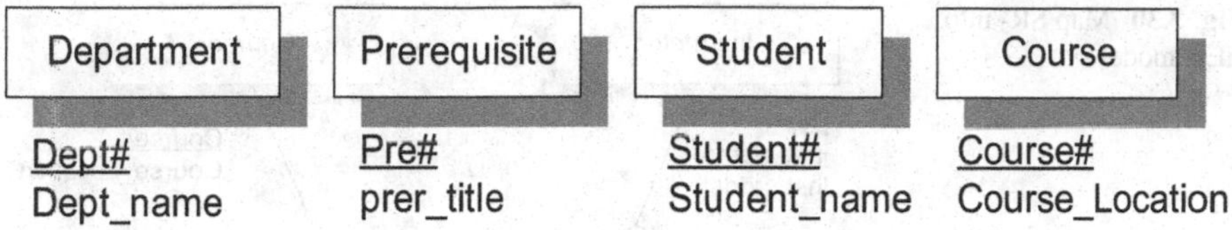

Fig. 3.27 Map primary relations to entities

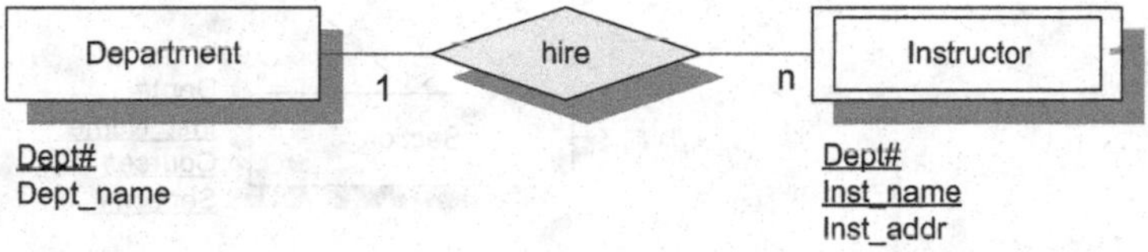

Fig. 3.28 Map PR_2 into EER model

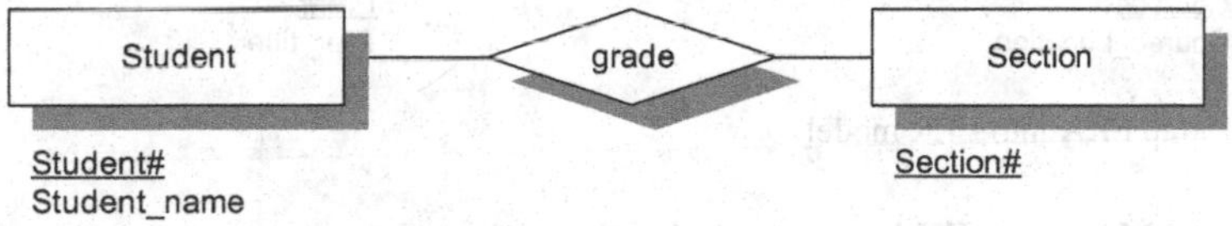

Fig. 3.29 Map SR_1 into EER model

attributes of the PR_2 relation will be attributes of the weak entity defined. For example, the PR_2 relational type in the classification table can be mapped to the following entities and their relationships in Fig. 3.28.

Substep 4 – Map SR_1 into a binary/n-ary relationship.

For each SR_1 secondary relation, identify the relationship by the primary key of the SR_1 relation. Define the NKA type attributes as the attributes of the relationship type. If the key of the SR_1 relationship is part of the primary key of another secondary relation, then it is mapped as an n-ary relationship in the EER model. For example, the SR_1 relational type in the classification table can be mapped to the following entities and their relationships in Fig. 3.29.

Substep 5 – Map SR_2 into a binary/n-ary relationship.

For each SR_2 relation, define an entity type for each of the KAG type attributes, with the KAG attribute as its entity key. Define a binary relationship type between all the entity types defined by the KAP and KAG attributes in the key of this SR_2 relation. The NKA attributes form the attributes of this binary relationship type. If the key of the SR_2 relationship is part of the primary key of another secondary relation, then it is mapped as an n-ary relationship in the EER model. For example, the SR_2 relational type in the classification table can be mapped to the following entities and their relationships in Fig. 3.30.

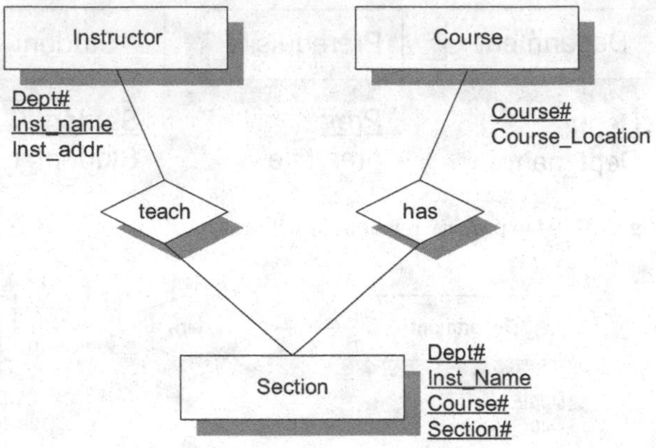

Fig. 3.30 Map SR_2 into EER model

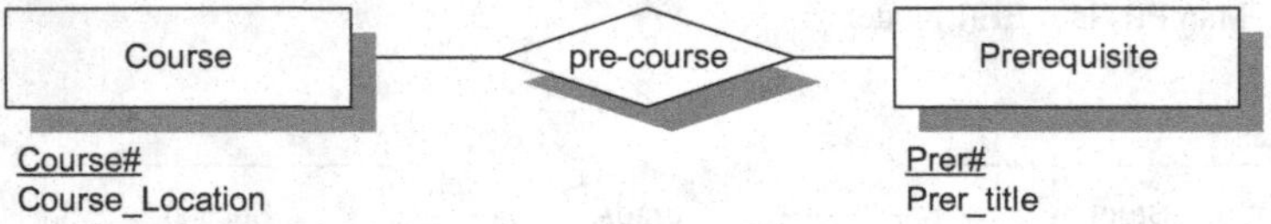

Fig. 3.31 Map FKA into EER model

Substep 6 – Map each FKA into a relationship.

For each FDA type attribute of a primary relation, R_1, define a relationship type between the entity defined from R_1 and the entity that has the FKA as its primary key.

The following entities and relationships can be derived from the classification table in Fig. 3.31.

Substep 7 – Map each inclusion dependency into semantics (binary/n-ary relationship).

If IDs have been derived between two entities, entity A with a as entity key and b′ as foreign key, and entity B with b as entity key and a′ as foreign key, then their semantics can be derived as follows:

Case 1. If given ID; a′ ⊆ a, then entity A is in a 1:n relationship with entity B.
Case 2. If given IDs: a′ ⊆ a, and b′ ⊆ b (optional), then entity A is in a 1:1 relationship with entity B.
Case 3. If given IDs: a′ ⊆ a, and b′ ⊆ b, and a′b′ is a composite key, then entity A is in an m:n relationship with entity B.

For example, Table 3.1 shows the derived semantics from the inclusion dependencies of the enrollment system:

Substep 8. Draw EER model.

Put together an EER model as a result of the above steps as shown in Fig. 3.32.

Table 3.1 Derive semantics from inclusion dependencies

Given derived inclusion dependency	Derived semantics
Instructor.Dept# ⊆ Department.Dept#	n:1 relationship between entities instructor and department
Section.Dept# ⊆ Department.Dept#	1:n relationship between entities instructor and section and between course and section.
Section.Inst_name ⊆ Instructor.Inst_name	
Section.Course# ⊆ Course.Course#	
Grade.Dept# ⊆ Section.Dept#	m:n relationship between relationship section and entity student.
Grade.Inst_name ⊆ Section.Inst_name	
Grade.Course# ⊆ Section.Course#	
Grade.Student# ⊆ Student.Student#	
Prerequisite.Course# ⊆ Course.Course#	1:1 relationship between course and prerequisite

3.6 Translating an EER Model to a UML

The following procedure transforms an EER model to a UML model (Fong and Kwan 1994):

Step 1 – Map entity to class.

An EER model works with entity types and their corresponding attributes. Attributes of a particular entity may be considered as instance variables of the class instance. For example, an entity type Student can be mapped into a class Student of UML as shown in Fig. 3.33.

Step 2 – Map relationship to the association.

In an EER model, relationships are represented as named associations among entities. In an object-oriented schema, they are links and associations between superclass(es) and subclass(es). A link is a physical conceptual connection between object instances. Association describes a group of link with common structure and semantics and can be represented as an attribute that explicitly references another object. The relationship in the EER model can be mapped into an association in the object-oriented schema on a 1:1 basis with its corresponding multiplicity of links and pointers. When constrained by cardinality, appropriate symbols must be specified by a line (link) with or without a solid dot sign. For example, the 1:n relationship in Fig. 3.34 can be mapped into the UML where "Cour-prer" is an association between the classes and prerequisite.

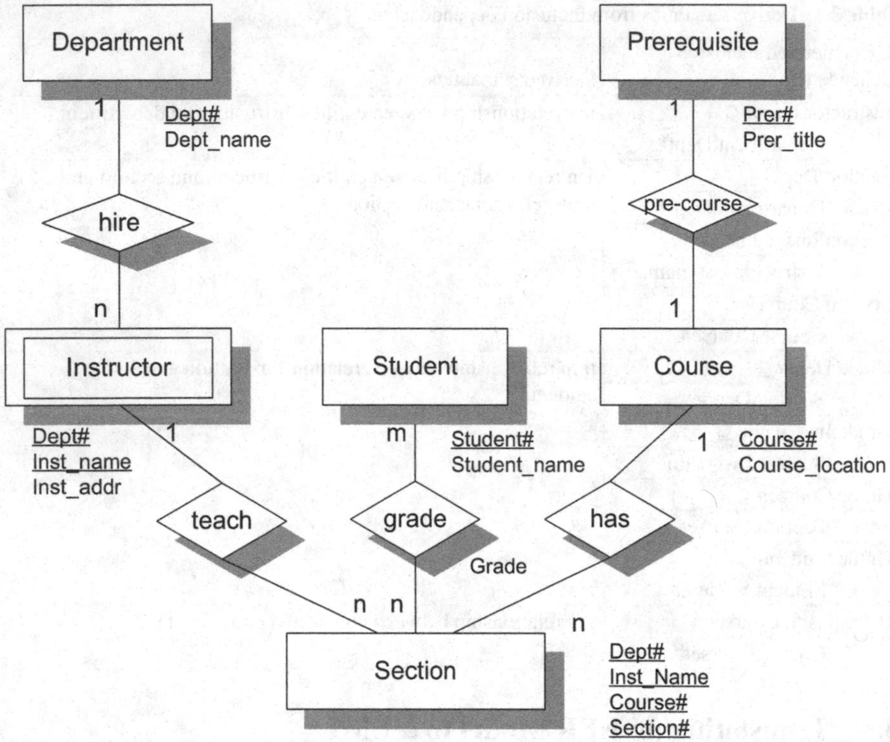

Fig. 3.32 Derived EER model in reverse engineering

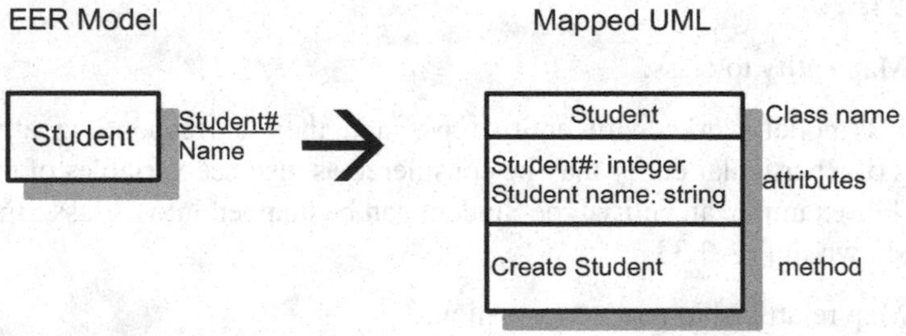

Fig. 3.33 Map an entity to a class

Step 3 – Map generalization to method.

For generalization, the variances among entities are suppressed and their commonalities are identified by generalizing them into one single class. The original entities with each of its unique differences are special subclass(es). The mutually exclusive subclass(es) are called disjoint generalizations. The mutually inclusive subclasses are called overlap generalization. For example, disjoint generalization in Fig. 3.35 can be mapped into the UML where subclass(es) Contract-Staff and

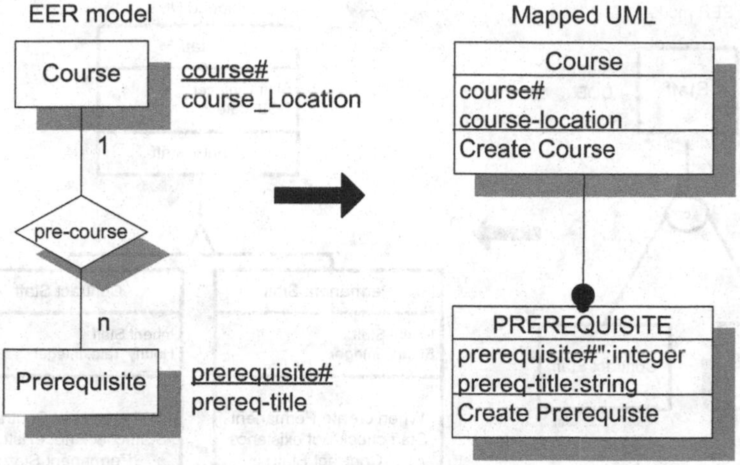

Fig. 3.34 Map a relationship to an association in UML

Permanent-Staff inherit the properties and operations of superclass Staff. The mapping of overlap generalization into the object-oriented schema is similar to the mapping of disjoint generalization into the object-oriented schema except that the check statement is omitted and a solid triangle is used to indicate overlapped subclass(es).

Step 4 – Map categorization to "Multiple" inheritance.

A categorization is derived by mapping isa relationships and their record types to a superclass/subclass such that a set of the superclass(es) can be united to form a superclass. All these superclass(es) may have different key attributes as they are originally independent classes. For example, the categorization in Fig. 3.36 can be mapped into the following UML model where the subclass Research-Assistant comes from one of the two superclass(es): Faculty or Graduate Student.

Step 5 – Map isa relationship to inheritance.

The concept of inheritance associated with a generalization (isa) relationship in object-oriented schema permits classes to be organized in which specialized class(es) inherit the properties and operations of a more generalized class. The class carries common properties while deriving a specialized subclass. For example, the isa relationship in Fig. 3.37 can be mapped into the following UML model where subclass Graduate_Student inherits the properties of its superclass Student.

Step 6 – Map weak entity to component class.

The existence of a weak entity in the EER model depends on its owner entity. For example, the weak entity Instructor in Fig. 3.38 can be mapped into UML where class Department is a composite object class that owns a component class Instructor. The own statement implies an existence dependency of component class Instructor such that if an instance of class Department is deleted, its corresponding component class Instructor instances are also deleted.

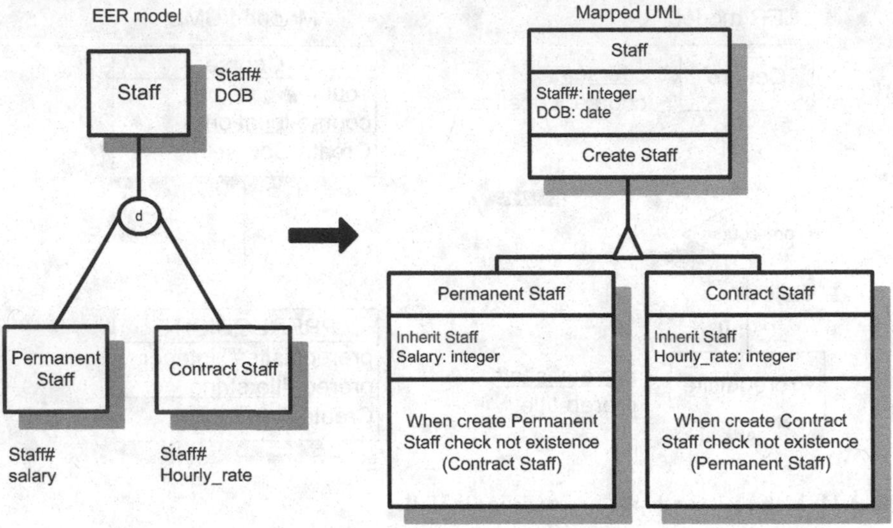

Fig. 3.35 Map disjoint generalization to method

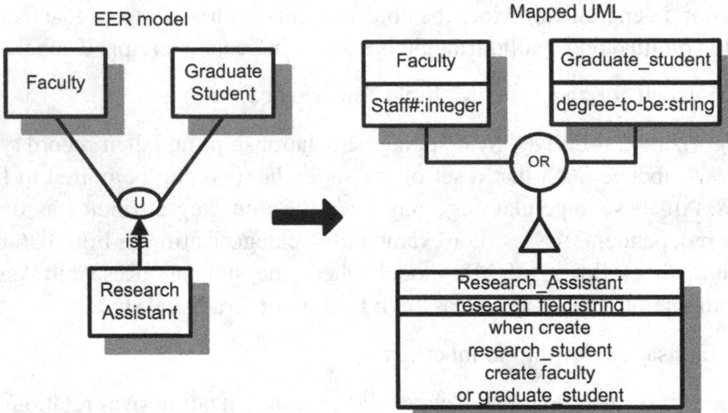

Fig. 3.36 Map categorization to method

Step 7 – Map aggregation to composite class.

The entities and their relationship in the EER model can be aggregated to form an entity. In an object-oriented model, this permits the combination of classes that are related into a higher-level composite class. For example, the aggregation in Fig. 3.39 can be mapped to the object-oriented schema where the composite class Section is an aggregation of two-component classes: class Instructor and class Course.

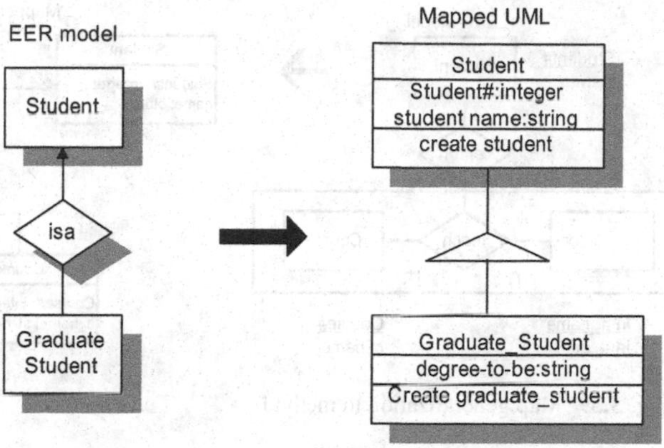

Fig. 3.37 Map isa relationship to inheritance

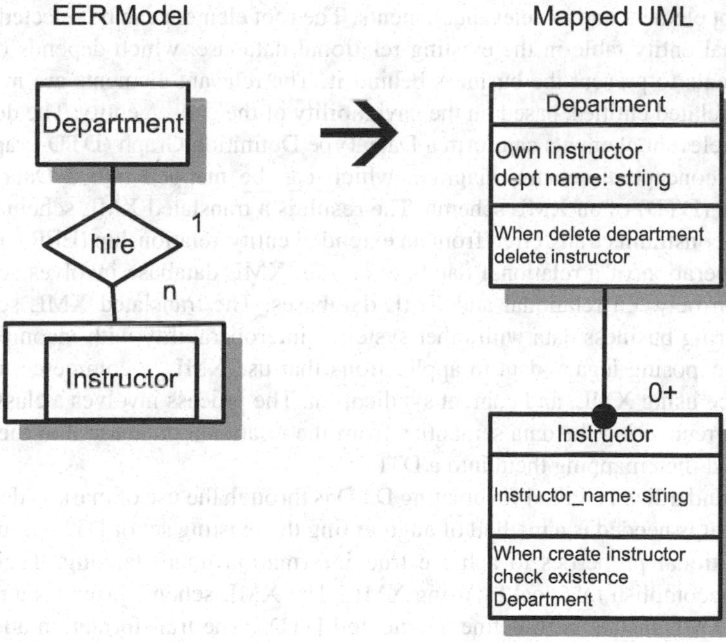

Fig. 3.38 Map weak entity to method

3.7 Translating a Relational Schema to a Document Type Definition

With XML adopted as the technology trend on the Internet, and with the investment in the current relational database systems, companies must convert their relational data into XML documents for data transmission on the Internet. In the process, to preserve the users' relational data requirements of data constraints into the converted XML documents, the user must define a required XML view as a root

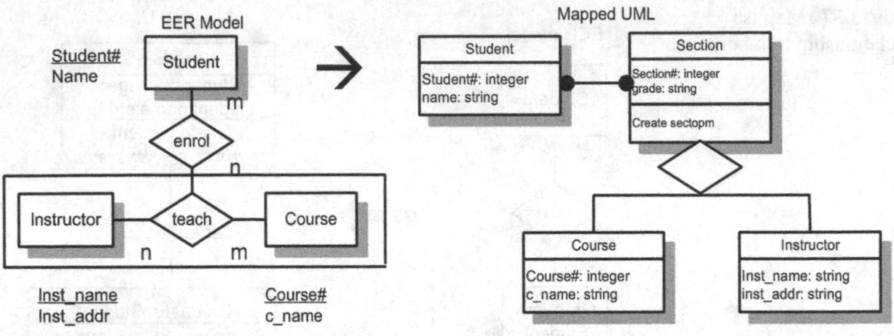

Fig. 3.39 Map generalization to method

element for each XML document. The construction of an XML document is based on the root element and its relevant elements. The root element can be selected from a relational entity table in the existing relational database, which depends on the requirements to present the business behind it. The relevant elements are mapped from the related entities, based on the navigability of the chosen entity. The derived root and relevant elements can form a Data Type Definition Graph (DTD-graph) as an XML conceptual schema diagram, which can be mapped into a Data Type Definition (DTD) of an XML schema. The result is a translated XML schema with semantic constraints transferred from an extended entity-relationship (EER) model.

Interoperation of a relational database and an XML database involves schema translation between relational and XML databases. The translated XML schema helps sharing business data with other systems, interoperability with incompatible systems, exposing legacy data to applications that use XML, e-commerce, object persistence using XML, and content syndication. The process involves a classification table recovering the data semantics from the relational database into the EER model, and then mapping them into a DTD.

The standardized method for creating DTD is through the use of markup declarations. What is needed is a method of augmenting the existing set of DTD properties with additional properties to achieve true information understanding. There are ways to accomplish this goal by using XML. The XML schema provides a means of using XML instances to define augmented DTDs. The transformation adopts a reverse engineering approach. It reconstructs the semantic model in an EER model from the logical relational schema by capturing the user's knowledge. It then reengineers the EER model into a DTD-graph (Funderburk et al. 2002).

To make relational schema compatible with the XML schema, based on each constraint in the relational schema, we map the relational schema with its semantic constraints into a DTD and a DTD-graph. A DTD-graph is an XML logical schema in the form of a hierarchical containment. To draw a DTD-graph, we select an element as a root and then put its relevant information into a document. The selection is usually driven by the business nature. In other words, it depends on the requirements to present the business behind. Relevance concerns which entities are related to the selected entity to be processed. The relevant classes include the selected and related entities that are navigable. Navigability specifies whether traversal from an entity to its related entity is possible. Relationships can be directional with navigability. Unidirectional means only one relationship end is navigable. Bi-directional means both relationship ends are navigable.

An XML document is in the form of a spool of text in a particular sequence and the sequence will affect the output statement and finally the whole database schema. An XML schema consists of a root element and then each element is laid down one by one as branches and leaves in the schema. There is a top-down relationship of the element in an XML schema. Even the element's attributes are also ordered in the schema.

On the other hand, a DTD-graph node diagram uses a graphical interface. Each node in a DTD-graph does not carry any ordering information. There is no explicit root-branch relationship between nodes in the DTD-graph nodes diagram.

In order to solve the problem due to this structural difference, an arbitrary XML view, a database object, has to be created in order to start the branching from the root. Branching from this root element are the basic classes and various constraints included in the DTD-graph specification. To prepare for the transformation, the non-ordered DTD-graph node diagram must be replaced with a listing of all related components in the entity diagram. This process is "decomposition." With the component list, a process sequence is drawn to transform each kind of DTD-graph component into its XML correspondence of DTD. The structural difference problem could be solved.

Figure 3.40 shows the general architecture of re-engineering relational schema into XML schema DTD.

By following the procedure in Fig. 3.40, we translate a relational schema into an XML schema based on a selected XML view and then load relational data into an XML schema. It consists of three steps:

1. Reverse engineering relational schema into an EER model.
2. Schema translation from an EER model into a DTD-graph and DTD.
3. Data conversion from a relational database to XML documents.

Step 1 – Reverse engineering a relational schema into an EER model.

By use of classification tables to define the relationship between keys and attributes in all relations, we can recover their data semantics in the form of an EER model. Refer to Sect. 3.5 for details.

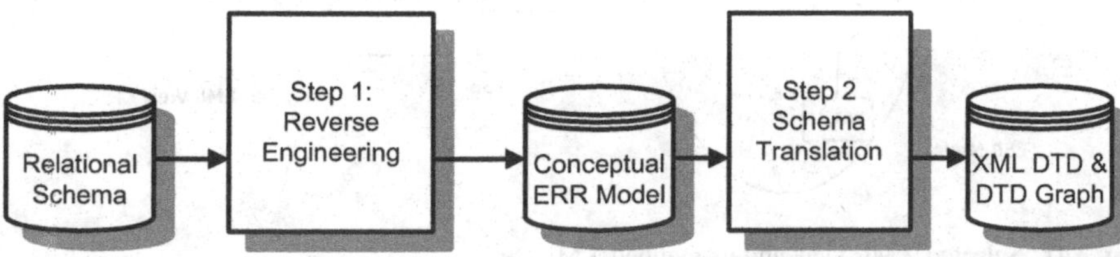

Fig. 3.40 Architecture of translating schema from relational into XML

Step 2 – Schema translation from the EER model into a DTD-graph and DTD.

We can map the data semantics in the EER model into a DTD-graph according to their data dependencies constraints. These constraints can then be transformed into a DTD as an XML schema as shown in the following:

Rule 1: Define an XML View Root Element in DTD

To select an XML view of the source relational schema as a root element, its relevant information must be transformed into an XML logical schema including the selected entity and all its relevant entities that are navigable.

Navigability specifies the feasibility of the traversal from an entity to its related entities. The relationship can be directional with navigability. The process is similar to the process when we walk the tree structure of a DTD-graph. We navigate each relationship, then each relationship from the children's table of the previous relationships, and so on.

In Fig. 3.41, entity E is the selected entity for an XML view, The navigable entities in the EER model are mapped as sub-elements under root elements in a hierarchy structure. Each attribute of the relevant entity is mapped into the attribute of the corresponding element. In the example, this selected XML view and its relevant relations can be mapped as elements of an XML schema. The relevance of the relations depends on the connectivity and the constraints of the hierarchical tree of the elements The one-to-many cardinality can be mapped into one parent and many child elements, and the many-to-one cardinality can be mapped into one parent and one child elements of a translated XML schema.

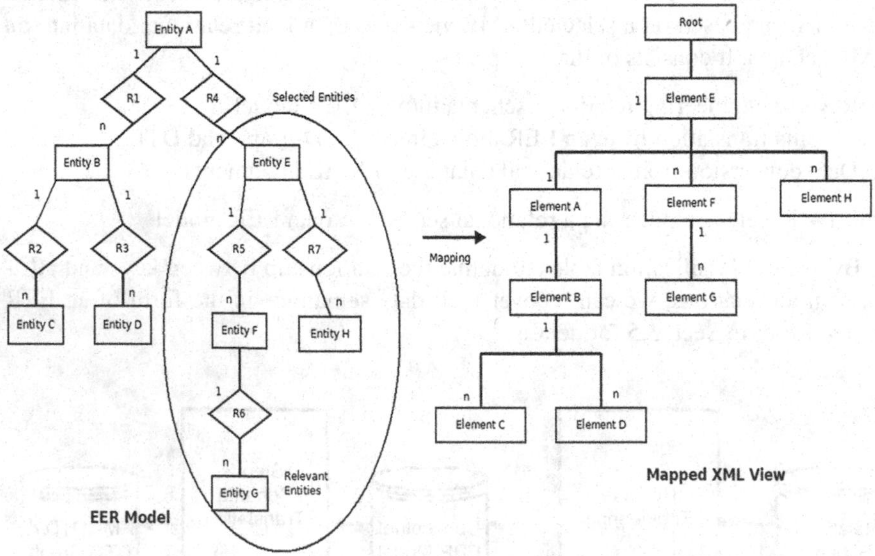

Fig. 3.41 Selected XML view and its mapped XML tree

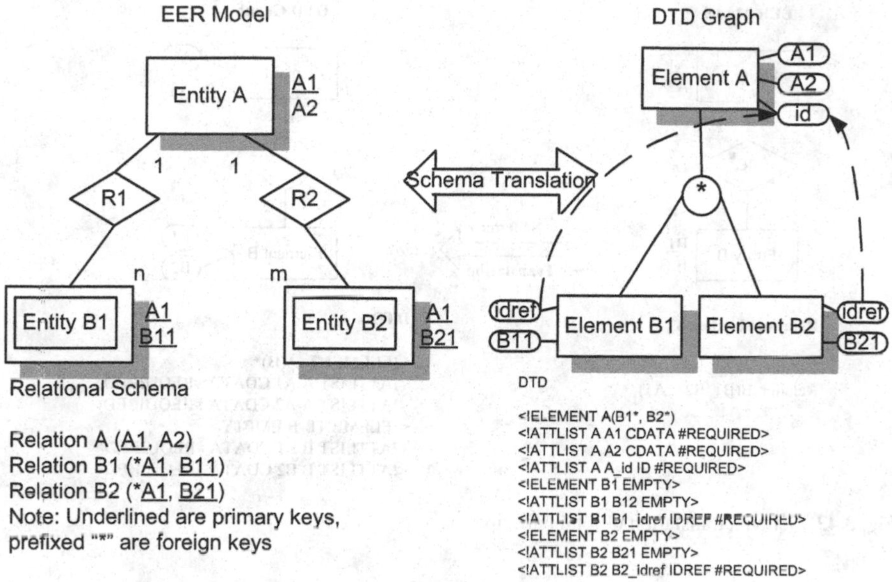

Fig. 3.42 Schema translation of weak entity

Rule 2: Mapping Weak Entity from RDB to DTD

A weak entity depends on its strong entity such that the primary key of the weak entity is also a foreign key addressing to the primary key of its strong entity, and cannot be a null value. In DTD, we transform the strong entity into an element with an ID and the weak entity into another element that refers to the ID element using IDREF as shown in Fig. 3.42.

Rule 3: Mapping Participation from RDB to DTD

A child table is in total participation with a parent table provided that all data occurrences of the child table must participate in a relationship with the parent table. A foreign key of a child table in total participation must address the primary key of its parent table and cannot be a null value. A child table is in partial participation with a parent table provided that the data occurrences of the child table are not totally participated in a relationship with the parent table. A foreign key of a child table in partial participation must address the primary key of its parent table and can be a null value. In DTD, we translate the total and partial participations into an optional occurrence as shown in Figs. 3.43 and 3.44.

Case 1: Total/Mandatory Participation

Case 2: Partial/Optional Participation.

Rule 4: Mapping Cardinality from RDB to DTD

One-to-one cardinality indicates that a foreign key of a child table addresses a primary key of a parent table in a one-to-one occurrence. One-to-many cardinality

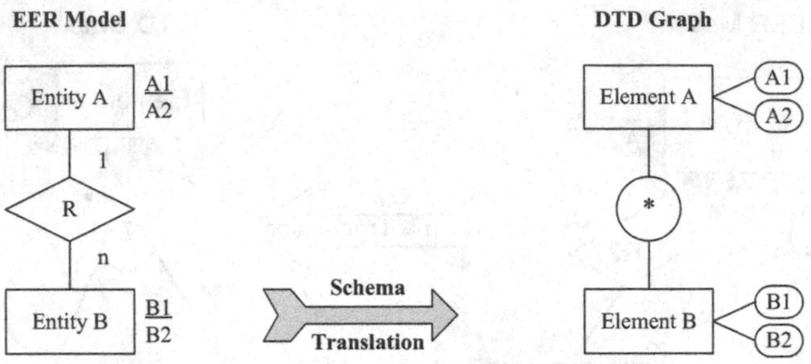

Relational Schema

Relation A(<u>A1</u>, A2)
Relation B(<u>B1</u>, B2, *A1)

DTD

```
<!ELEMENT  A(B)*>
<!ATTLIST A A1 CDATA #REQUIRED>
<!ATTLIST A A2 CDATA #REQUIRED>
<!ELEMENT  B EMPTY>
<!ATTLIST B B1 CDATA #REQUIRED>
<!ATTLIST B B2 CDATA #REQUIRED>
```

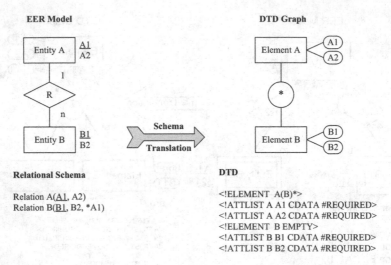

Fig. 3.43 Schema translation of total participation

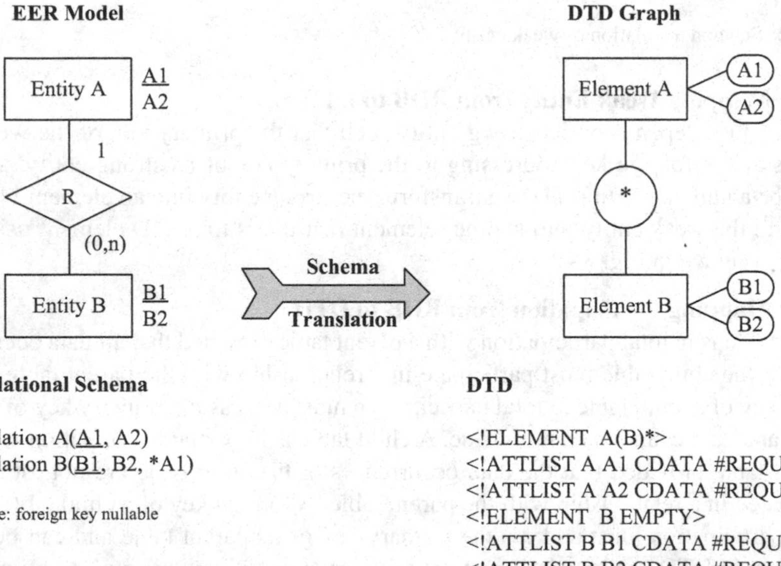

Relational Schema

Relation A(<u>A1</u>, A2)
Relation B(<u>B1</u>, B2, *A1)

Note: foreign key nullable

DTD

```
<!ELEMENT  A(B)*>
<!ATTLIST A A1 CDATA #REQUIRED>
<!ATTLIST A A2 CDATA #REQUIRED>
<!ELEMENT  B EMPTY>
<!ATTLIST B B1 CDATA #REQUIRED>
<!ATTLIST B B2 CDATA #REQUIRED>
```

Fig. 3.44 Schema translation of partial participation

indicates that a primary key of a parent table is addressed by many foreign keys of a child table in a one-to-many occurrence. Many-to-many cardinality indicates that a primary key of a parent table is addressed by many foreign keys of a child table and vice versa. This pair of tables are thus in a many-to-many cardinality. In DTD, we translate one-to-one cardinality into parent and child element (Fig. 3.45) and

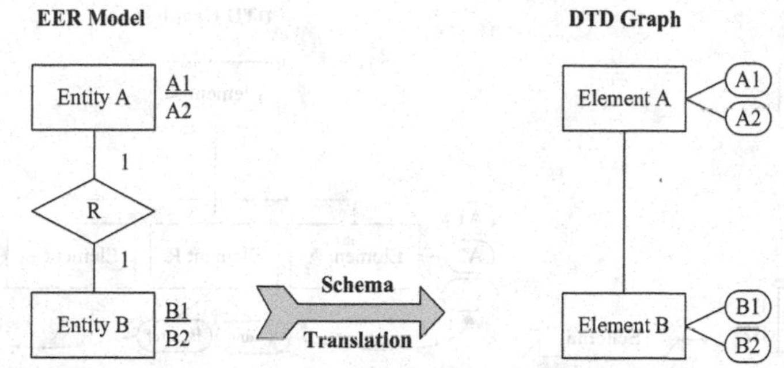

Relational Schema

Relation A(<u>A1</u>, A2)
Relation B(<u>B1</u>, B2, *A1)

DTD

```
<!ELEMENT A(B)>
<!ATTLIST A A1 CDATA #REQUIRED>
<!ATTLIST A A2 CDATA #REQUIRED>
<!ELEMENT B EMPTY>
<!ATTLIST B B1 CDATA #REQUIRED>
<!ATTLIST B B2 CDATA #REQUIRED>
```

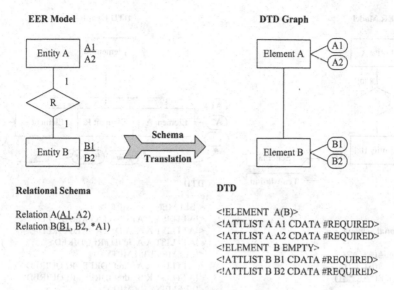

Fig. 3.45 Schema translation of One-to-One cardinality

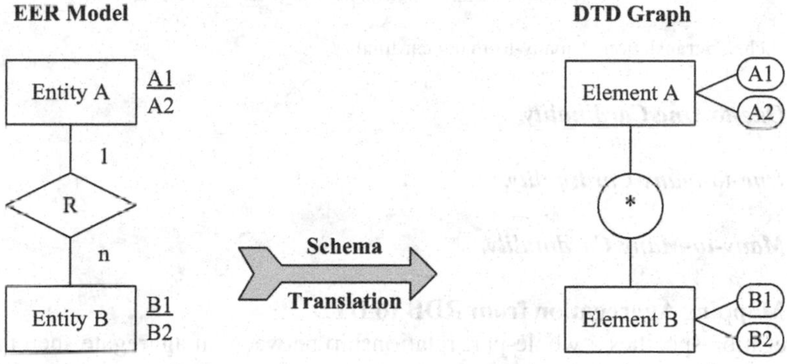

Relational Schema

Relation A(<u>A1</u>, A2)
Relation B(<u>B1</u>, B2, *A1)

DTD

```
<!ELEMENT A(B)*>
<!ATTLIST A A1 CDATA #REQUIRED>
<!ATTLIST A A2 CDATA #REQUIRED>
<!ELEMENT B EMPTY>
<!ATTLIST B B1 CDATA #REQUIRED>
<!ATTLIST B B2 CDATA #REQUIRED>
```

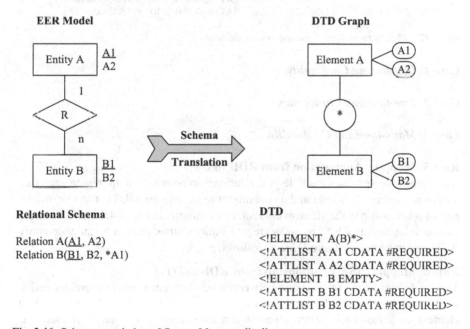

Fig. 3.46 Schema translation of One-to-Many cardinality

one-to-many cardinality into a parent and child element with multiple occurrences (Fig. 3.46). In many-to-many cardinality, it is mapped into DTD of a hierarchy structure with ID and IDREF as shown in Fig. 3.47.

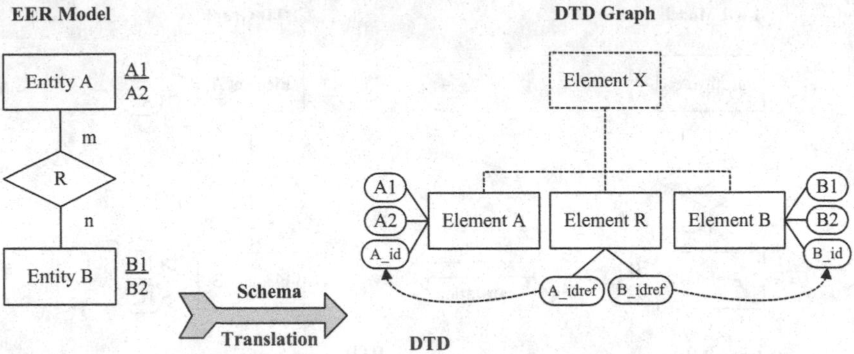

Relational Schema

Relation A(<u>A1</u>, A2)
Relation B(<u>B1</u>, B2)
Relation R(*<u>A1</u>, *<u>B1</u>)

DTD

```
<!ELEMENT A EMPTY>
<!ATTLIST A A1 CDATA #REQUIRED>
<!ATTLIST A A2 CDATA #REQUIRED>
<!ATTLIST A A_id ID #REQUIRED>
<!ELEMENT R EMPTY>
<!ATTLIST R A_idref IDREF #REQUIRED>
<!ATTLIST R B_idref IDREF #REQUIRED>
<!ELEMENT B EMPTY>
<!ATTLIST B B1 CDATA #REQUIRED>
<!ATTLIST B B2 CDATA #REQUIRED>
<!ATTLIST B B_id ID #REQUIRED>
```

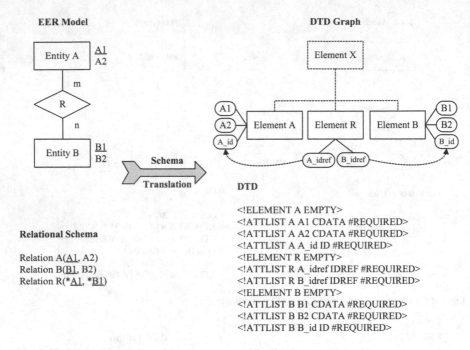

Fig. 3.47 Schema translation of many-to-many cardinality

Case 1: One-to-One Cardinality.

Case 2: One-to-many Cardinality.

Case 3: Many-to-Many Cardinality.

Rule 5: Mapping Aggregation from RDB to DTD

An aggregation specifies a whole-part relationship between an aggregate such that a class represents the whole and a constituent represents part. DTD can construct a part of relationship in the element content. For example, in Fig. 3.48, entity B, entity C, and relationship R1 form an aggregate entity that is related to another entity A. They can be mapped into DTD as follows:

Rule 6: Mapping ISA Relationship from RDB to DTD

The isa defines as the relationship between a subclass entity to a superclass entity. In DTD, we transform each subclass entity as a child element that refers to its parent element such that each parent element can have zero to one child elements as (Fig. 3.49):

Rule 7: Mapping Generalization from RDB to DTD

The generalization defines a relationship between entities to build a taxonomy of classes: One entity is a more general description of a set of other entities. In DTD, we transform the general superclass entity into an element, the element type originating from the superclass. For example, in Fig. 3.50 and Fig. 3.51, we present the generalization of entity B and entity C into entity A in DTD.

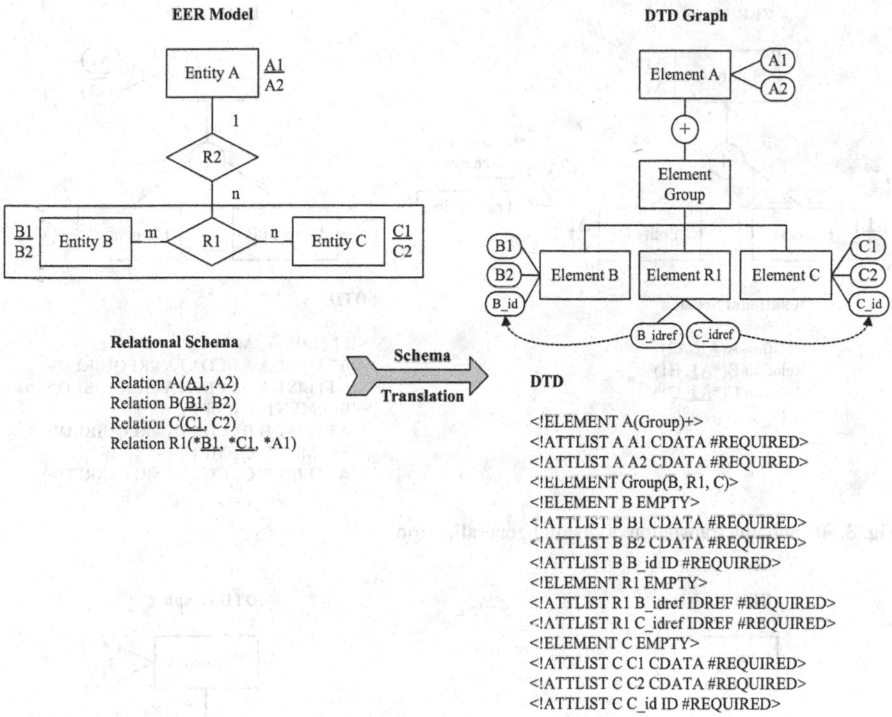

Fig. 3.48 Schema translation of aggregation

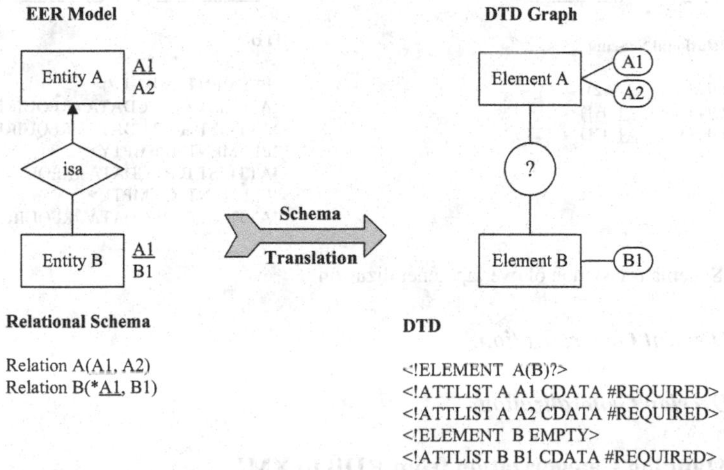

Fig. 3.49 Schema translation of ISA relationship

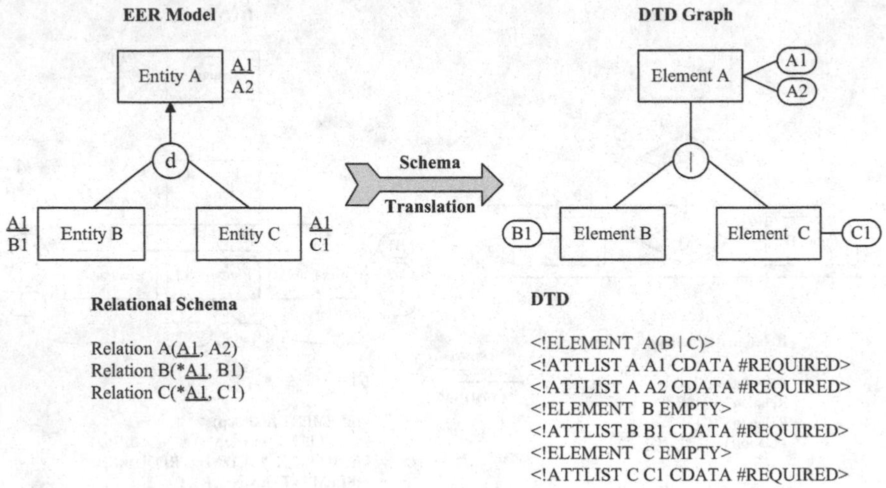

Fig. 3.50 Schema translation of disjoint generalization

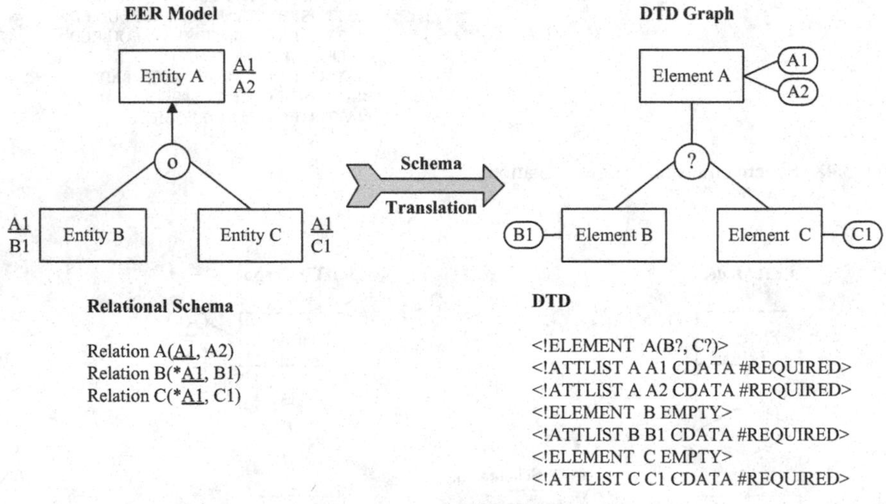

Fig. 3.51 Schema translation of overlap generalization

Case 1: Disjoint Generalization.

Case 2: Overlap Generalization.

Rule 8: Mapping Categorization from RDB to XML

A subclass table is a subset of categorization of its superclass tables. In other words, a subclass table is a subset of a union superclass tables such that the data occurrence of a subclass table must appear in one and only one superclass table. In DTD, we

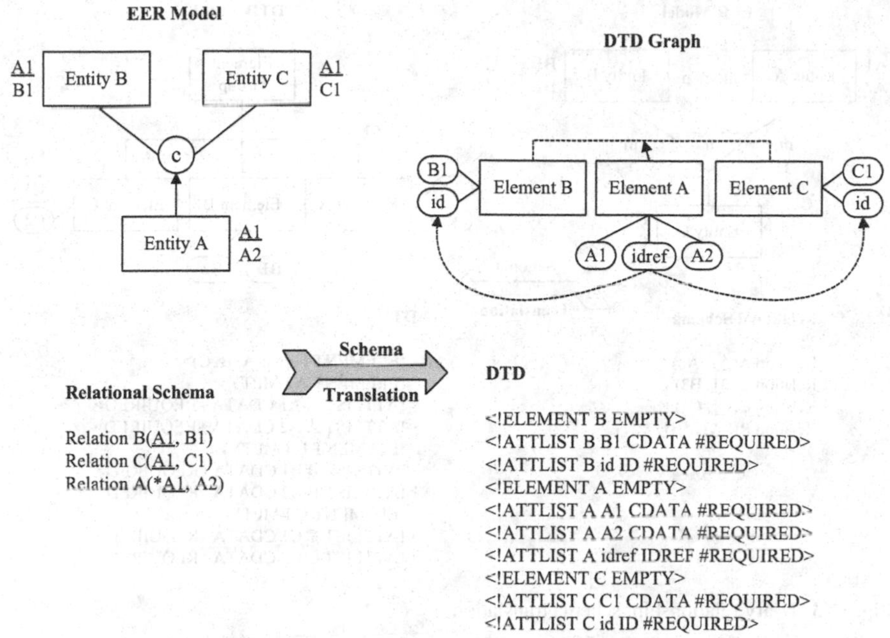

Fig. 3.52 Schema translation of categorization

transform the super classes into elements, and their common subclass into an element on the same level. Each element receives an additional "artificial" ID attribute declared as #REQUIRED referred by their common element's IDREF in DTD as shown in Fig. 3.52.

Rule 9: Mapping N-ary Relationship from RDB to XML

Multiple tables relate to each other in an n-ary relationship. An n-ary relationship is a relationship relation for multiple tables such that components of the former's compound primary key addressing to the primary keys of the latter, which are related to each other. In DTD, we transform the n-ary relationship into group of element as shown in Fig. 3.53.

3.8 Case Study of Translating a Relational Schema to a Document Type Definition

Consider a case study of a hospital database system. In this system, a patient can have many record folders. Each record folder can contain many different medical records of the patient. The AE, a ward, and an outpatient record can be generalized as a medical record. A country has many patients. A borrower of the record folder of the patient can be a department, a doctor, or other hospital for their references or

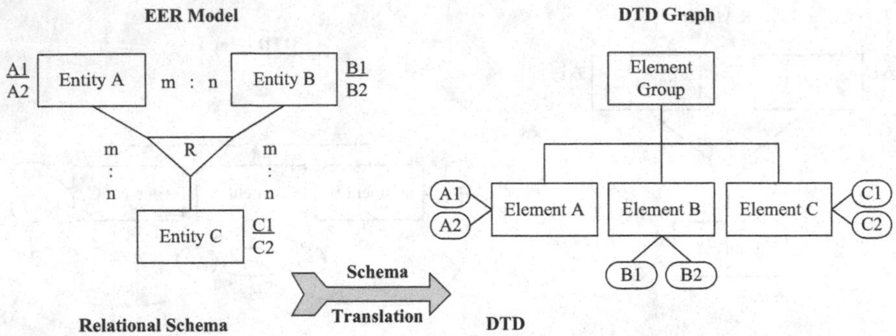

Relational Schema

Relation A(A1, A2)
Relation B(B1, B2)
Relation C(C1, C2)
Relation R(*A1, *B1, *C1)

DTD

```
<!ELEMENT Group(A, B, C)>
<!ELEMENT A EMPTY>
<!ATTLIST A A1 CDATA #REQUIRED>
<!ATTLIST A A2 CDATA #REQUIRED>
<!ELEMENT B EMPTY>
<!ATTLIST B B1 CDATA #REQUIRED>
<!ATTLIST B B2 CDATA #REQUIRED>
<!ELEMENT C EMPTY>
<!ATTLIST C C1 CDATA #REQUIRED>
<!ATTLIST C C2 CDATA #REQUIRED>
```

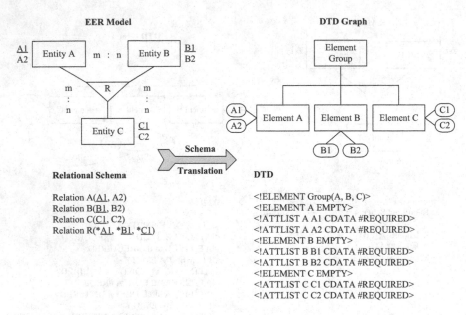

Fig. 3.53 N-ary relationship: schema translation

checking. Once a record folder is borrowed, a loan history is created to record the details about it. The relational schemas for this case study are shown below. *Notice that underlined and italic means primary key and * means foreign key.*

Relation Country	(Country_No, Country_Name)
Relation Patient	(HKID, Patient_Name, *Country_No)
Relation Record_Folder	(Folder_No, Location, *HKID)
Relation AE_Record	(*Medical_Rec_No, AE_No)
Relation Medical_Record	(Medical_Rec_No, Create_Date, Sub_Type *Folder_No)
Relation Borrower	(*Borrower_N, Borrower_Name)
Relation Borrow	(*Borrower_No,*Folder_No)
Relation Loan_History	(*Borrower_No, *Folder_No, Loan_Date)
Relation Department	(Borrower_No, Department_Name)
Relation Doctor	(Borrower_No, Doctor_Name)
Relation Other_Hospital	(Borrow_No, Hospital_Name)

By following the procedures that were mentioned before, we now translate this relational schema into DTD as shown below.

Step 1 – Reverse Engineering Relational Schema into an EER Model

By using the classification table, we can recover the EER model from the given relational schemas as shown in Fig. 3.54.

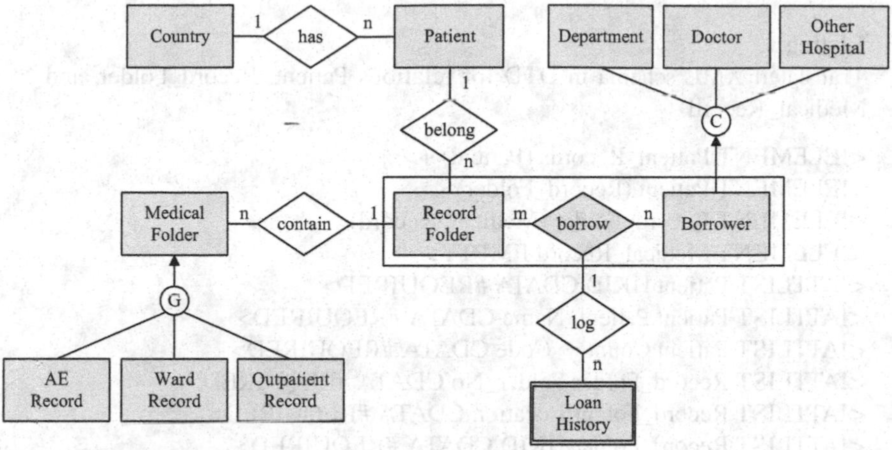

Fig. 3.54 EER model for a hospital database system

Step 2.1 – Defining an XML View
In this case study, suppose we concern the patient medical records, so the entity Patient is selected. Then we define a meaningful name for the root element, called Patient_Records. All patients are under the root element as shown below.

XML Schemas (DTD):

```
<!ELEMENT Patient_Records (Patient)+>
```

We start from the entity Patient in the EER model and then find the relevant entities for it. The relevant entities include the related entities that are navigable from the parent entity. Entities Record Folder, Medical Record, and Borrow are considered relevant entities because they are navigable from the entity Patient. Since the relationship between the entity Patient and the entity Country is many-to-one, then the entity County is considered not navigable from the entity Patient according to our methodology. As a result, a DTD-graph that starts from the entity Patient is formed and shown in Fig. 2.9 in Chap. 2.

Entity Patient is a direct child of the root element, Patient_Records. Since the entities Record Folder and Medical Record are navigable from the Patient entity, then we map all those entities into the elements of the XML DTD. We then define the attributes of those elements by using the definition of the relational schema as shown below:

Step 2.2 – Mapping Weak Entity into Content Model
It is not applicable in this step.

Listing 1
Translated XML schema in DTD for relations Patient, Record_Folder, and Medical_Record

```
<!ELEMENT Patient_Records (Patient) +>
<!ELEMENT Patient (Record_Folder)>
<!ELEMENT Record_Folder (Medical_Record)>
<!ELEMENT Medical_Record EMPTY>
<!ATTLIST Patient HKID CDATA #REQUIRED>
<!ATTLIST Patient Patient_Name CDATA #REQUIRED>
<!ATTLIST Patient Country_Code CDATA #REQUIRED>
<!ATTLIST Record_Folder Folder_No CDATA #REQUIRED>
<!ATTLIST Record_Folder Location CDATA #REQUIRED>
<!ATTLIST Record_Folder HKID CDATA #REQUIRED>
<!ATTLIST Medical_Record Medical_Rec_No CDATA #REQUIRED>
<!ATTLIST Medical_Record Create_Date CDATA #REQUIRED>
<!ATTLIST Medical_Record Sub_Type CDATA #REQUIRED>
<!ATTLIST Medical_Record Folder_No CDATA #REQUIRED>
```

Step 2.3 – Mapping Participation into Content Model
The relationship between the entities, Patient and the Record Folder, is total participation. The relationship between the entities, Record Folder and the Medical Record, is also in total participation. Therefore, the content model of the XML schema is translated as shown below. *Notice that all foreign keys in the relational schema will not be mapped into XML DTD because they will be represented in containment or ID and IDREF.*

Listing 2
Translated XML Schema for relations Patient, Record_Folder and Medical_Record:

```
<!ELEMENT Patient (Record_Folder*)>
<!ELEMENT Record_Folder (Medical_Record*)>
<!ELEMENT Medical_Record EMPTY>
<!ATTLIST Patient HKID CDATA #REQUIRED>
<!ATTLIST Patient Patient_Name CDATA #REQUIRED>
<!ATTLIST Patient Country_Code CDATA #REQUIRED>
<!ATTLIST Record_Folder Folder_No CDATA #REQUIRED>
<!ATTLIST Record_Folder Location CDATA #REQUIRED>
<!ATTLIST Medical_Record Medical_Rec_No CDATA #REQUIRED>
<!ATTLIST Medical_Record Create_Date CDATA #REQUIRED>
<!ATTLIST Medical_Record Sub_Type CDATA #REQUIRED>
```

Step 2.4 – Mapping Cardinality into Content Model

The relationship between entities Borrower and entity Record_Folder is in many-to-many cardinality. It is because a borrower can borrow many record folders and a record folder can be borrowed by many borrowers. In this many-to-many cardinality, we will not include the relationship between entities borrow and borrower since they are in a many-to-one relationship. The translated DTD together with the many-to-many relationship is shown below:

Listing 3

Translated XML schema for relations Record_Folder and Borrow

```
<!ELEMENT Record_Folder (Borrow*, Medical_Record*)>
<!ELEMENT Medical_Record EMPTY>
<!ELEMENT Borrow EMPTY>
<!ATTLIST Borrow Borrower_No CDATA #REQUIRED>
```

Since the entity Loan_History is also navigable from the Borrow entity and they are in a one-to-many relationship, so the modified XML schema will be:

Listing 4

Translated XML Schema for relation Loan_History

```
<!ELEMENT Borrow (Loan_History*)>
<!ELEMENT Loan_History EMPTY>
<!ATTLIST Loan_History Folder_No CDATA #REQUIRED>
<!ATTLIST Loan_History Loan_Date CDATA #REQUIRED>
```

Step 2.5 – Mapping Aggregation into Content Model

It is not applicable in this case study.

Step 2.6 – Mapping ISA into Content Model

It is not applicable in this case study.

Step 2.7 – Mapping Generalization into Content Model

Since the medical record can be an AE, a ward or an outpatient record, so it is a disjoint generalization. Then the translated DTD for the entity Medical Record is shown below:

Step 2.8 – Mapping Categorization into Content Model

Although there is a categorization in this case study, it is not navigable from the entity Patient. Thus, it is not applicable.

Step 2.9 – Mapping N-ary Relationship into Content Model

It is not applicable in this case study.

Listing 5
Translated XML schema for relations Medical_Record, AE_Record, Ward_Record, and Outpatient_Record

```
<!ELEMENT Medical_Record (AE | Ward | Outpatient)>
<!ATTLIST Medical_Record Medical_Rec_No CDATA #REQUIRED>
<!ATTLIST Medical_Record Create_Date CDATA #REQUIRED>
<!ATTLIST Medical_Record Sub_Type CDATA #REQUIRED>
<!ELEMENT AE EMPTY>
<!ATTLIST AE AE_No CDATA #REQUIRED>
<!ELEMENT Ward EMPTY>
<!ATTLIST Ward Ward_No CDATA #REQUIRED>
<!ATTLIST Ward Admission_Date CDATA #REQUIRED>
<!ATTLIST Ward Discharge_Date CDATA #REQUIRED>
<!ELEMENT Outpatient EMPTY>
<!ATTLIST Outpatient Outpatient_No CDATA #REQUIRED>
<!ATTLIST Outpatient Specialty CDATA #REQUIRED>
```

As a result, the final XML DTD is shown in Listing 6.

Listing 6
Patient Records DTD

```
<!ELEMENT Patient_Records (Patient+)>
<!ELEMENT Patient (Record_Folder*)>
<!ATTLIST Patient
            HKID                  CDATA        #REQUIRED
            Patient_Name          CDATA        #REQUIRED>
            Country_No            CDATA        #REQUIRED
<!ELEMENT Record_Folder (Borrow*, Medical_Record*)>
<!ATTLIST Record_Folder
            Folder_No             CDATA        #REQUIRED
            Location              CDATA        #REQUIRED
<!ELEMENT Borrow (Loan_History*)>
<!ATTLIST Borrow
            Borrower_No           CDATA        #REQUIRED>
<!ELEMENT Loan_History EMPTY>
<!ATTLIST Loan_History
            Loan_Date             CDATA        #REQUIRED>
<!ELEMENT Medical_Record (AE_Record | Outpatient_Record | Ward_Record)>
<!ATTLIST Medical_Record
            Medical_Rec_No        CDATA        #REQUIRED
            Create_Date           CDATA        #REQUIRED
            Sub_Type              CDATA        #REQUIRED>
<!ELEMENT AE_Record EMPTY>
<!ATTLIST AE_Record
            AE_No                 CDATA        #REQUIRED>
```

(continued)

```
<!ELEMENT Outpatient_Record EMPTY>
<!ATTLIST Outpatient_Record
          Outpatient_No        CDATA        #REQUIRED
          Specialty            CDATA        #REQUIRED>
<!ELEMENT Ward_Record EMPTY>
<!ATTLIST Ward_Record
Ward_No                        CDATA        #REQUIRED>
          Admission_Date       CDATA        #REQUIRED
          Discharge_Date       CDATA        #REQUIRED
```

3.9 Translating a Relational Schema to an Xml Schema Definition

We can also translate a relational schema into an XML Schema Definition (XSD). Like DTD, an XSD is also an XML logical schema, and it has more features than DTD. The translation process is also very similar to Sect. 3.7. As shown in Sect. 3.7, the three processes of mapping relational schema into an XSD are through an EER model and XSD graph as follows (Fong and Cheung, 2005).

Step 1 – Reverse engineering a relational schema into an EER model.

Same as in the step 1 of Sect. 3.7.

Step 2 – Reengineering an EER model to an XSD graph:

The transformation between an EER model and an XSD graph is a semantic-based methodology. The transformation consists of the following nine rules outlining the basic framework between the EER model and the XSD graph. The steps are defined for capturing relationships and constraints among entities. Besides mapping an EER model to an XSD graph, we preserve the data semantics of the source relational schema in a target XSD in a hierarchical tree model.

Rule 1: Define an XML View in XSD
Similar to rule 1 in Sect. 3.7, we can abstract an XML view of EER model upon user supervision into an XML tree as shown in Fig. 3.55.

Rule 2: Mapping Foreign Key from RDB to XSD
The "Entities" and "Attributes" of the EER model are represented as Elements and Attributes of an XML model. We use the sub-element for applying the cardinality primitive in the XML model. If we find the multi-valued attributes, we place them as sub-elements with "maxOccurs = unbounded" in the XSD. In an XML model, a unique attribute can be represented as a "key." Thus, the primary key of an EER model is presented by a <key> tag in the XML model. A foreign key d is eliminated in the translated XSD because the foreign key between a parent relation and child relations in the relational schema is mapped into the hierarchical structure between a parent element and its child elements in an XSD. See Fig. 3.56.

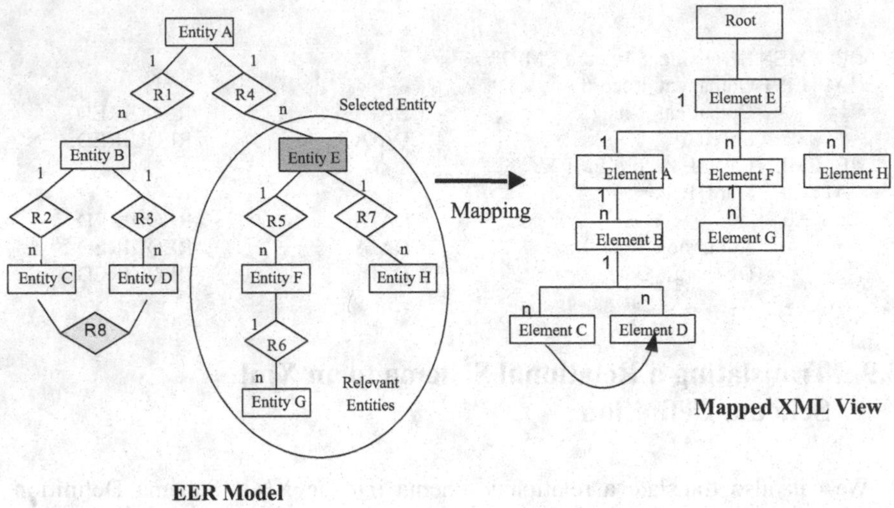

Fig. 3.55 Map selected entities in EER model into an XML tree

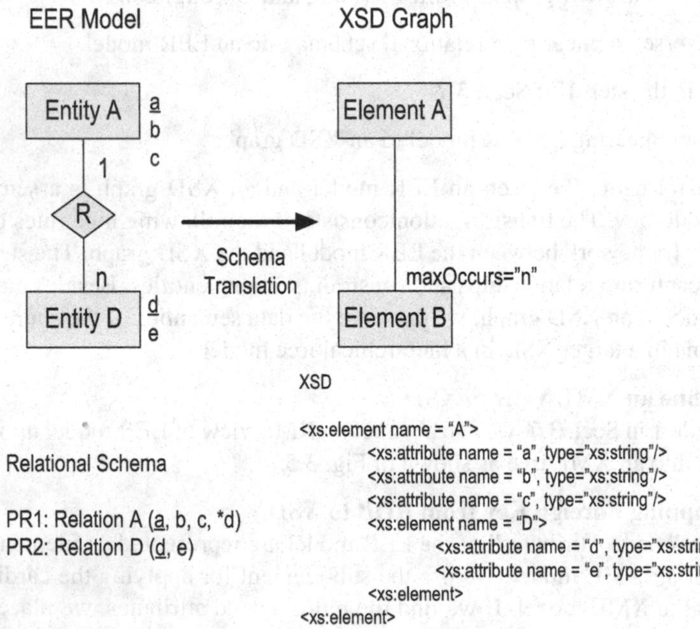

Fig. 3.56 Map a foreign key into parent-child elements in XSD

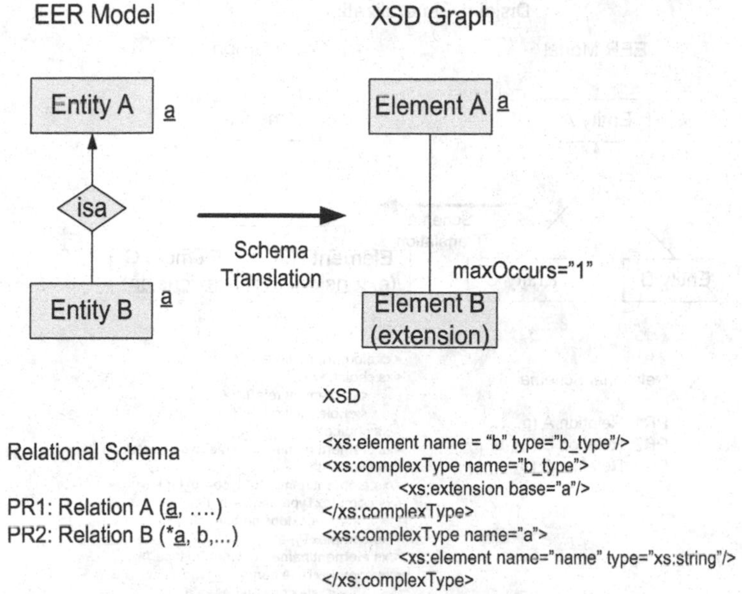

Fig. 3.57 Map isa relationship into element extension in XSD

Rule 3: Mapping Isa Relationship from RDB to XSD
The relationship between the sub-type and super-type is an "isa" relationship. When we map an EER model to an XSD graph, we can use the "extension" tag for the "isa" relationship. The "complexType" feature can be applied for this primitive in the XML model. The child "complexType" inherits properties of the parent "complexType" by applying the "extension" tag on the child definition. Its attributes can be added on to complete the "complexType" definition. See Fig. 3.57.

Rule 4: Mapping of Generalization from RDB to XSD
Generalization is a concept that some entities are subtypes of other entities. The disjoint generalization is mapped into a complex element such that its component elements are mutually exclusive by a "choice" keyword. The overlap generalization is mapped into a complex element such that its component elements are mutually inclusive. See Fig. 3.58.

Rule 5: Mapping of Aggregation from RDB to XSD
Aggregation is an abstraction through which relationships are treated as higher-level entities. In an XML schema, the transformation of the aggregation is to group child elements under a parent element. In the whole-class element definition, the part-class element is included in the attribute list of the whole class by using the "ref" keyword for the type parameter. See Fig. 3.59.

Rule 6: Mapping of Categorization from RDB to XSD
Categorization is a relationship in connection with multiple superclass elements and one subclass element. The key in the subclass element instance must refer to one of

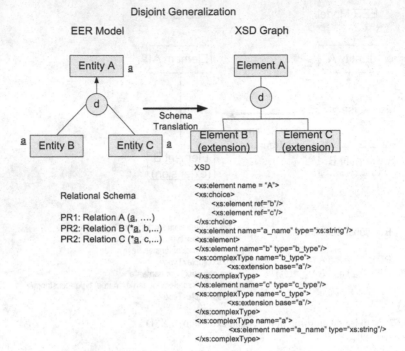

Disjoint Generalization

EER Model XSD Graph

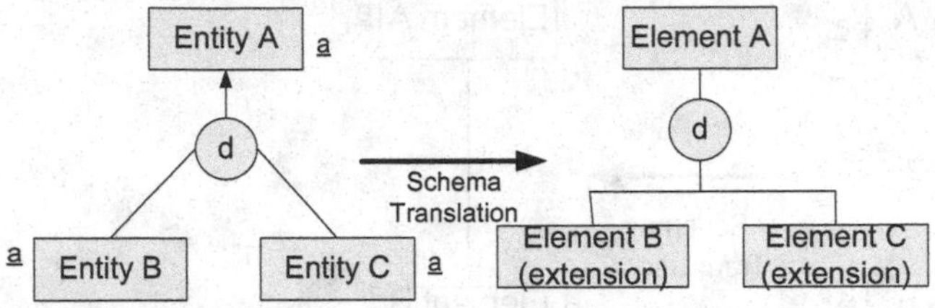

Relational Schema

PR1: Relation A (<u>a</u>, ….)
PR2: Relation B (*<u>a</u>, b,...)
PR2: Relation C (*<u>a</u>, c,...)

XSD

```
<xs:element name = "A">
<xs:choice>
    <xs:element ref="b"/>
    <xs:element ref="c"/>
</xs:choice>
<xs:element name="a_name" type="xs:string"/>
<xs:element>
</xs:element name="b" type="b_type"/>
<xs:complexType name="b_type">
        <xs:extension base="a"/>
</xs:complexType>
</xs:element name="c" type="c_type"/>
<xs:complexType name="c_type">
        <xs:extension base="a"/>
</xs:complexType>
<xs:complexType name="a">
        <xs:element name="a_name" type="xs:string"/>
</xs:complexType>
```

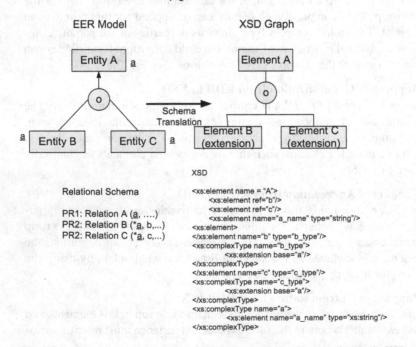

Overlap generalization

EER Model XSD Graph

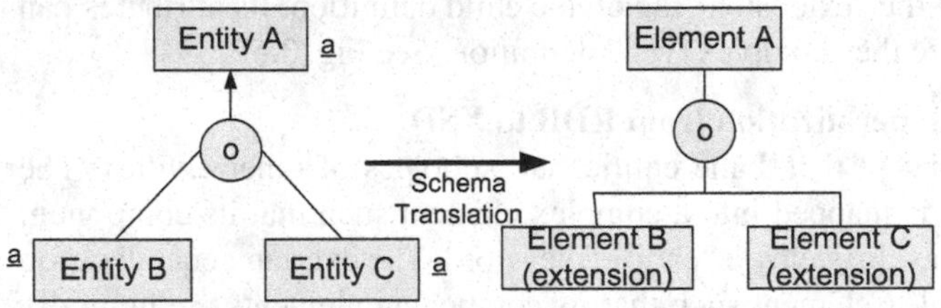

XSD

Relational Schema

PR1: Relation A (<u>a</u>, ….)
PR2: Relation B (*<u>a</u>, b,...)
PR2: Relation C (*<u>a</u>, c,...)

```
<xs:element name = "A">
    <xs:element ref="b"/>
    <xs:element ref="c"/>
    <xs:element name="a_name" type="string"/>
<xs:element>
</xs:element name="b" type="b_type"/>
<xs:complexType name="b_type">
        <xs:extension base="a"/>
</xs:complexType>
</xs:element name="c" type="c_type"/>
<xs:complexType name="c_type">
        <xs:extension base="a"/>
</xs:complexType>
<xs:complexType name="a">
        <xs:element name="a_name" type="xs:string"/>
</xs:complexType>
```

Fig. 3.58 Map generalization into multiple references of a complex element in XSD

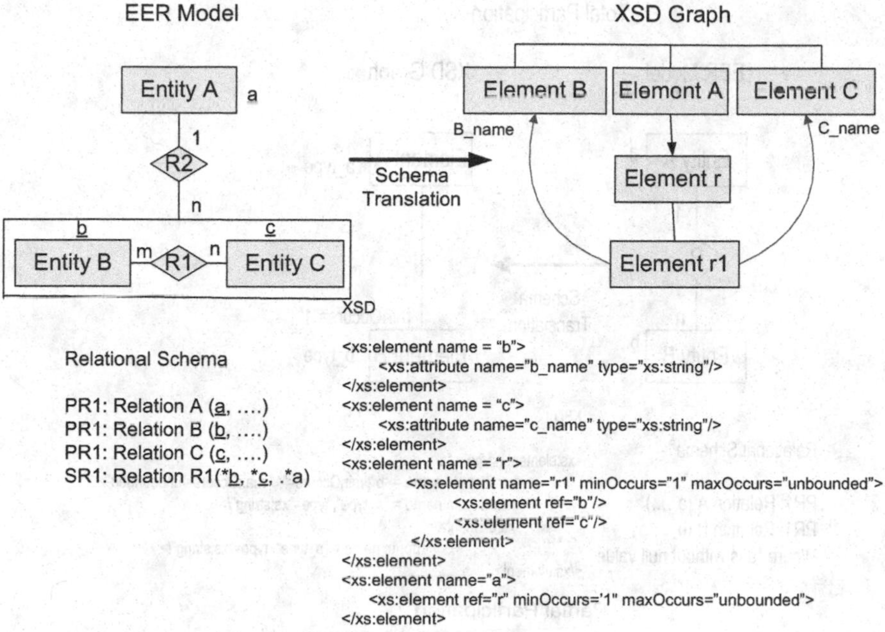

Fig. 3.59 Map aggregation into a complex element sequence in XSD

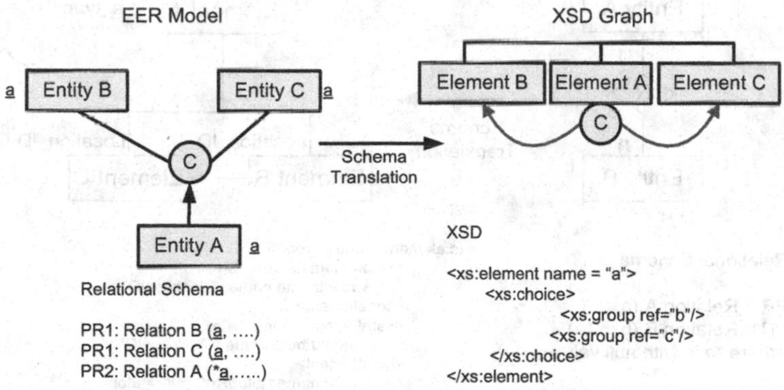

Fig. 3.60 Map categorization into a complex element choice in XSD

the superclass elements. By using the "choice" keyword for making a constraint, this primitive can function in an XSD. Either element B or element C must appear as a superclass in the subclass element A. We use the "group" feature for defining the properties on the element side. See Fig. 3.60.

Rule 7: Mapping of Participation from RDB to XSD
The partial and total participations can be used for distinguishing two types of relationships between parent and child entities. Total participation means a mandatory relationship between parent and child elements. In an XSD, there is a more flexible way to maintain the referential integrity by using an attribute group, element group, or global element with "minOccurs" and "maxOccurs." See Fig. 3.61.

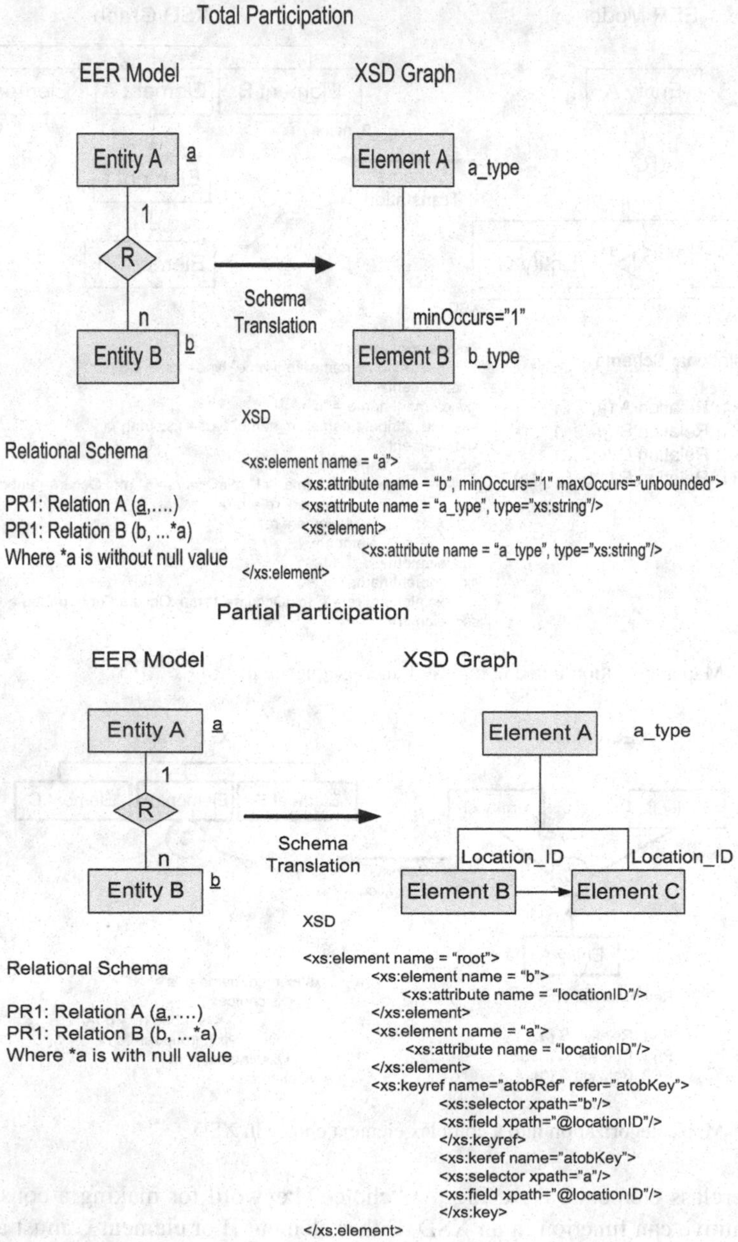

Fig. 3.61 Map participation into a parent-child relationship in XSD

Rule 8: Mapping of Cardinality from RDB to XSD
We capture 1:1, 1:n, and m:n cardinalities in this step. A cardinality in the XSD graph is represented as a sub-element or a global element. The name of the associating element is the association name in an m:n relationship. The associating element could be treated as a pointer referring to the associated elements and is assisted by the keyword of "minOccurs" defined on the element declaration. If an element is referred to by two or many elements, it is treated as a global element in the 1:1 and 1:n cardinalities. See Fig. 3.62.

Rule 9: Mapping of n-ary Relationship from RDB to XSD
We apply the concept of a ternary relationship from an EER model into an XSD graph. The relationship relation is placed at the center of three related relations in an

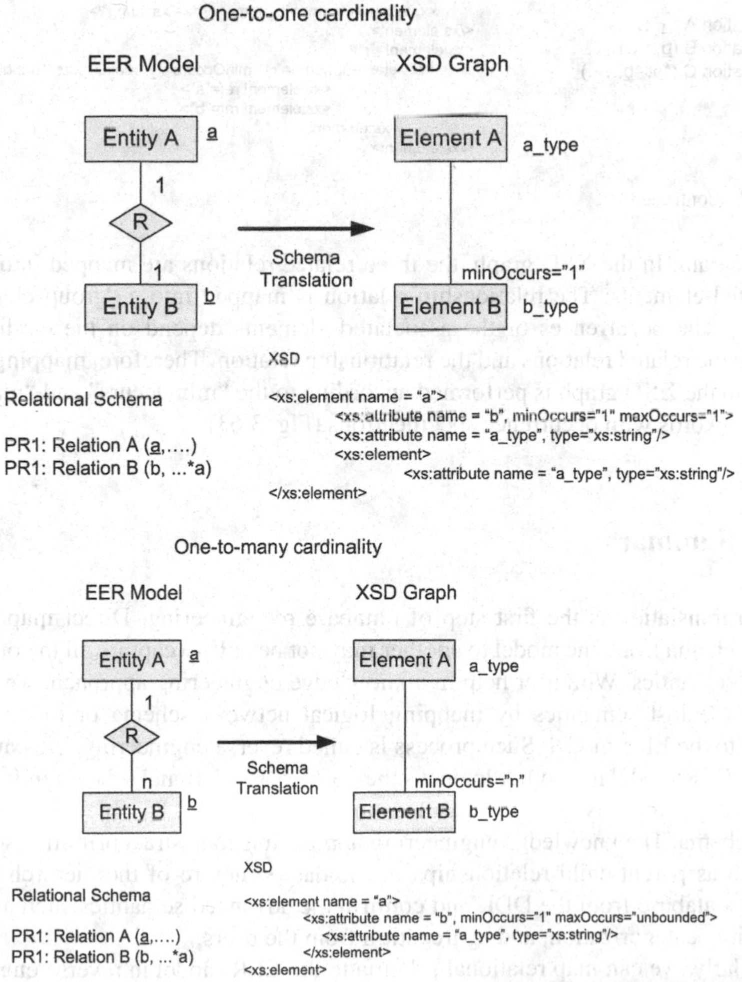

Fig. 3.62 Map cardinality into the parent-child elements in XSD

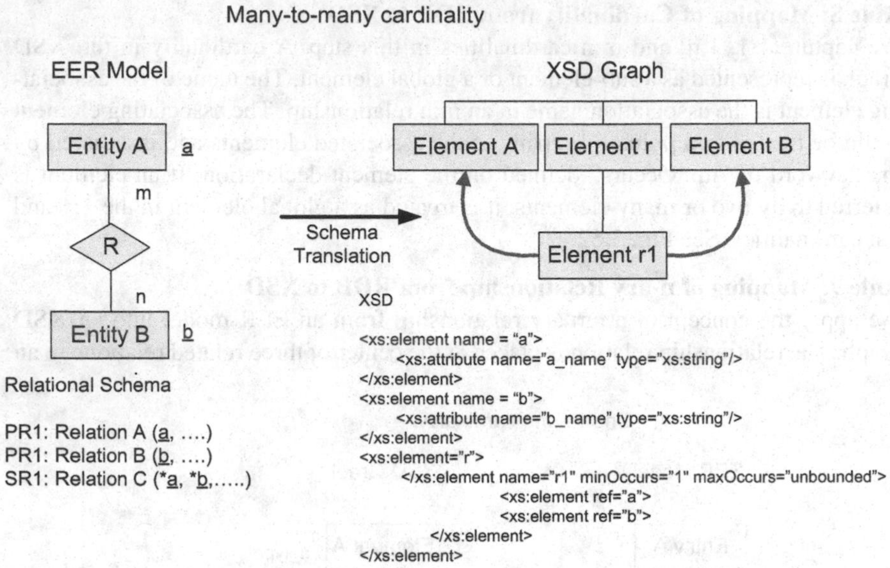

Fig. 3.62 (continued)

EER diagram. In the XSD graph, the three related relations are mapped into three associated elements. The relationship relation is mapped into a "group element" function. The occurrences of the associated elements depend on the cardinality between the related relations and the relationship relation. Therefore, mapping relations into the XSD graph is performed according to the "minOccurs" and "maxOccurs" keywords with occurrence specifications (Fig. 3.63).

3.10 Summary

Schema translation is the first step of database reengineering. Direct mapping a logical schema from one model to another may not be able to capture all the original schema semantics. With user help in a knowledge engineering approach, we could recover the lost semantics by mapping logical network schema or hierarchical schema to the EER model. Such process is called reverse engineering. We can then map the EER model to another logical schema such as relational schema in forward engineering. Similarly, we can map relational schema into an object-oriented or XML schema. The knowledge engineering approach is to abstract primitive semantics such as parent-child relationships in the data structure of the hierarchical or network database from the DDL and confirm the advanced semantics such as generalization, categorization, and aggregation from the users.

Similarly, we can map relational schema to the EER model in reverse engineering with users' assistance to recover the lost semantics. The process is to make use

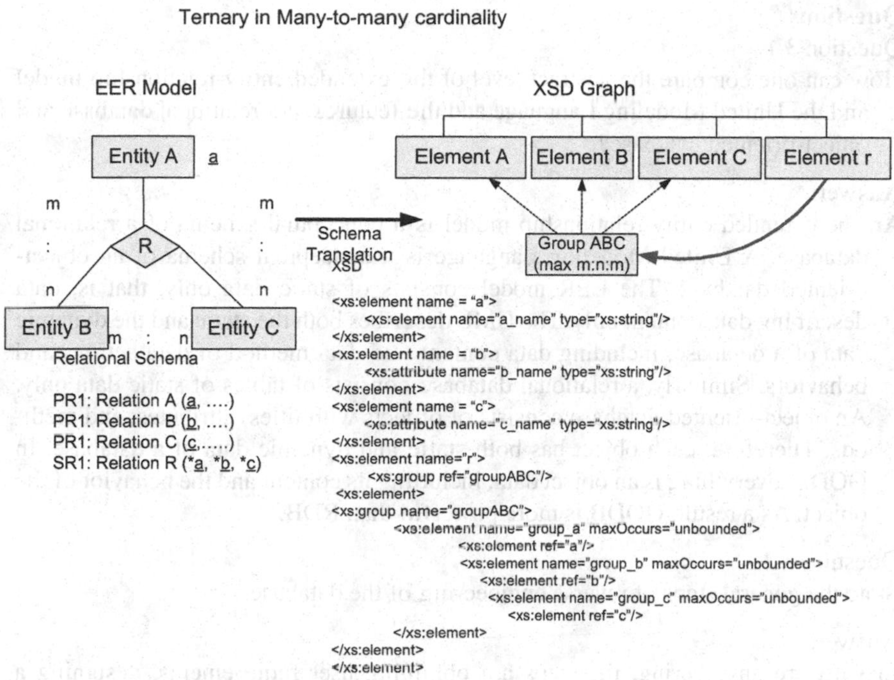

Fig. 3.63 Map n-ary relationship into a group element in XSD

of the various keys in the existing relation, for example, primary keys, foreign keys, composite keys, and the components of the composite keys. These keys, along with the inclusion dependencies, the constraints of the relations, can be used to reconstruct primitive semantics of the schema. For the advanced semantics, users' inputs are also needed. Once the EER model is reconstructed, we can then map the EER model to the UML model, a conceptual model for an object-oriented database, in forward engineering. From the UML model, we can map to an object-oriented database schema. Similarly, we can map an EER model into a DTD graph or XSD graph.

The translation from an XML view of the relational schema into an XML schema can be accomplished by recovering data semantics from the relational schema into its conceptual schema in an extended entity-relationship model. Once these constraints are defined, we can select relations that can represent the XML view from the relational schema. The other relevant relations can also be extracted according to the one-to-many and superclass-to-subclass navigability of the XML tree. Together, these relations are then mapped into the XML conceptual schema in the DTD graph and then to DTD. The DTD graph and DTD are XML schemas but in a diagram form for DTD graph as XML conceptual schema and in text form for DTD as XML logical schema.

Similarly, we can also map relational schema into an XSD and XSD graph. The XSD and XSD graph not only have the same functions as the DTD and DTD graphs but also are richer in features and are more adaptable in the industry.

Questions

Question 3.1.

How can one compare the abstract level of the extended entity-relationship model and the United Modeling Language and the features of a relational database and object-oriented database?

Answer:

An the extended entity-relationship model is a conceptual schema of a relational database. A United Modeling Language is a conceptual schema of an object-oriented database. The EER model consists of static data only, that is, data describing data content only. The UML describes both the static and the dynamic data of a database, including data content and data method of data actions and behaviors. Similarly, a relational database consists of tables of static data only. An object-oriented database consists of objects with titles, attributes, and methods. Therefore, each object has both static and dynamic data of a database. In OODB, everything is an object data, including its content and the behavior of the object. As a result, OODB is more powerful than RDB.

Question 3.2.

State the general steps of reverse engineering of the database.

Answer:

In software engineering, the steps are obtaining user requirements, designing a computer system, and then implementing the system accordingly. Therefore, forward engineering is from user requirements to design and then implementation. Reverse engineering is vice versa, from implementation to design and then back to user requirements. In developing a database system, one needs to capture user requirements in data modeling in a conceptual schema. Then the developer implements the conceptual schema design in a logical schema. Reverse engineering is from implementation, for example, relational schema, to a conceptual schema, for example, the extended entity-relationship model.

In general, the steps in reverse engineering are to analyze the lower-level database implementation to recover the original database design. For example, reverse engineer relational schema into the extended entity-relationship model is to analyze the relational schema keys in a classification table as follows:

Step 1 Define each relation key and field.
Step 2 Map each type 1 primary relation into an entity.
Step 3 Map secondary relation into a weak entity.
Step 4 Map each secondary relation into a binary relation.
Step 5 Map each foreign key into a relationship.
Step 6 Map each inclusion dependency into a semantic relationship.
Step 7 Draw an extended entity-relationship model.

Another example of reverse engineering is a decompiling database program. A database developer writes a higher-level database language to access a database because it is more user-friendly. The program needs to be compiled into a lower-level database program to access a database, which is called forward engineering. Reverse engineering is to decompile a lower-level database program into a higher-level database program. For example, decompiling a lower level accessing one record at a time DL/1 database program to a higher level accessing multiple tuples at a time SQL statement. The steps are to analyze multiple DL/1 statements and combine them into one SQL statement. Therefore, reverse engineering involves many uncertainties, and is not recommended.

Bibliography

Booch G (1994) Object-oriented analysis design with application. The Bensamin/Cummings Publishing Co, Inc, p 15

Elmasri R, Navathe S (1989) Fundamentals of database systems. The Benjamin/Cummings Publishing Company

Fong J (1992) Methodology for Schema translation from hierarchical or network into relational. Inf Softw Technol 34(3):159–174

Fong J, Cheung SK (2005) Translating relational schema into XML schema definition with data semantic preservation and XSD graph. Inf Softw Technol 47(7):437–462

Fong J, Kwan I (1994) An re-engineering approach for object-oriented database design. In: Proceedings of first IFIP/SQI international conference on software quality and productivity (ICSQP'94). Chapman and Hall, 5–7, pp 139–147

Funderburk JE, Kierman G, Shanmugasundaram J, Shekita E, Wei C (2002) XTABLES: bridging relational technology and XML. IBM Syst J 41(4):616–641

Navathe S, Awong A (1988) Abstracting relational and hierarchical data with a semantic data model. Entity-relationship Approach:305–333

Quizon A (1990) End-user computing in Multi-environment systems. In: Proceedings of South-East Asia regional computer confederation conference on information technology, pp 602–617

Zaniolo C (1979) Design of relational views over network schemas. In: Proceedings of ACM SIGMOD 79 conference, pp 179–190

Chapter 4
Data Conversion

The objective of data conversion is to convert between database systems without any loss of information. The data conversion process must transform the data from one data structure to another whilst preserving its semantics. Data conversion uses the data structure of the schema that results from schema translation.

As the relational model, object-oriented, and XML models become more popular, there is a need to convert production nonrelational databases to relational databases, and from relational databases to object-oriented databases and XML databases, i.e., XML documents stored in a native XML database or XML enabled database, to improve productivity and flexibility. The changeover includes schema translation, data conversion, and program translation. The schema translation consists of static data structure transformation from nonrelational to relational schema or from relational database schema to an object-oriented or an XML schema. This chapter describes a data conversion methodology to unload production nonrelational or a relational database to sequential files, and then upload them into a relational, object-oriented, or XML database. There are basically four techniques in data conversion: customized program, interpretive transformer, translator generator, and logical level translation. These are described in the following sections.

4.1 Customized Program Approach

A common approach to data conversion is to develop customized programs to transfer data from one environment to another (Fry et al. 1978). However, the customized program approach is very expensive because it requires a different program to be written for each M source file and N target, which sums up as m × n programs for all of them. Furthermore, these programs are used only once. As a result, totally depending on a customized program for data conversion is unmanageable, too costly, and time-consuming.

J. S. P. Fong, K. Wong Ting Yan, *Information Systems Reengineering, Integration and Normalization*, https://doi.org/10.1007/978-3-030-79584-9_4

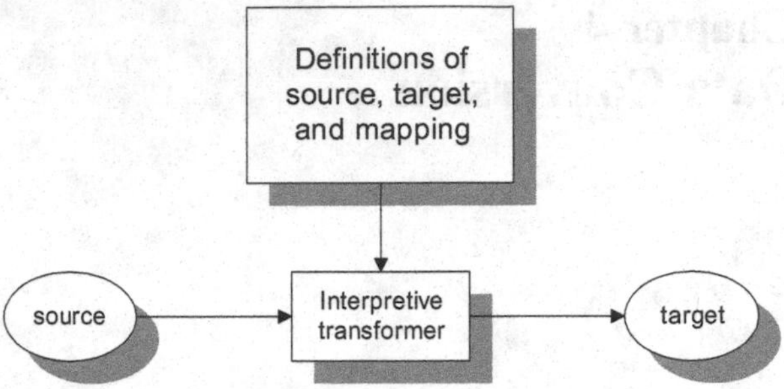

Fig. 4.1 Interpretive transformer

4.2 Interpretive Transformer Approach

An interpretive transformer accepts a source definition, a target definition and a mapping definition, and then maps the stored data from the source to the target database (Lochovsky and Tsichritzis 1982) as shown in Fig. 4.1.

Suppose that the database of a source nonrelational schema S_s is mapped to a target relational schema S_t. There are three distinct processes in this approach. One process accesses the source data (reading). Another process performs logical transformations on the data to place it into an internal form. A third process creates the target data (writing).

For example, Fry et al. (1978) describe a method that uses two specialized languages, the Stored Data Definition Language (SDDL) and the Translation Definition Language (TDL), to define the structure of the two databases and the source to target translation parameters. Using these definitions, a series of programs (refer to Fig. 4.2) are used to perform the data conversion process.

In order to separate the restructuring process from the source and target conversion function of the Translator, The Normal Form of Data is introduced. A data structure expressed in the Normal Form will be viewed as a set of N-tuples of the form.

Ref-Name <Item, Item……>

The Normal Form presented here has two types of N-tuples: a data structure instance N-tuple and a relationship N-tuple.

The data structure instance N-tuple consists of the following: Data Structure Instance Name (Ref-Name), Identifier (unique), and Data Item(s).

The relationship N-tuple consists of: Relationship Name (Ref-Name) and Identifiers of all data instances involved in the relationship.

For instance, the following Cobol structure:

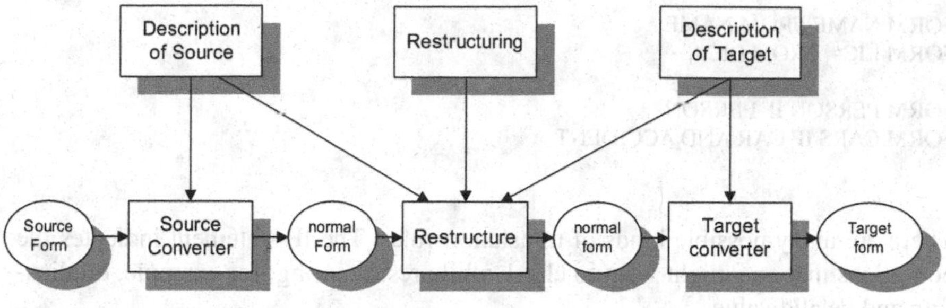

Fig. 4.2 The general model for data translator

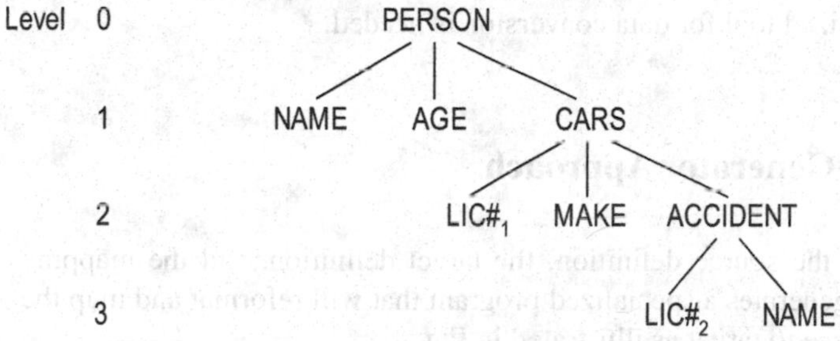

Can be expressed in using these SDDL statements:

Data Structure	PERSON <NAME, AGE>
Instance	CARS <LIC#$_1$, MAKE>
N-tuples	ACCIDENTS <LIC#$_2$, NAME>
Relationship	PERSON-CAR <NAME, LIC#$_1$>
N-tuples	CAR-ACCIDENT <LIC#$_1$, LIC#$_2$>

To translate the above three levels to the following two levels data structure:

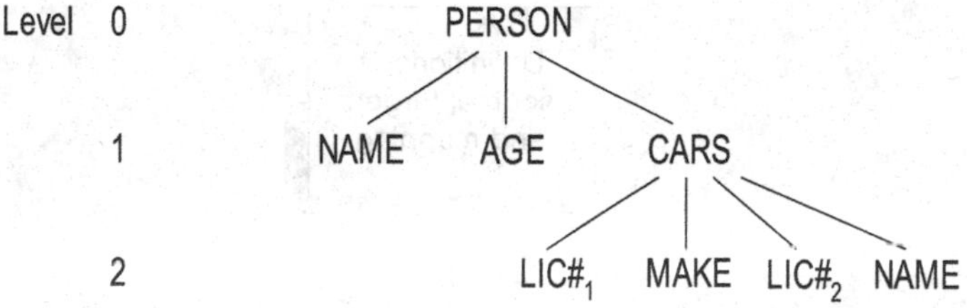

The TDL statements are

FORM NAME FROM NAME
FORM LIC#$_1$ FROM LIC#$_1$
:
FORM PERSON IF PERSON
FORM CARS IF CAR AND ACCIDENT

There are many possible kinds of translation rules. The IF statement indicates the conditions that one might want to check while restructuring; for example, duplication and invalid values.

The data conversion problem can basically be resolved by available software tools. However, these tools are DBMS dependent and are supplied by the vendors only. A more generalized tool for data conversion is needed.

4.3 Translator Generator Approach

The translator reads the source definition, the target definition, and the mapping definition, and then generates a specialized program that will reformat and map the stored data from source to target as illustrated in Fig. 4.3.

As in the case of the interpretive translator approach, two languages are used. One describes the source and target database file and the other describes the mapping between source and target database files. There are two phases to the translation process; the compile time phase and the run time phase. In the compile-time phase, the specialized translator program is generated; in the run time phase, this program is executed.

For example, Shu et al. (1975) implemented EXPRESS, which can access a wide variety of data and restructure it for new uses by program generation techniques. The function of the EXPRESS system is to translate and execute the specification languages DEFINE and CONVERT. The DEFINE description is compiled into a

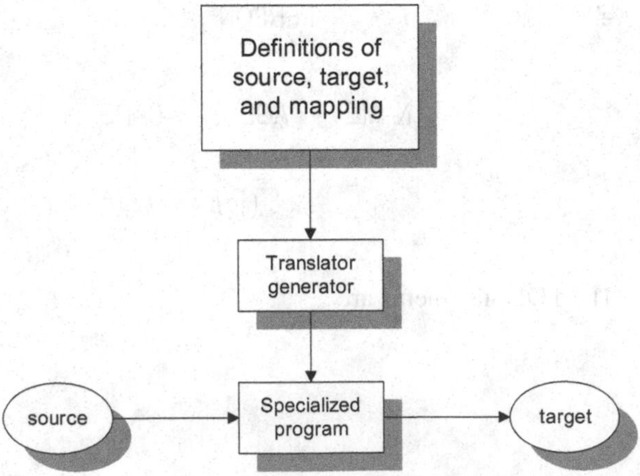

Fig. 4.3 Translator generator

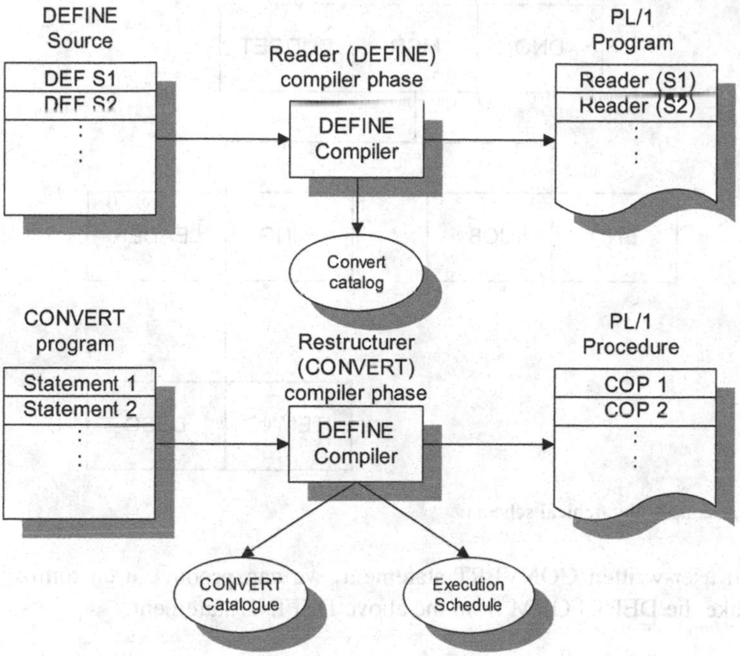

Fig. 4.4 DEFINE and CONVERT compile phase

customized PL/1 program for accessing source data. The restructuring specified in CONVERT is compiled into a set of customized PL/1 procedures to derive multiple target files from multiple input files. The general architecture of the DEFINE compile-time phase and the general architecture of the CONVERT compile-time system is shown in Fig. 4.4.

As an example, consider the following hierarchical database (Fig. 4.5):

Its DEFINE statements can be described in the following where for each DEFINE statement, code is generated to allocate a new subtree in the internal buffer.

```
GROUP DEPT:
   OCCURS FROM 1 TIMES;
   FOLLOWED BY EOF;
   PRECEDED BY HEX '01';
   :
   END EMP;
   GROUP PROJ:
         OCCURS FROM 0 TIMES;
         PRECEDED BY HEX '03';
   :
   END PROJ;
END DEPT;
```

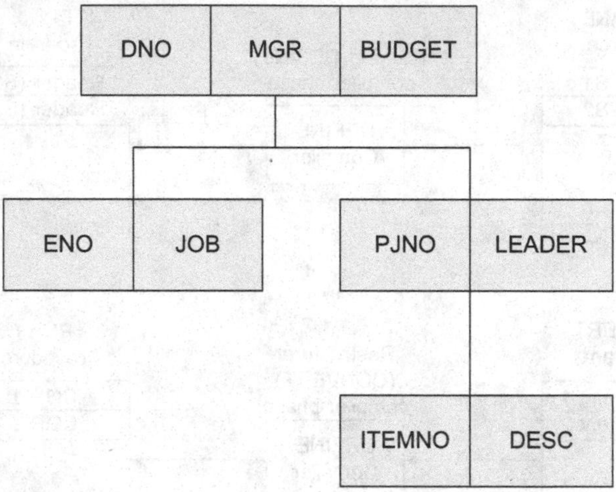

Fig. 4.5 A sample hierarchical schema

For each user-written CONVERT statement, we can produce a customized program. Take the DEPT FORM from the above DEFINE statement:

```
T1 = SELECT (FROM DEPT WHERE BUDGET GT '100');
```

will produce the following program:

```
/* PROCESS LOOP FOR T1 */
DO WHILE (not end of file);
  CALL GET (DEPT);
  IF BUDGET > '100'
         THEN CALL BUFFER_SWAP (T1, DEPT);
END
```

However, this approach is proprietary, language-oriented (not user-friendly), and too expensive to adopt.

4.4 Logical Level Translation Approach

This approach is similar to the interpretive approach but proposes the reduction of storage and physical costs and without the need for specialized description languages. Instead, it considers only the logical level of data representation. For

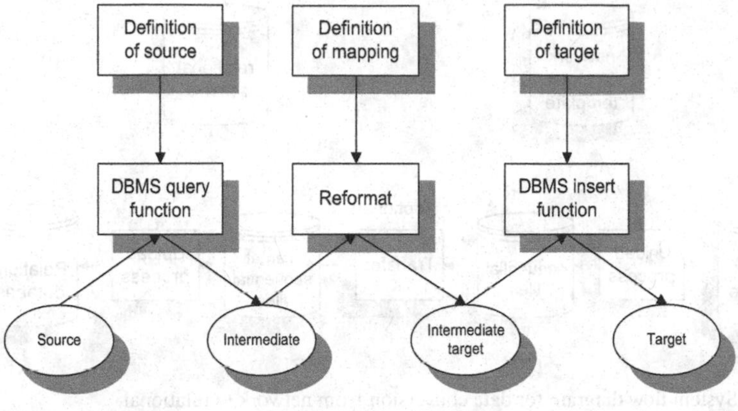

Fig. 4.6 Logical level approach for data conversion

example, Shoshani (1975) used a source definition of the network database and the network DML to read the data from the network database and store it in a convenient, intermediate target. The intermediate target format was then read and stored in the relational database using the definition of the relational database and the relational DML as illustrated in Fig. 4.6.

There are two parts to this problem: unloading the data from the nonrelational or relational database and uploading the data into the relational database or from the relational to object-oriented or XML database. The two steps are independent since most vendor load utilities accept a simple flat file as input. Any available utility that can read the source database and creates a flat output file can be used for this purpose. These output sequential files should be reorganized into a logical sequence for the uploading process after the generation of the new database definition. Generally, the load utility can be applied in the upload process.

The logical level approach is more commonly used in the industry because it is easier to implement than the others. The later sections describe using the logical approach to convert data from a network database to a relational database, from a hierarchical database to a relational database, and from a relational database to an object-oriented or XML database.

4.5 Data Conversion from Network to Relational

As described before, the logical approach consists of an unload step and an upload step. For the purpose of automation, we must convert data from a network database to a semantically richer relational database. The primitive semantics of record types and record keys in network schema can be mapped into relations and relation keys in the relational schema. Other more advanced semantics, such as generalization and categorization, are considered not the main component of the database and can

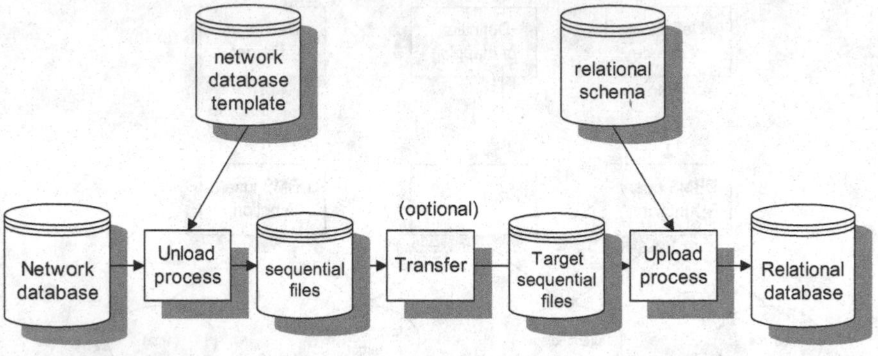

Fig. 4.7 System flow diagram for data conversion from network to relational

be handled later. Thus, a preprocess of direct schema translation from network to relational is needed before the data conversion. These steps are shown in Fig. 4.7 (Fong and Bloor 1994).

Conversion is automated by database navigation. The process includes unloading the network database into sequential files. The unload process reads all the records of the network database and writes them to the files.

The procedure to convert the network database into relational is:

Preprocess step 1 – Direct schema translation from network to relational.

- Rule 1. Map each record type to a relation.
- Rule 2. Map each record "Navigational" key (i.e., concatenate owner record key to member record key) to the relation key.

The translated relational schema will then be used as a template to map the network database content to a target relational database.

Step 1 – Create a template file to define the network database and its translated relational schema.

A template file can be created from an input network schema together with user input to specify the record identifier. The template file consists of network schema record types, their linkages to each other through different set types, and their record identifier. The record identifiers will contain the concatenation of record keys and will be mapped into the relational database as primary keys or composite keys. The template file will be used to unload the network database into sequential files.

The following shows the structure of a template file.

Record type template file.

Name	Key_1,.ey_n	Identifier type	$Identifier_1$..$Identifier_n$	$Attr_1$..$Attr_n$

Name = network schema record type name
Key_1,.Key_n = record key of the record type
Identifier Type = record identifier type, 'F' for fully internally identified, 'P' for partially internally identified
and 'I' for internally unidentifier.
$Identifier_1$..$Identifier_n$ = concatenated record keys with owner record keys.
$Attr_1$..$Attr_n$ = attributes of the record type.

Besides the above template file, another template file is used to store all the set linkage information. The following is the structure of the set linkage template file.

Set linkage template file.

Owner	Member	Set linkage name

Owner = owner record type name within the set
Member = member record type within the set
Set Linkage = name of the set that connects the owner and member

Step 2. Unload network database into sequential files.

In the unload process, with the help of template files from step 1, an Unload program will read all record occurrences of each record type of the network database from the bottom up and map each record type into a sequential file. The Unload algorithm is as follows:

```
Program Unload network database to sequential files
begin
 /*      n = number of record types
         m = number of levels in each path expression
 */
 Get all record type N1, N2....Nn within input network schema;
 For i = 1 to n do /* for each target record type Ni */
   while Ni record occurrence found do
    begin
      If it is first occurrence
        then obtain first record Ni within area
        else obtain next record Ni within area;
        For j = m-1 to 1 do
        /* read target record owner records by database navigation
        from level m-1 to level 1, a system-owned records */
        Obtain owner records keys Ki(1), Ki(2),...Ki(j)
         /* obtain the record keys of all owners of record Ni along
        database access path from bottom up to the system owned
        record*/
       end-for;
    Case record identifier_type of
'F': begin
        If m = 1
        then output Ni record with Ki(m) as record identifier to
                   sequential  file i
         else output Ni record with Ki(1), Ki(2)....Ki(m-1), Ki(m)
                   as foreign key to sequential file  i /*   Ki(m) = key of
                   owner record key in level m */
   end;
'P': output Ni  record with Ki(1), Ki(2),.., Ki(m-1), Ki(m) as
       record identifier to sequential file i;
'I':  output Ni record with Ki(1), Ki(2),.., Ki(m-1),
      Sequence# as record identifier to sequential file i;
    end-case;
 end-while;
 end-for;
end;
```

The algorithm reads each record occurrence by database navigation. For each record occurrence of fully internally identified read, it reads its owner record occurrences from the bottom up to the system owned record types. It then concatenates the owner record keys for the record type of partially internally identified or internally unidentified. For owner record keys with a record type of fully internally identified, the concatenation of owner record keys is not required. The objective is to concatenate owner record identifiers as foreign keys in the target record when mapped to the relational database.

Step 3 – (optional) Transfer sequential files to the target computer.

We must transfer the unloaded sequential files into another computer if the target relational database is residing in a different physical location or another machine. The data format may need to be changed due to different bit sizes per word and/or character sizes per record. This is a straightforward task for which many software utilities already exist.

Step 4 – Upload sequential files into a relational database.

Finally, we upload the sequential files into a relational database according to the translated relational schema. The relational schema must be created before the upload process.

Case Study of Data Conversion from Network to Relational

Before converting data from the network to relational, a translated relational schema must be defined. We apply the previously described method to the university enrollment system for illustration. Figure 4.8 shows a network schema and its database.

The following steps show the different stages in the conversion process:

Step 1 – Create a template file to define the network databases and its translated relational schema:

During the template creation process, the user is prompted to input the record class of each entity. The following shows the user input for each entity type in the university enrollment system.

The identify type (F, P, I) of:	COURSE#	F
The identify type (F, P, I) of	PREREQUISITE	F
The identify type (F, P, I) of	DEPARTMENT	F
The identify type (F, P, I) of	INSTRUCTOR	P
The identify type (F, P, I) of	SECTION	P
The identify type (F, P, I) of	STUDENT	F
The identify type (F, P, I) of	GRADE	P

The template file is shown below with record name, existing record keys, record identifier type ('F' = fully internally identified, 'P' = partially internally identified, and 'I' = internally unidentified), derived record identifier, and attributes for each record type.

Record name	Record key	Identifier type	Record identifier	Attributes
Course	Course#	F	Course#	Course#
				Course_location
Prerequisite	Prerequisite#	F	Prerequisite#	Prerequsite#
				Prerequsite_title
Department	Department#	F	Department#	Department#
				Department_name
Instructor	Instructor_name	P	Department#	Instructor_name
			Instructor_name	Instructor_address

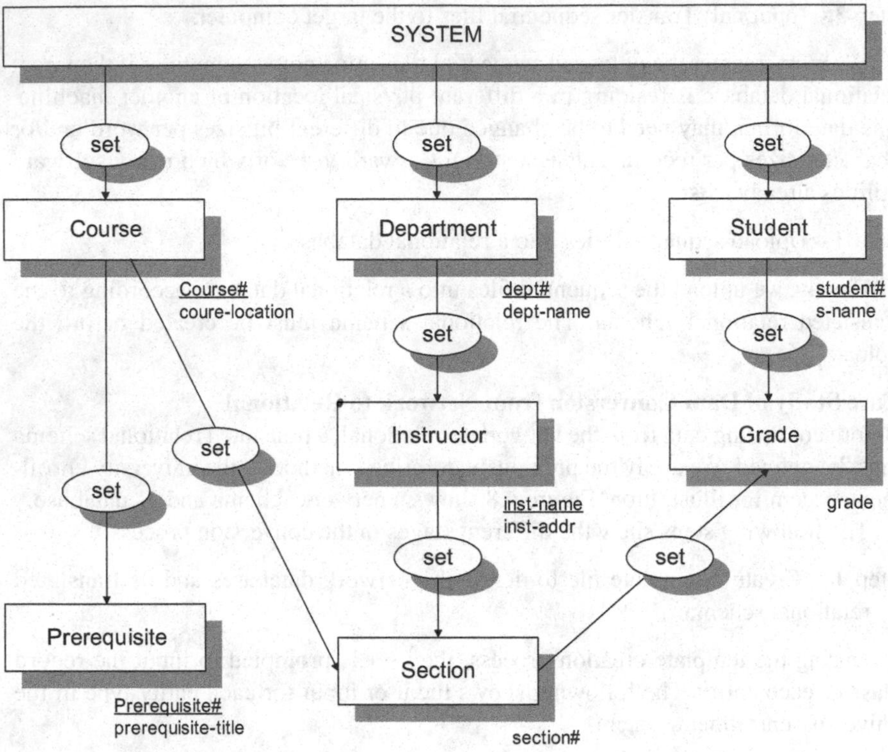

Record Course

COURSE#	COURSE_LOCATION
CS101	LECTURE THEATRE1
IS201	LECTURE THEATRE2
IS301	ROOM P7818

Record Student

STUDENT#	STUDENT_NAME
025056	JOHN F. SMITH
312788	FRANK. H. FRAN
217228	JANE E. BUNDY

Record Prerequisite

PREREQUISITE#	PREREQUISITE_TITLE
IS201	SYSTEM ANALYSSIS

Record Section

SECTION
SECTION1
SECTION2

Record Department

DEPARTMENT#	DEPARTMENT_NAME
CS	COMPUTEER SCIENCE
IS	INFORMATION SYSTEM

Record Section

GRADE
A
B

Record Instructor

INSTRUCTOR_NAME	INSTRUCTOR_ADDRESS
A.B.ADAMS	WHITE PLAINS
J.S. FINK	BROOKLYN
A.M. JONES	LONG ISLAND

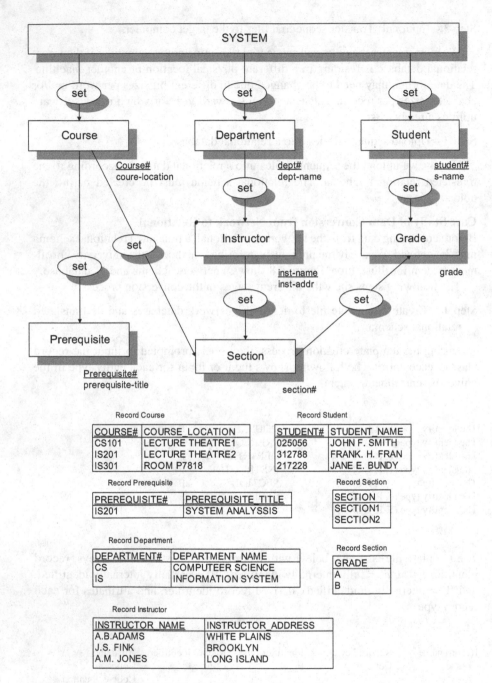

Fig. 4.8 A network database for university enrollment system

Record name	Record key	Identifier type	Record identifier	Attributes
Section		P	Department# Course# Instructor_name Section#	
Student	Student#	F	Student#	Student# Student_name
Grade		P	Department# Instructor_name Course# Student# Section#	Grade

The Set Linkage template file is shown below:

Owner	Member	Set Linkage Name
COURSE	PREREQUISITE	Course_Prerequisite
COURSE	SECTION	Course_Section
DEPARTMENT	INSTRUCTOR	Department_Instructor
INSTRUCTOR	SECTION	Instructor_section
STUDENT	GRADE	Student_grade
SECTION	GRADE	Section_grade

Step 2 – Unload records of each record type in the network database, with the record identifier into a sequential file.

Record COURSE

COURSE#	COURSE_LOCATION
CS101	LECTURE THEATRE 1
IS201	LECTURE THEATRE 2
IS301	ROOM P7818

Record PREREQUSITE

PREREQUISITE#	PREREQUISITE_TITLE	*COURSE#
IS201	SYSTEM ANALYSIS	IS301

Record DEPARTMENT.

DEPARTMENT#	DEPARTMENT_NAME
CS	COMPUTER SCIENCE
IS	INFORMATION SYSTEM

Record INSTRUCTOR

DEPARTMENT#	INSTRUCTOR_NAME	INSTRUCTOR_ADDRESS
CS	A.B. ADAMS	WHITE PLAINS
CS	J.S. FINK	BROOKLYN
IS	A.M. JONES	LONG ISLAND

Record SECTION

DEPARTMENT#	COURSE#	INSTRUCTOR_NAME	SECTION#
CS	CS101	A.B. ADAMS	SECTION 1
CS	CS101	J.S. FINK	SECTION 2

Record STUDENT

STUDENT#	STUDENT_NAME
025056	JOHN F. SMITH
312788	FRANK H. FRAN
217228	JANE E. BUNDY

Record GRADE

DEPARTMENT#	INSTRUCTOR_NAME	SECTION#	COURSE#	STUDENT#	GRADE
CS	A.B. ADAMS	Section 1	CS101	025056	A
CS	J.S. FINK	Section 2	CS101	312788	P

Step 3 – Upload the unloaded sequential files into the relational database.

The relational schema will be created with one create statement for each relation. For example, the following is a create statement for the relation table DEPARTMENT. Each unloaded sequential file is loaded to a relation.

```
CREATE TABLE DEPARTMENT
                    (DEPARTMENT                 CHAR(2),
                    DEPARTMENT_NAME             CHAR (20))
CREATE TABLE COURSE
                    (COURSE#                    CHAR(5),
                    COUSE_LOCATION              CHAR (20))
CREATE TABLE PREREQUISITE
                    (PREREQUISITE#              CHAR(5),
                    PREREQUISITE_TITLE          CHAR (20),
                    COURSE#                     CHAR(5))
CREATE TABLE INSTRUCTOR
                    (DEPARTMENT                 CHAR(2),
                       INSTRUCTOR_NAME
  CHAR(20),
                    INSTRUCTOR_ADDRESS          CHAR (40))
```

```
CREATE TABLE SECTION
                    (DEPARTMENT                         CHAR(2),
                    COURSE#                             CHAR(5),
                       INSTRUCTOR_NAME
  CHAR(20),
                    SECTION#                            CHAR(10))
CREATE TABLE STUDENT
                    (STUDENT#                           INTEGER(5),
                    STUDENT_NAME                        CHAR (40))
CREATE TABLE GRADE
                    (DEPARTMENT                         CHAR(2),
                    INSTRUCTOR_NAME                     CHAR (20),
                    COURSE#                             CHAR (5),
                    STUDENT#                            INTEGER(5),
                    SECTION#                            CHAR(8),
                    GRADE                               CHAR (1))
```

4.6 Data Conversion from Hierarchical to Relational

In a similar manner to the data conversion from network to relational, data conversion from hierarchical to relational requires some initial processing followed by a sequence of three steps, as shown in Fig. 4.9.

Preprocess step 1 – Translate hierarchical schema to relational schema by mapping each segment type to a relation and each segment "Access path" key to a relation key.

Step 1 – Unloading the hierarchical database, writing each segment type data into a file.

The algorithm for this process is shown below.

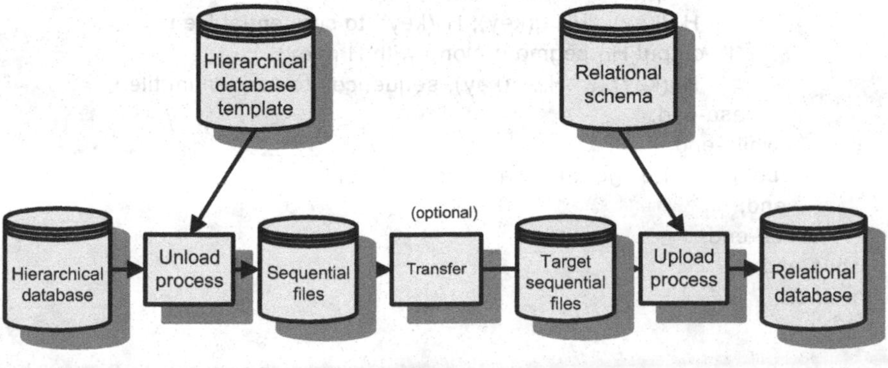

Fig. 4.9 System flow diagram for data conversion from hierarchical to relational

```
Program Unload hierarchical database to sequential files
Begin
  /* H = the number of segment types */
  Get all segment type H1, H2,..Hh from the hierarchical input schema;
  For i = 1 to h do /* for each target segment type */
  begin
     Get Hi1, Hi2... Hii segment types;
         /* get target segment Hii parent segments Hi1...Hi(i-1)  */
    Let j = 1 /* start from level 1 of root segment */
    While j > 0 do /* processing all target segment occurrences */
     begin
       case j of
    j=1: begin /* process all root segment occurrences */
         Get next Hi1 segment;
          If segment found
            then Let j = j + 1 /* go down toward target segment */
            else Let j = j - 1 /* go up to get out of the loop */
         end
   i>j>1: begin /* set up parentage position */
              Get next within parent Hij segment;
               If segment found
                then Let j = j + 1 /*go down toward target segment*/
                 else Let j = j - 1; /* go up toward root segment */
             end;
    j=i: begin /* process target segment */
         while Hii segment found do
           begin
            Get next within parent Hii segment; /*set up parentage */
              case Hii segment identifier type of
                 "F": output Hii segment with its parent segment
                      keys Hm to sequential file i;
                             /*Hm=the concatenation of parent
                                                segment keys of Hi segment*/
                 "P": output Hii segment along with Hi1(key),
                       Hi2(key)...Hi(i-1)(key), Hii(key)  to sequential file i;
                 "I": output Hi1 segment along with Hi1(key),
                       Hi2(key)......Hi(i-1)(key),.sequence# to sequential file i;
              case-end;
            while-end;
            Let j = j - 1; /* go up toward root segment */
           end;
        case-end;
   while-end;
  for-end;
  end;
```

Step 2 – (optional) Transfer sequential file to a target computer.

Step 3 – Upload sequential files to the relational database.

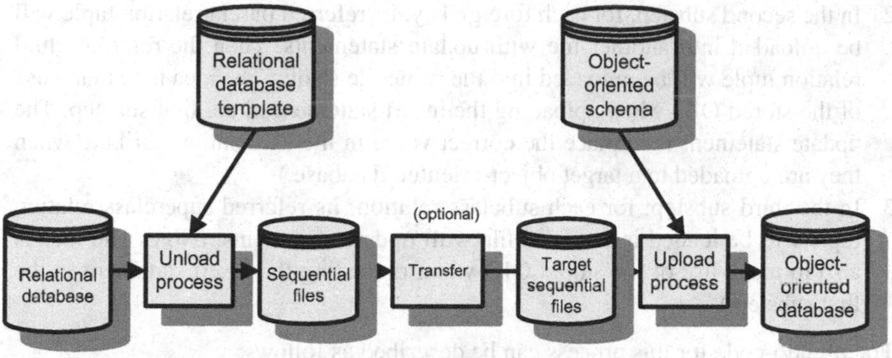

Fig. 4.10 System flow diagram for data conversion from relational to object-oriented

4.7 Data Conversion from Relational to Object-Oriented

Similar to the procedure for data conversion from network to relational, we must perform schema translation from relational to object-oriented in preprocess, and then unload and upload the relational database to a target object-oriented database as shown in Fig. 4.10.

There are four steps in converting data from relational to object-oriented. They are:

Preprocess step 1 – Translate relational schema into an object-oriented schema.

Rule 1: Map Relation to the Class Object
This rule maps relations into class objects. The resulting classes contain all the attributes of the source relations.

Rule 2: Map Foreign Keys to Association Attribute
This mapping takes the value determined relationships of the relational model and maps them into association attributes in the object-oriented model. The foreign key attributes are then dropped from the class, leaving the class with semantically meaningful attributes and association attributes with other classes.

Rule 3: Map isa Relationship to Inheritance
The subclass-to-superclass (i.e., isa) relationships in a relational schema are represented by a class hierarchy in the object schema with inheritance statements.

Step 1 – Unload relations' tuples into sequential files.

According to the translated object-oriented schema, the tuples of each relation will be unloaded into a sequential file. The unload process is divided into three steps:

1. The first substep is to unload each relation tuple into a file using insert statements (Note: These statements will later be uploaded back to a target object-oriented database such that each class will be initially loaded from the tuples of a corresponding relation.)

2. In the second substep, for each foreign key, its referred parent relation tuple will be unloaded into another file with update statements. Then the referred child relation tuple will be unloaded into the same file (Note: The idea is to make use of the stored OID when uploading the insert statement in the first substep. The update statement is to place the correct value in the association attribute when they are uploaded to a target object-oriented database.)
3. In the third substep, for each subclass relation, its referred superclass relation tuple will be loaded into a third file with update statements. (Note: The idea is also to make use of the stored OID when uploading the insert statement in the first substep.)

The pseudo-code for this process can be described as follows:

```
Begin
Get all relation R1, R2....Rn within relational schema;
For i = 1 to n do /* first substep: load each class with
                  corresponding relation tuple data */
 begin
  while Rj tuple found do
    output non-foreign key attribute value to a sequential file Fi
          with insert statement;
  end;

For j = 1 to n do /* second substep: update each loaded class with
                  its association attribute value */
begin
  while Rj tuple with a non-null foreign key value found do
  begin
     Get the referred parent relation tuple from Rp where Rp is
                  a parent relation to Rj;
      Output the referred parent relation tuple to a sequential
                  file Fj with update statement;
       Get the referred child relation tuple from Rj;
       Output the referred child relation tuple to the same file
                  Fj with update statement;
  end;

  For k = 1 to n do /* third substep; update each subclass to
                  inherit its superclass attribute value */
  begin
     while a subclass relation Rk tuple found do
      begin
        Get the referred superclass relation tuple from Rs
                  where Rs is a superclass relation to Rk;
          Output the referred superclass relation tuple to a
                  sequential file Fk with update statement;
       end;
  end;
```

Step 2 – (optional) Transfer sequential files to target computer.

The unloaded sequential file can be transferred to another computer if the target object-oriented database resides on another machine. The data format may need to be changed due to different bit sizes per word and/or character sizes per record. This is a straightforward task for which many software utilities already exist.

Step 3 – Upload sequential files to an object-oriented database.

As a prerequisite of the data conversion, a schema translation from relational to object-oriented schema will be carried out beforehand. Then, the translated object-oriented schema is mapped into the object-oriented databases DDL. The sequential file F_i will first be uploaded into an object-oriented database to fill in the class attributes' values. The sequential file Fj will then be uploaded into the object-oriented database to fill in each class association attribute value. Lastly, the sequential file F_k will be uploaded to fill in each subclass inherited attributes value.

Step 4 – (optional) Normalize object-oriented database to normal form if necessary (Ling and Teo 1994).

A poorly designed relation incurs the overhead of handling redundant data and the risk of causing update anormalities. We can decompose a relation into fully normalized relations. Similarly for an object-oriented schema, since complex attributes and multivalued attributes make a class object in an unnormal form, we must normalize them into normal form to avoid update anormalities. For example, the following is a class object with update anormalities.

```
Class Employee
                attr Employee#: integer
                attr Employee_name: string
                attr Salary: integer
                attr dept_name: string
                attr dept_budget: integer
                attr dept_location: set(string)
end
```

If we delete a department, we must update all the department employees' data. If we change the data of a department, we must change all the department data of the employees working in the department. Such update anormalities create the need to normalize the object-oriented schema. The solution is to remove these update anormalities by decomposing a class object into two class objects so that they can function independently of each other. The procedure to perform a normalization is as follows:

- Create a referenced class if one does not exist.
- Introduce an object reference if one does not exist.
- Move decomposed attributes to the referenced class.

In the example, we can normalize the class Employee by decomposing into two classes: Employees and Department as follows:

```
Class Employee                                   Class Department
  attr Employee#: integer                          attr Dept_name: string
  attr Employee_name: string                       attr Dept_budget: integer
  attr Salary: integer                             attr location: set(string)
  association attr hired_by ref Department           association attr hire ref
end                                                    set(Employee
                                                 end
```

After the normalization, the update anormalities are eliminated since the decomposed two class objects can be updated independently.

Case Study of Data Conversion from Relational to Object-Oriented

To illustrate the application of the above methodology, we can use a modified university enrollment system as an example.

Relation Course

Course	Course_title	Location
CS101	Intro to Computer Science	Lecture Theatre 1
IS201	System Analysis	Lecture Theatre 2
IS301	Decision Support System	Room P7818

Relation Prerequisite

*Course#	Prerequisite	Prereq_title
IS301	IS201	System Analysis

Relation Instructor

SS#	Inst_name	Inst_addr
415223641	A.B.Adams	White Plains
613557642	J.S. Fink	Brooklyn
452113641	A.M.Jones	Long Island

Relation Section

SS#	*Course	Section#	Lecture_hour
415223641	CS101	1	30
613557642	CS101	2	30

Relation Graduate Student

Student#	Degree_to_be
012888	M.Sc.
120008	Ph.D.

Relation Student

Student#	Student_name	Sex
012888	Paul Chitson	M
120008	Irene Kwan	F
117402	John Lee	M

Relation Enroll

*Student	*Course	SS#	Section#	Year	Grade
012888	CS101	415223614	1	1995	A
120008	CS101	613557642	2	1996	B

Its semantic model can be represented by the following extended entity-relationship model in Fig. 4.11.

By using the methodology in Chap. 3, we can convert these relations into class objects as follows:

Step 1 – Translate relational schema to object-oriented schema.

The result of translating the relational schema into the object-oriented model is shown in a UML diagram in Fig. 4.12.

Its translated object-oriented schema is as follows:

```
Class Student
  attr student#: integer
  attr student_name: string
  attr sex: string
end
```

```
Class Graduate student
inherit Student
attr degree_to_be: string
end
```

```
Class Section
  attr section#: integer
  attr lecture_hour: integer
  association attr divided_by ref course
  association attr taught_by ref instructor
end
```

```
Class Instructor
  attr inst_name: string
  attr ss#: integer
attr inst_addr: string
end
```

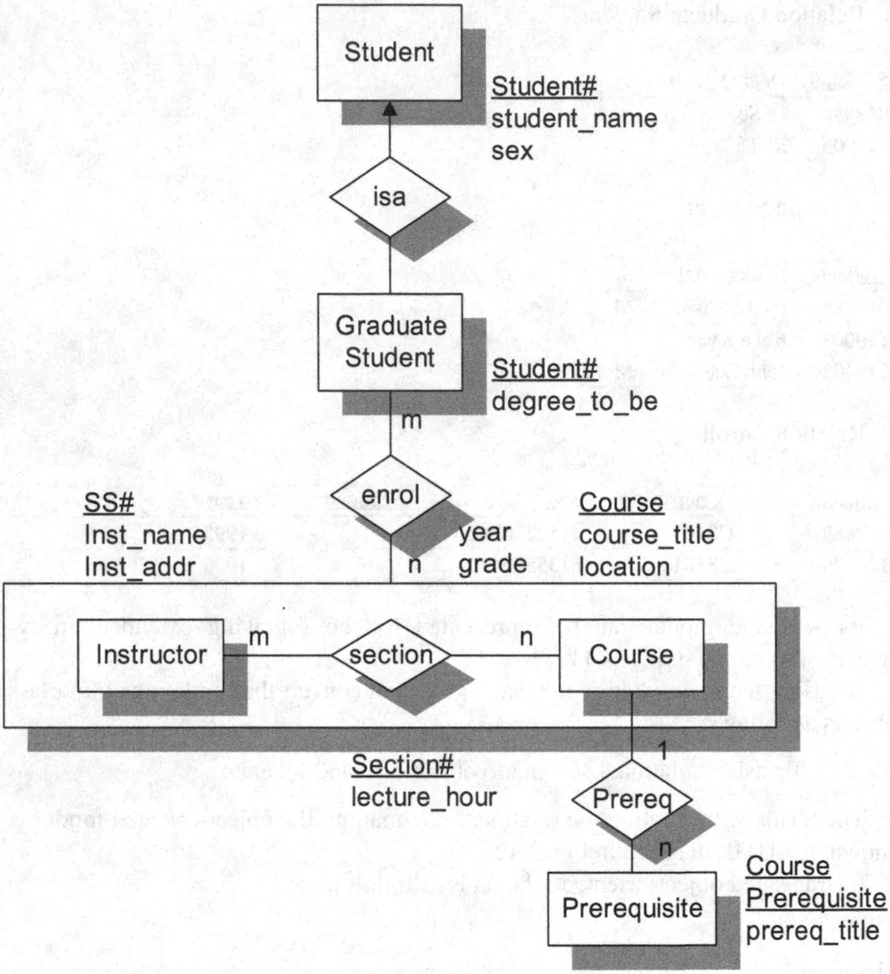

Fig. 4.11 An EER model for the modified university enrollment system

```
Class Course
  attr course: string
  attr course_title: string
  attr location: string
  association attr prer_by ref set(prerequisite)
end
```

```
Class Prerequisite
  attr course: string
  attr prerequisite: string
  attr prereq_title: string
association attr prere ref course
end
```

```
Class Enrol
  attr year integer
  attr grade: string
  association attr register ref graduate_student
  association attr provide ref section
end
```

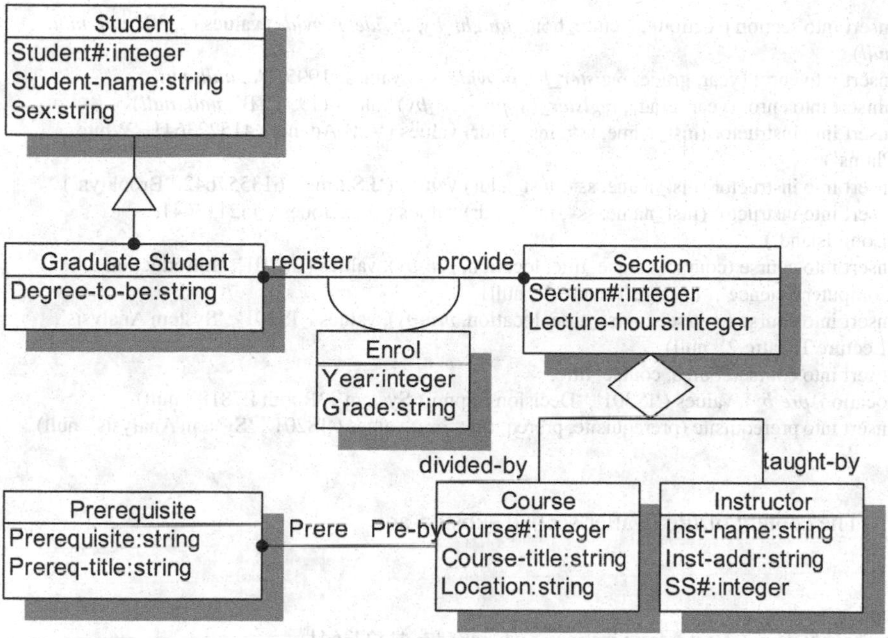

Fig. 4.12 Translated object-oriented schema in UML

Step 2 – Unload data into sequential files.

By applying the algorithm specified, this step unloads data from each relation into a sequential file along with its association data from other relations.

The idea is to load the attribute data from the input relation, and the association attribute data from the loaded object-oriented database. The Select statement is to retrieve class occurrences that have been loaded into the object-oriented database with the stored OID. The association attributes are in italic.

For implementation, a foreign key will be loaded with referred data using the stored OID. The insert and select statements in the following are from a prototype written using UniSQL (UniSQL 1992).

The content of file F_i after the first substep in unload process are the following insert statements:

insert into student (student#, student_name, sex) values (‘012888’, ‘Paul Chitson’, ‘M’)
insert into student (student#, student_name, sex) values (‘120008’, ‘Irene Kwan’, ‘F’)
insert into student (student#, student_name, sex) values (‘117402’, ‘John Lee’, ‘M’)
insert into graduate_student (student#, degree_to_be, *register*) values (‘012888’, ‘M.Sc.’, null)
insert into graduate_student (student#, degree_to_be, *register*) values (‘120008’, ‘Ph.D.’, null)
insert into section (section#, lecture_hour, *taught_by, divide, provide*) values (1, 30, *null, null, null*)

insert into section (section#, lecture_hour, *taught_by, divide, provide*) values (2, 30, *null, null, null*)
insert into enrol (year, grade, *register_by, provide_by*) values (1995, 'A', *null, null*)
hinsert into enrol (year, grade, *register_by, provide_by*) values (1996, 'B', *null, null*)
insert into instructor (inst_name, ss#, inst_addr) values ('A.B.Adams', 415223641, 'White Plains')
insert into instructor (inst_name, ss#, inst_addr) values ('J.S.Fink', 613557642, 'Brooklyn')
insert into instructor (inst_name, ss#, inst_addr) values ('A.M.Jones', 452113641, 'Long Island')
insert into course (course, course_title, location, *pre-by*), values ('IS101', 'Introduction to Computer Science', 'Lecture Theatre 1', null)
insert into course (course, course_title, location, *pre-by*), values ('IS201', 'System Analysis', 'Lecture Theatre 2', null)
insert into course(course, course_title, location, *pre-by*), values ('IS301', 'Decision Support System', 'Room P7818', null)
insert into prerequisite (prerequisite, prereq_title, *pre*) values ('IS201', 'System Analysis', null)

The content of file F_j after second substep are:

update section
set *taught_by* = (select * from instructor where ss# = 415223641)
set *divided_by* = (select * from course where course = 'IS101')
where ss# = 415223614 and course = 'IS101' and section# = 1

update section
set *taught_by* = (select * from instructor where ss# = 613557642)
set *divided_by* = (select * from course where course = 'IS101')
where ss# = 613557642 and course = S101' and section# = 2)

update enroll
set *register_by* = (select * from graduate_student where student# = '012888')
set *provide_by* = (select * from section where ss# = 415223641 and course = 'IS101' and section# =1)
where ss# = 415223641 and course = S101' and section = 1 and year = 1995

update enroll
set *register_by* = (select * from graduate_student where student# = '120008')
set *provide_by* = (select * from section where ss# = 613557642 and course = 'IS101' and section# = 2)
where ss# = 613557642 and course = 'IS101' and section = 2 and year = 1996

```
update course
set pre_by = (select * from prerequisite where course = 'IS301')
where prerequisite = 'IS301'
```

```
update prerequisite
set prereq = (select * from course where course = 'IS301')
where prerequisite = 'IS201'
```

The content of file F_k after third substep are:

```
update graduate_student
set student_name = (select * from student where student# = '012888')
set sex = (select * from student where student# = '012888')
where student# = '012888'
```

```
update graduate_student
set student_name = (select * from student where student# = '120008')
set sex = (select * from student where student# = '1200008')
where student# = '1200008'
```

Step 3 – (optional) Transfer sequential files to the target computer.

Not applied in this case study.

Step 4 – Upload sequential files into the object-oriented database.

The three files F_i, F_j, and F_k are then uploaded into an object-oriented database to fill in the classes and their attributes' values.

Step 5 – (optional) Normalize the translated object-oriented schema.

Since there is no redundant data in the object-oriented schema, this step can be skipped.

As a result, the converted object-oriented database is.

Class Course

OID	Course	Course_title	Location
001	CS101	Intro to Computer Science	Lecture Theatre 1
002	IS201	System Analysiss	Lecture Theatre 2
003	IS301	Decision Support System	Room P7818

Class Prerequisite

OID	Stored_OID	Course#	Prerequisite	Prereq_title
014	003	IS301	IS201	System Analysis

Class Instructor

OID	Inst_name	SS#	Inst_addr
004	A.B.Adams	415223641	White Plains
005	J.S. Fink	613557642	Brooklyn
006	A.M.Jones	452113641	Long Island

Class Section

OID	SS#	Stored OID	Section#	Lecture_hour
007	415223641	001	1	30
008	613557642	001	2	30

Class Graduate Student

OID	Student#	Degree_to_be
009	012888	M.Sc.
010	120008	Ph.D.

Class Student

OID	Student#	Student_name	Sex
009	012888	Paul Chitson	M
010	120008	Irene Kwan	F
011	117402	John Lee	M

Class Enrol

OID	Stored OID	Stored OID	SS#	Section#	Year	Grade
012	009	001	415223614	1	1995	A
013	010	001	613557642	2	1996	B

4.8 Data Conversion from Relational to Xml Document

As the result of the schema translation in Chap. 3, we translate an EER model into different views of XML schemas based on their selected XML view. For each translated XML schema, we can read its corresponding source relation sequentially by embedded SQL; that is, one tuple at one time, starting a parent relation. The tuple can then be loaded into an XML document according to the mapped XML DTD. Then we read the corresponding child relation tuple(s), and load them into an XML document. The procedure is to process corresponding parent and child relations in the source relational database according to the translated parent and child elements in the mapped DTD as follows:

```
Begin
    While not end of element do
    Read an element from the translated target DTD;
    Read the tuple of a corresponding relation of the element from
    the source relational database;
    load this tuple into a target XML document;
    read the child elements of the element according to the DTD;
    while not at end of the corresponding child relation in the
            source relational database do
            read the tuple from the child relation such that the child's
  corresponding to the processed parent relation's tuple;
        load the tuple to the target XML document;
    end loop    //end inner loop
  end loop    //end outer loop
end
```

As a result, the data can be converted into an XML according to each preserved data semantic in the translated DTD as shown in the following rules:

Notice that each rule of data conversion must be processed after each rule of schema translation in Sect. 3.7 in Chap. 3.

Rule 1: Mapping Weak Entity from RDB to XML
In converting relational data of a weak entity into an XML instance, we must ensure that each child element's IDREF refers to its strong element's ID (Fig. 4.13).

Rule 2: Mapping Participation from RDB to XML
In converting relational tuples with total participation into XML instances, we must ensure that each child element (converted from child relation tuples) is under its corresponding parent element (converted from parent relation tuples). Similarly, we can convert partial participation tuples into XML instances. However, for those

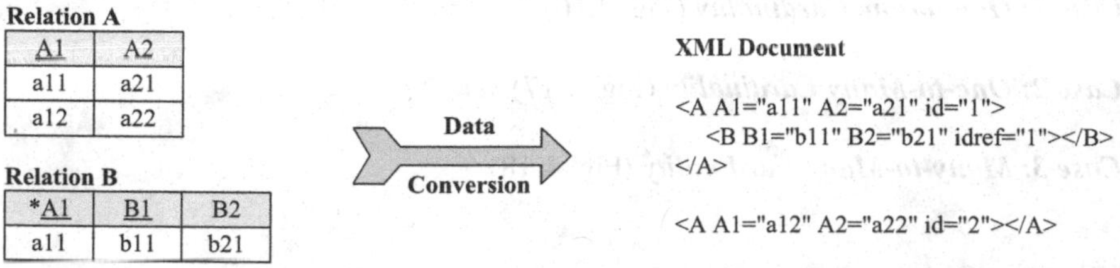

Fig. 4.13 Weak entity: data conversion

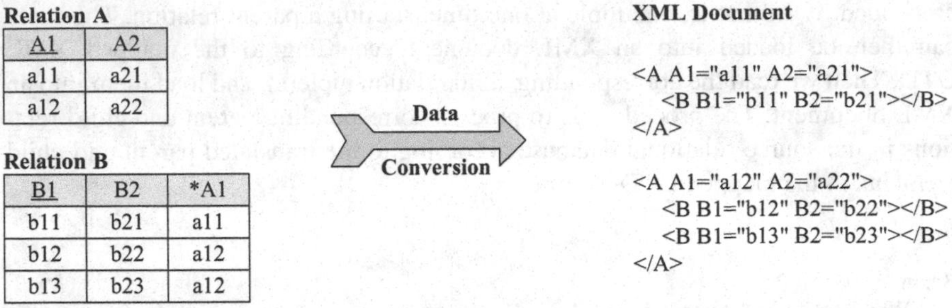

Fig. 4.14 Total participation: data conversion

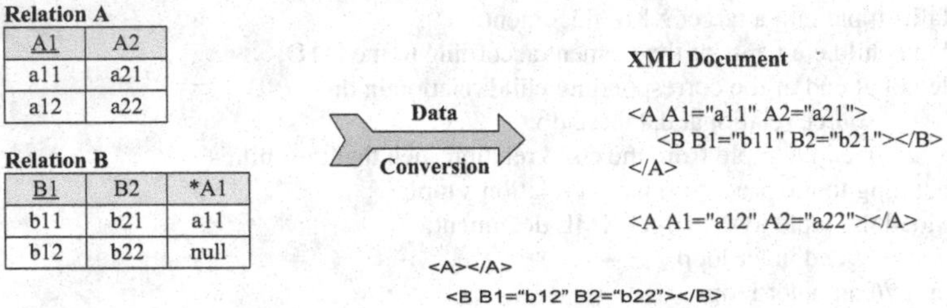

Fig. 4.15 Partial participation: data conversion

standalone (nonparticipating) child relation tuples, they can only be converted into child element instances under an empty parent element instance.

Case 1: Total/Mandatory Participation (Fig. 4.14).

Case 2: Partial/Optional Participation (Fig. 4.15).

Rule 3: Mapping Cardinality from RDB to XML

In converting one-to-one relational tuples into XML instances, we must ensure that each parent element instance consists of one child element instance only. In converting one-to-many relational tuples into XML instances, each parent element instance can have multiple child element instances. In converting many-to-many relational tuples into XML instances, a pair of ID and IDREF in two element types are applied such that they refer to each other in many-to-many associations.

Case 1: One-to-one Cardinality (Fig. 4.16).

Case 2: One-to-Many Cardinality (Fig. 4.17).

Case 3: Many-to-Many Cardinality (Fig. 4.18).

Relation A

A1	A2
a11	a21
a12	a22

Relation B

B1	B2	*A1
b11	b21	a11
b12	b22	a12

Data Conversion

XML Document

```
<A A1="a11" A2="a21">
   <B B1="b11" B2="b21"></B>
</A>

<A A1="a12" A2="a22">
   <B B1="b12" B2="b22"></B>
</A>
```

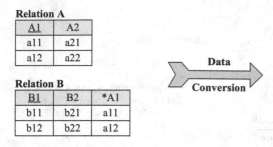

Fig. 4.16 One-to-one cardinality: data conversion

Relation A

A1	A2
a11	a21
a12	a22

Relation B

B1	B2	*A1
b11	b21	a11
b12	b22	a12
b13	b23	a12

Data Conversion

XML Document

```
<A A1="a11" A2="a21">
   <B B1="b11" B2="b21"></B>
</A>

<A A1="a12" A2="a22">
   <B B1="b12" B2="b22"></B>
   <B B1="b13" B2="b23"></B>
</A>
```

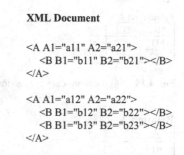

Fig. 4.17 One-to-Many cardinality: data conversion

Relation A

A1	A2
a11	a21
a12	a22

Relation B

B1	B2
b11	b21
b12	b22

Relation R

*A1	*B1
a11	b11
a12	b12

Data Conversion

XML Document

```
<A A1="a11" A2="a21" A_id="1"></A>
<B B1="b11" B2="b21" B_id="2"></B>
<R A_idref="1" B_idref="2"></R>

<A A1="a12" A2="a22" A_id="3"></A>
<B B1="b12" B2="b22" B_id="4"></B>
<R A_id="3" B_idref="4"></R>
```

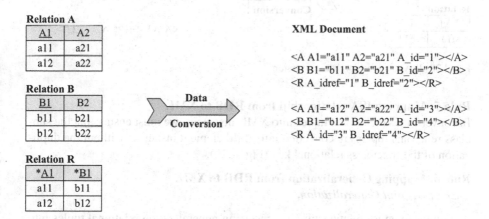

Fig. 4.18 Many-to-many cardinality: data conversion

Rule 4: Mapping Aggregation from RDB to XML

In converting aggregation relational tuples into XML instances, we must ensure the component relational tuples are converted into the component elements under a group element in an XML document (Fig. 4.19).

Relation A

<u>A1</u>	A2
a11	a21
a12	a22

Relation B

<u>B1</u>	B2
b11	b21
b12	b22

Relation C

<u>C1</u>	C2
c11	c21
c12	c22

Relation R1

*<u>B1</u>	*<u>C1</u>	*A1
b11	c11	a11
b12	c12	a12

Data Conversion

XML Document

```
<A A1="a11" A2="a21">
  <Group>
    <B B1="b11" B2="b21" B_id="1"></B>
    <R1 B_idref="1" C_idref="2"></R1>
    <C C1="c11" C2="c21" C_id="2"></C>
  </Group>
</A>

<A A1="a12" A2="a22">
  <Group>
    <B B1="b12" B2="b22" B_id="3"></B>
    <R1 B_idref="3" C_idref="4"></R1>
    <C C1="c12" C2="c22" C_id="4"></C>
  </Group>
</A>
```

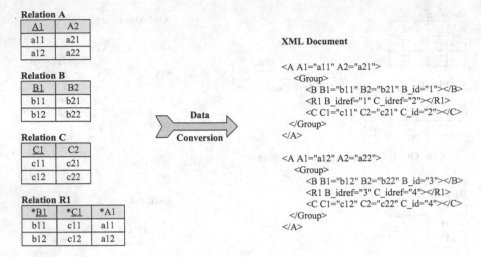

Fig. 4.19 Aggregation: data conversion

Relation A

<u>A1</u>	A2
a11	a21
a12	a22

Relation B

*<u>A1</u>	B1
a11	b11

Data Conversion

XML Document

```
<A A1="a11" A2="a21">
    <B B1="b11" ></B>
</A>

<A A1="a12" A2="a22"></A>
```

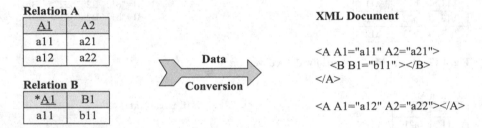

Fig. 4.20 ISA relationship: data conversion

Rule 5: Mapping ISA relationship from RDB to XML

In converting isa relational tuples into XML instances, we must ensure that the subclass relational tuples are converted into child element instances without the duplication of the superclass relational key (Fig. 4.20).

Rule 6: Mapping Generalization from RDB to XML

Case 1: Disjoint Generalization.

Similar to an isa relationship, in converting generalization relational tuples into XML instances, we must ensure that the subclass relational tuples are converted into child element instances without the duplication of the superclass relational key. However, in disjoint generalization, there are no duplicate element instances in two different element type instances under the same parent element instance. On the other hand, there is no such restriction in overlap generalization (Fig. 4.21).

Case 2: Overlap Generalization (Fig. 4.22).

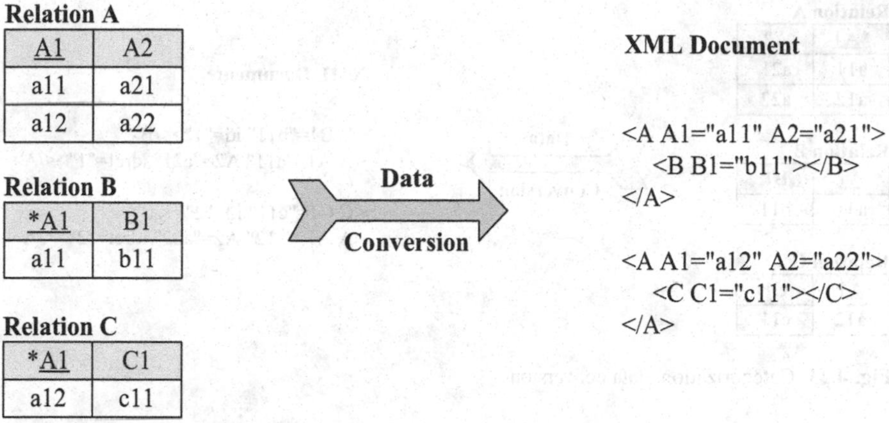

Fig. 4.21 Disjoint generalization: data conversion

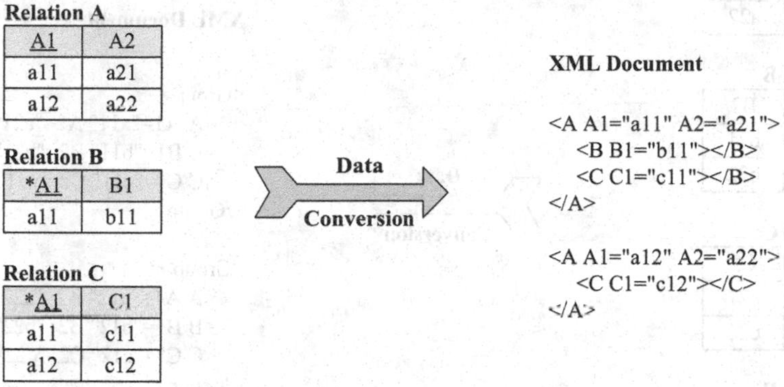

Fig. 4.22 Overlap generalization: data conversion

Rule 7: Mapping Categorization from RDB to XML
In converting categorization relational tuples into XML instances, we must ensure that each child tuple is converted into one only child element instance under a parent element instance (Fig. 4.23).

Rule 8: Mapping n-ary Relationship from RDB to XML
In converting n-ary relational tuples into XML instances, we must ensure that the parent relations are converted into component element instances under a group element in an XML document (Fig. 4.24).

Relation A

*<u>A1</u>	A2
a11	a21
a12	a22

Relation B

<u>A1</u>	B1
a11	b11

Relation C

<u>A1</u>	C1
a12	c11

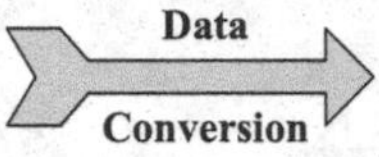

XML Document

```
<B B1="b11" id="1"></B>
<A A1="a11" A2="a21" idref="1"></A>

<C C1="c11" id="2"></C>
<A A1="a12" A2="a22" idref="2"></A>
```

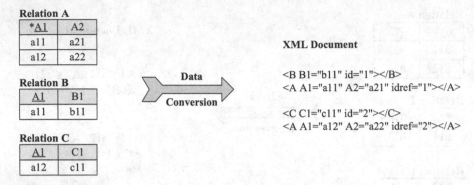

Fig. 4.23 Categorization: data conversion

Relation A

<u>A1</u>	A2
a11	a21
a12	a22

Relation B

<u>B1</u>	B2
b11	b21
b12	b22

Relation C

<u>C1</u>	C2
c11	c21
c12	c22

Relation R

*<u>A1</u>	*<u>B1</u>	*<u>C1</u>
a11	b11	c11
a12	b12	c12

XML Document

```
<Group>
    <A A1="a11" A2="a21"></A>
    <B B1="b11" B2="b21"></B>
    <C C1="c11" C2="c21"></C>
</Group>

<Group>
    <A A1="a12" A2="a22"></A>
    <B B1="b12" B2="b22"></B>
    <C C1="c12" C2="c22"></C>
</Group>
```

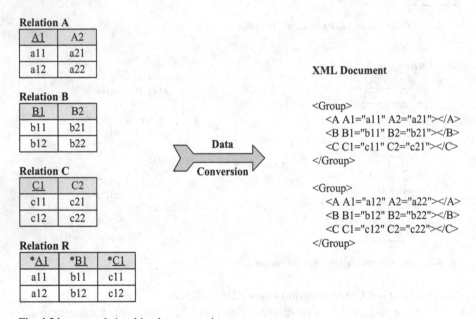

Fig. 4.24 n-ary relationship: data conversion

4.9 Summary

This chapter shows the various methods of data conversions, which include the customer program approach, interpretive transformer approach, translator generator approach, and logical level translation approach. The customer program approach is too costly because each customized program needs to be written for each file, and can only be used once. The interpretive transformer approach and the translator generator approach are language-dependent and also very limited in their functions. They provide a simulator (or compiler) approach to convert from a file format to another. The users need to learn how to use their simulation language, and even so, the language cannot be used to serve for general database file conversion purposes. The logical level translation approach seems to be more general. Actually, many software utilities in the market apply this approach. However, these software tools are proprietary.

Algorithms have been developed by converting a hierarchical database to a relational database, a network database to a relational database, and a relational database to an object-oriented database. They all apply the logical level translation approach by using unload source database to sequential files in the target database data structure sequence and then upload them to the target database.

The algorithm of converting network databases to relational databases is to read through all the network database record types from the bottom up. Each record type accessed will be concatenated with its owner record keys. The objective is to create the record identifier in each unload process. The foreign keys can also be unloaded into the sequential file. They can then be uploaded into a relational database.

The algorithm of converting a hierarchical database to a relational database is similar. The objective is also to create segment identifiers from each database access to each segment type.

The algorithm of converting a relational database to an object-oriented database is to make use of stored OID. In other words, the superclass is stored first. Its OID can then be used to store its subclass. Similarly, the composite class data is stored first and then followed by their component (or associated) class by using the stored OID.

Data conversion must be done after schema mapping. The data conversion from relational into an XML document is to automate the data loading according to the translated XML schema in the document type definition. For each rule of schema mapping for each data semantic, we can read the tuples from the relational database and then load them into the XML elements and their sub-elements according to their translated XML schema. We can apply pair of ID and IDREF in DTD or a pair of Key and Keyref in XSD to implement a many-to-many relationship in an XML document.

Questions

Question 4.1.

When we convert relational tuples into an XML document, can we avoid converting duplicate elements instances in the XML documents?

Answer:

Whenever a database has duplicate data instances, we call it an XML document, the duplicate tuples will be converted into duplicate XML element instances. In order to avoid duplicate elements, we must normalize a relational database before converting it into an XML document to ensure no duplicate XML elements. Relational database normalization includes first normal form, second normal form, third normal form, Boyce Codd Normal form, fourth normal form, and fifth normal form. An alternative to avoid duplicate XML elements is to apply pointer structure by transforming duplicate elements into pointers pointing to a unique XML element.

Question 4.2.
What is XML parse? How to make it?

Answer:
XML parser provides a way to access or modify data in an XML document. For example, the DOM parser parses an XML document by loading the complete contents of the document and creating its complete hierarchical tree in memory. The Document Object Model (DOM) is an official recommendation of the World Web Consortium (W3C). It defines an interface that enables programs to access and update the style structure and contents of an XML document. XML parsers support DML (data manipulation language) of DL/1 into one SQL statement. The steps are:

Step 1 Analyze DML steps.
Step 2 Combine multiple lower level DML statement of DL/1 into one higher-level database SQL statement.

Question 4.3.
What are the steps needed to perform data conversion from Network database to Relational database using logical level translation?

Answer:
The steps using the logical level approach for data conversion from Network database to Relational database are:

Step 1: Perform schema translation from Network database schema to Relational database schema.
Step 2: Unload the Network database record data into a sequence file. A program must be written to read Network database data into multiple sequential files, one record type data per one sequential file. For example, this step produces ten sequential files for a Network database with ten record types.
Step 3: Upload the download sequential files into the target Relational database. Another program must be written to read each sequential file into each target Relational table. In this case, this step will read ten sequential files into ten Relational tables.

Therefore, the key for data conversion between different databases is to read the input database according to its schema into sequential files, and then read these sequential files into the output target database according to the translated target database schema.

Bibliography

Fong J, Bloor C (1994) Data conversion rules from network to relational database. Inf Softw Technol 36(3):141–153

Fry J et al (1978) An assessment of the technology for data and program related conversion. In: Proceedings of 1978 national computer conference, vol 4, pp 887–907

Ling TW, Teo PK (1994) A normal form object-oriented entity relationship diagram. In: Proceedings of the 13th international conference on the entity-relationship approach, LNCS 881, pp 241–258

Lochovsky F, Tsichritzis D (1982) Data models. Prentice Hall, Inc., pp 300–336

Shoshani A (1975) A logical-level approach to data base conversion. In: 1975 ACM SIGMOD international conference on management of data, pp 112–122

Shu N, Housel B, Lum V (1975) CONVERT: a high level translation definition language for data conversion. Commun ACM 18(10):557–567

UniSQL (1992) UniSQL/X user's manual. UniSQL Inc

Chapter 5
Database Program Translation

The concept of a relational database was first proposed by E.F. Codd in 1970. It was almost instantaneously recognized as a more user-friendly model than the previous nonrelational (e.g., hierarchical or network model) database model. However, it was not adopted by the industry until the early 1980s because of its poor performance. Throughout the 1980s, the performance of relational databases improved and gained wider industry acceptance. This created a need to convert existing databases into a relational structure. Yet database conversion is both a costly and time-consuming process. The majority of time spent on such conversion projects is spent on the process of program translation.

To translate a program, it is necessary to determine the functions and semantics of the program. Programmers often make assumptions about the state and order of the data in the database without stating these assumptions explicitly in their programs. Therefore, it will usually be necessary to provide more information about the semantics of the program than can be extracted from the program text and its documentation alone. Also needed in the program conversion process is information about the data structure of the program before translation, the new structure of the program after translation, and how the two are related.

In general, there are five basic approaches in program translation: emulation, software interface (bridge program), decompiling, coexistence, and rewriting. We develop a relational interface as the software interface for our proposed methodology. We have improved the performance by implementing an internal schema that lets both relational and nonrelational database programs access a common data structure *without* database navigation. Database navigation is not user-friendly because the users can only access a record by following through its access path. It is also inefficient because each database access may take several I/Os.

The five basic approaches and our "enhanced interface" approach are described in the following sections.

J. S. P. Fong, K. Wong Ting Yan, *Information Systems Reengineering, Integration and Normalization*, https://doi.org/10.1007/978-3-030-79584-9_5

5.1 Rewriting

This approach requires the entire database system to be redeveloped from scratch in a relational format. One must translate the nonrelational schema into relational schema; rewrite all the application programs to run on the relational database; and throw away the old application programs.

5.2 Software Interface

Vendors may provide relational interface software to their nonrelational DBMSs. For example, Logical Record Facility (LRF), a software tool from Computer Associates (CA 1992a), is a run-time facility that allows application programs to access IDMS (a network database) data without knowing the physical structure of the database. It converts IDMS into IDMS/R, a relational-like database. Under LRF, programmers do not use database navigation statements to access the database. It is possible to combine processes in a macro that acts as a relational DML statement. Views are defined by the relational operators select, project, and join. A view is implemented as a logical record. Figure 5.1 shows a diagram of the processing retrieval paths of LRF.

As an example, to implement a join operation for three records. (Department, Office, and Employee) in a company's network database, using the foreign key, Employee-ID, the DBA must define the paths table as shown in Fig. 5.2 (CA 1992b). Only after this table has been defined in the subschema can the user retrieve the rows from the results of the join operation.

A logical path EMP-LR using LRF is defined in subschema below:

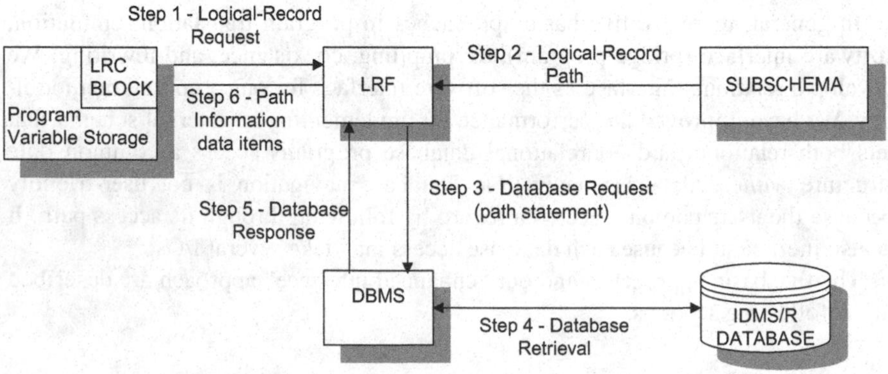

Fig. 5.1 LRF processing retrieval path (steps 3, 4, and 5 are repeated until all path-DML statements have been executed)

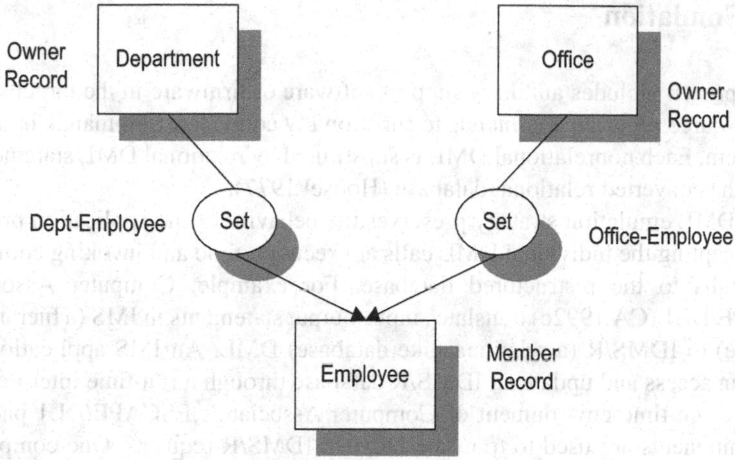

Fig. 5.2 An employee system in network schema

PROGRAM REQUEST	SUBSCHEMA PATH GROUP
OBTAIN FIRST EMP-LR WHERE EMP-ID EQ '1234'	ADD PATH-GROUP NAME IS OBTAIN EMP-LR SELECT FOR EMP-ID OF EMPLOYEE OBTAIN FIRST EMPLOYEE WHERE CALCKEY EQ EMP-ID OF LR ON 0000 NEXT ON 0326 ITERATE IF DEPT-EMPLOYEE MEMBER ON 0000 NEXT ON 1601 ITERATE OBTAIN OWNER WITHIN EPT-EMPLOYEE ON 0000 NEXT FIND CURRENT EMPLOYEE ON 0000 NEXT IF OFFICE-EMPLOYEE MEMBER ON 0000 NEXT ON 1601 ITERATE OBTAIN OWNER WITHIN OFFICE-EMPLOYEE ON 0000 NEXT

Path-group EMP-LR is the logical-record name. It enables users to retrieve Employee, Department, and Office records of the same employee. Database navigation is done in the subschema, retrieving a sequence of Employee, Department, and Office records. The "Next" statement validates the return code of DML. 0000 indicates a successful operation. LRF locates an appropriate path by matching the selection criteria specified in the program request to the selectors specified in the path.

5.3 Emulation

This approach includes auxiliary support software or firmware in the target system to map source program commands to functionally equivalent commands in the target system. Each nonrelational DML is substituted by relational DML statements to access the converted relational database (Housel 1977).

The DML emulation strategy preserves the behavior of the application program by intercepting the individual DML calls at execution time and invoking equivalent DML calls to the restructured database. For example, Computer Associate's ESCAPE/DL1 (CA 1992c) translates input-output statements in IMS (a hierarchical database) to IDMS/R (a relational-like database) DML. An IMS application program can access and update an IDMS/R database through a run-time interpreter.

In the run-time environment of Computer Associate's ESCAPE/DL1 package, two components are used to translate DL/1 to IDMS/R requests. One component, the ESCAPE DL/1 Run-time Interface, receives DL/1 requests from the application program; it then accesses the IDMS/R database and presents the appropriate IMS segments to the application program. The other component, the Interface Program Specification Block (IPSB) Compiler, describes the correspondence between the IDMS/R database structure and the simulated IMS database structure that the application program will view. The IPSB Source contains user-supplied control information that is compiled by the IPSB Compiler; the resulting IPSB Load Module is loaded by the ESCAPE/DL1 Run-time Interface as shown in Fig. 1.4.

5.4 Decompilation

This approach first transforms a program written in a low-level language into an equivalent but more abstract version and then, based on this abstract representation, implements new programs to fit the new environment, database files, and DBMS requirements. Decompilation algorithms have been developed to transform programs written with the procedural operators of CODASYL DML into programs that interact with a relational system via a non-procedural query specification. This is done through the analysis of the database access path.

For example, Katz and Wong (1982) designed a decompilation method that proceeded in two phases. The first phase is analysis. During this phase, a network database program is partitioned into blocks of statements for which an entry can only occur at the first statement. The user then seeks to group together a sequence of FIND statements that reference the same logically definable set of records and to aggregate these sets whenever possible. The result is the mapping of a DML program into access path expressions. The second phase is embedding, where the access path expression is mapped into a relational query and interfaced with the original program.

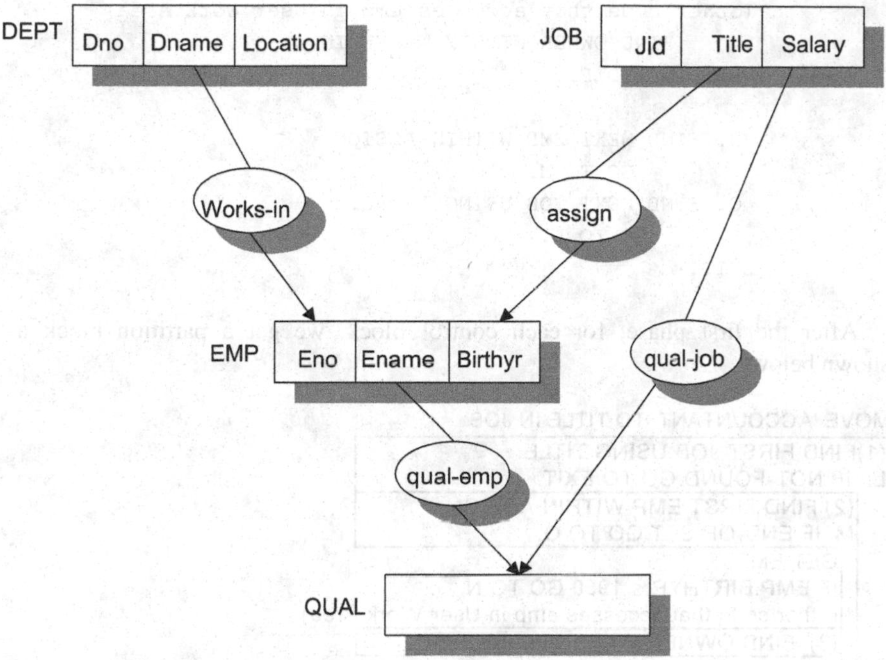

Fig. 5.3 A sample network schema for decompilation

For instance, consider a program that finds the departments for which accountants born after 1950 are assigned, using the following network schema in Fig. 5.3.

The corresponding relational schema is:

```
Relation DEPT (Dno, Dname, Location)
Relation JOB (Jid, Title, Salary)
Relation EMP (Eno, Ename, Birthyr, Dno, Jid)
Relation QUAL (*Eno, *Jid)
```

A sample network database program to be decompiled is as follows:

```
     MOVE 'ACCOUNTANT' TO TITLE IN JOB.
     FIND FIRST JOB USING TITLE.
L.  IF NOT-FOUND GO TO EXIT.
     FIND FIRST EMP WITHIN ASSIGN.
M. IF EMP-OF-SET GO TO O.
     GET EMP.
     IF EMP.BIRTHYR ≤ 1950 GO TO N.
```

```
(other code that accesses emp in User Work Area)
              FIND OWNER WITHIN WORKS-IN.
              GET DEPT.
                 :
 N. FIND NEXT EMP WITHIN ASSIGN.
         GO TO M.
 O. FIND NEXT JOB USING TITLE.
        GO TO L.
EXIT.
```

After the first phase, for each control block, we get a partition block as shown below:

```
MOVE 'ACCOUNTANT' TO TITLE IN JOB
(1)FIND FIRST JOB USING TITLE.
L.  IF NOT-FOUND GO TO EXIT.
    (2) FIND FIRST EMP WITHIN ASSIGN.
    M. IF END-OF-SET GO TO O.
       GET EMP.
       IF EMP.BIRTHYR ≤ 1950 GO TO N.
       (other code that accesses emp in User Work Area)
       (3)  FIND OWNER WITHIN WORKS-IN.
         GET DEPT.
    N.FIND NEXT EMP WITHIN ASSIGN.
    GO TO M.
O.     FIND NEXT JOB USING TITLE.
   GO TO L.
   EXIT.
```

After the second phase, blocks 1 and 2 are translated into the first SQL select statement and block 3 is translated into secondary SQL select statements as shown below:

```
LET C1 BE
SELECT E.TID, E.ENO, E.ENAME, E.BIRTHYR FROM JOB, EMP
WHERE J.TITLE = JOB.TITLE AND E.ASSIGN = J.JID.
LET C2 BE
SELECT D.DNO, D.NAME, D.LOCATION FROM EMP, DEPT
WHERE E.TID = EMP.TID AND E.WORKS-IN = D.DNO.
MOVE 'ACCOUNTANT' TO TITLE IN JOB.
L.
```

```
        OPEN C1.
        SELECT C1.
    M.    IF end of set GO TO EXIT.
            FETCH C1.
            IF EMP.BIRTHYR ≤ 1950 GO TO N.
    ------ other code ------
            OPEN C2.
            SELECT C2.
            FETCH C2.
          :
            CLOSE C2.
    N. SELECT C1.
          GO TO L.
      EXIT.  CLOSE C1.
```

5.5 Coexistence

This approach continues to support the nonrelational database while developing an information-capacity-equivalent relational database for the same application. Developers maintain an incremental mapping from the nonrelational database to the relational database. For example, Mark et al. (1992) present an incrementally maintained mapping from a network to a relational database. In the beginning, the applications on the relational database are restricted to retrievals. Gradually, applications on the network database are rewritten and moved to the relational database, while the incremental mapping continues to maintain the relational database for the applications still running on the network database. The basic idea of the incremental maintained mapping is illustrated in Fig. 5.4.

The initial network to relational database mapping algorithm takes as input the network schema defined in terms of the network DDL. The algorithm generates an equivalent relational schema definition in terms of the relational DDL, a program for unloading the network database to a temporary file and a program for uploading the temporary file to the relational database. After the relational database is defined using the generated relational DDL statements, the network database is mapped to the temporary file by using the generated unloading program. Finally, the uploading program reads the data in the temporary file and inserts them into the relational database.

At the network site, DML statements that update the database are monitored. Every time an update operation changes the database, the changes are also recorded in the differential file. This transformer is referred to as NETMAP.

At the relational site, all DML statements are monitored. Before a retrieval operation retrieves data from the database or an update operation changes the database, all changes recorded in the differential file, but not yet installed in the database, are first installed in the database. This transformer is referred to as RELMAP.

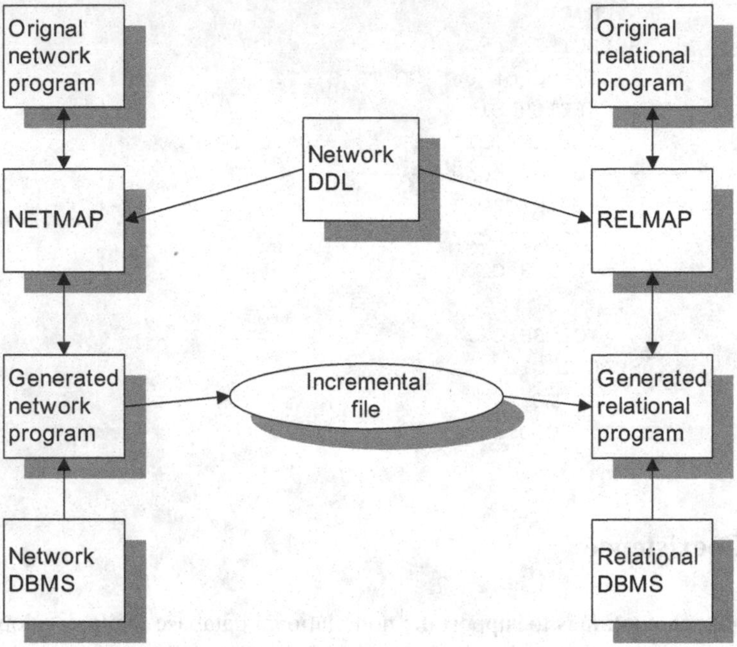

Fig. 5.4 Incrementally converting the network to the relational database system

5.6 Translate SQL to Network Data Manipulation Language

Emulation adds more workload to the database administrator because of the pre-compile macro call design of each database access. Decompilation is not feasible because of the nature of reverse engineering from lower-level database management language to higher-level database management language. Rewriting is very costly due to the number of bridge program(s) needed for each application program. Co-existence requires companies to maintain two different database management systems at the same time, which requires much manpower. As a result, the relational interface approach is the preferred option.

Our approach applies a preprocess to map a network schema to an information-capacity-equivalent relational schema. This open schema includes the derivation of primary and foreign keys in the transformed relational tables. Our objective is to implement the mapped relational schema over the existing network schema to form an open internal schema that can be used concurrently by both relational and network database programs.

Before program conversion, we must translate the network schema to a relational schema without loss of information. Translation from network to relational schema involves a one-to-one mapping between the record type and the relation. The Set structure of the network schema is translated into the referential relationship between child and parent relations. For example, Zaniolo (1979) designed a set of relations that recast the network schema in terms of a relational model. In this structure, each network record type is mapped to a relation on a one-to-one basis. The record key of the network schema is mapped to a primary key in the relational table. However, if the existing network record key is not unique, then we must concatenate it with its owner record key in order to create the primary key. The owner record key is also mapped as a foreign key in the relational table to link the parent and child records. If the set membership in the network schema is manual, then the record key of the member record will be mapped as a candidate key in the relational table.

Our approach enhances this schema translation by putting the translated relational record keys into secondary indices. The implementation of such secondary indices in each nonrelational record forms an open schema so that the access path of each record type takes only one I/O, the same as in the relational database primary indices. Secondary indices are composed of the record identifier that was derived from the primary keys of the owner records. The target of the secondary indices is each record type of the network database.

Basically, there are three types of record identifiers: fully internally identified, partially internally identified, and internally unidentified as described in Chapter 3. The record identifier is derived from the semantics of the existing network database. However, once a real-world situation has been modeled in a network schema, some of the semantics are irretrievable. We thus need user input to distinguish each type of record identifier so that we can recover its semantics. Figure 5.5 shows that such record identifiers are stored in the secondary indices in an existing nonrelational database (where F = fully internally identified, P = partially internally identified, I = internally unidentified, and IX = secondary indices).

In Fig. 5.6, we show a system flow diagram for an embedded SQL program that accesses the existing network database as an *open* database. Open in this context means that a network database with secondary indices can be accessed by both network and relational database programs.

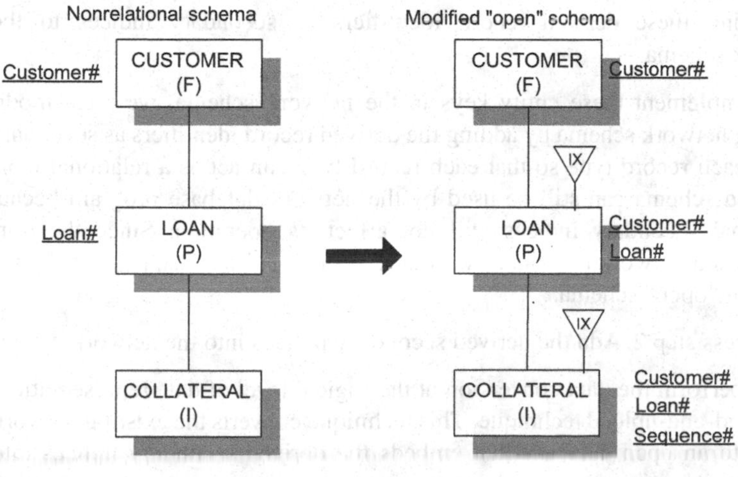

Fig. 5.5 Add derived secondary indices

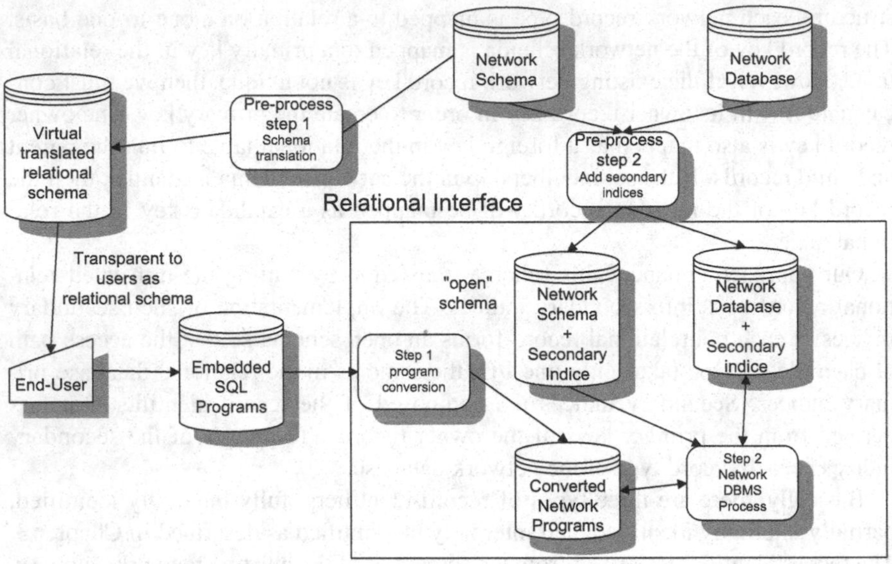

Fig. 5.6 Relational interface provision for network databases

The overall procedure for creating this relational interface involves the following steps:

Preprocess step 1. Map network schema to a relational schema and derive secondary indices.

We first map the original network schema into a corresponding relational schema by:

- Deriving a corresponding relational record key for each network record type, confirmed with the users then
- Adding these derived record identifiers as secondary indices to the network schema

To implement these entity keys in the network schema, we must modify the existing network schema by adding the derived record identifiers as secondary indices to each record type so that each record type can act as a relational table. The modified schema can still be used by the network database program because the additional secondary indices will not affect its operation. Since the translated schema is a network schema as well as a "Relational-like" schema to the user, we call it an "open" schema.

Preprocess step 2. Add the derived secondary indices into the network database.

We perform the data conversion at the logical level of data representation using an unload-and-upload technique. This technique converts the existing network database into an open database that embeds the derived secondary indices into each record. The conversion first unloads the data from each network database record type into a sequential file, adding the derived record identifier. Then it uploads each sequential file into the network database according to the modified "Relational-like" schema with secondary indices composed of the derived record identifiers.

Step 1. Translate SQL to network DML.

The main process of interface creation begins with program translation. To effect the translation process, we must define the algorithm and syntax for translating the relational DML (SQL, for example) to the network DML (IDMS, for example). After we complete the schema translation and create an open database by adding secondary indices to the internal schema, each SQL statement can be mapped to a series of IDMS statements.

The completed program translation will have a one-to-one mapping between each record type of the nonrelational database and each relation in the relational database, which ensures that the output of both DMLs will be the same. The following sections show the detail of the actual translation algorithms.

The user can now apply SQL statements to access the nonrelational database. Each SQL (the DML of a relational database) statement is translated at the run time into the lower-level DML of the network database. The following are the major SQL statements for the Join, Select, Update, Insert, and Delete operations and their translation into the equivalent DML language of IDMS, a network DBMS (CA 1992b).

Relational Operation Project

The general algorithm for projection translation follows, in which all attributes in a relation R, which corresponds to a record type N, are projected.

<u>Algorithm</u> Projection

1. <u>find</u> first N record by secondary indices IX
2. get D_j values, j = 1, 2,..n /* get referenced data */
3. <u>find</u> next N record
4. <u>exit if</u> none
5. <u>continue</u> from 2

The syntax for the algorithm Project is:

Relational	Network
Exec SQL Declare C cursor for Select * from Table-T End-Exec.	Obtain first N within IX. If return-code ≠ 0 error-exit else Display N Perform Loop until end-of-record.
Exec SQL Open C end-exec.	
Exec SQL Fetch C into T.	Loop. Obtain next N within IX. Display N.
Display T.	

Relational Operation Join

In the relational model, a join operation is allowed between two relations if the joined attributes are compatible. Users may form joins from any two record types in the network database. In general, the Join operation for two record types N_i and N_k are as follows:

<u>Algorithm</u> Join

```
1.  find first Ni record by secondary indices IXi
2.  exit if none
3.  LOOP1: get referenced data item values in buffer
4.     LOOP2: find Nk record by secondary indices IXk
5.        evaluate compatible attributes /* if f1 = v1 and f2 = v2 */
6.        continue from 8 if evaluation fails
7.        get referenced data item values /* obtain joined record */
8.        find next Nk record within secondary indices IXk
9.        exit if none
10.        continue from LOOP2
11. find next Ni record within secondary indices IXi
12. exit if none
13. continue from LOOP1
```

The syntax for the algorithm Join is:

Relational	Network
Exec SQL Declare C cursor for Select F1, F2....Fn from Table-T1, Table-T2. End-exec.	Find first N_i record within IX_i. Find first N_k record within IX_k. If record-found perform LOOP1 until end-of-record.
Exec SQL Open C end-exec.	LOOP1. If f1=v1 and f2=v2 Obtain N_i record Obtain N_k record. Perform LOOP2 until end-of-record. Find next N_i record within IX_i.
Exec SQL Fetch C into T end-exec	
	LOOP2. Find next N_k record within IX_k. If f1=v1 and f2=v2 Obtain N_i record Obtain N_k record.

Relational Operation Insertion

Attribute values are specified for a tuple to be inserted in a relation R^k. We denote by v^1 ,$v^{2....}$ v^n the values for attributes corresponding to fields in N^k and with V^1.$V^{2...}$ V^f the values of the foreign keys in $R^{k.}$

<u>Algorithm</u> Insertion

1. <u>locate</u> the owner record type N_{k-1} of to-be-inserted record N_k within secondary indices IX_{k-1} using $ID_{k-1.}$ /* ID_{k-1} = record identifier value in IX_{k-1} */
2. <u>locate</u> to-be-inserted record types N_k within secondary indices IX_k using ID_k ./* ID_k is the record identifier value in IX_k */

3. Establish contents of all N_k record data items in working storage (v_1, $v_{2....}$ v_n, V_1, $V_{2...}$ V_f).
4. <u>store</u> N_k record
5. <u>connect</u> N_k record to all owners record N_{k-1} in manual sets that have been established its currency in 2.

The syntax for the algorithm Insert is:

Relational	Network
Exec SQL Insert into Table-T(F1, F2,….Fn) Values (V1, V2…..Vn) End-Exec.	Find first N_{k-1} within Ix_{k-1} using ID_{k-1}. If return-code ≠ 0 error-exit-1 else Move V1 to F1 Move V2 to F2 … Move Vn to Fn Find first N_k within IX_k using ID_k If return-code = 0 error-exit-2 else Store N_k If set membership between N_k and N_{k-1} is manual connect N_k to N_{k-1}.

Relational Operation Deletion

A simple delete-only statement in the network database corresponds to the relational database delete statement for a given relational schema. The delete-record-N-only statement has the following properties:

- Remove record N_k from all set occurrences in which it participates as a member.
- Remove but do not delete all optional members N_{k+1}, for each set where N_k participates as an owner record.
- Do not delete record N_k if there are fixed or mandatory members record N_{k+1} for each set S where N_k participates as an owner record.
- The syntax for the algorithm Delete is:

Relational	Network
Exec SQL Delete from Table-T where F1 = V1 and F2 = V2 and … and Fn = Vn End-Exec.	Obtain first N_k within IX_k using ID_k. If return-code ≠ 0 error-exit-1 else Find current N_{k+1} within S If return-code = 0 error-exit-2 else Erase N_k.

Relational Operation Update

Suppose we want to replace the value of an attribute A in the relation R with the value V. Basically, we consider two cases. In the first case, A is not a foreign key. It corresponds to a data item in the corresponding record type N and thus we need a modified network command to perform the replacement. In the second case, A is a foreign key. Replacing a value, in this case, involves changing the set linkages, rather than the attribute value. Value (A) is the content of attribute A in the record type N before the update.

Algorithm Update

```
If A ∈ {A1, A2,… An} /* A is a non-foreign key attribute */
  then if A = K(R) /* K(R) = key field in record R */
    then drop the update /* disallow update record key */
    else do
           get Nk record by secondary indices IXk
           modify Nk record /* update non-key field by A=V */
         end
 else if V ≠ null and value(A) = null /* A is a foreign key */
       then connect Nk to new-owner-record Nn /* insert Nk into
                                                 new owner record set */
 else if V = null and value(A) ≠ null
       then disconnect Nk from old-owner-record Nk-1
                              /* remove Nk from old owner record set */
 else if V≠ null and value(A) ≠ null
       then reconnect Nk from old-owner-record Nk-1 to new-
                               owner-record Nn. /* change Nk owner */
```

Other functions implied by the network IDMS include:

- Mandatory or fixed set membership will disallow the disconnect operation in order to preserve the original inherent constraint of the network database.
- Fixed set membership will disallow foreign key change.

The syntax for the algorithm Update is:

Relational	Network

Exec SQL Update Table-T
set F1 = V1
and F2 = V2
and Fn = Vn
End-Exec.
	Obtain first N_k within IX_k using ID_k.
	If return-code ≠ 0
	    error-exit
	else
	if A ≠ foreign key
	    Move V1 to F1
	    .....
	    Move Vn to Fn
	    Modify N_k
	else
	if V ≠ null and value(A) = null
	    Find first N_n within Ix_n
	    Connect N^k to N^n
	else
	if V = null and value(A) ≠ null
	    Find first N^{k-1} within IX^{k-1}
	    Disconnect N^k from N^{k-1}
	else
	if V≠ null and value (A) ≠ null
	    Find first N^{k-1} within IX^{k-1}
	    Find first N^n within Ix^n
	    Reconnect N_k from N_{k-1} to N_n.

Step 2. Processing network database data manipulation language.

The translated network database program is now ready for processing. From the users' point of view, they are executing an embedded-SQL program. However, from the system point of view, the embedded SQL program has been translated into a network database program, to access the network DBMS. Because of the equivalent translated network DML statements (compared with the embedded SQL statements), the result of the translated network database program is the same as the result of the embedded SQL program. Such processing can be successful if accomplished by changing the execution environment, i.e., mapping the relational schema of the embedded SQL program to the network schema of the translated network database program in the preprocess step 1 and adding secondary indices to the translated network schema and the network database in the preprocess step 2.

On the other hand, even with the secondary indices added to the network database, the existing network database program, after recompilation with the modified secondary-indices-add network schema, can still access the modified network database as it did before the addition, as Fig. 5.7 shows (Fig. 5.7 is an extension of Fig. 5.6). As a result, the modified network DBMS acts as a relational interface to the relational database program and as a network DBMS to the network database program. The benefit of this relational interface is that the users can write new programs using an embedded-SQL (relational database) program while the existing (out-of-dated) network database programs are still in use. The out-of-dated network database programs should be gradually phased out or rewritten to use an embedded-SQL program.

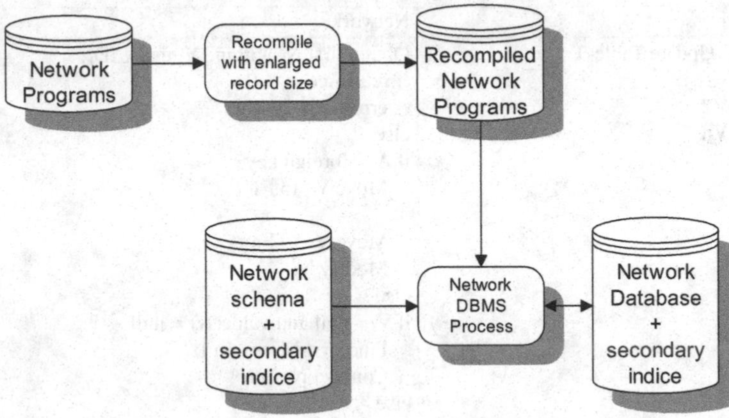

Fig. 5.7 Existing network database programs access "open" database

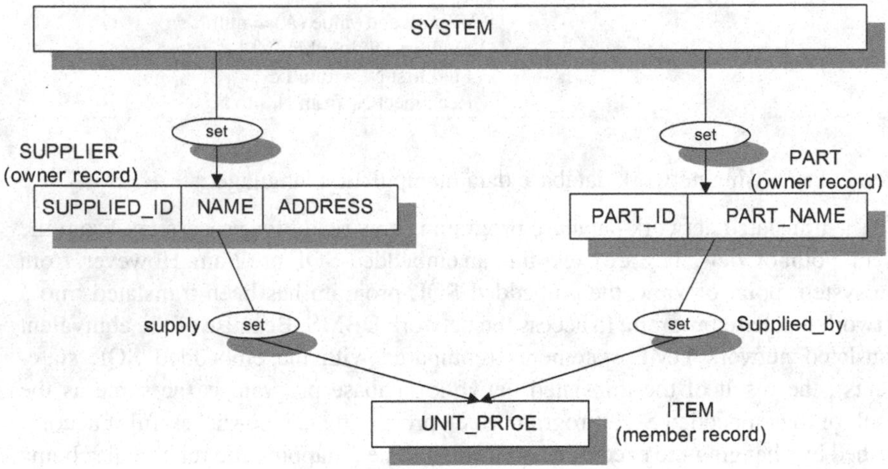

Fig. 5.8 Network schema

Case Study of Translating Embedded SQL to Network Database Program
To illustrate the emulation algorithm in a case study, the following is an embedded SQL program that will be able to access the network database for the manufacturer's part supplier system of Fig. 5.8.

Sample data from the Network database could be as follows:

SUPPLIER

SUPPLIER_ID	SUPPLIER_NAME	ADDRESS
S1	John's Co.	32 Ivy Road
S2	Michael Lee	61 Clark Road
S3	Jack's Store	90 Dicky Road
S4	Michael Lee	61 Clark Road

PART

PART_ID	PART_NAME
P1	Sugar
P2	Orange Juice
P3	Beer
P4	Chocolate

ITEM

UNIT_PRICE
4
5
6

After schema transformation, the modified network schema acting as an "open" internal schema is as shown in Fig. 5.9.

The data of the converted database are:

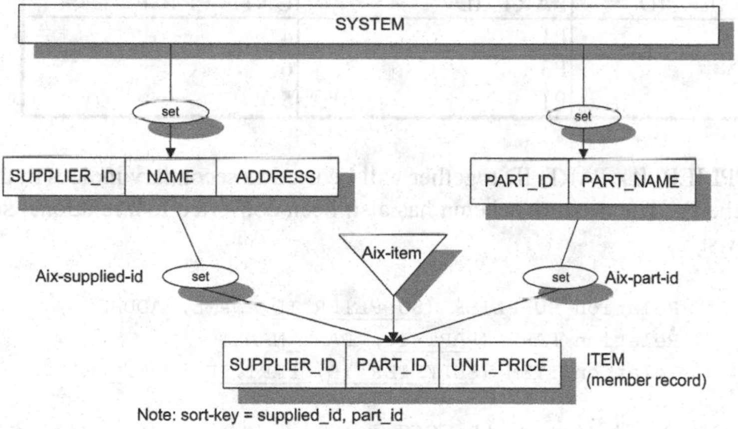

Fig. 5.9 Network schema with secondary indices as "open" schema

SUPPLIER

SUPPLIER_ID	SUPPLIER_NAME	ADDRESS
S1	John's Co.	32 Ivy Road
S2	Mic hael Lee	61 Clark Road
S3	Jack's Stare	90 Dicky Road
S4	Michael Lee	61 Clark Road

PART

PART_ID	PART_NAME
P1	Sugar
P2	Orange Juice
P3	Beer
P4	Chocolate

ITEM

SUPPLIER_ID	PART_ID	UNIT_PRICE
S1	P1	4
S2	P3	6
S3	P1	5

SUPPLIER_ID, PART_ID together will be used as secondary indices in the network schema. The network schema has also been converted to a relational schema as follows:

```
Relation SUPPLIER (SUPPLIER_ID, NAME, ADDRESS)
Relation PART (PART_ID, PART_NAME)
Relation ITEM (SUPPLIER_ID, PART_ID, UNIT_PRICE)
```

We can thus write an embedded-SQL program with two SQL statements (Select and Insert) to access the translated relational schema as follows:

```
ID DIVISION.
PROGRAM-ID.   RELATIONAL-DATABASE-PROGRAM.
ENVIRONMENT DIVISION.
CONFIGURATION SECTION.
SOURCE-COMPUTER. DG MV10000.
OBJECT-COMPUTER. DG MV10000.
DATA DIVISION.
WORKING-STORAGE SECTION.
```

```
    EXEC SQL DECLARE C1 CURSOR FOR
         SELECT * FROM SUPPLIER
    END-EXEC.
 01 SUPPLIER.
     05  SUPPLIER-ID     PIC X(4).
     05  SUPPLIER-NAME     PIC X(20).
     05  ADDRESS     PIC X(20).
 01 PART.
     05  PART-ID     PIC X(4).
     05  PART-NAME     PIC X(20).
 01 ITEM.
     05  SUPPLIER-ID     PIC X(4).
     05  PART-ID  PIC X(4).
     05  UNIT-PRICE     PIC 9(4).
 01 PRICE     PIC ZZ9.
 77 NO-DATA     PIC S9(9) COMP VALUE +100.
 77 END-OF-SET     PIC S9(9) COMP VALUE +100.
 77 ACCESS-OK     PIC S9(9) COMP VALUE +0.
 PROGRAM DIVISION.
 000-MAIN-ROUTINE.
          PERFORM 100-SELECT-ITEM.
          PERFORM 300-INSERT-ITEM.
          EXEC SQL CLOSE C1 END-EXEC.
          STOP RUN.
 100-SELECT-ITEM.
      EXEC SQL OPEN C1 END-EXEC.
      EXEC SQL FETCH C1 INTO :ITEM END-EXEC.
      IF SQLCODE = NO-DATA
         DISPLAY 'NO SELECTED RECORD IN ITEM TABLE'
      ELSE
         MOVE UNIT-PRICE TO PRICE
         DISPLAY 'SUPPLIER ' ITEM.SUPPLIER-ID
              ',  PART  ' ITEM.PART-ID, ':  PRICE ' PRICE
         PERFORM 150-SELECT-NEXT-ITEM
      UNTIL SQLCODE = END-OF-SET.
 150-SELECT-NEXT-ITEM.
      EXEC SQL FETCH C1 INTO :ITEM END-EXEC.
      IF SQLCODE = ACCESS-OK
         MOVE UNIT-PRICE TO PRICE
         DISPLAY 'SUPPLIER ' ITEM.SUPPLIER-ID
              ', PART '   ITEM.PART-ID, ': PRICE '  PRICE.
```

```
300-INSERT-ITEM.
    MOVE 'S3' TO SUPPLER-ID.
    MOVE 'P1' TO PART-ID.
    MOVE 5 TO UNIT-PRICE.
    EXEC SQL INSERT INTO ITEM
         (SUPPLIER-ID, PART-ID, UNIT-PRICE)
         VALUES (:SUPPLIER-ID, :PART-ID, :UNIT-PRICE)
    END-EXEC.
    IF SQLCODE = NO-DATA
       DISPLAY 'NO RECORD INSERTED'
    ELSE
       MOVE UNIT-PRICE TO PRICE
       DISPLAY 'SUPPLIER ' ITEM.SUPPLIER-ID
               ', PART    ' ITEM.PART-ID
               ': PRICE   ' PRICE ' INSERTED'.
```

After program translation, the above embedded-SQL program will be translated into a network database program containing the emulated Network DML statements of OBTAIN and STORE as shown below:

```
IDENTIFICATION DIVISION.
PROGRAM-ID. CONVERTED-NETWORK-DATABASE-PROGRAM.
ENVIRONMENT DIVISION.
  CONFIGURATION SECTION.
  SOURCE-COMPUTER. DG MV10000.
  OBJECT-COMPUTER. DG MV10000.
DATA DIVISION.
SUBSCHEMA SECTION.
COPY "SUBSUPPLY.COB"
WORKING-STORAGE SECTION.
77 TXT-NO    PIC 9(10).
01 PRICE    PIC ZZ9.
77 NO-DATA    PIC S9(9) COMP VALUE +100.
77 END-OF-SET    PIC S9(9) COMP VALUE +100.
77 ACCESS-OK    PIC S9(9) COMP VALUE +0.
```

```
PROCEDURE DIVISION.
MAIN-CNV SECTION.
INIT.
    READY UPDATE.
    INITIATE TRANSACTION TX-NO USAGE UPDATE.
000-MAIN-ROUTINE.
        PERFORM 100-SELECT-ITEM.
        PERFORM 300-INSERT-ITEM.
        COMMIT.
        FINISH.
        STOP RUN.
100-SELECT-ITEM.
    OBTAIN FIRST ITEM WITHIN AIX-ITEM.
    IF DBMS-STATUS NOT = 00000
        DISPLAY 'NO RECORD IN ITEM TABLE'
    ELSE
        MOVE UNIT-PRICE TO PRICE
        DISPLAY 'SUPPLIER ' AIX-SUPPLIER-ID
                ', PART    ' AIX-PART-ID
                ': PRICE   ' PRICE
        PERFORM 150-SELECT-NEXT-ITEM
    UNTIL DBMS-STATUS =17410.
150-SELECT-NEXT-ITEM.
    OBTAIN NEXT ITEM WITHIN AIX-ITEM.
    IF DBMS-STATUS = 00000
        MOVE UNIT-PRICE TO PRICE
        DISPLAY 'SUPPLIER ' AIX-SUPPLIER-ID
                ', PART    ' ,AIX-PART-ID, ': PRICE   ' PRICE.
300-INSERT-ITEM.
    MOVE 'S3' TO SUPPLIER-ID.
    MOVE 'P1' TO PART-ID.
    MOVE 5    TO UNIT-PRICE.
    FIND FIRST PART WITHIN AIX-PART USING SORT KEY.
    IF DBMS-STATUS NOT = 00000
    DISPLAY 'NO RECORD INSERTED - MISSING OWNER
    IN PART'
    ELSE
      FIND FIRST SUPPLIER WITHIN AIX-SUPPLIER
    USING SORT KEY
      IF DBMS-STATUS NOT = 00000
         DISPLAY 'NO RECORD INSERTED -
    MISSING OWNER IN SUPPLIER'
    ELSE
      MOVE SUPPLIER-ID TO AIX-SUPPLIER-ID.
    MOVE PART-ID TO AIX-PART-ID.
```

```
OBTAIN FIRST ITEM
WITHIN AIX-ITEM USING SORT KEY.
IF DBMS-STATUS = 00000
   DISPLAY 'NO RECORD INSERTED'
ELSE
   STORE ITEM
   MOVE UNIT-PRICE TO PRICE
   DISPLAY 'SUPPLIER ' AIX-SUPPLIER-ID
           ', PART    ' AIX-PART-ID
           ': PRICE   ' PRICE ' INSERTED'.
```

5.7 Translate SQL to Hierarchical Data Manipulation Language

The hierarchical to relational schema mapping is based on key-propagation, which is very similar to the process of normalizing a relational schema. There is a one-to-one correspondence between segment types and relations. In addition, the key fields of higher-level segment types are propagated to lower-level segment types. Because of database navigation, the user needs to use a parent segment key in order to access its child segment. As a result, the parent segment key is concatenated with the child segment key to identify the child segment. When we map hierarchical schema to relational schema, the parent segment key will appear in both the parent relation and child relation, which leads to the existence of redundant data. For example, the CUSTOMER# in Fig. 5.5 will appear in both relation Customer and relation Loan when mapping the left-hand-side hierarchical schema to right-hand-side relational schema. However, semantically, if CUSTOMER# is not needed to identify the relation Loan, then the relation Customer and relation Loan are not normalized.

Any hierarchical link is an inherent integrity constraint, which ensures that a child segment occurrence is connected automatically to a parent segment occurrence and may not be removed unless deliberately deleted. Following the DBTG (database task group, a database committee in the 1960s and 1970s) terminology, the hierarchical link is of type: fixed-automatic.

To illustrate the program translation from relational to hierarchical, we must show the syntax for translating each SQL to a hierarchical database management language of IMS (Information Management System, a hierarchical DBMS). There are four parameters in the IMS database management language. They are:

- Function Code, which defines the database access function.
- Program Control Block, which defines the external subschema access path.
- I-O-Area, which is a target segment address.

- Segment Search Argument, which defines the target segment selection criteria as follows:

```
CALL "CBLTDLI" USING FUNCTION-CODE
                                        PCB-MASK
                                        I-O-AREA
                                        SSA-1
                                        ...
                                        SSA-n.
```

After the schema translation, we create an open database by adding secondary indices to the IMS schema. Next, at runtime, we map an SQL statement to a series of IMS DML statements. The overall methodology for program translation from a relational to a hierarchical model can be described with a procedure similar to those previously described for converting from the network model to the relational model:

Preprocess step 1. Schema translation.
Preprocess step 2. Data conversion.

Step 1. Translate SQL to hierarchical database DML:

Program translation can be completed in a similar manner to the network database. By the addition of secondary indices, we can translate the relational SQL into the hierarchical database DML.

The algorithms and procedures are similar, except for the Update operation. An update operation that alters the value of a foreign key in the relational database cannot be directly translated to a hierarchical database such as IMS. This is because the linkages between parent and child segments are fixed and the parentage, once established, cannot be changed. To change the linkage, we must write a special program that copies the child segment and its dependent segments to a new child segment, and then deletes the old child segment. On the other hand, if we update a non-key field, the process is simple. The Update operation in a relational database can be translated to the hierarchical database using the following algorithm:

Algorithm Update

1. Set up the position of target segment H.
2. Set up new values of target segment H.
3. Update target segment H.

The syntax for the algorithm Update is:

Relational	Hierarchical
Exec SQL Update Table-T set F1 = V1 and F2 = V2 and …… Fn = Vn End-Exec.	Move Vk1 to Fk1. Move Vk2 to Fk2. …… Move Vkn to Fkn. Exec DLI GHU using PCB(1) Segment T into Segment-area where S1=Fk1 and S2=Fk2 … and Sn=Fkn. If return-code = space Move V1 to F1 ….. Move Vn to Fn Exec DLI REPLACE else error-exit.

Step 2. Processing hierarchical database DML.

The translated hierarchical database programs are now ready for processing. The result of processing the translated hierarchical database program will be the same as the result of processing the embedded SQL program before translation. Similarly, Fig. 5.6 shows (if we substitute all occurrences of "network" with "hierarchical") that even with the secondary indices added to the hierarchical database, the existing hierarchical database program, after recompilation with the modified secondary-indices-added hierarchical schema, can still access the modified hierarchical database as it did before. As a result, the modified hierarchical DBMS acts as a relational interface to the relational database program and as a hierarchical DBMS to the hierarchical database program. The out-of-date hierarchical database programs should be phased out or rewritten to the embedded SQL programs.

5.8 Translate SQL to OSQL

We can implement the relational interface by translating an embedded SQL Cobol program source to DL/1 Cobol program source code. The types of relational operations addressed include Select, Join, Update, Insert, and Delete. Figure 5.10 shows the data flow diagram of the relational interface.

The relational interface software scans the Cobol source program, filtering embedded SQL commands and passing them to the SQL command analyzer. The software determines the type of operation in the extracted SQL command by

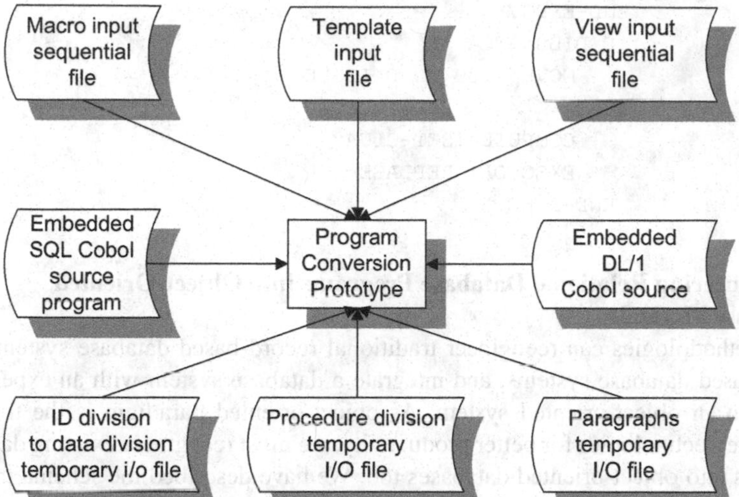

Fig. 5.10 System diagram of the program translation

analyzing the command tokens. Some tokens, such as Table Name, Field Name, Conditions, and Host Variable, are saved. The recognized relational operation type is used to find the corresponding template macro in the macro file.

The macro file contains the embedded DL/1 (Data Language I, IMS database management language) in Cobol statements for emulating one embedded SQL Cobol command. Each operation has its own macro for the segment and field to be changed depending on the operation. The use of the macro variables lets the segment names be substituted when the macro is expanded. Each variable indicates where a parameter is required. The variable name is preceded by ! and delimited by ^ and has a maximum length of eight as required by DL/1. For example, TAB_NAME on the first line of the following sample macro is the name of a variable that is replaced, in this case, by a table name.

The template macro then generates the emulation source code, with the dummy variable being replaced by the saved tokens selected earlier.

A sample macro is shown below:

```
UPDATE PERFORM !TAB-NAME^-REPLACE-!SERIALNO^
                                           !FULLSTOP^
UPDTWH !TAB-NAME^-REPLACE-!SERIALNO^.
     EXEC DLI GHU USING PCB(1)
                                          SEGMENT (!TAB-NAME^)
                                          INTO (!TAB-NAME^-AREA)
                                          SEGLENGTH (!TAB-NAME^-LEN)
                                          WHERE (!WHERE-CL^)
                                          FIELDLENGTH(!FLD-NAME^-LEN)
```

```
END-EXEC.
IF DIBSTAT = 'E'
    MOVE +100 TO DLICODE
ELSE
    COMPUTE !SET-CLUA^
    EXEC DLI REPLACE
  END-EXEC.
```

Reengineering Relational Database Programs into Object-Oriented Database Methods

Our methodologies can reengineer traditional record-based database systems into table-based database systems, and integrate a database system with an expert system into an object-oriented system. As object-oriented paradigm is the trend of computer technologies for better productivity, we must reengineer existing database systems into object-oriented databases too. We have described the schema translation and data conversion from a relational database to an object-oriented database. This section describes how to translate relational database programs (i.e., embedded SQL programs) into object-oriented database programs.

Relational database programs can be defined as program logic with a non-procedural call of embedded-SQL statements. In general, object-oriented database programs are encapsulated methods in each object. The participated boundary of relational database programs is more general. However, the participated boundary of object-oriented database methods is bounded by each object. As a result, the functional specification of relational database programs is multi-threaded with many outputs (i.e., many inputs and many outputs), while the functional specification of object-oriented database methods is one in, one out (i.e., one input, one output). To convert a relational database program into object-oriented methods, we must therefore break down the relational database into modules such that each module accesses only one object. The program logic of a relational database program can be converted into program logic of messages among objects.

The translation steps can be as follows:

The Relational Database

```
Relation Supplier (supplier-id, supplier-name, address)
Relation Part (part-id, part-name)
Relation Item (supplier-id, part-id, unit-price)
```

Step 1. Schema translation from relational into object-oriented as described in Chapter 3.

Step 2. Data conversion from relational into an object-oriented database as described in Chapter 4.

Step 3. Break down the logic of each relational database program into messages logic such that each message invokes an object by translating each module into an object's method and translating the other program logic into message processing logic among objects.

For example, the example of the following embedded-SQL program can be translated into the following object-oriented methods using UniSQL as a sample (UniSQL 1992):

Step 1. Relational tables SUPPLIER, PART, and ITEM are translated into the following objects:

```
create supplier                      create part
(supplier_id string,                 (part_id string,
 supplier_name string,               part_name string));
  address string));

create unit_price
(unit_price integer,
 supplied_by supplier,
 supplemented_by part));
```

Step 2. Data on relational tables SUPPLIER, PART, and UNIT_PRICE are unloaded and uploaded into data of object students under an object-oriented database management system.

Step 3.1. The relational database programs to select and insert items are translated into messages that access object ITEM in different methods using UniSQL, an object-oriented database.

As an example, an embedded SQL program is as follows:

```
ID DIVISION.
PROGRAM-ID. Relational-DATABASE-PROGRAM.
ENVIRONMENT DIVISION.
DATA DIVISION
WORKING-STORAGE SECTION.
    EXEC SQL DECLARE TEST1 CURSOR FOR
        SELECT * FROM SUPPLIER
    END-EXEC.
01 SUPPLIER.
    05   SUPPLIER-ID    PIC X(4).
    05 SUPPLIER-NAME    PIC X(20).
    05   ADDRESS   PIC x(20).
01    PART.
    05    PART-ID    PIC X(4).
    05    PART-NAME    PIC X(20)
01    ITEM.
    05    SUPPLIER-ID    PIC X(4).
    05    PART-ID    PIC X(4).
    05    UNIT-PRICE    PIC 9(4).
```

```
01   PRICE          PIC Z99.
77   NO-DATA              PIC S9(9) COMP VALUE +100.
PROGRAM DIVISION.
000-MAIN-ROUTINE.
    MOVE 'S3' TO SUPPLIER-ID.
    MOVE 'P1' TO PART-ID.
    MOVE 5 TO UNIT-PRICE.
    EXEC SQL INSERT INTO ITEM
        (SUPPLIER-ID, PART-ID, UNIT-PRICE)
    VALUES (:SUPPLIER-ID, :PART-ID, :UNIT-PRICE)
    END-EXEC.
          IF SQLCODE = NO-DATA
        DISPLAY 'NO RECORD INSERT'
    ELSE
        MOVE UNIT-PRICE TO PRICE
        DISPLAY 'SUPPLIER' ITEM.SUPPLIER-ID
        ', PART ' ITEM.PART-ID
        ': PRICE ' PRICE ' INSERTED'.
```

Step 3.2. The emulation method of this embedded-SQL program can be converted into an UniSQL C program as follows:

```
void
in_info(DB_OBJECT *class_object, DB_VALUE *return_arg, DB_
VALUE *supplier_id, DB_VALUE *supplier_name, DB_VALUE *sup-
plier_address, DB_VALUE *part_id, DB_VALUE *part_name,
DB_VALUE *unit_price)

{
EXEC SQLX BEGIN DECLARE SECTION;
DB_OBJECT *class_obj = class_object;
const char *supplier_id;
const char *supplier_name;
const char *supplier_address;
  const char *part_id;
  const char *part_name;
  const char *unit_price;
  DB_OBJECT *new_instance = NULL;
  EXEC SQLX END DECLARE SECTION;
  DB_MAKE_NULL(return_arg);
```

```
supplier_id = DB_GET_STRING(supplier_id);
supplier_name = DB_GET_STRING(supplier_name);
supplier_address = DB_GET_STRING(supplier_address);
part_id = DB_GET_STRING(part_id);
part_name = DB_GET_STRING(part_name);
unit_price = DB_GET_STRING(unit_price);

if (supplier_id != NULL && part_id != NULL && unit_price
!= NULL)
   EXEC SQLX INSERT INTO item(supplier_id, supplier_name,
   supplier_address,  part_id,  part_name,  unit_price)
   VALUES  (::supplier_id,  ::suplier_name,  ::supplier_
   address,  ::part_id,  ::part_name,  ::unit_price)  TO
   :new_instance;

if (new_instance != NULL)
DB_MAKE_OBJECT(return_arg, new_instance);
};
```

Step 3.3 Message of invoking this object can be translated into the following message command file.

```
Call main
```

Transaction Translation

To translate transactions from RDB to OODB, we can apply a symbolic transformation technique that contains syntax translation and semantic translation for SQL. For syntax translation, an SQL statement will be modified. For semantic translation, the navigational syntax will be modified. For example, the join operation in RDB can be replaced by class navigation (association) in OODB. Queries of the source language are built in our model. We navigate the query graph (QG) of SQL and then map it to the QG of OSQL (object-oriented SQL or OQL) (Cattell et al. 1997) with reference to the intermediate result of schema translation. Semantic rules (transformation definition) for query transformation from the source language to the target language will be applied. Then, the query of the target language will be produced. The output query OSQL should be the syntactic and semantic equivalent to the source SQL.

The OSQL, the object-oriented extension to SQL, allows data retrieval using path expressions, and data manipulation using methods. In query transformation, a syntax-directed parser converts the input OSQL into multi-way trees. The transformation process is then performed, based on the subtree matching and replacement technique. The process of SQL to OSQL transformation is in Fig. 5.11.

After schema mapping from RDB to OODB, we can transform an RDB transaction (SQL) to an OODB transaction (OSQL). The following sections detail the

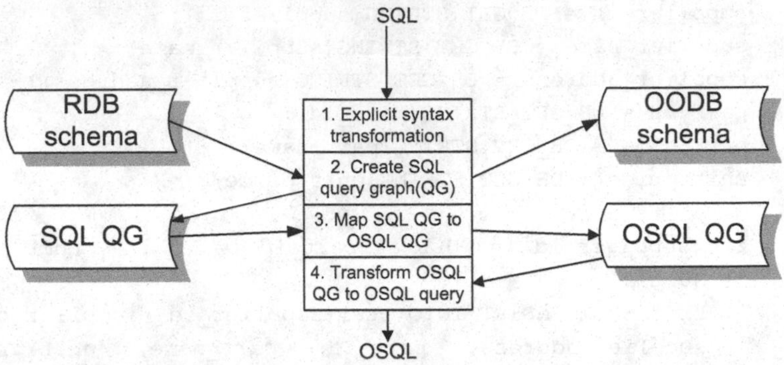

Fig. 5.11 Process for SQL to OSQL translation

major SQL statements for the Join, Update, Insert, and Delete operations and their translation into the equivalent OSQL statements.

Relational Operation Join

In the relational model, a join operation is allowed between two relations if the joined attributes are compatible. Users may transform a join operation in RDB to class navigation in OODB. The technique is to convert the database access path from SQL's query graph of joining relations: R_1,R_2,……R_n to the OSQL's query graph of navigating classes: C_{anchor}, C_2,……C_n. The join operation can be transformed to class navigation for class C_{anchor} (first class in class navigation path) (Fong and Chitson 1997) as:

Step 1. Decompose SQL query transaction.

During this step, the SQL query transaction is decomposed into groups by parsing its syntax as:

```
        SELECT {attribute-list-1} FROM {R1,R2,......Rn}
        WHERE {join-condition} AND/OR {search-condition-1}
        ORDER BY {attribute-list-2} GROUP BY {attribute-list-2}
HAVING {search-condition-2}
```

Step 2. Create the query graph of SQL through the input relations join path.

Based on the input relations, a join graph can be created to indicate the join condition from one relation to another. The join condition can be based on the natural join, i.e., the value match of common attributes of the input relations, or, based on the search condition specified in the SQL statement. The join path can be described as:

$R_1 \underset{J_1}{\rightarrow} R_2 \underset{J_2}{\rightarrow} \ldots\ldots \underset{J_n}{\rightarrow} R_n$ where J_1, J_2.....J_n are join and search conditions

Step 3. Map the SQL query graph to the OSQL query graph.

We can map each relation to a corresponding class from the preprocessing. The first relation in the join graph (in step 2) can be mapped to an anchor class. We can then form a class navigation path to follow from the anchor class to its associated class, and so on, until all the mapped classes are linked. The class navigation graph is the mapped OSQL query graph as shown below:

$C_{anchor} \rightarrow C_2 \rightarrow .. \rightarrow C_n$ where $^{P1}, {}^{P2} .... {}^{Pn}$ are aggregate attributes of class $C_{anchor}, C_2 .... C_n$

For example, Fig. 5.12 shows how a SQL query graph among three relations' join query graph is mapped into an OSQL query graph among two classes associated by the Stored OID of class Student addressing to the OID of class Course. Note that query graphs are in the direction of the arrows.

Step 4. Transform SQL to OSQL query transaction

From the query graph of SQL, a corresponding OSQL transaction can be constructed by:

- Replacing the target attribute of relations by the target attribute of classes in the navigation path.
- Replacing the input relations in the FROM clause by the anchor class.

The translated OSQL statement can be described as:

```
SELECT {attributes in classes navigation path into OID} FROM
{Canchor}
WHERE {transformation of join-condition} AND/OR {transforma-
tion of search-condition-1}
ORDER BY {transformation of attribute-list-2} GROUP BY {trans-
formation of attribute-list-2}
HAVING {transformation of search-condition-2}
```

Refer to the case study for an example.

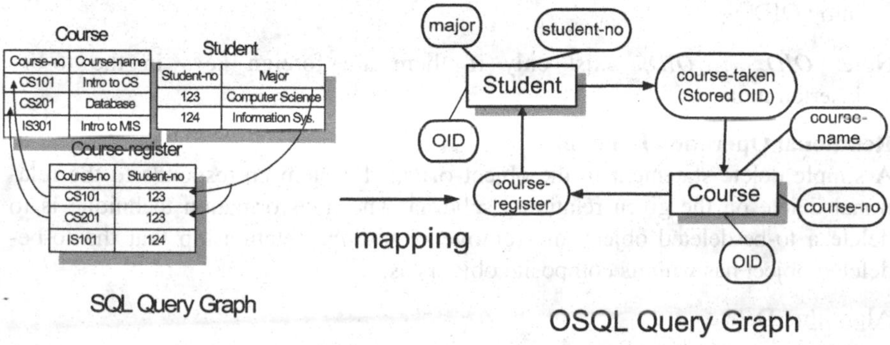

Fig. 5.12 A SQL query graph is mapped to an OSQL query graph

Relational Operation Insertion
Attribute values are specified for a tuple to be inserted in a relation R_k. We denote by v_1, $v_2 \ldots v_n$ the values corresponding to attributes in R_k and, if any, with V_{f1}, $V_{f2} \ldots V_{fm}$ corresponding to the foreign keys in R_k. The transformation technique is to preserve the referential integrity between parent relations and child relations through foreign keys V_{f1}, $V_{f2} \ldots V_{fm}$ in RDB to the association between class C_k and its associated class through aggregate attributes $^{P}{}_{c1}$, $^{P}{}_{c2} \ldots ^{P}{}_{cm}$ in OODB as follows (Zhang and Fong 2000):

Step 1. Locate the to-be-inserted object.

According to the preprocess, we can map the to-be-inserted tuple in RDB to a corresponding to-be-inserted object in OODB as follows:

SQL: INSERT into R (v_1, $v_2 \ldots v_n$, V_{f1}, $V_{f2} \ldots V_{fm}$) value ($V(v_1)$, .. $V(v_n)$, $V(V_{f1}) \ldots V(V_{fm})$)

Pre-process(schema translation): Relation R_k (v_1, $v_2 \ldots v_n$, V_{f1}, $V_{f2} \ldots V_{fm}$) → Class C_k (A_1, $A_2 \ldots A_n$, P_{c1}, $P_{c2} \ldots P_{cm}$)

Step 2. (optional). Locate composite objects that contain the to-be-inserted object.

The aggregate attributes of a composite object contain the stored OID of another object. We can locate, if any, the parent relations R_{p1}, $R_{p2} \ldots R_{pm}$ of the relation R_k with the to-be-inserted tuple by matching its foreign keys V_{f1}, $V_{f2} \ldots V_{fm}$ against their parent relations' primary keys. We can map these parent relations to the associated class C_{a1}, $C_{a2} \ldots C_{am}$ class of the to-be-inserted class C_k by matching the values of foreign keys as follows:

*SELECT * from* C_{a1} *where* $A_{a1} = V_{f1}$ *into:* $OID_{C_{a1}}$

.....

SELECT * from C_{am} where $A_{am} = V_{fm}$ into: $OID_{C_{am}}$

Step 3. Insert the to-be-inserted object.

We can then put the OID of the composite objects (in step 2) into the aggregate attributes of the to-be-inserted object and insert it as:

INSERT into C^k (A^1,…A^n, P^{c1},…P^{cm}} values ($V(v^1)$,…$V(v^n)$, $OID_{C_{a1}}$,…. $OID_{C_{am}}$) into : OID^{Ck}

Note: $OID_{C_{a1}}$,…. $OID_{C_{am}}$ exist only if there are foreign keys in the to-be-inserted tuple.

Relational Operation Deletion
A simple delete statement in the object-oriented system corresponds to the relational delete on the given relational schema. The transformation technique is to delete a to-be-deleted object and remove if any, the relationship that the to-be-deleted object has with its composite objects as:

<u>Algorithm</u> Delete

Step 1. Locate the to-be-deleted object.

We can map a to-be-deleted tuple in relation R_k to a corresponding to-be-deleted object in class C_k as:

SQL: DELETE from R_k where $v_1=V(v_1)$ and $v_2=V(v_2)\ldots$ $v_n=V(v_n)$

Preprocess (schema translation): Relation R_k $(v_1, v_2 \ldots v_n, V_{f1}, \ldots V_{fm}) \rightarrow$ Class C_k $(A_1, A_2 \ldots A_n, {}^{P}{}_{c1}, \ldots {}^{P}{}_{cm})$

Step 2 (optional). Delete aggregate attribute of composite objects containing the to-be-deleted object.

We can locate the parent relation $R_{p1}, R_{p2} \ldots R_{pm}$ of the relation R_k of the to-be-deleted tuple by matching its foreign keys $V_{f1}, V_{f2} \ldots V_{fm}$ against the parent relations' primary keys. Similarly, there may be an aggregate attribute P_k in the to-be-deleted object that points to a set of associated classes $C_{b1}, C_{b2} \ldots C_{bp}$. We can then delete the aggregate attribute of these composite objects in the associated class $C_{a1}, C_{a2} \ldots C_{am}$, $C_{b1}, C_{b2} \ldots C_{bp}$.

SELECT P_k from C_k where $A_1=V(v_1)$ and...$A_n=V(v_n)$ into : OID_{C_k}
UPDATE C_{a1} set $P_{a1} = P_{a1}$ - { OID_{C_k} } where $A_{a1} = V(V_{f1})$
.....

UPDATE C_{am} set $A_{am} = A_{am}$ - { OID_{C_k} } where $A_{am} = V(V_{fm})$
UPDATE C_{b1} set $P_{b1} = P_{b1}$ - { OID_{C_k} }
.....

UPDATE C_{am} set $P_{bp} = P_{bp}$ - { OID_{C_k} }

Step 3. Delete the to-be-deleted object.

We can then delete the to-be-deleted object from its class C_k as:

DELETE ALL from C_k where $A_1=V(v_1)$ and... $A_n=V(v_n)$

Note: ALL is needed to delete all the subclasses' objects only if deleting a superclass object.

Relational Operation Update

Suppose we want to replace the value of an attribute v_k from value $V(v_{k1})$ to $V(v_{k2})$ in the relation R_k (which maps to class C_k). Basically, we consider two cases. In the first case, v_k if not a foreign key. It corresponds to an attribute in the corresponding object, and thus we need an update statement of OSQL to perform the replacement. In the second case, v_k is a foreign key. Replacing a value, in this case, involves changing the aggregate attributes of its composite as shown below:

Step 1. Locate the to-be-updated object.

We can map a to-be-updated tuple in relation R_k to a corresponding to-be-updated object in class C_k as:

SQL: UPDATE R_k set $v_k = V(v_{k2})$ where $v_1=V(v_1)$ and $v_2=V(v_2)\ldots$ $v_n=V(v_n)$

Pre-process(schema translation): Relation R_k (v_1, v_2…v_n, V_{f1}, …V_{fm}) → Class C_k (A_1,A_2…A_n, P_{c1}, …P_{cm}, P_p)

Step 2 (optional). Update aggregate attribute of composite objects containing to-be-updated object.

If the to-be-updated attribute is an aggregate attribute (P_c or P_p), we can locate the aggregate attribute P_c or P_p in the to-be-updated object, and then delete (the existing) and insert (the new) aggregate attribute of these composite objects in the associated class C_{a1}, …C_{am}, C_{b1}, …C_{bp} as.

SELECT P_{c1},..P_{cm}, P_p from C_k where A_1=V(v_1) and…A_n=V(v_n) into : OID_{C_k}

UPDATE C_{ak} set $P_{ak} = P_{ak} - OID_{C_k}$
UPDATE $C_{a'k}$ set $P_{a'k} = P_{a'k} + OID_{C_k}$

UPDATE C_{bk} set $P_{bk} = P_{bk} - OID_{C_k}$

UPDATE $C_{b'k}$ set $P_{b'k} = P_{b'k} + OID_{C_k}$

Step 3. Update the to-be-updated object.

We can then update the to-be-updated object from its class C_k as:

UPDATE C_k set v_k = V(v_{k2}) where v_1=V(v_1) and v_2=V(v_2)… v_n=V(v_n)

Case Study of Transaction Translation from SQL to OSQL

Suppose we have an enrollment system with the following RDB schema:

```
Relation PERSON (SS#, Name)
Relation COURSE (Course-no, Course-name)
Relation STUDENT (SS#, @Student#, Major)
Relation COURSE-REGISTER (*Course-no, *Student#)
Relation DEPARTMENT (Dept-name, Faculty)
Relation STAFF (SS#, @Staff#, *Dept-name, Position)
Relation OFFICE (Office#, Office-name, Office-loc, *Staff#)
```

where underlined words are primary keys, words with @ prefixes are candidate keys, and words with * pprefixes are foreign keys.

By following the preprocess step 1, we map each relation to a class such that, each primary key of a tuple is transformed into an OID and an attribute in an object. In step 2, each attribute of a tuple is mapped to an attribute in an object. In step 3, the foreign keys Dept-name and Staff# are mapped to aggregate attribute P_{dept}, P_{staff} with values pointing to the OID of DEPARTMENT and STAFF. In step 4, the relationship relation COURSE-REGISTER is mapped to aggregate P_{course} and $P_{student}$ with set values pointing to the OID of COURSE and STUDENT. In step 5, the subclasses STUDENT and STAFF copy the attributes of superclass PERSON. The translated OODB schema can be shown below:

```
Class PERSON (OID, SS#: integer, Name: string)

Class COURSE (OID, Course-no: integer, Course-name: string,
Pstudent: set(STUDENT))

Class STUDENT (OID, Student#: integer, Major: string, Pcourse:
set(COURSE)) as subclass of PERSON

Class DEPARTMENT (OID, Dept-name: string, Faculty: string,
Pstaff: set(STAFF))

Class STAFF (OID, Staff#: integer, Position: string,
Pdepartment: DEPARTMENT, Poffice: set (OFFICE)) as subclass
of PERSON

Class OFFICE (OID, Office#: integer, Office-name: string, Office-
loc: string, Poccupant : STAFF)
```

Assuming we are to hire a new staff 'John Doe' for the Computer Science Department. The SQL transaction for the insert statement is:

```
INSERT PERSON (SS#, Name) value (452112345, 'John Doe')

INSERT STAFF (Dept-name, Position) value (CS, Professor)
```

By following the algorithm insert, we can translate the SQL statement to the following OSQL statement by locating the composite objects that contain the to-be-inserted object, and insert the to-be-inserted object with the aggregate attributes pointing to the composite objects as:

```
INSERT into PERSON (SS#, Name) value (452112345, 'John Doe')

SELECT * from DEPARTMENT where Dept-name = 'CS' into :OIDcs

INSERT into STAFF (Staff#, Position, Pdepartment) value (123,
Professor, OIDcs)
```

However, if John Doe resigns, we need to remove his record from the CS department. The SQL for the delete statement is:

```
DELETE from STAFF where Staff# = 123
```

By following the algorithm delete, we can translate the SQL statement to the following OSQL statements by deleting the aggregate attribute of the composite objects that contain the to-be-deleted object, and also by deleting the set of OFFICE that John Doe occupies, and then delete the to-be-deleted object with the aggregate objects pointing to the composite objects as:

SELECT $P^{department}$, P^{office} from STAFF where SS# = 452112345 into :OID^{staff}

UPDATE DEPARTMENT set $P_{staff} = P_{staff} - OID_{staff}$
UPDATE OFFICE set $P_{occupant} = P_{occupant} - \{OID_{staff}\}$
DELETE ALL from PERSON where SS# = 452112345

Now, suppose John Doe actually wants to transfer from the CS department to the IS department. The SQL for the update statement is:

```
UPDATE STAFF set dept-name = 'IS' where SS# = 452112345
```

By following the algorithm update, we can translate the SQL statement to sets of OSQL statements as:

SELECT P^{office} from STAFF where SS# = 452112345 into :OID^{staff}
UPDATE DEPARTMENT set $P_{staff} = P_{staff} - OID_{staff}$ where Dep="CS"
UPDATE OFFICE set $P_{staff} = P_{staff} - \{OID_{staff}\}$ where Dep="CS"
UPDATE DEPARTMENT set $P_{staff} = P_{staff} + OID_{staff}$ where Dep="IS"
UPDATE OFFICE set $P_{staff} = P_{staff} + \{OID_{staff}\}$ where Dep="IS"
UPDATE STAFF set dept-name = 'IS' where SS# = 452112345

Query Translation from SQL TO XQL
An XQL (XML Query Language) is a query language for XML documents and can be implemented by XPath. The SQL allows data retrieval using table join and data manipulation using methods. In query transformation, a syntax-directed parser converts the SQL into multi-way trees. The transformation process is performed, based on the subtree matching and replacement technique. The process of SQL query transformation is given in Fig. 5.13.

Translation of SQL Query to XPath Query
After the schema is done, SQL query can be translated to XPath query by the following steps:

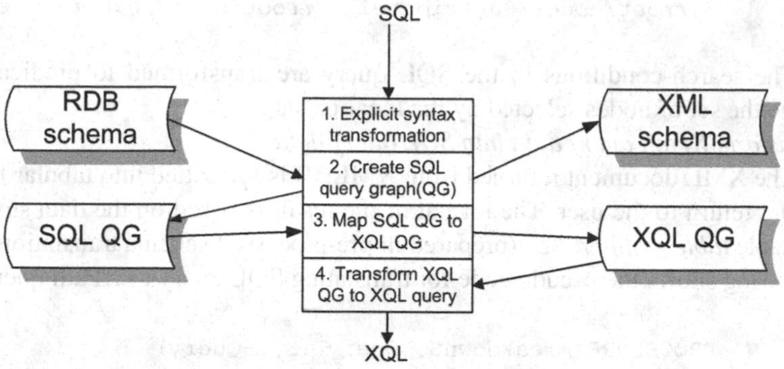

Fig. 5.13 Process for SQL to XQL transformation

1. *Decompose SQL query transaction.*

   The basic syntax SQL SELECT statement is in the form of:

```
SELECT {attribute-list-1} FROM {relation-list} WHERE
{join-condition} AND / OR {search-condition-1} ORDER BY
{attribute-list-2} GROUP BY {attribute-list-3}
HAVING {search-condition-2}
```

   The SQL query is decomposed into groups by parsing its syntax into the identifier-list, relation-list, and search conditions from the SQL query.

2. *Create the SQL query graph.*

   Based on the relation-list and the join-condition in the SQL query transaction, the SQL query graph is created. The join condition is based on the natural join or based on the search condition specified in the SQL query.

3. *Map the SQL query graph to the XPath query graph.*

   The SQL query graph is mapped to the XPath query graph. The table joins from the SQL query graph forms the XPath location path, which are the steps for navigating down the document tree from the root node.

4. *Transform SQL to XPath query.*

   In this step, the SQL query is transformed into XPath syntax as:

```
/root/node1[@attribute1=condition]/…/node2[@
attribute2=condition]/@attribute3
```

The attribute-list in the SQL query is mapped to the leaf attribute node at the bottom of the document tree. If all the attributes of the element node are selected, "@*" is mapped to select all the attributes from the leaf element node.

If more than one attributes are selected, the union operator is used to get the result. For example:

```
/root/node1/@attribute1 | /root/node1/@attribute2
```

The search-conditions in the SQL query are transformed to predicates to refine the set of nodes selected by the location step.

5. *Transform XPath query data into SQL query data.*

   The XML document returned from XMLDB is formatted into tabular format before return to the user. The format of the result is based on the data stored in the table *table_column_seq* (prepared in pre-processed schema translation). The following shows the pseudo code for translating SQL query to XPath query:

```
PROCEDURE BreakdownSQLQuery (SQL-Query)
  Initialize the array identifier-array,
  Initialize the array relation-array to empty array
  Initialize the array search-condition-array to
  empty array
   Initialize the array XQL-query-array to empty array
   Extract the portion of the SQL-Query from keyword
   'SELECT' to keyword 'FROM' into variable identifiers
   Extract the portion of the SQL-Query from keyword
   'FROM' to keyword 'WHERE' into variable relations
   Extract the portion of the SQL-Query from keyword
   'WHERE' to then end of the query into variable
    search-conditions
```

Identify each search condition from the variable search-conditions and put them into the array search-condition-array.

```
FOR EACH search-condition-array element DO
BEGIN
Remove the search-condition from search-condition-
array if it is a table join.
  IF search-condition is the function 'EXISTS( )' THEN
  Break down the subquery within 'EXISTS( )' by
  recursively calling procedure BreakdownSQLQuery
  Replace 'EXISTS' with XPath function 'count( ) > 0'
        END IF
    END
```

Identify each identifier from the variable identifier and put them into array identifier-array

```
FOREACH identifier-array element DO
BEGIN
    Locate the element node which the identifier
    belongs to
    construct the XQL query from the root node to the
    element node the identifier belongs to
    IF the identifier is '*' THEN
        Append '@*' to the end of the XQL query
        ELSE
    Append the identifier to the end of the XQL query
        END IF
    Store the XQL query to the array
    XQL-query-array
        END
    Concatenate the elements of the array XQL-query-
    array with the union sign '|' to form a single
    XQL query
    RETURN the concatenated XQL query.
  END PROCEDURE

PROCEDURE mainProcedure (User input SQL query)
  XQL-Query = EXEC PROCEDURE BreakdownSQLQuery (User
  input QL query)
  Submit the XQL-Query to the XMLDB Server
      IF no XML document returned THEN
    RETURN
      ELSE
    Retrieve the corresponding column headers
    Format the returned XML document into tabu-
    lar format
    RETURN the data to user
      END IF
  END PROCEDURE
```

Case Study of Translating an SQL Query into XPath Query

Case studies of queries for security trading client statements are used to illustrate query translation between XPath and SQL.

Table record sequence number column

For any table to be used for query translation, an extra column – *seqno* is required. These columns are used by the XML gateway and therefore, the following paragraphs first explain the usage and maintenance of these columns.

For each table, the last column is *seqno*. These *seqno* columns are used to ensure the records returned from the database are in the right order and this column is used for translation XQL location index functions (e.g., position( )).

These *seqno* columns are incremented by one for each new record. For example, for the CLIENTACCOUNTEXECUTIVE table. The *seqno* is 1 and 2 for clientid 600001 (Fong et al. 2006).

On inserting a new record to a table, the insert trigger first finds out which column is used for counting *seqno* from the node_tablecolumn_mapping table. Then, the trigger selects the maximum *seqno* value for the new record. The maximum *seqno* value plus one will be assigned as the *seqno* value of the new record. For example, a new record inserted to the table CLIENTACCOUNTEXECUTIVE on the next page for clientid 600001 gets a new *seqno* value 3 since the maximum *seqno* for clientid 600001 already in the table is 2.

There is no need to update the seqno value in case the record is deleted. In XQL, the location index function (e.g., position()) counts the order of the record relative to the parent node.

Client Table

Clientid	**Title**	**lastname**	**firstname**
600001	Mr	Chan	Peter
600002	Mrs	Wong	Ann
600003	Miss	Lee	Jane
Phone	**fax**	**email**	**seqno**
27825290	27825291	Peter@tom.com	1
24588900	21588200	Ann@ibm.com	1
27238900	36225555	Jane@msn.com	1

Clientorder Table

clientid	**orderid**	**Tradedate**	**stockid**	**Inputquantity**
600001	300001	20020403	000003	10000
600002	300002	20020403	000004	10000
600003	300003	20020404	000003	20000
600003	300004	20020405	000004	6000
600002	300005	20020405	000941	6000
Action	**ordertype**	**Allornothing**	**inputdatetime**	**Seqno**
Buy	Limit	N	200204031001	1
Buy	Limit	N	200204031002	2
Sell	Limit	N	200204041101	1
Buy	Limit	N	200204051408	2
buy	Limit	N	200204051506	1

Balance Table

Clientid	Stockid	Bookbalance	seqno
600001	000001	10000	1
600001	000941	1000	2
600002	000001	1000	1
600003	000011	1000	1
600003	000012	500	2

AccountExecutive Table

aeid	Lastname	firstname	Seqno
AE0001	Franky	Chan	1
AE0002	Grace	Yeung	1
AE0003	Paul	Ho	1

The relational schema is preprocessed and translated to the XML schema. From the relational tables above, the EER model is created (Fig. 5.14):

An XML view of the relational schema on the selection of Client as root is translated from the EER model into a DTD Graph as follows (Fig. 5.15):

Query for selecting all the *ClientID* and *OrderID*

SQL Query:

```
SELECT Client.ClientID, Order.OrderID
FROM        Client, Order
WHERE       Client.ClientID = Order.ClientdID
```

Translated XPath query:

```
/ClientStatement/Client/@ClientID
/ClientStatement/Client/Order/@OrderID
```

Result from XPath Result:

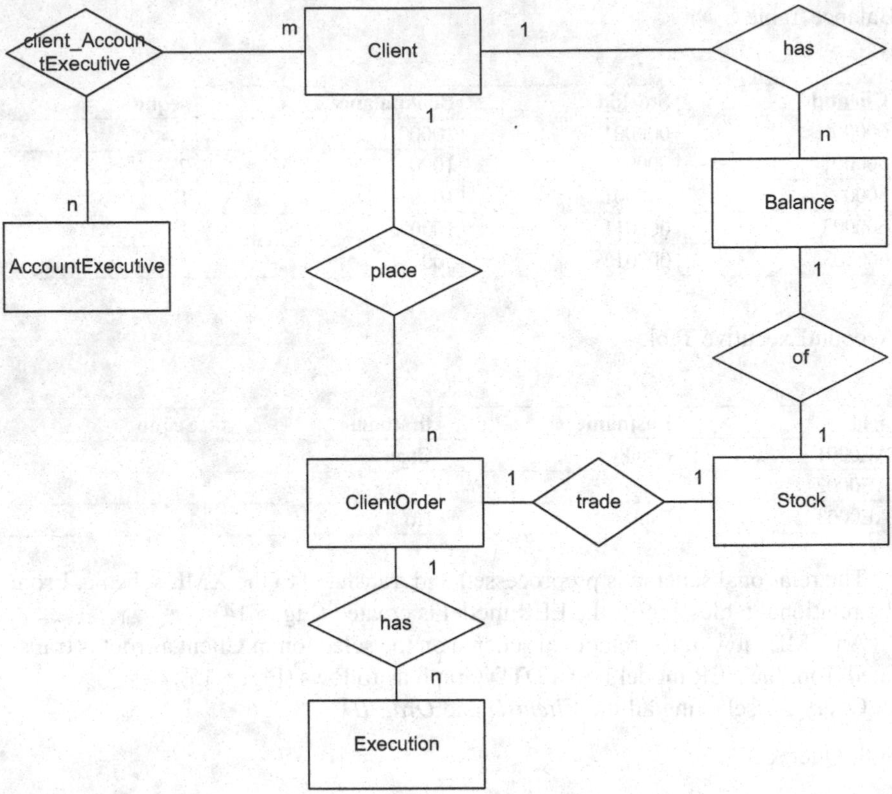

Fig. 5.14 EER Model of the relational tables

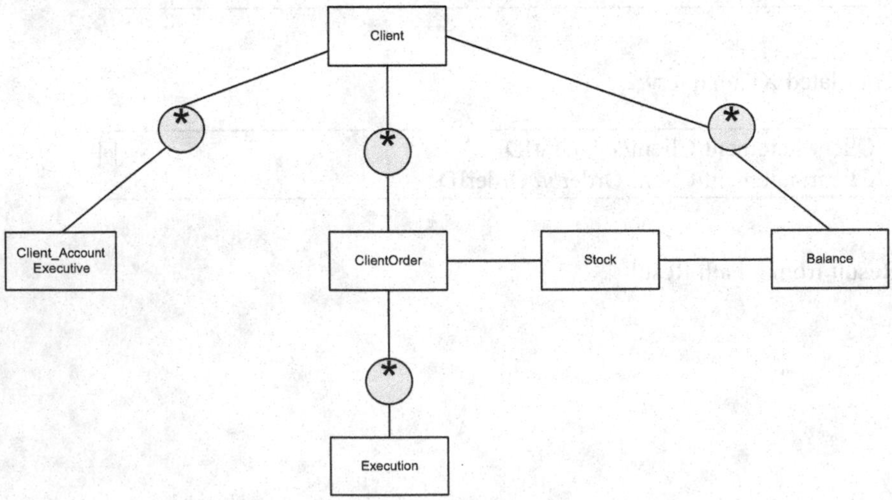

Fig. 5.15 An XML client view in EER model is mapped to a DTD

```
<Client ClientID="600001"
    <Order OrderID="300001"></Order>
</Client>
<Client ClientID="600002">
    <Order OrderID="300002"
    <Order OrderID="300005"
</Client>
<Client ClientID="600003">
    <Order OrderID="300003"
    <Order OrderID="300004"
</Client>
```

5.9 Summary

This chapter describes techniques in program translation, including rewriting, software interface, emulation, decompilation, and coexistence. Rewriting is to redevelop a new program, and is too costly. The software interface is to add a software layer atop of DBMS to translate source DML to target DML before run time processing. This technique results in additional work for DBA (database administrator).

Decompilation translates a lower-level DML to a higher-level DML, not feasible due to the nature of reverse engineering. Coexistence adds a target DBMS running parallel with the source DBMS. It is too labor-intensive and complicated for companies to support two DBMSs at the same time. Emulation translates source DML to target DML during run time. The technique is attractive due to its simplicity.

As a result of the above analysis, we decide, not to translate the hierarchical or network database DML to a relational database DML directly. Such translation is not possible at present. Instead, we adopt an indirect program translation to solve the problem. We will emulate embedded-SQL programs to hierarchical or network database programs. The benefit is for the users to write embedded-SQL programs to run against a hierarchical or network database. Such a process can let the users develop new programs in SQL while letting the old hierarchical or network database programs slowly get phased out.

The emulation includes transaction translation of Select, Join, Update, Modify, Insert, and Delete DML statements from SQL to IMS (hierarchical database DML) or IDMS (network database DML). The technique expands the non-procedural SQL to a series of procedural IMS or IDMS DMLs. Secondary indices are imposed on the hierarchical or network database for the purpose of eliminating database navigation in the translation process.

For transaction translation from SQL to OSQL or XQL, the query can be processed by mapping a non-procedural SQL DML to a navigational procedural OSQL DML or XQL according to the mapped OSQL or XQL query graph. The transaction translation can be processed by replacing foreign key updates with Stored OID (an OID stored in the database) update in OSQL, or to a navigation path in XPath.

Questions

Question 5.1

In database program translation, can we translate the higher-level database program into a lower-level database program or vice versa?

Answer:

A higher-level database program consists of a relatively rich and powerful database manipulation language such that a simple verb involves many movements. For example, a keyword Select in relational DML SQL means selecting multiple tuples from a relational database. However, a keyword Move in Hierarchical database DML means getting a record a time from Hierarchical database. Therefore, Select is a higher-level DML in relational database relatively when compared with Move as a low-level DML in Hierarchical database. In database program translation, it is much easier to translate from Select to Move, rather than vice versa. The reason is that translating a high DML to a low DML statement is to map a higher DML statement to multiple low DML statements, which is logically simple. On the other hand, the vice versa is much more complicated with the logic and also with many uncertainties for one to recover the higher-level DML SQL statement's original intention from a low-level DML DL/1 in Hierarchical database.

Question 5.2

Explain key propagation of Hierarchical database?

Answer

The Hierarchical database schema is in a top-down tree structure such that each parent record can be connected to multiple child records, but each child record is connected to one parent record only. Furthermore, the child record key must concatenate its parent record key. As a result, a child record key must concatenate its parent record key, and a grant child record key must concatenate the child record key plus its grant parent record, which is called key propagation because the concatenation of parent record can be propagated down to many levels of child record key and grant child record key, that is, a grant child record key must concatenate its parent record key, and its grant parent record key, all the way up to the top root record of a hierarchical database, which is called key propagation.

Bibliography

CA (1992a) Logical Record Facility of CA-IDMS/DB 12.0. Computer Associates International Limited

CA (1992b) SQL Reference of CA-IDMS/DB 12.0. Computer Associates International Limited

CA (1992c) Escape DL/1 user's guide. Computer Associates International Limited

Cattell RRG et al (eds) (1997) The object database standard: ODMG 2.0. Morgan Kaufmann Publishers

Fong J, Chitson P (1997) Query translation from SQL to OQL for database reengineering. Int J Inf Technol 3(1):83–101

Fong J, Ng W, Cheung SK, Au I (2006) Positioning-based query translation between SQL and XQL with location counter. Proceedings of APWeb2006 XRA06, Lecture notes in computer science, LNCS 3842, pp 11–18

Housel B (1977) A unified approach to program and data conversion. Proceedings of international conference on very large data base, pp 327–335

Katz R, Wong E (1982) Decompiling CODASYL DML into relational queries. ACM Trans Database Syst 7(1):1–23

Mark L, Roussopoulos N, Newsome T, Laohapipattana P (1992) Incrementally maintained network → relational database mapping. Softw Pract Exp 22(12):1099–1131

UniSQL (1992) UniSQL/X user's manual. UniSQL Inc

Zaniolo, C. (1979) Design of relational views over network schemas. Proceedings of ACM SIGMOD 79 Conference, pp 179–190

Zhang X, Fong J (2000) Translating update operations from relational to object-oriented databases. J Inf Softw Technol 42(3)

Bibliography

Chapter 6
Schemas Integration

Over the last two decades, a number of database systems have come into the market by using predominant data models: hierarchical, network, relational, object-oriented, and XML. As the performance of the Relational Database (RDB) is improved, it has been accepted by the industry and created the need of converting companies' hierarchical or network databases to RDB and XML. To meet users' requirements, there is a need to support various data models in a single platform. However, due to the implied constraints of the various data models, it is difficult for organizations to support heterogeneous database systems.

Survey results show that coexistence and integration of database systems is an option to solve the problem. These databases are created and managed by the various units of the organization for their own localized applications. Thus, the global view of all the data that is being stored and managed by the organization is missing. Schema integration is a technique to present such a global view of an organization's databases. There has been a lot of work done on schema integration. Batini et al. (1992) and Özsu amd Valduriez (1991) present surveys of work in this area. But all these techniques concentrate on integrating database schemas without taking into consideration new database applications. This chapter presents a practical approach to schema integration to support new database applications by comparing the existing databases against the data requirements of the new applications. If the existing databases are inadequate to support new applications, then they are evolved to support them.

Relational database system (RDB) has been dominant in the industry for the last two decades. Object-oriented database application (OODB) is recognized as a post-relational technology that can improve productivity. Hence, most companies need to enhance their existing relational database systems to support new object-oriented applications as and when needed. The current trend is to implement an object-relational database system (ORDB) using a relational engine with OO features. This chapter proposes a methodology to integrate existing ORDB systems based on user

J. S. P. Fong, K. Wong Ting Yan, *Information Systems Reengineering, Integration and Normalization*, https://doi.org/10.1007/978-3-030-79584-9_6

requirements. We can recover and verify schema semantics by data mining and store it in metadata. A frame model metadata is used to enforce constraints for solving semantic conflicts arising from schema integration. The frame model metadata is an object-relational like metadata that can specify static data semantic as well as dynamic data operation based on four relational tables.

6.1 Schemas Integration for Relational Databases

In any schema integration methodology, all the database schemas have to be specified using the same data model. The proposed approach uses an extended entity relationship (EER) data model. Therefore, the first step in the schema integration methodology is to translate a non-EER database schema to an EER database schema.

In our approach, a successful schema integration process should require the information capacity of the original schemas to be equivalent or dominated by the transformed schemas. To achieve this, we must prove that each proposed integrated process can preserve data semantics constraints to ensure information completeness. The following three major steps must be followed in its sequence. However, the sequence of sub-steps in each major step is immaterial.

Step 1. Resolve conflicts among conceptual schema in EER models.

Sub-step 1.1 Resolve conflicts on synonyms and homonyms

This step is subject to user input during the transformation process. The role, by definition, is the functional usage of an entity. However, to define the role, in the case of synonyms, either A.x or B.x dominates one another in their data type and size. The only trigger here is the user identification of its semantics equivalence. Similarly, once a user has identified that the attributes are of homonyms, the data types and their size can be redefined into a different data structure (Kwan and Fong 1999). (Fig. 6.1)

Rule 1:

IF A.x and B.x have different data types or sizes

THEN x in A and B may be homonyms, let users clarify x in A and B

ELSE IF x ≠ y, and A.x and B.y have the same data type and size

THEN ((x,y) may be synonyms, let users clarify (x, y));

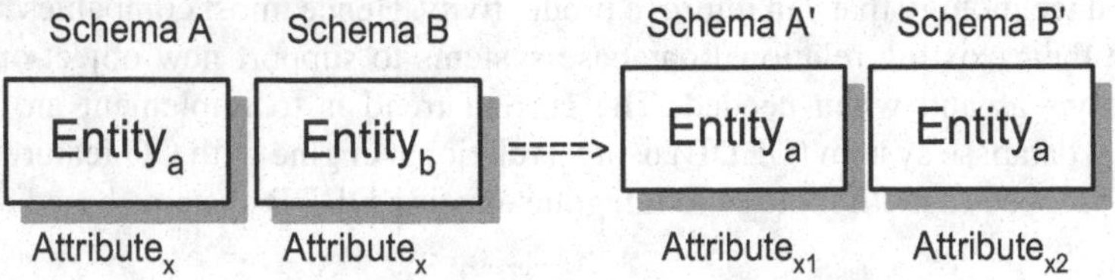

Fig. 6.1 EER model with synonyms and homonyms

(Note: Classa and Classb are synonyms, Attributex are homonym)

Sub-step 1.2 Resolve conflicts on data types

Case 1 conflict occurs when an attribute appears as an entity in another schema. Case 2 conflict occurs where a key appears as an entity in another schema and case 3 conflict occurs when a component key appears as an entity in another schema. To verify case 1, since the translation process has preserved the information capacity in both the original schema A and schema B into the transformed schema A = (A, R(A,A'), A'), the transformed schema A has proved to dominate original schemas. The transformation process is information preserved. This transformation mapping between schema A and schema B resolves conflicts on data types since schema B remains its original structure. The verification of case 2 and case 3 is similar for all cases that are transforming entities with attributes as an entity in another schema. The only difference is the cardinality between the created entity A' and the original entity. (Fig. 6.2)

Rule 2:

IF x ∈ (attribute(A) ∩ entity(B))
  THEN entity A' ← entity B such that cardinality (A, A') ← n:1
  ELSE IF x ∈ (keys(A) ∩ entity(B))
    THEN entity A' ← entity B such that cardinality (A, A') ← 1:1
    ELSE IF (x ⊂ keys(A)) ∩ (entity(B))
    THEN entity A' ← entity B such that cardinality(A, A') ← m:n

Sub-step 1.3 Resolve conflicts on key

The conflict exists where a key appears as a candidate key in another schema. The verification of this rule is subject to the users' input. Users will have to decide on whether schema B dominates schema A. If so, schema A will take the key of

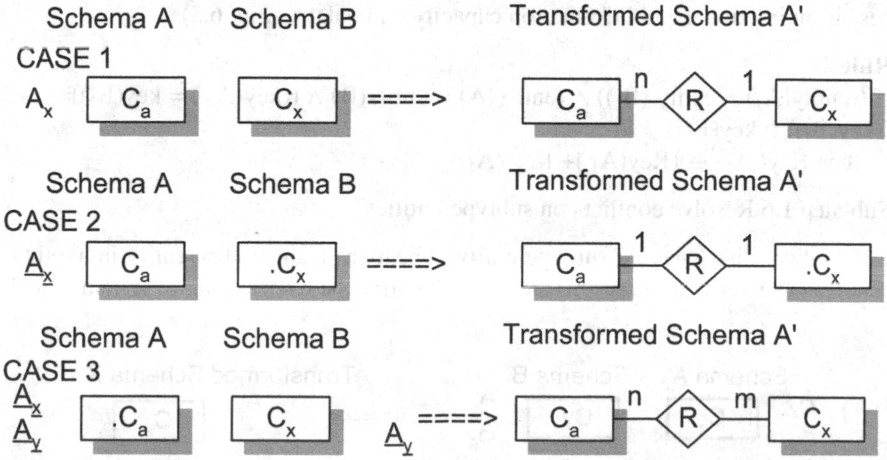

Fig. 6.2 EER model with data types conflicts in three cases

schema B as its own key, or vice versa. Hence, this translation process is information capacity preserved and bidirectional. (Fig. 6.3)

Rule 3:
IF x ∈(key(A) ∩ candidate_keys(B))
THEN let users clarify x in A and B

Sub-step 1.4 Resolve conflicts on cardinality

Conflict exists where identical entities are of different cardinality in two schemas. The verification of this step is subject to which schema has higher cardinality. Schema with higher cardinality naturally dominates the other schema with identical entities. Hence, higher cardinality will override the lower cardinality conflicts. This translation process is therefore information capacity equivalent and is bidirectional with the feasible recovery of original schema from transformed schema. (Fig. 6.4)

Rule 4:
IF (entity(A_1) = entity (B_1)) ∧ (entity(A_2) = entity (B_2)) ∧ (cardinality(A_1, A_2) = 1:1) ∧ (cardinality(B_1, B_2) = 1:n)
THEN cardinality(A_1, A_2) ← 1:n;
ELSE IF (entity(A_1) = entity(B_1)) ∧ (entity(A_2) = entity(B_2)) ∧ (cardinality(A_1, A_2) = 1:1 or 1:n) ∧ (cardinality(B_1, B_2) = m:n)
THEN cardinality(A_1, A_2) ← m:n;

Sub-step 1.5 Resolve conflicts on weak entities

Conflict occurs when a strong entity appears as a weak entity in another schema. The verification of this resolution step is subject to the interdependence between entities. The schema has a weak entity that is similar to another strong entity in another schema but with an additional key component from its strong entity. The former dominates the latter. Hence, a weak entity overrides the strong entity by transforming the strong entity to a weak entity for consistency. This translation process is bidirectional and information capacity equivalent. (Fig. 6.5)

Rule 5:
If ((entity(A_1) = entity (B_1)) ∧ (entity(A) = entity(B) ∧ ((key(A_2) = key(B_2))=0) ∧ ((key(B_1)) ∩ key(B_2)) ≠ 0)
then Key(A_2) ← (Key(A_1)+ Key (A_2))

Sub-step 1.6 Resolve conflicts on subtype entities

Conflict exists where a subtype entity appears as a super type entity in another schema. The verification of this step is to identify the overlapping of two identical

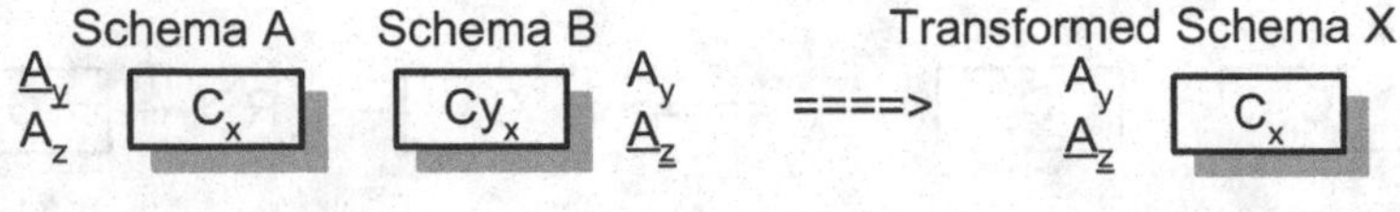

Fig. 6.3 EER models with key conflicts

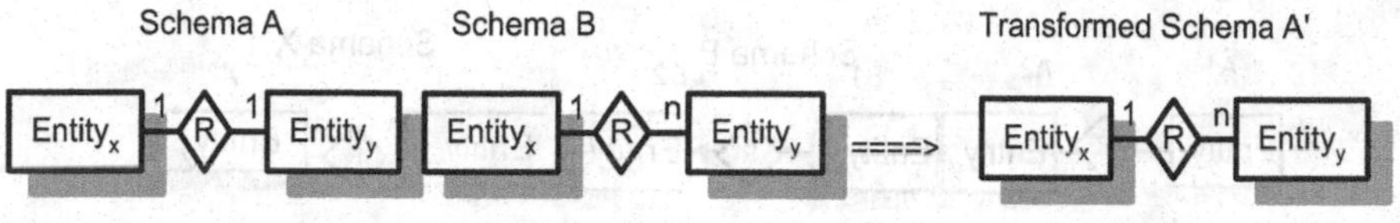

Fig. 6.4 EER model with cardinality conflicts

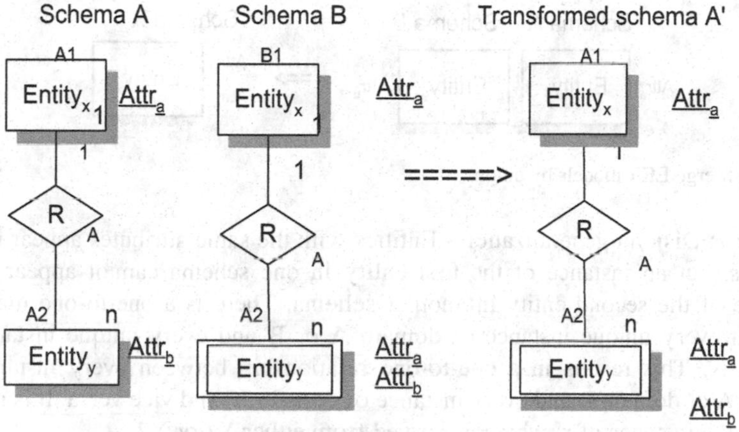

Fig. 6.5 EER model with weak entity conflict

entities in bidirectional in two different schemas. A1 isa A2 in one schema and A2 isa A1 in another schema. This translation process is transformed into the schema with 1:1 cardinality. (Fig. 6.6)

Rule 6:

IF ((entity(A_2) $\subseteq$ entity(A_1)) $\wedge$ (entity(B_1) $\subseteq$ entity(B_2)) $\wedge$ (entity (A_1) = entity (B_1)) $\wedge$ (entity (A_2)= entity (B_2)))

THEN begin entity $X^1 \leftarrow$ entity A^1

In step 2 and step 3, the transformation processes are totally based on their pre-condition without users' interference during the integration process.

Step 2. Merge entities.

Sub-step 2.1 Merge entities by union

In this step, there is a one-to-one mapping between every instance of domain A∪B and every instance of domain X and vice versa. (Fig. 6.7)

Rule 7:

IF ((domain(A) $\cap$ domain(B)) $\neq$ 0)

THEN domain(X) $\leftarrow$ (domain(A) $\cup$ domain(B))

Sub-step 2.2 Merge entities by generalization

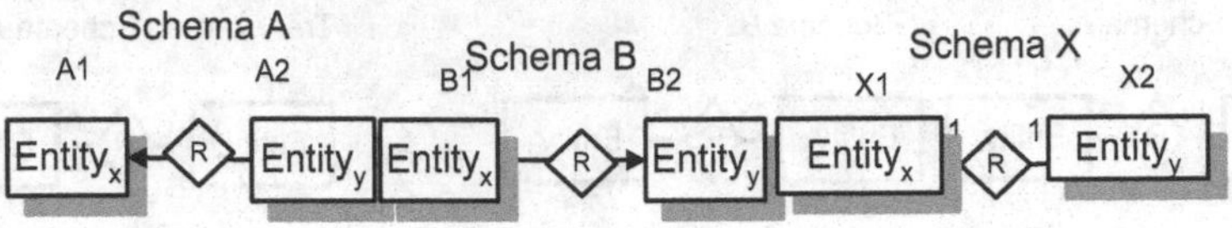

Fig. 6.6 EER model with subtype conflict

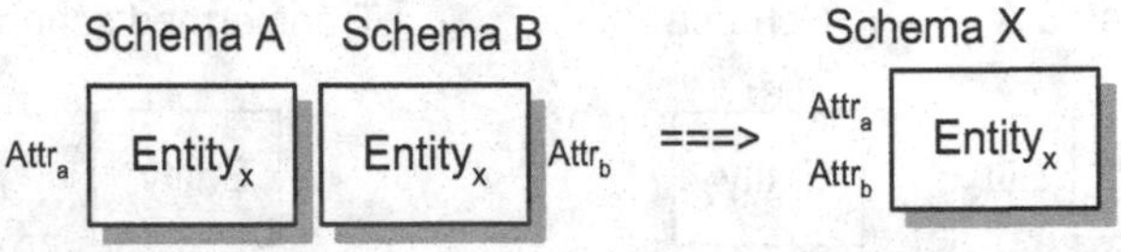

Fig. 6.7 Merge EER models by union

Case 1: Disjoint generalization - Entities with the same attributes appear in two schemas, but an instance of the first entity in one schema cannot appear as an instance of the second entity in another schema. There is a one-to-one mapping between every unique instance of domain A or B and every unique instance of domain X. This results in a one-to-one relationship between every instance of domain A or domain B and every instance of domain X, and vice versa. It is able to recover the instance of x, which is derived from either X1 or X2.

Case 2: Overlap generalization - Entities with the same attributes appear in two schemas, but an instance of the first entity in one schema can appear as an instance of the second entity in another schema. There is a one-to-one mapping between every unique instance of domain A and B and every unique instance of domain X. This results in a one-to-one relationship between every instance of domain A and B and every instance of domain X. It is able to recover the instance of x, which is derived from either domain A or B. (Fig. 6.8)

Rule 8:

IF ((domain(A) $\cap$ domain(B)) $\neq$ 0) $\wedge$ ((I(A) $\cap$I (B))=0)

THEN begin entity $X_1 \leftarrow$ entity A

entity $X_2 \leftarrow$ entity B

domain(X) $\leftarrow$ domain(A) $\cap$ domain(B)

(I (X_1) $\cap$ I(X_2))=0

end

ELSE IF ((domain(A) $\cap$ domain(B)) $\neq$ 0) $\wedge$ ((I(A) $\cap$I (B)) $\neq$ 0)

THEN begin entity $X_1 \leftarrow$ entity A

entity $X_2 \leftarrow$ entity B

domain(X) $\leftarrow$ domain(A) $\cap$ domain(B)

(I (X_1) $\cap$ I(X_2)) $\neq$ 0

end;

Sub-step 2.3 Merge entities by subtype relationship

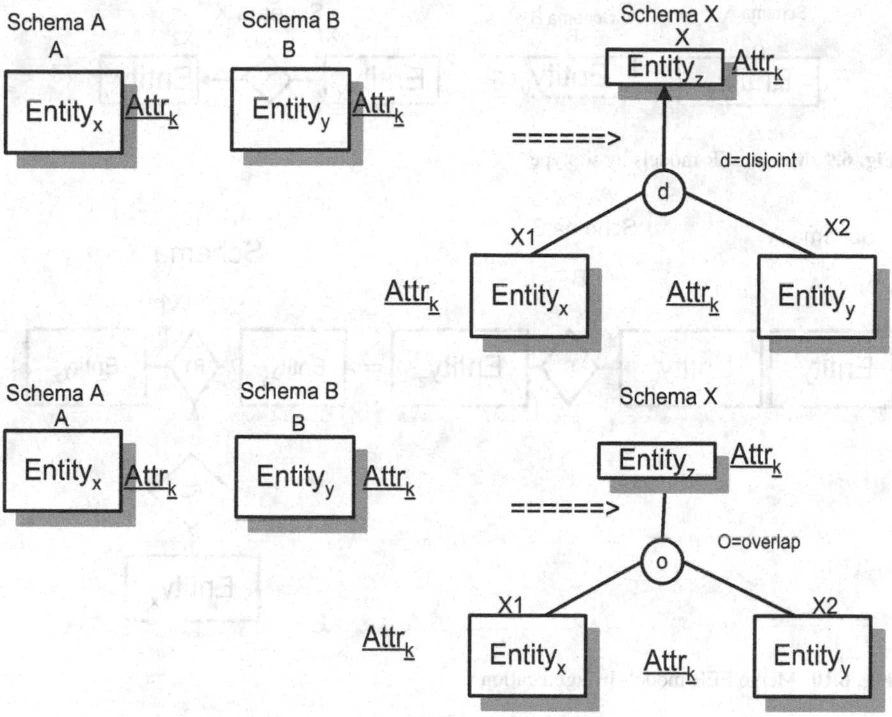

Fig. 6.8 Merge EER models by generalizations

There is a one-to-one relationship between every instance of domain A and every instance of domain X1 and between every instance of domain B and every instance of domain X2. It is able to recover the instance of x, which is derived from either A or B. The practical recovery search logic is that any element that does not exist in domain B will be in domain A only, and any element that exists in domain B will be also in domain A. (Fig. 6.9)

Rule 9:

IF domain(A) $\subset$ domain(B)

THEN begin entity $X_1 \leftarrow$ entity A

entity $X_2 \leftarrow$ entity B

entity X_1 isa entity X_2

end;

Sub-step 2.4 Merge entities by aggregation

X is an aggregation of B1, B2, and R(B). Entity A and entity B and their relationships are preserved in the transformed schema X. There is a bidirectional one-to-one mapping between elements of A, (B1, B2, R(B)) and (X1, X2, R(X)) by introducing a common key field. It is able to recover the instance of x, which is derived from either B1 or B2. X1 dominates the (B1and B2) to ensure that

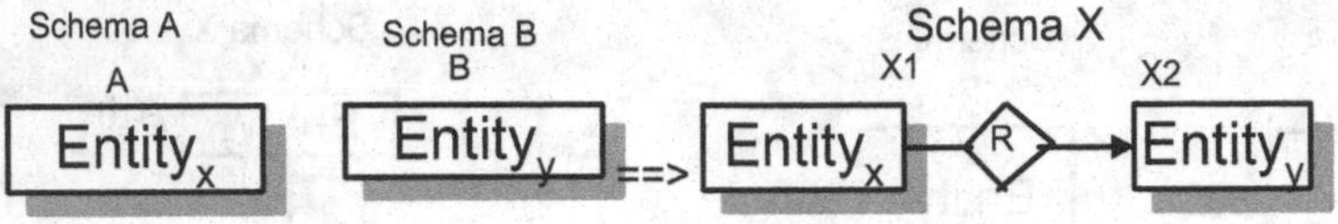

Fig. 6.9 Merge EER models by subtype

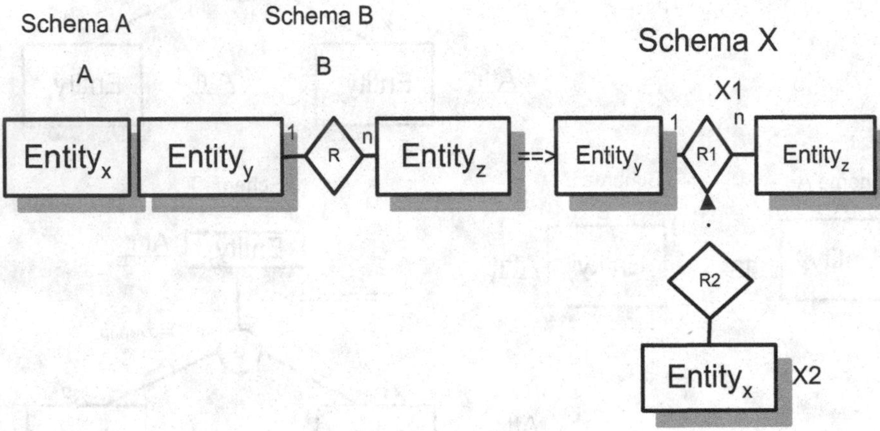

Fig. 6.10 Merge EER models by aggregation

information is preserved after the schema is transformed and X is proved to be equivalent to (A,B). (Fig. 6.10)

Rule 10:

IF relationship B →→ entity A /*MVD →→ means multi-value dependency/
THEN begin aggregation X_1 ← (entity B_1 , relationship B, entity B_2)
entity X_2 ← entity A
cardinality (X_1, X_2) ← 1:n
end;

Sub-step 2.5 Merge entities by categorization

X provides a view to schema A and schema B. X1 is a union of A1 and A2. There is a one-to-one mapping between every unique instance of domain A1 or A2 and every instance of domain X1. Entity X1 dominates entity (A1, A2) ⇒ entity (A1, A2) ≤ entity X1, entity X2 dominates entity B ⇒ entity B ≤ entity X2 to ensure that there is no information loss during transformation. It is able to recover the instance of x1, which can be derived from either A1 or A2. (Fig. 6.11)

Rule 11:

IF $(I(B) \subset I(A_1)) \vee (I(B) \subset I(A_2))$
THEN begin entity X_2 ← entity B
entity X_{c1} ← entity A_1
entity X^{c2} ← entity A^2

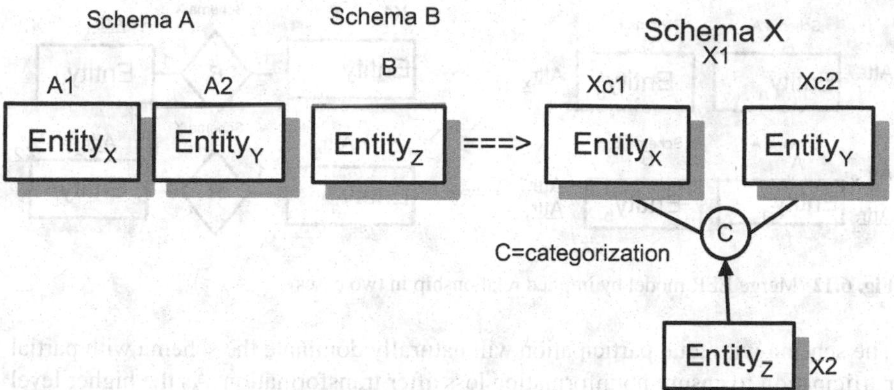

Fig. 6.11 Merge schemas into categorization

categorisation $X_1 \leftarrow$ (entity X_{c1} , entity X_{c2})
$(I(X_2)$ isa $I(Xc_1)) \vee (I(X_2)$ isa $I(Xc_2))$
/* X_2 is subtype to X_{c1} or X_{c2} */
end;

Sub-step 2.6 Merge entities by implied binary relationship

X provides a view to A and B. There is a mapping between every unique instance of entity A and B and every instance of entity X. There is a common field of entity key to enabling relationships built at each pair of instances in the entity (A,B) and instance in entity X . It is able to recover the instance of entity X, which is derived from the entity(A, B). (Fig. 6.12)

Rule 12:
IF x $\in$ (attribute(A) $\cap$ key(B))
THEN begin entity $X_1 \leftarrow$ entity A
entity $X_2 \leftarrow$ entity B
cardinality $(X_1, X_2) \leftarrow$ n:1
end
ELSE IF ((attribute(A) $\cap$ key(B)) $\neq 0$) $\wedge$ ((attribute(B) $\cap$ key(A)) $\neq 0$)
THEN begin entity $X_1 \leftarrow$ entity A
entity $X_2 \leftarrow$ entity B
cardinality $(X_1, X_2) \leftarrow$ 1:1
end;

Step 3. Merge relationships.

Sub-step 3.1 Merge relationships by subtype relationship

Case 1: Two relationships A, B are in the same role with different levels of participation. The verification of this step is to identify the participation of two identical schemas A and B with different levels of participation but with the same role.

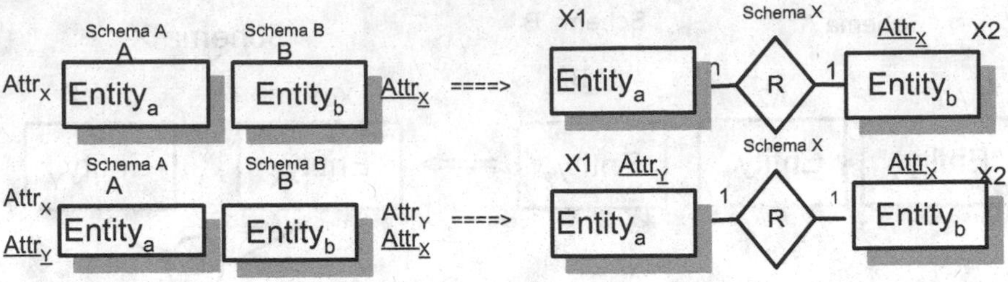

Fig. 6.12 Merge EER model by implied relationship in two cases

The schema with total participation will naturally dominate the schema with partial participation to ensure no information loss after transformation. As the higher level of participation has absorbed the lower level of participation in the transformed schema with a new entity and relationship created, no alteration of data semantics is necessary.

Case 2: Two relationships have different semantics but with an intersecting relationship. The verification of this step is to identify two relationships that have different semantics but with an intersecting relationship. The schema which has overlapping relationships of different kinds of semantics would naturally dominate these schemas by assigning an overlap generalization relationship to its intersecting schemas. Hence, information about its original semantics and relationships should both be preserved. (Fig. 6.13)

Rule 13:

/* Case 1 */

IF (entity(A_1) = entity(B_1)) ∧ (entity(A_2) = entity(B_2)) ∧ (participation(A_1 , A) = total) ∧(participation(B_1 ,B) = partial)

THEN begin entity X^1 ← entity A^1

entity X_2 ← entity A_2

entity X_3 isa entity X_1

relationship X ← entity($X_{3,}$ X_2)

participation(X_3, X) ← total

end

ELSE

/* Case 2 */

IF (entity (A_1)=entity(B_1)) ∧ (entity(A_2) = entity(B_2)) ∧((relation(A) ∩ relation(B)) ≠ 0)

THEN begin entity X^1 ← entity A^1

entity X^2 ← entity A^2

entity X^3 isa entity X^2

entity X^4 isa entity X^2;

relationship Xa ← Relationship A

relationship Xb ←Relationship B

end

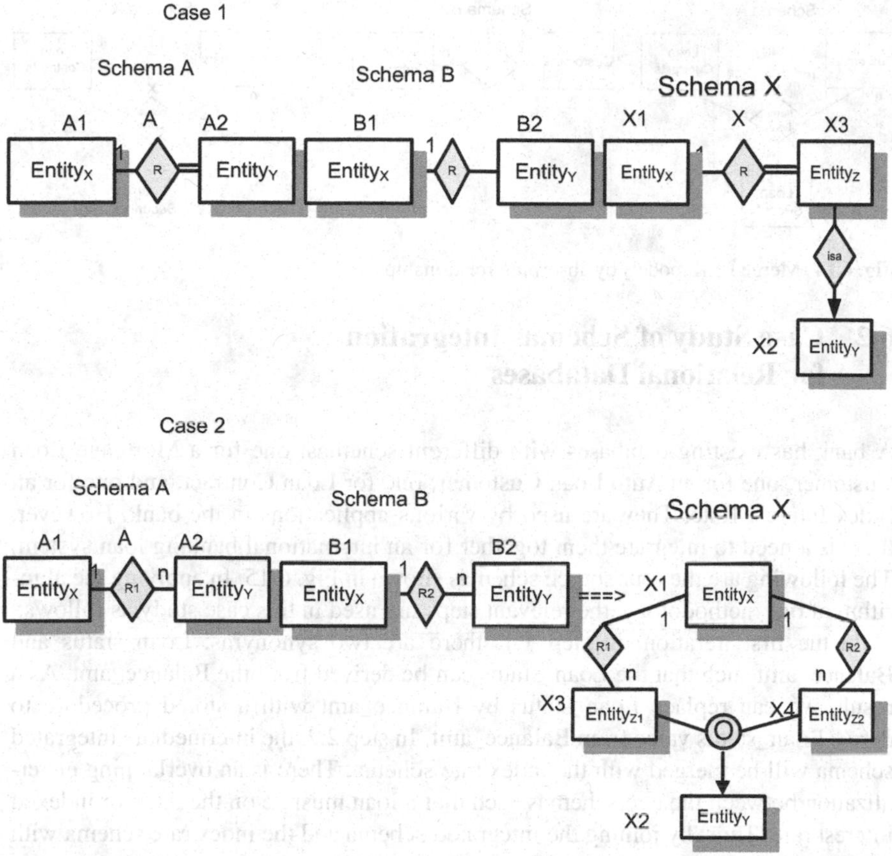

Fig. 6.13 Merge EER models by subtype relationship

Sub-step 3.2 Absorbing a lower degree relationship into a higher degree relationship

This step is to identify the inconsistent degree level of two identical entities in different schema A and B. The schema with the higher degree naturally dominates the schema with the lower degree to ensure that there is no information loss after transformation. This translation process is to absorb the schema with the lower degree relationship by the schema with the higher degree relationship. (Fig. 6.14)

Rule 14:

IF ((relationship(A) ⊃ relationship (B) ∧ (degree(A) > degree(B)) ∧(entity(A1)=entity(B1)) ∧ (entity (A2)=entity (B2))

THEN begin relationship(X) ← relationship(A)

entity X1 ← entity A1

entity X2 ← entity A2

entity X3 ← entity A3

end;

.

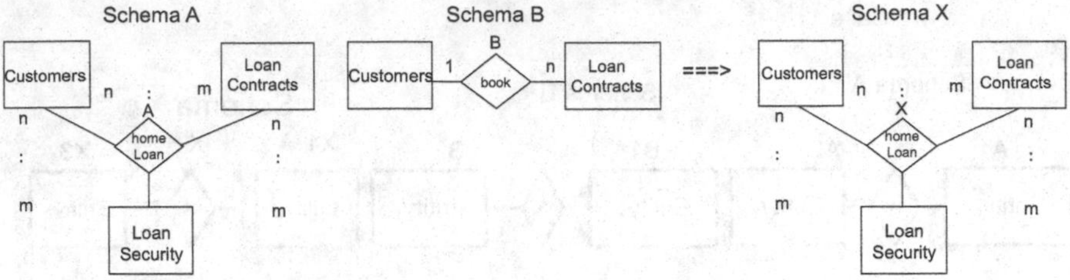

Fig. 6.14 Merge EER models by absorbing relationships

6.2 Case Study of Schemas Integration for Relational Databases

A bank has existing databases with different schemas: one for a Mortgage Loan Customer, one for an Auto Loan Customer, one for Loan Contract, and one for an Index Interest Rate. They are used by various applications in the bank. However, there is a need to integrate them together for an international banking loan system. The following are the four source schemas shown in Fig. 6.15. In applying the algorithm of our methodology, the relevant steps are used in this case study as follows:

In the first iteration, in step 1.1, there are two synonyms: Loan_status and Balance_amt such that the Loan_status can be derived from the Balance_amt. As a result, we can replace Loan_status by Balance_amt with a stored procedure to derive Loan_status value from Balance_amt. In step 2.2, the intermediate integrated schema will be merged with the index rate schema. There is an overlapping generalization between the two schemas such that a loan must be on the fixed or indexed interest rate. Thus, by joining the integrated schema and the index rate schema with overlap generalization, the two schemas can be integrated.

In the second iteration, in step 2.6, there is an implied relationship between the Loan Contract schema and (Mortgage loan) Customer segment such that ID# is used as an attribute in loan schema but as an entity key in customer schema. Thus, we can derive cardinality from the implied relationship between these entities, and integrate the two schemas into one EER model.

In the third iteration, in step 2.6, there is an implied relationship between the Loan Contract schema and (Auto loan) Customer segment and integrate the two schemas into one EER model. In step 3.1, the relationships between the loan contract and the two customer entities can be merged into an overlap generalization as shown in Fig. 6.16.

6.3 Schema Integration for Object-Relational Databases

The relational database system (RDB) has been dominant in the industry for the last two decades. Object-oriented database application (OODB) is recognized as a post-relational technology that can improve productivity. Hence, most companies need to

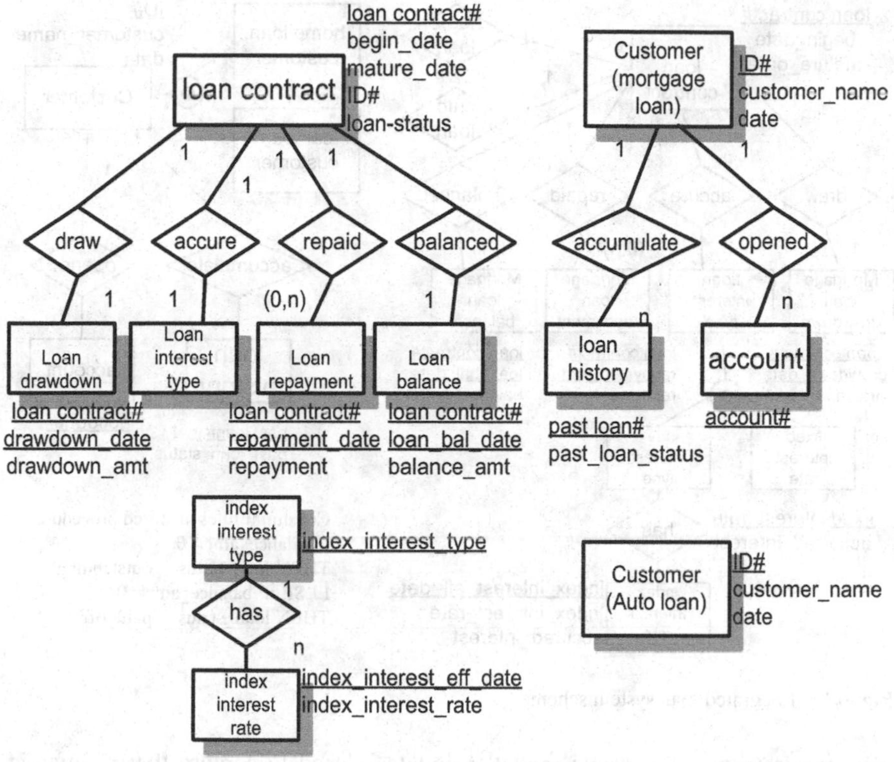

Fig. 6.15 EER models of the loan system

enhance their existing relational database systems to support new object-oriented applications as and when needed. The trend of the current industrial is to implement an object-relational database system (ORDB) using a relational engine with OO features. This section proposes a methodology to integrate existing ORDB based on user requirements. Frame metadata is used to enforce constraints for solving semantic conflicts arising from schema integration. The metadata is object-relational metadata that can specify static data semantics as well as dynamic data operation based on four relational tables.

In order to have coherence between new OO database applications and the existing database systems, leading database manufacturers gradually modify their relational database system to support OO features. It results in the so-called object-relational database management System (ORDBMS) in the current market. Most of these ORDBMS are powered by a relational database engine with extensions to the OO interface and features. When designing a database using these systems, a user employs either a relational view with some OO features or uses an OO view under a relational core. We propose a practitioner approach to integrate this kind of ORDBMS. A simplified schema integration technique is applied to the source database schemas, either in relational or object-oriented structure, based on

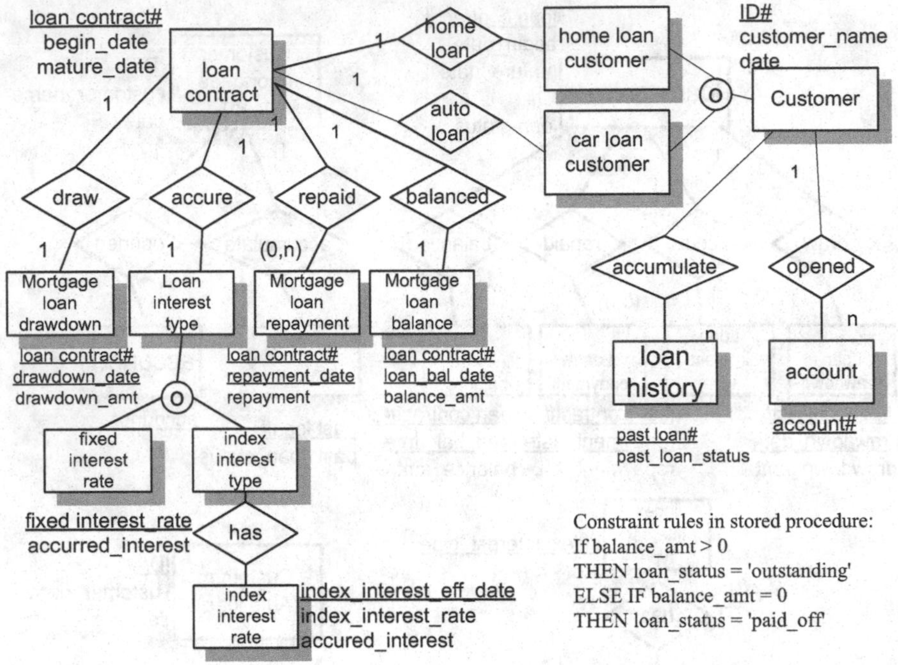

Fig. 6.16 Integrated loan system schema

user requirements. The frame model metadata is used to capture these semantic constraints and other abstractions result from the integration. The resultant system is an integrated schema of the object-relational database system (Fong 2000).

Frame Model Metadata The frame model metadata follows an object-oriented paradigm, based on frame. All conceptual entities are modeled as objects and group in object types called classes. The frame model metadata is implemented with a knowledge representation schema that represents the taxonomy inheritance structure (i.e., abstract relationship), properties of objects (i.e. classes and attributes), and the relationship between those objects in a standardized form. The details can be referred in Fig. 7.2 in Chapter 7.

Schema integration provides a global view of multiple schemas. Our approach uses a bottom-up approach to integrate an existing database into a global database by pairs. The main objective is to provide an integrated schema based on user requirements with no loss of information. The general algorithm is as follows:

Begin
For each existing database do
        Begin
    If its conceptual schema does not exist
            then reconstruct its conceptual schema by reverse engineering;
            For each pair of existing database schema A and schema B do

```
        begin
      resolve semantic conflicts between schema A and schema B;
      /*step1*/
   Merge classes/entities and relationship relations between schema
      A and B;
      /*step2a*/
  Capture and resolve the semantic constraints arising from
  integration using Frame Model metadata
      /*step2b*/
            end
            end
   end
```

The input schemas must analyze in pairs and resolve semantic conflicts in different areas. Conflicts are resolved using well-defined semantic rules with user supervisions. Classes are merged by union or abstractions like subtype, generalization, aggregation, and others. To demonstrate this step, UML diagrams are used to represent the conceptual schema of relational and object-oriented, respectively. The constraints arising from the integration are then captured and enforced in the frame model metadata. The details of each of the above steps are demonstrated as follows.

Step 1. Identify and resolve the semantics integrity conflicts among input schemas.

Input: Schema A and B with classes and attributes in conflict with each other on semantics.

Output: Integrated Schema Y after data transformation.

In dealing with definition-related conflicts like inconsistency in keys or synonyms/homonyms in names, user supervision is essential. For instance, two entities may have some candidate keys overlapping with each other but using different keys as the primary key. The user has to clarify this kind of situation.

On the other hand, for conflicts arising from structural differences, the goal is to capture as much information from the input schemas as possible. The most conservative approach is to capture the superset from the schemas. For example, in dealing with cardinality, the cardinality of the same relationship relation in schema A is 1:1 while the other one in schema B is 1:n. Since a 1:n relationship is the superset of a 1:1 relationship, the 1:n cardinality is used for the integrated relation. Another example is the participation constraint. If the same relationship relation in different schemas has different levels of participation constraints, partial participation always overrides total participation in the integrated schema. It is because total participation is a subset of partial participation.

When dealing with data type and subtype conflicts, the association/relationship relation is used for resolution. To illustrate this, assume we have an attribute *Department* of the entity *School* in one schema and an entity *Department* in another schema. To resolve the data type conflict, a 1:n relationship is formed in the integrated schema to link up these two entities.

Step 2. Merge classes and relationships into frame model metadata

Input: Existing schema A and B

Output: Merged (integrated) schema X with semantic constraints captured by frame model metadata

Classes are merged using the union operator if their domain is the same. Otherwise, abstractions are used under careful user supervision. By examining the same keys with the same class name in different database schemas, we can merge the entities by union. The integrated class takes all the attributes from both entities. Abstractions like generalization and aggregation are used in merging classes in different input schemas when they fulfill the semantic condition. The details are as follows.

Sub-step 2.1 Merge associations by capturing cardinality

The integration can be based on the richer data semantics of 1:n association and which can be specified in the cardinality attribute of the Attribute class in the frame model metadata. (Fig. 6.17)

Rule 1:

IF (class(A_1) = class (B_1)) ∧ (class(A_2) = class (B_2)) ∧
(cardinality(A_1, A_2) = 1:1) ∧ (cardinality(B_1, B_2) = 1:n)
THEN cardinality(A_1, A_2) ← 1:n;
ELSE IF (class(A_1) = class(B_1)) ∧ (class(A_2) = class(B_2)) ∧
(cardinality(A_1, A_2) = 1:1 or 1:n) ∧ (cardinality(B_1, B_2) = m:n)
THEN cardinality(A_1, A_2) ← m:n;

Frame Model Metadata Implementation
Header class

Class Name	Parents	Primary key	Operation	Class Type
X	0	A_1		Static
Y	0	A_3		Static

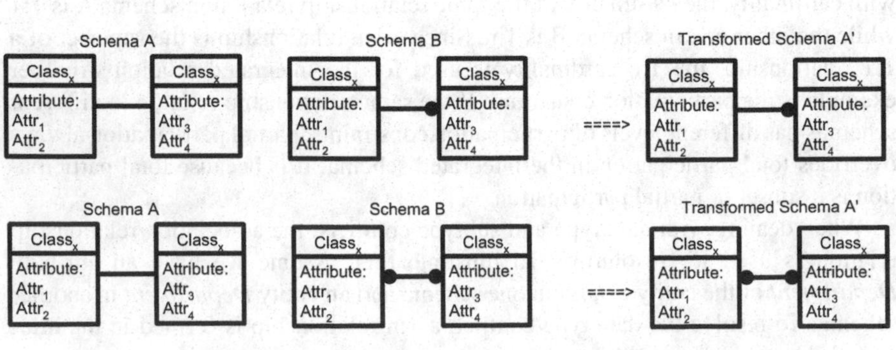

Fig. 6.17 Merge classes by associations

Attribute class

Attribute Name	Class Name	Method_ Name	Attribute Type	Default Value	Cardinality	Description
A[1]	X		String			Attribute
A[2]	X		String, Y		1	Pointer to Y
A[3]	Y		String, X		N	Attribute, Pointer to X
A[4]	Y		String			Attribute

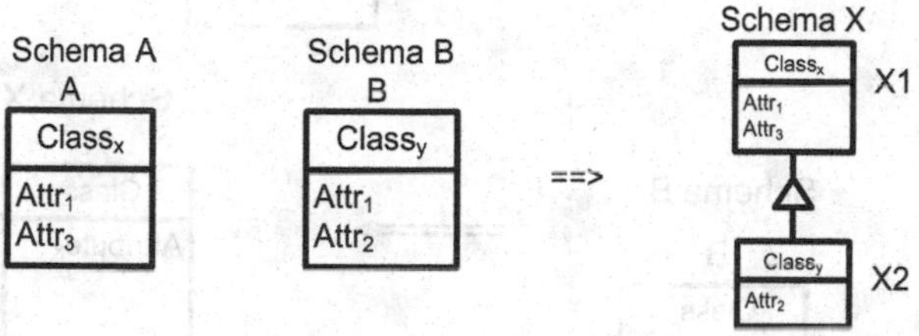

Fig. 6.18 Merge classes by subtype class

Sub-step 2.2 Merge classes by subtype

The integration can be based on the subtype relationship between two classes and that can be specified in the Parent attribute of the Header class in the frame model metadata. (Fig. 6.18)

Rule 2:

IF domain(A) $\subset$ domain(B)

THEN begin Class(X_1) $\leftarrow$ Class(A)

Class(X_2) $\leftarrow$ Class(B)

Class(X_1) isa Class(X_2)

End;

Frame Model Metadata

Header class

Class Name	Parents	Primary key	Operation	Class Type
Y	X	A_1		Static
X	0	A_1		Static

Attribute class

Attribute Name	Class Name	Method Name	Attribute Type	Default Value	Cardinality	Description
Y	A_1		Integer			Superclass primary key
Y	A_2		Date			Subclass non-key attribute
X	A_3		Date			Superclass non-key attribute

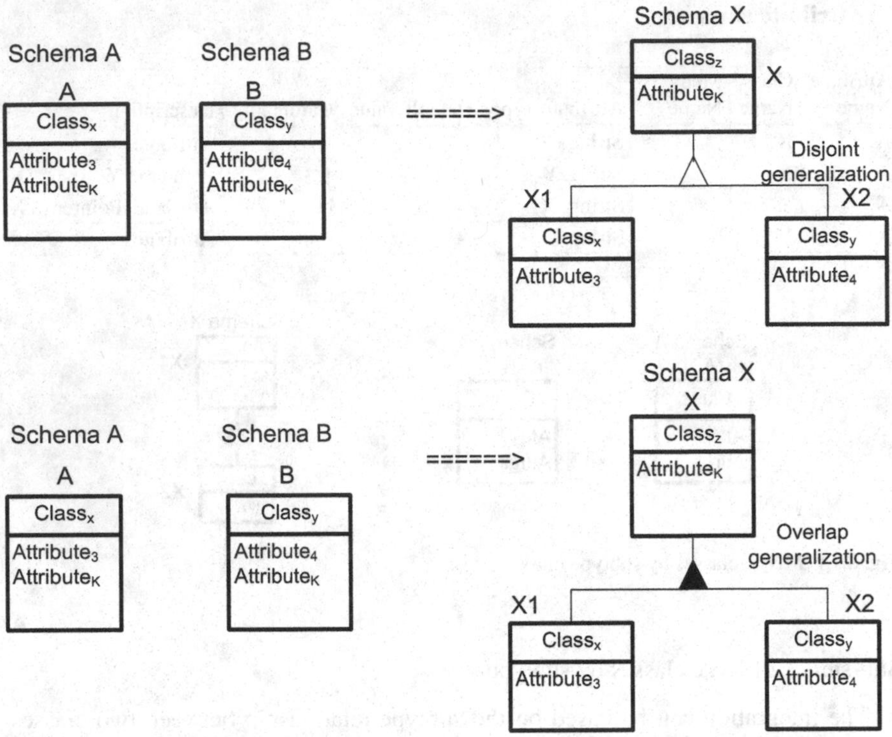

Fig. 6.19 Merge classes by generalization

Sub-step 2.3 Merge classes by generalization

The integration can be based on the subtype relationship between two subclasses and one superclass and which can be specified in the Parent attribute of the Header class and the method class in the frame model metadata. (Fig. 6.19)

Rule 3:

IF ((domain(A) ∩ domain(B)) ≠ 0) ∧ ((I(A) ∩ I(B))=0)
  THEN begin Class(X_1) ← Class(A)
      Class($X_{2)}$ ← Class(B)
      Domain(X) ← domain(A) ∩ domain(B)
      (I (X_1) ∩ I(X_2))=0 /* disjoint generalization
    end
  ELSE IF ((domain(A) ∩ domain(B)) ≠ 0) ∧ ((I(A) ∩ I(B)) ≠ 0)
    THEN begin Class(X_1) ← Class(A)
        Class(X_2) ← Class(B)
        domain(X) ← domain(A) ∩ domain(B)
        (I (X_1) ∩ I(X_2)) ≠ 0 /* overlap generalization
      end;

Frame Model Metadata Implementation

Header class

Class Name	Parents	Primary key	Operation	Class Type
Z	A_k	0		Static
X	A_k	Z	Call Ins_X	Active
Y	A_k	Z	Call Ins_Y	Active

Attribute class

Attribute Name	Class Name	Method 000000000Name	Attribute Type	Default Value	Cardinality	Description
Z	A_k		Integer			Superclass primary key
X	A_3		Date			Subclass non-key attribute
Y	A_4		Date			Subclass non-key attribute

Constraint class

Constraint_ Name	Method_ Name	Class_ Name	Parameters	Ownership	Event	Sequence	Timing
Ins_X	Insert_X	X	A_k	Self	Insert	before	Repeat
Ins_Y	Insert_Y	Y	A_k	Self	Insert	before	Repeat

Method class

Method_ Name	Class_ name	Parameter	Seq_ no	Condition	Action	Description
Insert_X	X	@A_k		If (Select * from Y where A_k = (@A_k) = null	Insert X (@ A_k, A_3)	
Insert_Y	Y	@A_k		If (Select * from X where A_k = @A_k) = null	Insert Y (@ A_k, A_4)	

Sub-step 2.4 Merge classes by aggregation

In the object-oriented view, aggregation provides a convenient mechanism for modeling the relationship *IS_PART_OF* between objects. By extending the semantics of slot values, an attribute stores either the reference of another object or a copy of that object to make it a composite value. An object becomes dependent upon another if the dependent object is referred to by an attribute in the "parent" object. When an object is deleted, all dependent objects it is related to are also deleted. Since the implementations of this abstraction are different in relational and OO models, the merging procedures are different as well. (Fig. 6.20)

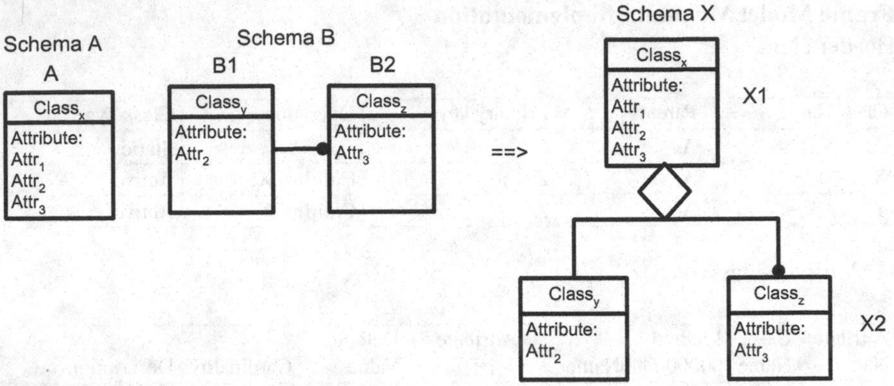

Fig. 6.20 Merge classes by aggregation

Rule 4:

If Domain (Key(B1)) ⊂ Domain (Attr(A)) AND
Domain (Key(B2)) ⊂ Domain (Attr(A))
THEN begin aggregation(X_1) ← Class(A)
Class(X_2)← Class(B1, association, B2)
End;

Frame Model Metadata Implementation

Header class

Class Name	Parents	Primary key	Operation	Class Type
X	A_1	0	Call Del_X, Ins_X	Active
Y	A_2	X		Static
Z	A_3	Y		Static

Attribute class

Attribute Name	Class Name	Method_ Name	Attribute Type	Default Value	Cardinality	Description
X	A_1		Integer		1	Superclass primary key
X	A_2		Y		1	Attribute pointer to Y
X	A_3		Z		N	Attribute pointer to Z
Y	A_2		Date		1	Superclass non-key attribute
Z	A_3		Date		N	Subclass non-key attribute

Constraint class

Constraint_ Name	Method_ Name	Class_ Name	Parameters	Ownership	Event	Sequence	Timing
Del_X	X	Delete_X	A_1, A_2, A_3	Self	Delete	Before	Repeat
Ins_X	X	Insert_X	A_1, A_2, A_3	Self	Insert	Before	Repeat

Method class

Method_ Name	Class_ name	Parameter	Seq_ no	Condition	Action	Description
Delete_X	X	@A_1, @A_2, @A_3			Delete from Z where A_3 = @A_3 Delete from Y where A_2 = @A_2 Delete from X where A_1 = @A_1	
Insert_X	X	@A_1, @A_2, @A_3		If ((Select * from Y where A_2=@A_2) <> Null) AND ((Select * from Z where A_3=@A_3) <> Null)	Insert X (@ A_1, @A_2, @A_3)	

6.4 Case Study of Object-Relational Schemas Integration

In a bank, there are existing databases with different schemas: one for the local mortgage customers, another for overseas banking customers, and one for local car loan customers. They are used by various applications in the bank. However, there is a need to integrate them into an international banking loan system. Assume the schema integration has to be done in both the relational representation as well as the OO representation. The following are the input schemas and final integrated schema for both models followed by the one frame model metadata representing the integrated schema of both models. (Figs. 6.21 and 6.22)

Frame Model Metadata:

Header class

Class Name	Parents	Primary key	Operation	Class Type
Customer	0	Cust_ID	Call Del_Cust	Static
Local Customer	Customer	Cust_ID	Call Ins_Local, Del_Local	Active
Oversea Customer	Customer	Cust_ID	Call Ins_Overseas	Static
Car Loan Customer	Local Customer	Cust_ID		Active
Home Loan Customer	Local Customer	Cust_ID		Active
Car Loan	Loan_Contract #	0		Static
Mortgage	Loan_Contract #	0		Static

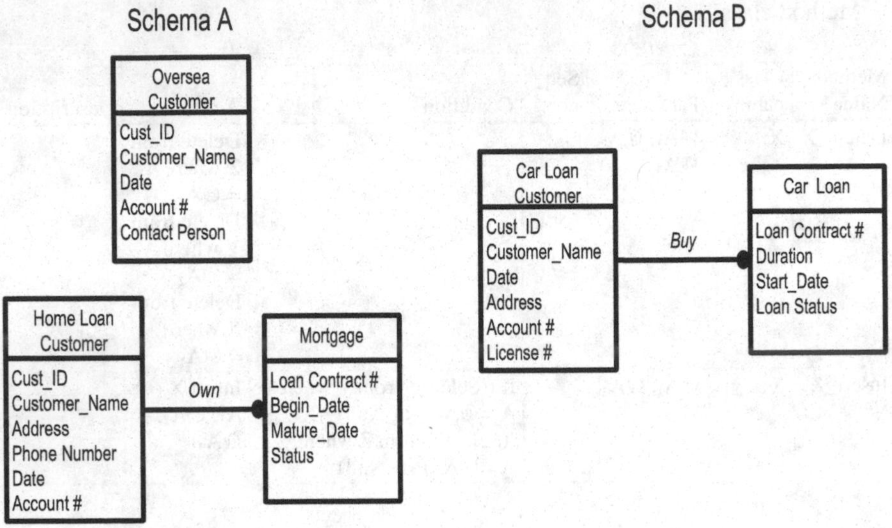

Fig. 6.21 Object-relational schemas to be integrated

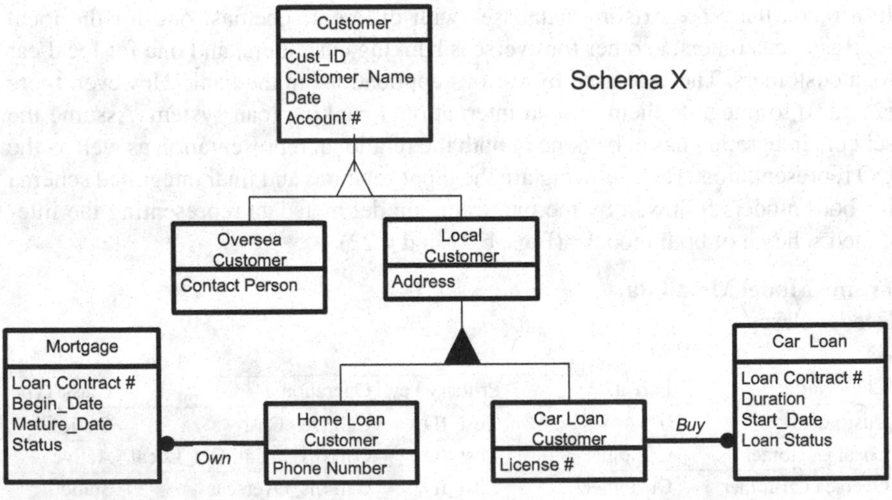

Fig. 6.22 Integrated object-relational schemas for loan system

Attribute class

Attribute Name	Class Name	Method Name	Attribute Type	Default Value	Cardinality	Description
Customer	Cust_ID		String			Superclass Key Attribute
Customer	Customer_ Name		String			Attribute
Customer	Date		Date			Attribute
Customer	Account #		String			Attribute
Local Customer	Address		String			Attribute
Oversea Customer	Contact_ Person		String			Attribute
Car Loan Customer	License #		String			Attribute
Home Loan Customer	Phone_ Number		Numeric			Attribute
Car Loan	Loan_ Contract #		String			Key Attribute
Car Loan	Duration		Integer	1		Attribute
Car Loan	Start_Date		Date			Attribute
Car Loan	Loan_ Status		String			Attribute
Mortgage	Loan_ Contract #		String			Key Attribute
Mortgage	Begin_ Date		Date			Attribute
Mortgage	Mature_ Date		Date			Attribute
Mortgage	Status		String			Attribute

Constraint class

Constraint_ Name	Method_ Name	Class_ Name	Parameters	Ownership	Event	Sequence	Timing
Del_Cust	Customer	Delete_ Customer	Cust_ID	Self	Delete	Before	Repeat
Ins_Local	Local Customer	Insert_ Local	Cust_ID	Self	Insert	Before	Repeat
Del_Local	Local Customer	Delete_ Local	Cust_ID	Self	Delete	Before	Repeat
Ins_ Overseas	Overseas Customer	Insert_ Overseas	Cust_ID	Self	Insert	Before	Repeat

Method class

Method_ Name	Class_ name	Parameter	Seq_ no	Condition	Action	Description
Delete_ Customer	Customer	@ Cust_ID		If (Select * from Local_ Customer where Cust_ID = @Cust_ID) then call Del_Local If (Select * from Oversea where Cust_ID = @ Cust_ID) then Delete Oversea_Customer(Cust_ ID)	Delete Customer (@Cust_ID)	
Insert_ Local	Local Customer	@ Cust_ID		If (Select * from Oversea_Customer where Cust_ID = @Cust_ID) = null	Insert Local_ Customer (@Cust_ID)	
Delete_ Local	Local Customer	@ Cust_ID		If (Select * from Car_ Loan_Customer where Cust_ID = @Cust_ID) then Delete Car_Loan_ Customer(Cust_ID) If (Select * from Home_Loan_Customer where Cust_ID = @ Cust_ID) then Delete Home_Loan_ Customer(Cust_ID)	Delete Local_ Customer (@Cust_ID)	
Insert_ Oversea	Overseas Customer	@ Cust_ID		If (Select * from Local_Customer where Cust_ID = @Cust_ID) = null	Insert Overseas_ Customer (@Cust_ID)	

6.5 Schemas Integration for XML Documents

We need to integrate XML schemas before we integrate XML documents because the integrated XML document must be compatible with the data structure of the integrated XML schemas. Since XML schema is in a tree structure which is top-down from root parent element to branch child sub-elements, in a fan out one-to-many structure. Furthermore, XML schema can use pointers to link associated elements together. For example, we can implement many-to-many cardinality data semantic by creating 3 sibling elements such that a middle sibling element pointing to the other two sibling elements. Each pointer links two elements together to form a one-to-many cardinality with the pointer element on the "many" side, and the pointed element on the "one" side. Two pairs of one-to-many elements with the same "many" side element can form a many-to-many cardinality between the two elements on the "one" side.

When we integrate XML schemas, we must locate their connectivity according to their relevance. Simple relevancy is to find their equivalent elements with the same key values. If such equivalent elements are found in the two to-be-integrated XML schemas, we can perform the union of the two equivalent elements into one element. In other words, if two elements' key value are matched, then we can integrate the two XML schemas with their connectivity of the union element. We will provide case study 2 in this situation.

If the key values of all elements cannot be matched between the two to-be-integrated XML schemas, we need to impose an artifact root element to connect the two schemas together as an integrated XML schema. We will provide a case study 1 in this situation.

If there are multiple pairs of domain equivalent elements found in the two to-be-integrated XML schemas, then we can perform union of the first pair of equivalent elements as one element, and factorize the other pair of equivalent elements by adding a new branch element under the root element, such that the key-matched elements referring to this new branch element under root element. We will provide case study 3 in this situation.

In the following three case studies, we will integrate two XML schemas A and B by matching their equivalent elements' key values. Then we will query the integrated XML schema and document with a global query which will be decomposed into sub-queries such that each sub-query will be executed on one of the schema A or schema B for access.

In the schema integration, it will integrate two XML Schemas, which call schema A and schema B. During the integration, it will try to find the matching element between schema A and schema B. For the matching element condition, it means both elements have the same key in XSD. Otherwise, the no matching element condition means both elements do not have the same key in XSD.

Case 1. No matching element between schema A and B

Step 1. Artificial root creation

In this step, it shows that the elements in schema A and B are no matching elements. The solution is to make an artificial root element to link the root of schema A and B, while the roots of schema A and B become the child element of the new root. (Fig. 6.23)

Step 2. Path expression to access integrated XML document

In this step, the query statement is analyzed as a path expression without predicates. The last element E_{A2} in path expression will be set as a root of the integrated XML document. As the last element E_{A2} belongs to document A, the subquery will not be generated. The query is executed without decomposition. (Fig. 6.24)

Step 3. Integration for two XML documents with an artificial root

In this step, it is no matching element between document A and B. The action of data integration is to create an artificial root element of the integrated document first. Then import the whole data of documents A and B under the root of the integrated document. (Fig. 6.25)

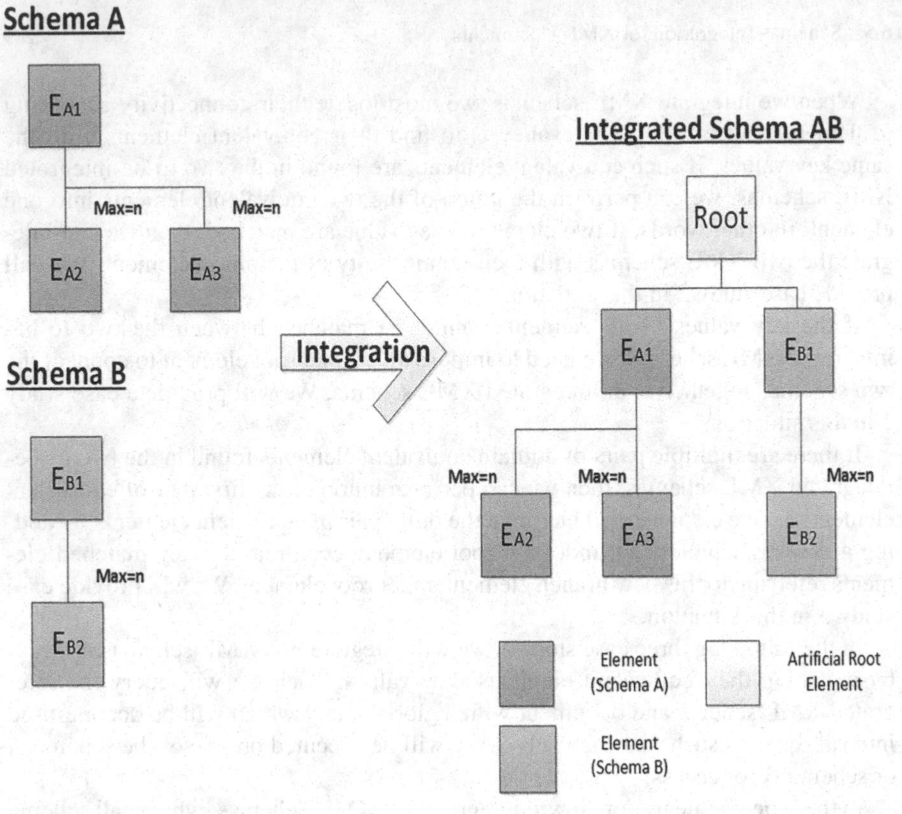

Fig. 6.23 XML Schema Integration – Case 1

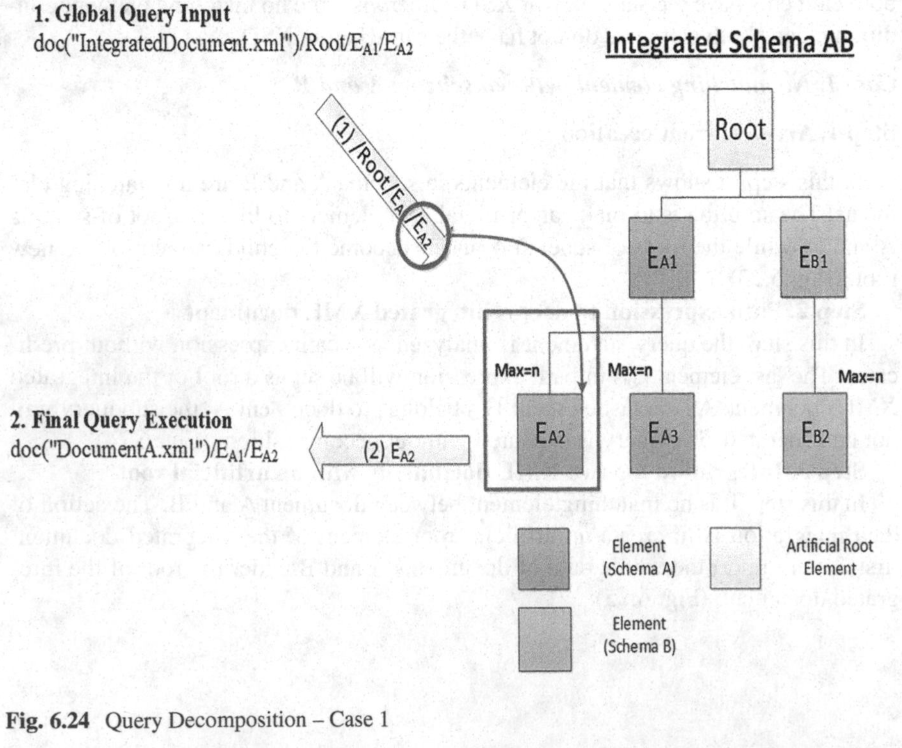

Fig. 6.24 Query Decomposition – Case 1

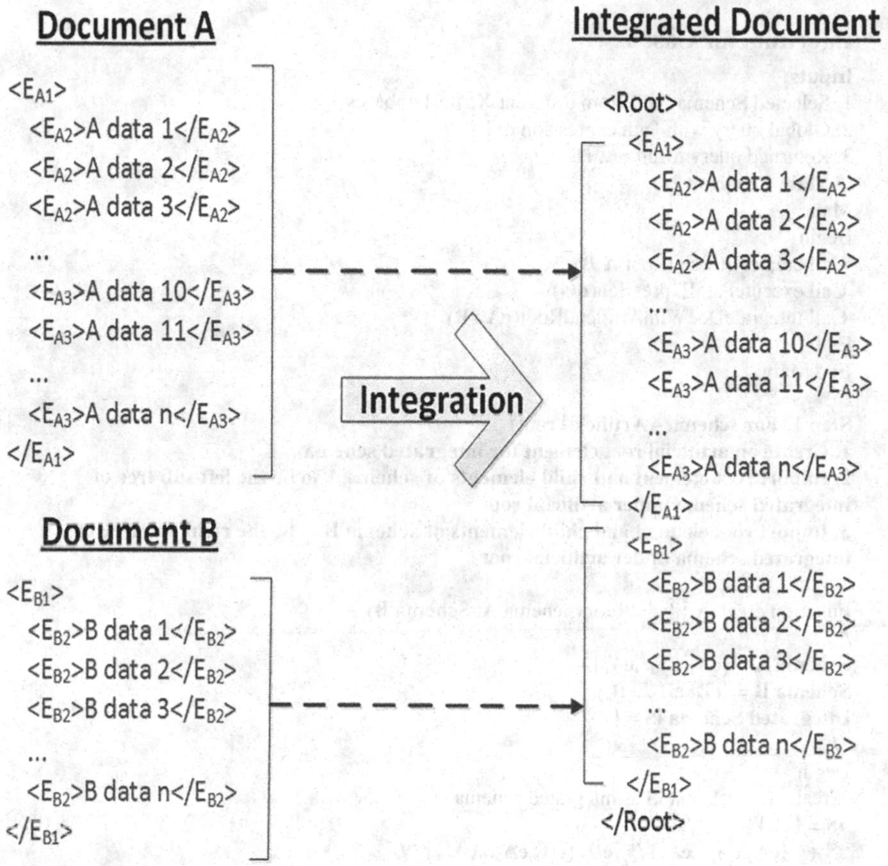

Fig. 6.25 XML documents Data Integration – Case 1

Algorithm for Case 1

Inputs:
1. Selected Schema **A**, **B** from different XML databases
2. Global query with Path expression **qG**
3. Returned query result **rA**, **rB**

```
/* Main Program */
Main
Begin
 Call createArtificialRoot(A,B)
 Call executePathExpression(qG)
 Call integrateDocWithArtificialRoot(rA,rB)
End
End Main
/*
Step 1 (For schema – Artificial root)
1. Create an artificial root element for integrated schema
2. Import root element and child elements of schema A to be the left sub tree of
integrated schema under artificial root
3. Import root element and child elements of schema B to be the right sub tree of
integrated schema under artificial root
*/
Function createArtificialRoot (Schema A, Schema B)
/*
Schema A = {eA1,eA2...eAn}
Schema B = {eB1,eB2...eBn}
Integrated Schema iS = {}
*/
Begin
 Create new schema iS as integrated schema
 iS = {eR}
 iS += {eA1,eA2...eAn} /* {eR, {eA1,eA2...eAn}} */
 iS += {eB1,eB2...eBn} /* {eR, {eA1,eA2...eAn},{eB1,eB2...eBn}} */
 Return iS
End
End Function
/*
Step 2 (For query – Path for single document)
```

(continued)

```
For executing Path with sub queries, please check in case 2.
*/
Function executePathExpression(Query qG)
Begin
 Element eL = Last element of expression path of qG
 dnA = documentName(eL) /* Get original document A name */
 pA = path(eL) /* Get original path expression */
 dbA = database(dnA) /* Get original database A connection */
 Update qG with dnA and pA /* qG = doc(dnA)/pA */
 Execute qG with connection dbA to retrieve returned result rA
 Return rA
End
End Function
/*
Step 3 (For data – Artificial root)
If the global query input is doc("Integrated.xml")/Root, this function will be
triggered to create an artificial root and import two whole documents. Otherwise,
the integrated document nD will import one query result only.
*/
Function integrateDocWithArtificialRoot(QueryResult rA, QueryResult rB)
/*
QueryResult rA = {eA1,eA2...eAn}
QueryResult rB = {eB1,eB2...eBn}
Integrated Document iD = {}
*/
Begin
 Create new document iD as integrated document
 iD = {eR}
 iD += {eA1,eA2...eAn} /* {eR,{eA1,eA2...eAn}} */
 iD += {eB1,eB2...eBn} /* {eR,{eA1,eA2...eAn},{eB1,eB2...eBn}} */
 Return iD
End
End Function
```

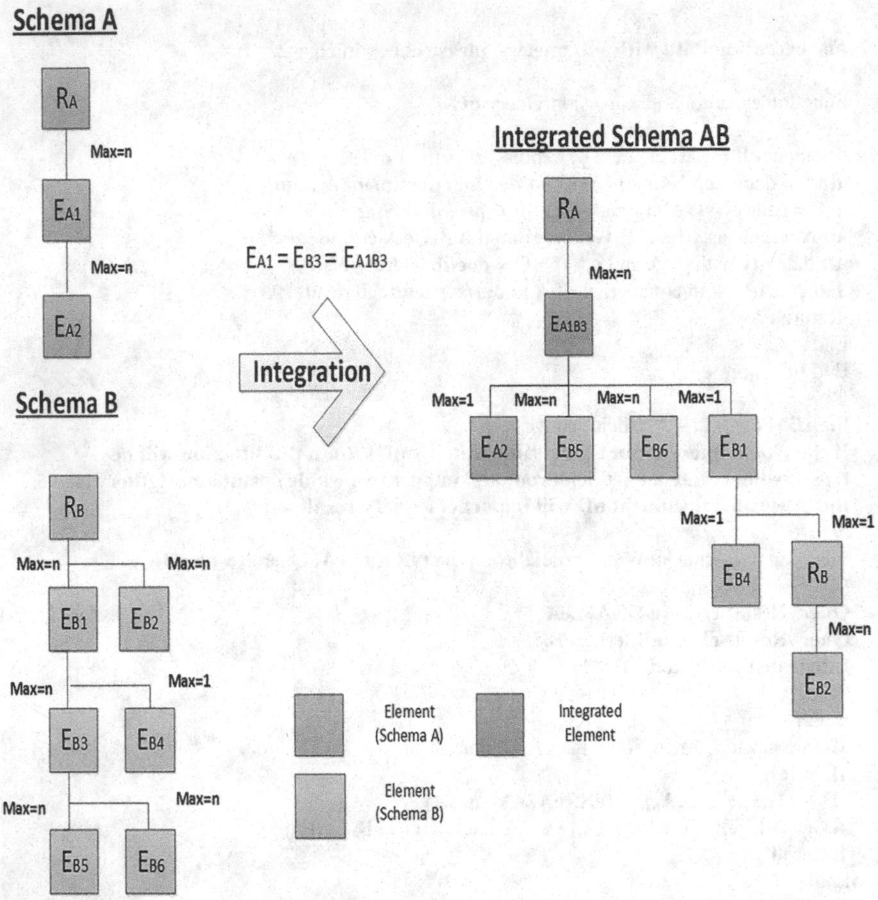

Fig. 6.26 XML Schemas Integration – Case 2

Case 2. One matching element between schema A and B

Step 1. One matching element integration

In this step, it shows one matching element in schema A and B. The solution is to merge the matching element in schema A and B which becomes an element E_{A1B3}. Schema A will be as a base. After that, the remaining child elements in schema A and B will under the element E_{A1B3}. And the sibling element of E_{B3} in schema B as child elements under the parent element of E_{B3} in schema B in 1: n data occurrences. Also, the parent element of element E_{B3} under element E_{A1B3} and become its child element in 1:1 data occurrence. (Fig. 6.26)

Step 2. Path expression to access two XML documents

In this case, the query statement is analyzed as a path expression without predicates. The last element E_{A1B3} in path expression will be set as a root of an integrated XML document. As the last element E_{A1B3} is a matching element which belongs to

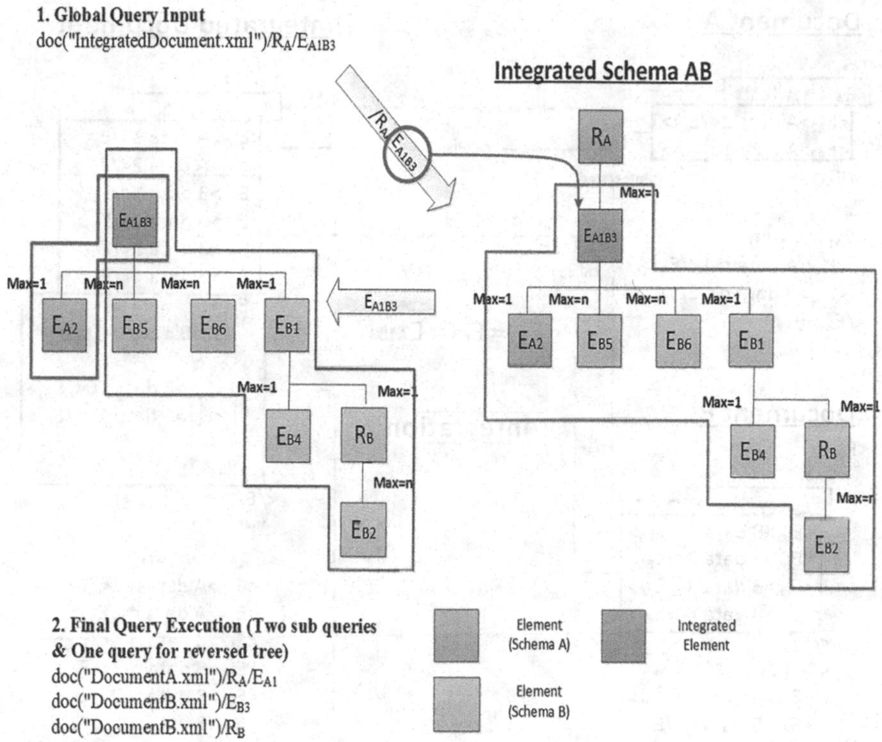

Fig. 6.27 Query Decomposition – Case 2

document A and B. The global query will be decomposed into two sub queries. Two sub queries will be executed to two different XML documents. In addition, the elements E_{B1}, E_{B4}, R_B, and E_{B2} are reversed. Therefore, the third query is required for generating reversed tree. (Fig. 6.27)

Step 3. Integration for matching element

In this case, the integrated document contains one matching element between documents A and B. The action of data integration will handle the combination of matching elements. For the combined matching element of the integrated document, the related child elements of documents A and B under the matching element will be grouped based on the same key value. In addition, some sub tree in the original document is reversed which make the data occurrence from 1:n to n:1. The reversed sub Tree will be formed first by getting the parent and sibling of the matching element. Then the reversed tree is appended under the matching element. (Fig. 6.28)

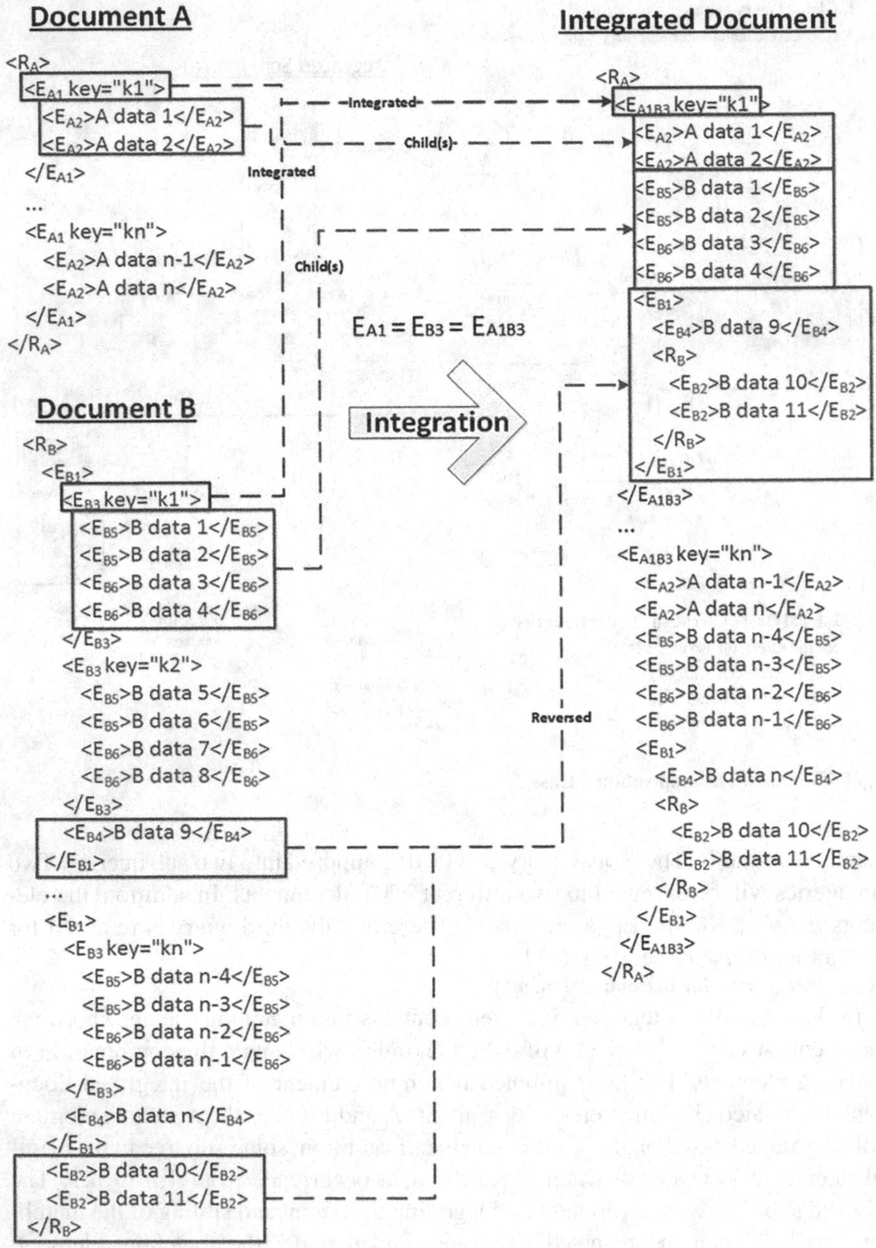

Fig. 6.28 Data Integration – Case 2

Algorithm for Case 2

Inputs:
1. Selected Schema **A**, **B** from different XML databases
2. Global query with Path expression **qG**
3. Returned query result **rA**, **rB**

/* Main Program */
Main
Begin
 Call integrateXSDWithMatchingElement(**A**,**B**)
 Call executePathExpressionWithSubQuery(**qG**)
 Call integrateDocWithOneMatching(**rA**,**rB**)
End
End Main
/*
Step 1 (For schema – One matching element)
m = matching element
Schema A = $\{eA_1, eA_2 \ldots, eA_m, \ldots eA_n\}$
Schema B = $\{eB_1, eB_2 \ldots, eB_m, \ldots eB_n\}$
*/
Function integrateXSDWithMatchingElement(Schema **A**, Schema **B**)
Begin
 /* Union matching element between schema A and B */
 Replace eA_m to $eAB_m = eA_m + eB_m$
 /* Move child elements of matching element from schema B */
 Move $\{eB_{m+1}, \ldots eB_n\}$ under eAB_m
 While (eB_m is not the root element)
Add parent element$\{eB_1, \ldots eB_{m-1}\}$of eB_m as a child element of eAB_m
Set parent element$\{eB_1, \ldots eB_{m-1}\}$under eAB_m in 1:1 occurrence
 End While
 Loop until all sibling elements of eB_m are added
Find the parent of sibling element $\{\ldots, eB_{m-1}, eB_{m+1}, \ldots\}$
Add sibling element$\{\ldots, eB_{m-1}, eB_{m+1}, \ldots\}$ under the parent element in 1:1/1:n data occurrence
 End Loop
 Return **A**
End
End Function/*
Step 2 (For query – Path for two documents)
Analyze query result which belongs to different documents by checking data dictionary. Sub query generation is required.
AnalyzedResult rQ = $\{eA_1, eA_2 \ldots eA_n, eB_1, eB_2 \ldots eB_n\}$
*/

(continued)

```
Function executePathExpressionWithSubQuery(AnalyzedResult rQ)
Begin
 Sub Query qA, qB
 For i=1 to n of rQ do
/* for each element of analyzed result */
 If ei belongs to {eA1,eA2...eAn} with the highest level then
 /* In case 2, eA1 is the highest level element */
 dnA = documentName(ei) /* Get original document A name */
 pA = path(ei) /* Get original path expression */
 dbA = database(dnA)/* Get original database A connection */
 Update qA with dnA and pA /* qA=doc(dnA)/pA */
 End If
 If ei belongs to {eB1,eB2...eBn} with the highest level then
 /* In case 2, eB3 is the highest level element */
 dnB = documentName(ei) /* Get original document B name */
 pB = path(ei) /* Get original path expression */
 dbB = database(dnB)/* Get original database B connection */
 Update qB with dnB and pB /* qB=doc(dnB)/pB */
 End If
 End For
 Execute qA, qB with connection dbA, dbB to retrieve returned result rA{eA1,eA2...
eAn}, rB{eB1,eB2...eBn}
 Return rA, rB
End
End Function
/*
Step 3 (For data – One matching element)
QueryResult rA = {eA1,eA2...,eAm,...eAn}
QueryResult rB = {eB1,eB2...,eBm,...eBn}
Integrated Document iD = {}
*/
Function integrateDocWithOneMatching(QueryResult rA, QueryResult rB)
Begin
 Create new document iD as integrated document
 iD += rA
 List mL = Get data of the matching element eAm from iD
 For i=1 to n of mL do
 Check the attribute name aN of eAmi
 Read the value aV of aN in eAmi
 Find the data of matching element eBm with value aV in rB
 Import child elements {eBm+1, eBm+2...} of eB to iD under eAmi
 If eBm is not a root element then
 ReversedTree rT = createReversedTree(eBm)
 Import rT to iD under eAmi in 1:1 data occurrence
 End If
 End For
 Return iD
End
End Function
```

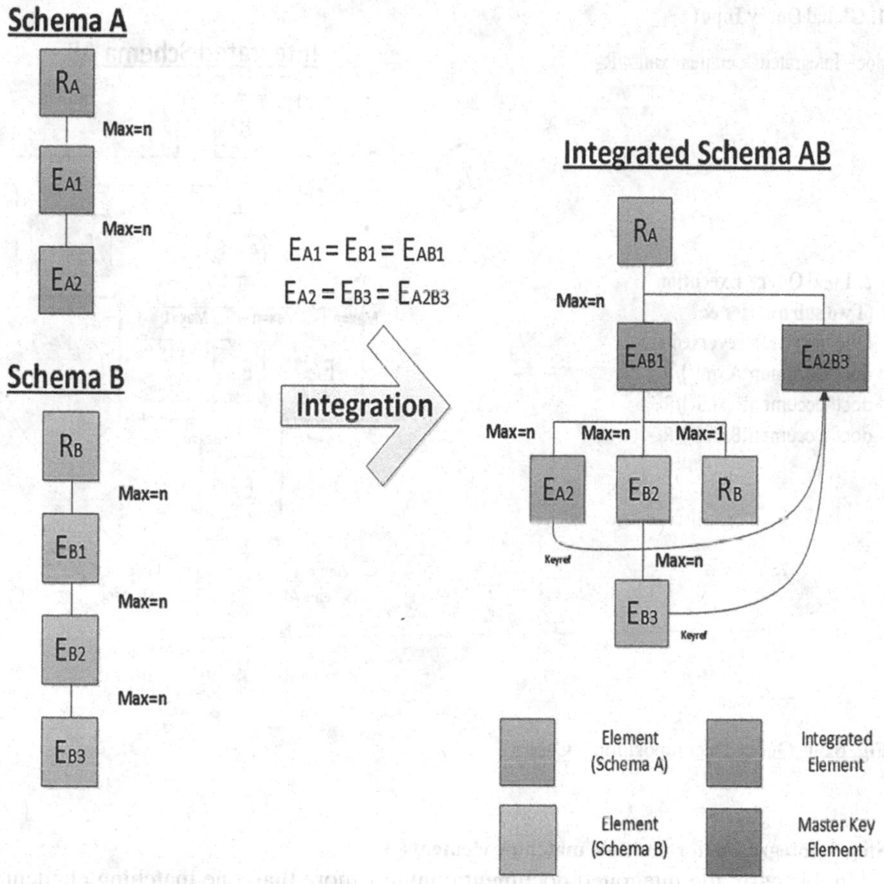

Fig. 6.29 Schema Integration – Case 3

Case 3. Multiple matching elements between schema A and B

Step 1. Multiple matching elements integration

In this step, it shows more than one matching element in schema A and schema B. For the first matching element, it is the same as case 2. For other matching elements, the solution is to add a new element for each pair of matching elements and under the root element of integrated schema AB, and add a key reference (**keyref**) to the matching element in schema A and schema B. (Fig. 6.29)

Step 2. Path expression to access two XML documents

In this case, the query statement is analyzed as a path expression without predicates. The last element R_A in path expression is a root of an integrated document. Therefore, the whole integrated XML document will be retrieved. As E_{AB1} is a first matching element which belongs to document A and B, the global query will be decomposed into two sub queries. Two sub queries will be executed to two different XML documents. In addition, the element R_B is reversed. Therefore, the third query is required for generating reversed tree. (Fig. 6.30)

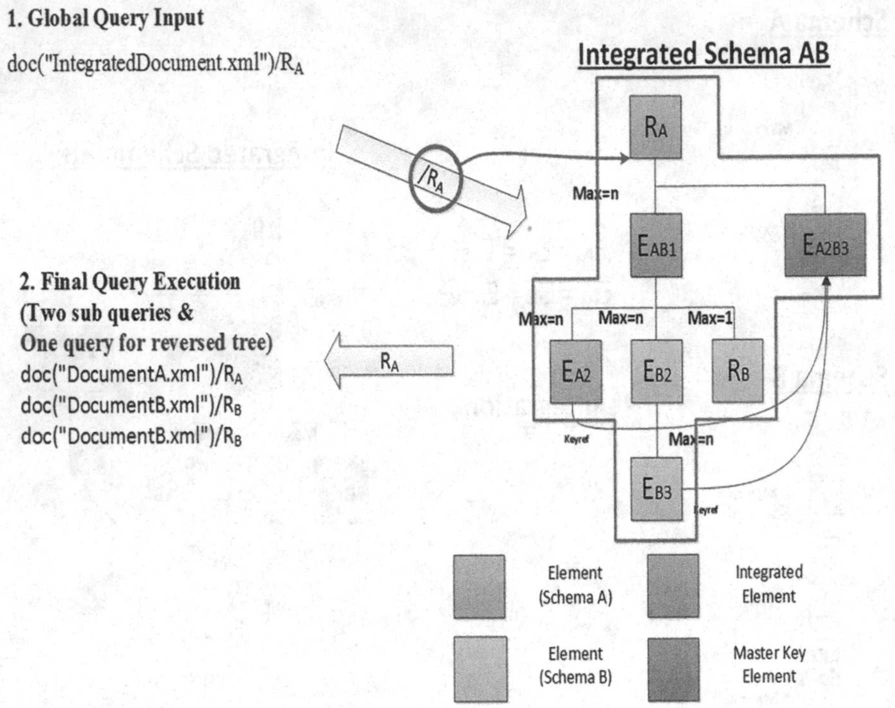

Fig. 6.30 Query Decomposition – Case 3

Step 3. Integration for multiple matching elements

In this case, the integrated document contains more than one matching element between documents A and B. For the first matching element, the action of data integration is the same as case 2. For the remaining matching elements, they will not be integrated and added a key reference. The collection of the key elements is created under the root. (Fig. 6.31)

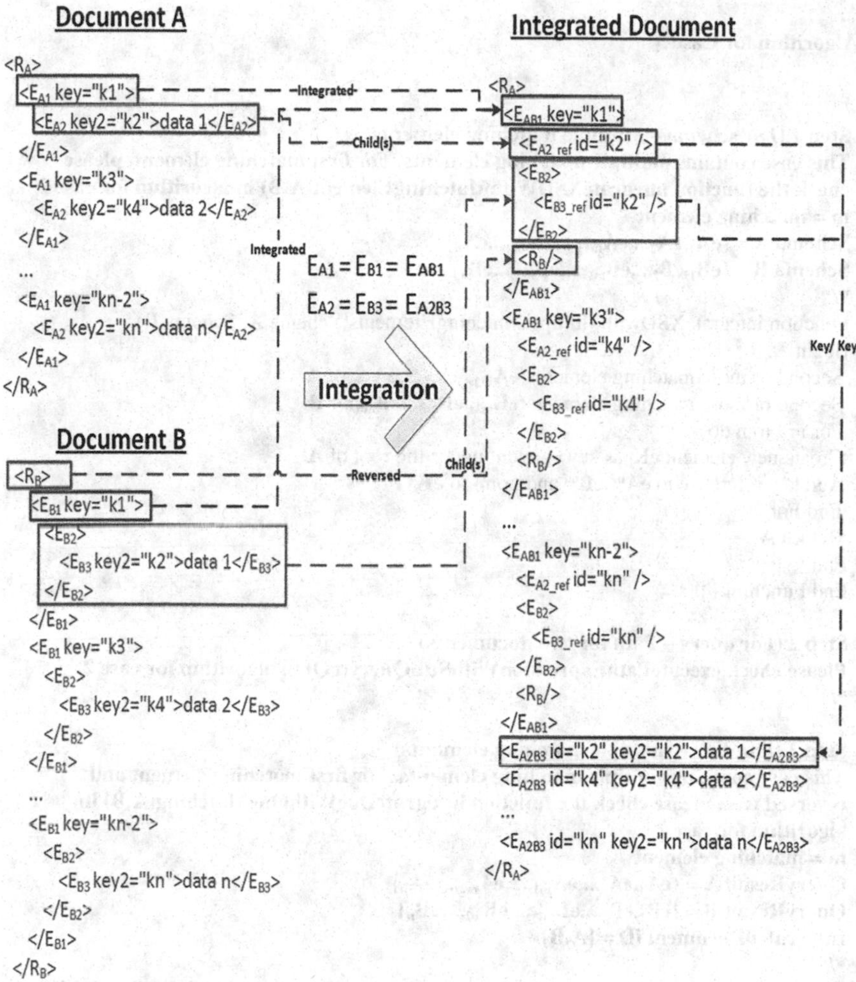

Fig. 6.31 XML document Data Integration - Case 3

Algorithm for Case 3

```
/*
Step 1 (For schema – Multiple matching elements)
This case contains multiple matching elements. For first matching element, please
check the function integrateXSDWithMatchingElement(A,B) in algorithm for case 2
m = matching element
Schema A = {eA_1,eA_2...,eA_m1,...,eA_m2,...eA_n}
Schema B = {eB_1,eB_2...,eB_m1,...,eB_m2,...eB_n}
*/
Function integrateXSDwithMultipleMatchingElements(Schema A, Schema B)
Begin
 Second or more matching elements(eA_m2, eA_m3...eA_mn)of A
 Second or more matching elements(eB_m2, eB_m3...eB_mn)of B
 For i=2 to n do
 Create new element eK_i as key element under the root of A
 Add key reference to eA^mi,eB^mi and point to eK^i
 End For
 Return A
End
End Function
/*
Step 2 (For query – Path for two documents)
Please check executePathExpressionWithSubQuery(rQ) in algorithm for case 2.
*/
/*
Step 3 (For data – multiple matching elements)
This case contains multiple matching elements. For first matching element and
reversed tree, please check the function integrateDocWithOneMatching(A,B) in
algorithm for case 2
m = matching element
QueryResult A = {eA_1,eA_2...,eA_m1,...,eA_m2,...eA_n}
QueryResult B = {eB_1,eB_2...,eB_m1,...,eB_m2,...eB_n}
IntegratedDocument iD = {A,B}
*/
Function integrateDocWithMultipleMatching(IntegratedDocument iD, QueryResult rA,
QueryResult rB)
Begin
 Second or more matching elements(eA_m2, eA_m3...eA_mn)of A
 Second or more matching elements(eB_m2, eB_m3...eB_mn)of B
 For i=2 to n do
 Create a new element eK_i as key element under the root of iD
 Set text content and attributes of eA^mi,eB^mi to eK^i
 Remove text content and attributes of eA_mi,eB_mi
 Add key reference to eA^mi,eB^mi, and point to eK^i
 End For
 Return iD
End
End Function
```

6.6 Case Study for XML Schemas Integration

Input multiple XML Schemas

Since a pair of matching elements Package and Warehouse contain the same key Location and Warehouseid, we can therefore merge them into one element Package by replacing element Warehouse as the element Package, and integrate both XML schemas Delivery.xsd and Inventory into an integrated schema Delivery.

Similarly, another pair of matching element Title in schema A and element Tag in schema B contain the same key Partid and Tagie with redundant data, therefore, we add a master element Itemkey which contains the data of these two equivalent elements.

As a result of resolving multiple matching elements as shown above, an integrated schema is shown in Fig. 6.28 in the following XSD (Fig. 6.32):

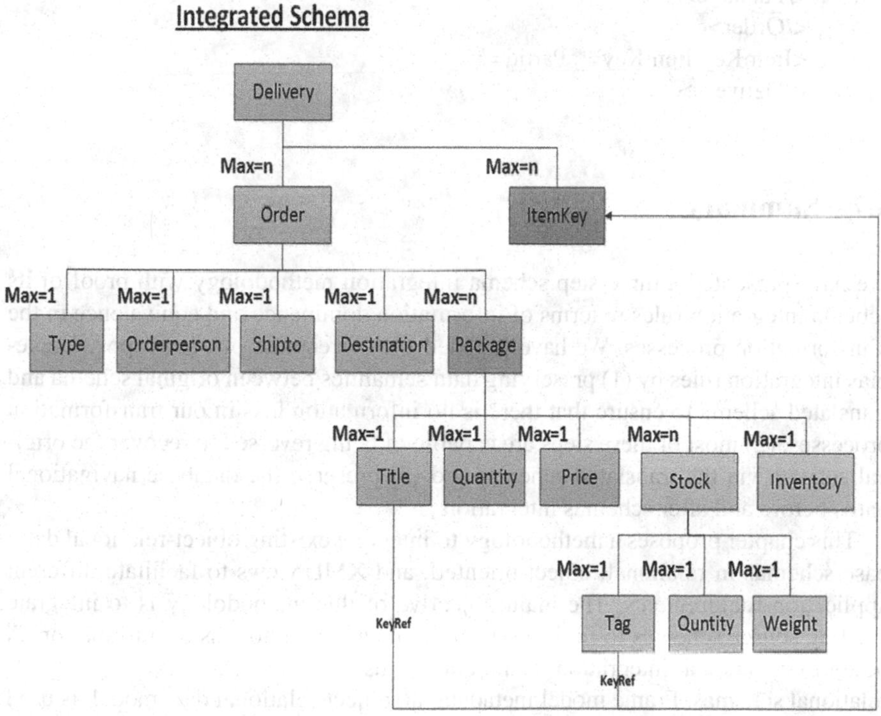

Fig. 6.32 XSD graph of integrated schema

Integrated Schema

<Delivery>
<Order Orderid=*>
<Type/>
<Orderperson/>
<Shipto/>
<Destination/>
<Package Location=*>
<Title ItemKey=* />
<Quantity/>
<Price/>
<Stock>
<Tag ItemKey=* />
<Quantity/>
<Weight/>
</Stock>
<Inventory/>
</Package>
</Order>
<ItemKey ItemKey=* Partid=*>
</Delivery>

6.7 Summary

We have presented a three-step schema integration methodology with proof of its schema integration rules in terms of information dominance and equivalence in the transformation processes. We have justified the correctness of our proposed schemas integration rules by (1) preserving data semantics between original schema and translated schema to ensure that there is no information loss in our transformation processes, (2) most of these steps are capable of being reversed to recover the original schema via the translated schema, and (3) preserve the database navigational paths before and after schemas integration.

This chapter proposes a methodology to integrate existing object-relational database schemas in relational, object-oriented, and XML views to facilitate different application requirements. The main objective of this methodology is to integrate existing source schemas to fulfill user requirements with no loss of information. A bottom-up schema integration technique is used to integrate existing object-relational schemas. Frame model metadata, an object-relational data model, is used to capture the semantic conflicts and other high-level abstract relationships arising from the integration process. In XML schemas integration, we preserve the data semantics according to their data navigation paths. For example, after schema integration, the original parent-to-child elements of the one-to-many structure may become child-to-parent of one-to-one structure. Therefore, the data semantics are preserved in the original parent and child elements association. The equivalent XML elements are matched according to their key values, which are the same criteria of a relational database for the compatibility of their relations in isa relationship.

Questions Question 6.1

Can multiple relational schemas be integrated into one logical schema? Give the rationale for your answer. How can the integration of relational schemas be compared with the integration of Extended Entity Relational Models with respect to meeting users' requirements?

Answer:

When multiple database schemas are integrated into one database schema, the rationale behind the integration is that they are related to meet users' requirements. The relational schema represents the data structure of a relational database, which misses the concept of how it can fulfill user data requirements. As a result, we cannot integrate relational schemas into one relational schema without regard to their data relationship conceptually. The reason is that user requirement is a concept whereas relational schema is an implementation of a concept. Without a clear concept, the implementation loses its most important information, that is, user requirements. On the other hand, we can integrate multiple EER modes into one EER model to meet users' requirements because the EER model represents user data requirements, and the fact that we can integrate multiple EER models into one EER model because the EER models are related to meet user requirements.

Question 6.2

What is the weak entity? What is the weak entity of the Relational database? What are aggregation relation tuples?

Answer:

An entity represents a unique important object in an Entity Relationship Model as a conceptual schema for a relational database. A weak entity is an entity in the ER model with a key dependence on a strong entity. The key of the weak entity must concatenate the key of its strong entity. For example, in an ER model, a hotel consists of many rooms. Both Hotel and Room are entities in an ER model in one (hotel) to many (room) cardinality relationships. Entity Hotel has a key called Hotel Name as a strong entity. Entity Room has a key called Room location which concatenates both Hotel Name and Room Number as a composite key.

An aggregation entity consists of component entities. An aggregation entity is mapped into a relationship relation in an Extended Entity-Relationship Model such that its key depends on its component entities' keys, that is, it is key concatenate all of its component entities' keys. For example, aggregation entity Teaching consists of two components: Teachers and Students. Therefore, aggregation entity Teaching concatenates component entity Student key Student ID and entity Teacher key Teacher Name.

Bibliography

Batini C, Ceri S, Navathe S (1992) Conceptual Database Design: An Entity Relationship Approach. The Benjamin/Cummings Publishing Company, Inc

Fong J, Pang F, Fong A, Wong D (2000) Schema Integration for Object-Relational Databases with Data Verification, Proceedings of the 2000 International Computer Symposium Workshop on Software Engineering and Database Systems, Taiwan, pp. 185–192.

Kwan I, Fong J (1999) Schema Integration Methodology and its Verification by use of Information Capacity. Information Systems 24(5):355–376

Özsu M, Valdariez P (1991) Principles of Distributed Database Systems., Prentice Hall International Edition.

Chapter 7
Database and Expert Systems Integration

System reengineering is broadly defined as the use of engineering knowledge or artifacts from existing systems to build new ones and is a technology for improving system quality and productivity. Traditionally, this work has focused on reusing existing software systems, (i.e., software programs, files, and databases). However, knowledge-based systems have also been developed within these organizations and are growing in popularity. It will soon be necessary for us not only to reuse existing databases but also to reuse the existing expert systems to create new expert systems and expert database systems.

Reusing or developing an integrated system for existing expert systems and database systems is a complex process. There are three possible scenarios that a system developer may encounter:

1. Reusing expert systems - The system developer reuses an existing expert system and builds new databases to create an integrated expert database system. This happens when:

- The existing expert system has difficulty handling a growing volume of factual data.
- A new database is required in the organization and this database can support the existing expert systems.
- A new database system is required to work underneath an existing intelligent interface, such as a natural language interface.

2. Reusing databases - The system developer reuses existing databases and builds a new expert system to create an expert database system. This happens when:

- There is a requirement to build intelligent components into an existing database (for example, integrity constraints, natural language interfaces, or intelligent interfaces, deductive rules, intelligent retrieval, or query optimization).

J. S. P. Fong, K. Wong Ting Yan, *Information Systems Reengineering, Integration and Normalization*, https://doi.org/10.1007/978-3-030-79584-9_7

- A new expert system is required and the existing databases can support this system.

3. Reusing both database and expert systems - The system developer reuses both existing database and expert systems to create an expert database system. For example, the company links expert systems and databases or the company has bought a new expert system and links it with their existing databases.

7.1 Using a Knowledge-Based Model to Create an Expert Database System

To provide a solution for the reengineering and/or the integration of DBSs and ESs, a knowledge-based model with the following properties is required (Huang 1994):

- A higher-level synthesis model - The best approach to integrate DBSs and ESs was to embrace the facilities of both DBSs and ESs technologies under one umbrella; that is, a higher-order synthesis was needed. The new model will combine high-level information modeling features, deductive capability, active capabilities (i.e., integrity constraints), and the flexibility of AI-based systems with the efficiency, security, and distributed and concurrent access provided by DBSs. Computer scientists have investigated the use of abstract data type concepts to define this richer data model that includes semantic data modeling concepts and object-oriented concepts and makes no real distinction between data and knowledge (in the form of rules).
- Reengineering capability - The most feasible approach to integrate DBSs and ESs was to enhance existing systems to couple both technologies. This is due to the concept of reengineering to save on the cost of implementation. The peer-to-peer architecture for the DBSs and ESs integration has been seen as the easiest way to achieve the reengineering of existing DBSs and ESs.
  The above criteria can be used to create a four-tier framework as depicted in Fig. 7.1. In this figure, the existing systems form the lower tier. The required data from these systems is extracted using coupling classes. The coupling classes extract, and possibly transform, the data of the lower tier into knowledge usable by the integrated system. The upper tier combines and enhances the knowledge of the existing system with additional knowledge to create an integrated expert database system.

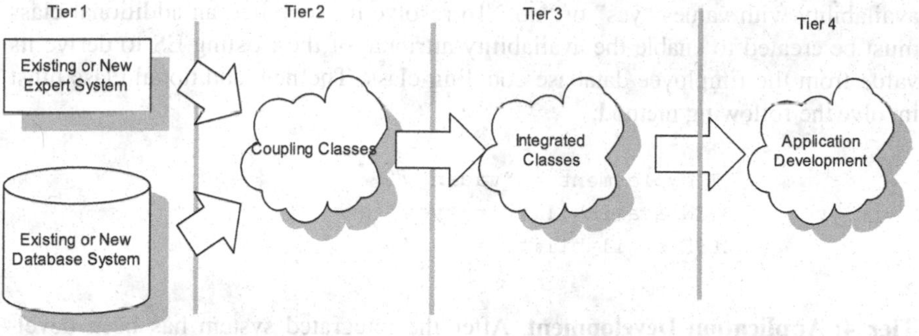

Fig. 7.1 The four-tier integrate expert database system model

Tier 1: Existing Systems The existing systems contain data to be reused in the new/integrated EDS. Only the data required for the operation of the integrated system is extracted. This data is brought into a consistent state through the coupling classes of tier 2.

Tier 2: Coupling Classes Coupling classes describe the information in existing systems. A coupling class provides the interface between the extension (or reengineered upper) layer and the existing systems. The uniformity of this interface layer insulates the upper layers from changes in the lower layers and can be used to bring information together so that data representing the same entities or attributes are consistent.

An attribute in a coupling class is derived from the values of the entities stored in the underlying systems. The derivation is a simple one-to-one mapping.

The coupling classes provide information from existing knowledge repositories, and additional information can also be stored by the integrated system. The information from the existing systems is only extracted on demand, as it would be unwise to copy information out of these repositories to store in the integrated systems without endangering the consistency of information across the organization.

Tier 3: Integrated Classes The third layer combines the components of the coupling classes with additional classes (and objects) to create an integrated system. To form an integrated system, name conflict and semantic conflict problems need to be solved. Since the system has a unified structure, (i.e., a higher-level synthesis model), the name conflict problem can be easily solved by using the synonym index. The synonym index creates a relationship between two different attributes with the same values.

To solve the semantic conflict problem between different attributes, additional classes must be appended into the integrated system. For instance, the value "vacancy" in the employment attribute of the Employee relation in an existing relational database indicates that the employee is available for assignment to a new project. In an existing ES, the same information is represented using an attribute availability with values "yes" or "no." To resolve this conflict, an additional class must be created to enable the availability attribute of the existing ES to derive its value from the Employee database coupling class. The new additional class must involve the following method:

```
IF employment = "vacancy"
THEN availability = "yes"
ELSE availability = "no"
```

Tier 4: Application Development After the integrated system has been developed, the system developer can use it as a knowledge base to develop its own application. The application system defines the components necessary to answer and give explanations for all problems that it is to solve.

7.2 A Knowledge-Based Model for the Integration of Expert Systems and Database Systems

An expert system frame model metadata (Huang 1994) is a good example of a knowledge-based model that fulfills the requirements for constructing an integrated EDS. The frame model metadata is an EER model framework used to construct an effective knowledge-based management system. It is a higher-order synthesis that includes frame concepts, semantic data modeling concepts, and object-oriented concepts to ensure no real distinction between "data" and "knowledge."

The frame model metadata is an object-oriented-like database that structures an application domain into classes. Classes are organized via generalization, aggregation, and user-defined relationships. Knowledge-based system designers can describe each class as a specialization (i.e., subclass) of its more generic superclass(es). Thus, attributes and methods of objects of one class are inherited by attributes and methods of another class lower in the ordering.

The ability to attach procedures to objects enables behavior models of objects and expertise in an application domain to be encapsulated in a single construct. The attached procedures follow an IF-THEN structure that enables the representation of production rules as well as normal procedures.

The constraints of database systems include integrity constraint enforcement, derived data maintenance, triggers, protection, version control, and so on. These are referred to as active database and deductive database systems. The frame model metadata unifies data and rules allowing these advanced features to be implemented. The knowledge processing mechanism (i.e., inference engine) and data retrieval mechanisms, have also been built into the frame model metadata. It also supports very strong integrity constraint enforcement.

The frame model metadata follows the object-oriented paradigm. All conceptual entities are modeled as objects. The same attribute and behavior objects are classified into an object type, called a class. An object belongs to one, and only one, class. Both facts and rules are objects in the frame model metadata.

The frame model metadata is implemented with a knowledge representation schema that includes object structure descriptions (i.e., classes), user-defined relationships between entities, and structure inheritance descriptions defined by taxonomies of structure that support data and behavior inheritance (i.e., abstract relationship) as shown in Fig. 7.2.

The components of the frame model metadata can be described as follows:

- Classes

The Frame model metadata consists of three classes: static classes, active classes, and coupling classes. Static classes represent factual data entities, active classes represent rule entities, and coupling classes represent the temporal entities imported from tier 1 and used by tier 3 to form an EDS. In other words, an active class is event driven, obtaining data from the database when invoked by certain events. Static classes store data in their own database. The three classes all use the same structure. Combining these three types of objects within the inheritance hierarchy structure enables the frame model metadata to represent and combine heterogeneous knowledge.

The structure of a class includes three main parts: attributes, methods, and constraints. An attribute may be an ordinary attribute as in the EER model, a complex attribute in the sense that it is structured or it may represent a set or a virtual attribute defined in the method part. A method can represent the behavior of the class, or give definitions of a virtual attribute, a deductive rule, or an active rule. Constraints represent additional knowledge concerning the attributes, the methods, and the class. Every class includes basic frame information to represent the class entity, called the header. The header of the class structure includes class name, primary key, parents, and a description. The Class_Name is a class identifier; that is, a unique name defined by the application developer. The Primary_Key assists the system to define the semantics of an object identifier. The frame model metadata supports a mechanism to deal with the Primary_Key and object name to ensure the object name is a unique name in the application. Parents represent the generalization/specialization relationship between the current class and its superclass. Each class also has a Description document, which contains a textual description of the class.

Figure 7.3 shows an example of a relational table and its correspondent coupling class structure in the frame model metadata for illustration.

The database coupling class mirrors the database structure (i.e. schema) but does not include all of the data in the database. The reason is that it is difficult to hold a large amount of data in the integration system. The expert system coupling class represents the communication that must be performed when data passes between the frame model metadata and an expert system. The expert system coupling class includes:

- Output Part Attributes: All the data that are required by the expert system.
- Input Part Attributes: All the results that are generated by the expert system.

```
Description: Class
Class { Class_Name   /* a unique name in all system */
        Primary_Key /*an attribute name or by default a
                                 class_name */
        Parents   /* a list of class names */
        Description  /* the description of the class */
        Attributes /*a list of attributes */
        Methods  /* a list of methods; */
        Constraints  /* constraint methods for the class */
        }
Description: Attribute
Attribute {
        Attribute_Name /* a unique name in this class */
        Attribute_Type /* the data type for the attribute */
        Default_Value /* predefined value for the attribute */
        Cardinality /* is the attribute single or multi-valued */
        Description /* a description of the attribute */
        Constraints /* constraint methods for the attribute */
        }
Description: Method
Method { Method_Name /* a unique name in this class */
        Parameters   /* a list of arguments for the method */
        Type /* the final result data type */
        Description /* the description of the method */
        Method_Body /* processing function of the method */
        {     If /* the rule conditions */
              Then /* the rule actions or normal methods */   }
        Constraints /* a list of constraints for this method */
        }
Description: Constraint
Constraints /* a list of constraint methods for this class */
      {   Method_Name /* constraint method name */
          Parameters     /* a list of arguments for the method */
          Ownership   /* the class name of the owner of the
                      method*/
          Event /* triggered event */
          Sequence  /* method action time */
          Timing /* the method action timer */ }
```

Fig. 7.2 The structure of the frame model metadata

Fig. 7.3 An example of a relation in the frame model metadata

```
Attributes:
    Name: Method(name)
    Sex: Method(sex)
    Father: Method(father)
    Mother: Method(mother)
Methods:
    name (): Text; {............}
    sex (): Text;{............}
    father (): Text;{............}
    mother (): Text;{............}
```

The conversion procedure will translate all input data variables that exist in the expert system into the output part attributes of the class. The program developer will decide the variable name in which to save the resultant information from the expert system. All the attributes of an expert system coupling class are represented as virtual variables. The communication functions between the frame model metadata and the external system are built into the method of each attribute. For example: Consider a credit assessment system called Credit that was built in the Crystal system. The expert system and its coupling class are shown below in Crystal format in Fig. 7.4.

- Attributes

These represent the properties of a class. A particular object will have a value for each of its attributes. The attribute values that describe each object become a major part of the data stored in the database. An attribute that is composed of several more basic attributes is called a composite attribute. Attributes that are not divisible are called simple or atomic attributes. An attribute value can also be derived or calculated from the related attributes or objects; for example, the Age and Date_of_Birth attributes of a person. For a particular person object, the value of Age can be determined from the current date and the value of the person's date of birth. This type of attribute is called a virtual attribute in the frame model metadata and is the result of a deductive rule or an active rule. For example, an attribute Generation of a person class can be deduced from the following rule:

```
If age > 40 then old person;
    if age < 16 then child;
        if 16 < age < 40, then young;
            on the event dead then dead person.
```

Most attributes have a single value for a particular object; such attributes are called single-valued. In some cases an attribute can have a set of values for the same object; for example, a College_Degrees attribute for a person. A person can have two or more degrees. A multivalued attribute may have lower and upper bounds on the number of values it can store. For example, the Colors attribute of a car may

```
* Credit Assessment Expert System in Crystal
* RULE LIST                    Thu Oct 21 22:13:33 1993  Page:   1
[  1] bank references are good
      IF        DO: Test Expression    customer_overdraft<50
        AND     DO: Test Expression    customer_history$="good"
[  2] credit rating
      + IF    [  4] customer status is house_owner
      +   AND [  3] customer salary is sufficient
      +   AND [  1] bank references are good
          AND   DO: Assign credit_rating$ = "good"
[  3] customer salary is sufficient
      IF   DO: Test Expression  monthly_salary>monthly_repayment
[  4] customer status is house_owner
      IF        DO: Test Expression  customer_status$="house-owner"
[  5]           CRYSTAL  MASTER  RULE
      +IF   [  2] credit rating is good
```

[<Number>] means rule number
$ means the variable is text

```
Class Name: Credit
Attributes:
    Customer_Status: Method(customer_status)            /*output part*/
    Monthly_Salary: Method(monthly_salary)              /*output part*/
    Monthly_Payment:Method(monthly_payment)             /*output part*/
    Customer_Overdraft:Method(customer_overdraft)/*output part*/
    Customer_History: Method(customer_history)          /*output part*/
    Customer_Credit: Method(customer_credit)            /*input part*/
Methods:
    customer_status (): Text; {.........................}
    monthly_salary (): Number; {.......................}
    monthly_payment (): Number; {........................}
    customer_overdraft (): Number; {........................}
    customer_history (): Text;{........................}
    customer_credit (): Text;{.......................}
```

Fig. 7.4 An expert system and its coupling class in the frame model metadata

have between one and five values. Figure 7.5 shows an example of attributes of an object Hector_Person:

- Methods

Rules extend the semantics of the data. The specification of rules is an important part of semantic data modeling since many of the facts in the real world are derived rather than consisting of pure data (Gray et al. 1992). It is increasingly important to

```
Attributes:
    Name="Hector"
    Date_of_Birth="06/02/65"
    Sex="M"
    Address="63 Chester Road, Sunderland, SR2 7PR"
    Age= Method(age)+
    Father= Object(Andrew)++
    Mother= Object(Anne)
```

+The syntax to represent a virtual value in an object is Method(<method>)

++ The syntax to represent an object value in an object is Object(<object>)

Fig. 7.5 An example of an attribute in the frame model metadata

Fig. 7.6 An example of a method in the frame model metadata

```
Object Identifier: Hector_Credit_Rating
Attributes:
    Customer= "Hector"
    Customer-Status= "House-Owner"
    Credit-Rating= Method(credit-rating)
Methods:
credit-rating (): Text;
    { IF Customer-Status = "House-Owner"
      Then Credit-Rating = "Good"}
```

integrate rules into data models in new information systems. A crucial characteristic of an object-oriented system is that the paradigm provides mechanisms for structuring and sharing not only data but also the programs (i.e., methods) that act on the data. The frame model metadata uses this characteristic to integrate rules into its model. The methods of the frame model metadata represent the behavior, the active rules, and the deductive rules of a particular object. Since the behavior representation of the object-oriented model is reflected by the different needs of different user communities, there is not an established way of representing behavior in object-oriented systems. The method body takes a production rule structure in the frame model metadata. Figure 7.6 shows an example of a method of the object Hector_Credit_Rating.

- Constraints

There are many properties of data that cannot be captured in the form of structures. These properties essentially serve as additional restrictions on the values of the data and/or how the data may be related (structured). For example, there may be a restriction that if a person is head of a department, the person must also belong to the department. Such restrictions cannot be expressed in terms of structures but must be captured by some additional mechanism. It is a primary consideration of database technology to ensure data (or knowledge) correctness and consistency. This requires the system to support integrity constraint functions. These functions are also required to allow proper handling of updates of knowledge for interrelated actions and active database rules. There are many semantics present in constraints that can be very useful when answering queries. Constraints can be used to prevent a possibly expensive database search operation or to answer otherwise unsolvable queries (Houtsma and Apers 1990). The constraint technology used in current database systems requires different levels of integrity constraint. There are two types of constraints used in database technology:

1. Static constraints that limit the allowable database states so as to accurately reflect the real-world situation.
2. Dynamic constraints that restrict the possible database state transitions.

For example, we can define an attribute constraint in the attribute salary. The constraint will be:

```
(salary_refuse ( ) Self Insert Before ( ) )
```

The method of salary_refuse is that no raise more than 500 is allowed. (note: salary@new is the data for new salary.)

```
If salary@new -    salary > 500
Then (fail)
```

7.2.1 The Hierarchical Structure

The frame model metadata uses the generalization relationship to build its hierarchical structure. There are three different types in the frame model metadata, i.e., static generalization, active generalization, and coupling generalization. These are discussed below.

1. Static Generalization

Static objects use the generalization relationship to represent abstract knowledge in their hierarchical structure. For example, we can use a static hierarchical structure to represent Male person knowledge by creating a new class called Male as shown in Fig. 7.7. The new class Male inherits all the features of the Person class and appends with it a constraint rule to ensure that the sex of the person is male. This type of generalization can be found in most semantic data models.

Fig. 7.7 The static hierarchy structure

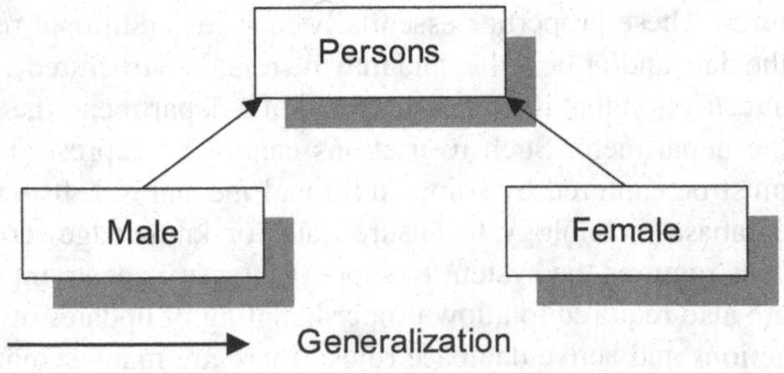

2. Active Generalization

Active classes use the generalization relationship to represent the hierarchical rule structure that is found in most production rule systems. This enables the system to represent complex knowledge. This also enables the system to easily trigger rules, since all related rules are clustered together, i.e., stored in the same object because of inheritance. For example, consider the family rule base system shown in Fig. 7.8. This rule base is presented in a format devised by the author.

Each rule is represented as an active class as shown in Fig. 7.9. The Son class inherits all the attributes and methods from the Malc class and the Child class. The system will easily trigger the child rule (i.e., method child) and the male rule (i.e., method male) in the Son class by using the inheritance hierarchy.

```
Rule Name: Male (X:Person) /* (X:Person) means the paramenter X
                                                   is a Person object */
      IF (X::sex="Male") /* X::sex means the sex attribute value of
                                                   the object X */
      Then true; /* The result of this rule is a boolean */
Rule Name: Child(X:Person, Y:Person) /* The parameters X and Y
                                                   are Person objects */
      IF (X::father=Y) .OR. (X::mother=Y)
      THEN true;
Rule Name: Son(X:Person, Y:Person)
      IF Child(X,Y) .AND. Male(X)
      THEN true;
```

Fig. 7.8 A family knowledge base

Fig. 7.9 The active generalization structure of the family knowledge base

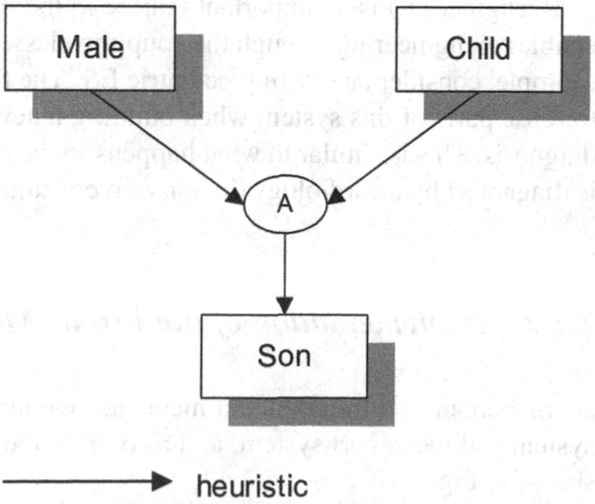

Active generalization is similar to Heuristics. Heuristics can combine logical operators (such as AND, OR, and NOT) to represent complex rules easily and clearly. The AND and OR logical operators combine multiple active entities together in active generalization. For example, the AND operator can combine the Child and Male entities via the active generalization relationship to produce the Son entity. Each active object is represented by a boolean value, i.e., true or false, in the frame model metadata. If the rule in an active class fails to be triggered, the active object will be false; otherwise, the active object will be true. The NOT entity allows negation, i.e., 'not false' is 'true'.

3. Coupling Generalization

The form of generalization between the coupling classes is the same as an active generalization. Different coupling classes can use the generalization relationship to combine to form a new coupling object. This hierarchical structure can represent distributed knowledge (or distributed DB) semantics. For example: Consider two databases, Person (in MS SQL Server) and Staff (in Oracle). The attributes for these two databases are:

Person (MS SQL Server)	Staff (Oracle)
Name	Name
Sex	Department
Father	Position
Mother	Age

The frame model metadata can be used to create two coupling classes to represent these two databases. We can then create a new class called Employee that inherits its properties from these two coupling classes. One problem that may occur during the process is when the same attribute name exists in two different parent classes; for example, Name exists in both the Person class and the Staff class. In such cases, the user needs to define which attribute has a higher priority.

Reengineering is an important feature in the frame model metadata. The system enables reengineering through the coupling classes and coupling generalization. For example, consider an existing pediatric ES. The frame model metadata can be used to reuse parts of this system when building a new ES for child cardiology medical diagnosis. This is similar to what happens in the real world. A child cardiology case is diagnosed by a cardiology doctor who consults with a pediatrician.

7.2.2 *Implementation of the Frame Model Metadata*

To implement the frame model metadata, we must include as inputs, the database system and the expert system, and as output, the Frame model metadata classes as shown in Fig. 7.10.

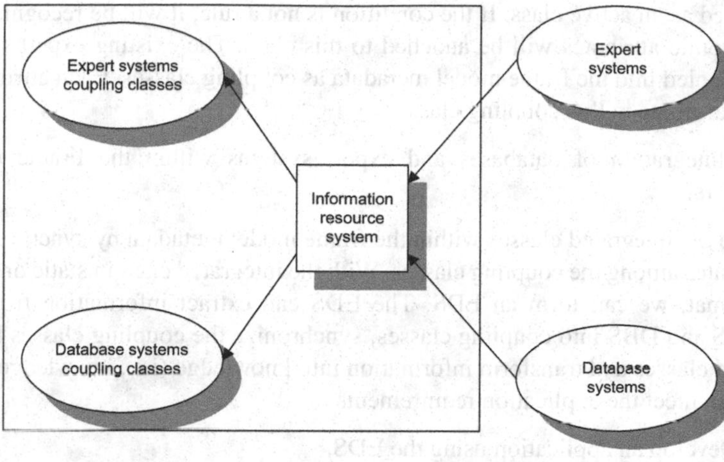

Fig. 7.10 The overview of the frame model metadata architecture

7.3 Steps for Using the Frame Model Metadata in Database and Expert System Integration

We can apply the frame model metadata as an object-oriented-like database in reengineering existing database systems and expert systems in the following:

7.3.1 Reusing Expert Systems

A company may have an expert system. The ES does not, however, store any data in a database. The system developer is required to create a database used by the expert system. This database could be built into a DBMS that has an interface with the existing expert system. This would require many changes to the source code of the existing expert systems. The steps for this implementation are:

Step 1. New application systems requirement analysis.

The system developer must analyze the existing expert system in order to understand what information is required. Database analysis is also required to implement the expert database system.

Step 2. Database creation within the Frame model metadata.

The system developer must develop a database for the expert system. The system developer then converts this database description within the frame model metadata as a static class. Again, the system developer can also add rules to the existing expert system. He/she then converts the rules into the Frame model metadata. Each rule is represented as an active class. Each condition of a multi-condition rule is also represented as an active class. If the condition is not a rule, it will be recognized as a fact. Atomic attributes will be attached to this class. The existing expert system can be coupled into the frame model metadata as coupling classes. Each attribute is a virtual attribute in this coupling class.

Step 3. Integration of databases and expert systems within the Frame model metadata.

Create the integrated classes within the frame model metadata by synchronizing the attributes among the coupling classes. With the integrated class in static or active class format, we can form an EDS. The EDS can extract information from the source ES and DBS into coupling classes, synchronize the coupling classes by the integrated classes and transform information into knowledge (i.e., knowledge engineering) to meet the application requirements.

Step 4. Develop an application using the EDS.

The EDS from the previous steps is a knowledge-based system. System developers can use it to develop new applications. The input to the EDS is the source ES and source DBS; the coupling classes and the integrated classes are temporal in the sense that their existence depends on the users' requirements, at run time only.

7.3.2 *Reusing Database*

In this case, a database exists in the company. The system developer is required to build a new expert system to interface an existing DBMS to access the database. The procedure is:

Step 1. Knowledge acquisition.

The system developer must perform the necessary knowledge acquisition. The result will be the rules of the expert system. The system developers must know the existing database structure, in order to understand what data exists to support the expert system.

Step 2. Create expert systems within the frame model metadata.

The system developer implements the expert system within the frame model metadata. The existing database will be used as "coupling classes."

Step 3. Integrate database systems and expert systems within the Frame model metadata.

The system developer will then integrate the existing database and the existing expert system within the Frame model metadata.

Step 4. Develop new applications using the EDS.

With the EDS, system developers can apply the rules from the source ES, using the data from the source DBS, and develop a knowledge-based system.

7.3.3 *Integrate Database System and Expert System*

In this case, a database system and an expert system already exist in the company. The system developer is required to build a communication channel between these two systems. The usual method to build this integrated system requires changes to some parts of the existing systems. The data can be passed into the existing system by the system I/O stream. The procedure is as follows:

Step 1. Knowledge acquisition.

The system developer must perform the necessary knowledge acquisition. The acquisition processing will focus on what is needed for the integration of the two existing systems. The knowledge acquisition will define what data will be integrated between the two systems.

Step 2. Create coupling classes.

The database system and the expert system will be coupled within the frame model metadata as two separate coupling classes.

Step 3. Integrate database systems and expert systems.

The system developer will then integrate these two subsystems into a system within the frame model metadata.

Step 4. Application development using the EDS.

The source ES and the source DBS can be integrated into an EDS, which transforms the input information into knowledge by developing a knowledge-based system; i.e., applying ES rules and extract data from a DBS.

7.4 A Case Study: Building an Intelligent Human Resource System

This section is concerned with an application of EDS in information processing—the Integrated Human Resource Management System (IHRMS) within a UK government agency. The IHRMS in this agency has been conceived as an information system. The benefits sought from EDS technology are greater flexibility and the ability to handle problems in terms of knowledge and symbolic reasoning.

The government agency employs approximately 4000 staff and is subdivided into a number of Directorates, each being responsible for specific services. Each Directorate has a resource manager who is responsible for a number of projects. The duty of the resource manager is to fit suitably qualified people to specific jobs within each of the projects for their Directorate. Project requirements and progress are monitored by Staff Management Units (SMUs) assigned to each project. It is the SMU who reports back to the resource manager within the directorate. Any vacancy that cannot be filled within the directorate is then considered across the other directorates. This involves staff being transferred between directorates, which is coordinated by the resource manager after consultation with the other directorate SMU and resource managers.

The main task of this project was to match staff with suitable placements and the ability to hold data relating to staff skills, location, availability, personal factors, and other human resource management knowledge. An EDS will be developed for this purpose. In order to keep this example simple, Table 7.1 is a subset of the knowledge base (only three rules) held in the Human Resource Management System (HRMS) ES, and Table 7.2 only shows a part of the personnel database sub-schema used by the EDS.

In this case study, the HRMS is to do the job-person matching. Its process includes the consideration of vacancy criteria, skills criteria, and staff's preferred next work areas. As shown in Table 7.1, the execution of a job-person match begins with the matching process in vacancy criteria, which includes staff type (internal or external), location, directorate, availability, and grade. Staff whose details match vacancy details in these aspects will be selected from the database as the first priority group staff for further evaluation.

Staff selected as the first priority group are then evaluated in their skill criteria. Each vacancy skill is used to match those of staff's skill attainment, and each skill level is checked if it meets the required level. During these processes, a skill qualification point is calculated for each staff and then evaluated to decide whether this staff will be selected as the candidate for this vacancy.

The third condition is to identify if this vacancy is one of the work areas that have been recommended as staff's next moves, and also, if this vacancy is one of staff's preferred next work areas. This information will be displayed together with result explanations for users' reference in decision-making.

The development environment of this EDS example could be any of the three cases as described above. In this case study, we assume that the situation is case 3,

Table 7.1 The sample rules for the HRMS ES

```
Rule Find-Employee:
        IF First-Priority-Group
            AND Skill-Sufficient
            AND Location = Preferred-Working-Area
        THEN    Display Person-id AND Name
Rule First-Priority-Group:
        IF Project-Directorate = Person-Directorate
            AND Staff-Type = "Internal"
            AND Age < Job-Required-Age
            AND Availability ="Yes"
            AND Average-Grade = "High"
        THEN True
Rule Skill-Sufficient:
        IF Job-Required-Skill-1 = Person-Skill-1
            AND Job-Required-Skill-2 = Person-Skill-2
        THEN    True
```

Table 7.2 Personnel Database Sub-Schema

Field Name	Type	Width
ID	Character	8
Name	Character	20
Age	Number	2
Staff-type	Character	15
Directorate	Character	20
Current-status	Character	15
Average-mark	Number	1
Skill-1	Character	20
Skill-2	Character	20

which means the system will reuse an existing ES and an existing database. The frame model metadata forms a communication bridge between the various subsystem.

7.4.1 EDS Development

Step 1. Knowledge Acquisition In this step, the attributes of existing ES and DB must be analyzed. The EDS developer also must define the characteristics of each attribute. Table 7.3 shows a table structure used to represent the result of the knowledge acquisition from an ES. The schema of the table includes four attributes: name, style, type, and memo. The name attribute represents the object name in the existing system. The object will exist in three different kinds of styles, i.e., atom, rule, and variable, in an ES. Atom means that the object is a fact. The rule means that the object is an inference rule. Variable means that the object value will be generated or supported by another event. The type attribute represents the content type of the object. The memo is to enable the developer to write down comments for the object. This will assist the developer to understand the meaning of the object during the development cycle. Table 7.3 shows the result of the knowledge acquisition for the HRM ES.

The EDS developer needs to know which existing databases will relate to the new system. The developer also must understand the existing database schema. There are three ways in which the developer can discover the existing database schema. One way is to go through the database documents to find out its schema. The second method is to retrieve the database schema from the data dictionary system of the existing database system. The final method is to use the database conversion or migration tools to reverse the database schema into a developer understandable format. In the case study, the existing database is stored in a relational DBMS. We used its data dictionary system to retrieve the database schema. The sub-schema of the personnel database can be seen in Table 7.2.

Table 7.3 The Result of the Knowledge Acquisition for the HRM ES

Name	Style	Type	Memo
Find-employee	Rule	Boolean	"Yes"or "no"
First-priority-group	Rule	Boolean	"High", "middle", or "low"
Skill-sufficient	Rule	Boolean	
Display	Rule	Boolean	
Person-id	Variable	Character	
Name	Variable	Character	
Location	Variable	Character	
Preferred-working-area	Variable	Character	
Project-directorate	Variable	Character	
Person-directorate	Variable	Character	
Staff-type	Variable	Character	
Age	Variable	Number	
Job-required-age	Variable	Number	
Availability	Variable	Character	
Average-grade	Variable	Character	
Job-required-Skill-1	Variable	Character	
Person-Skill-1	Variable	Character	
Job-required-Skill-2	Variable	Character	
Person-Skill-2	Variable	Character	
"Internal"	Atom	Character	
"High"	Atom	Character	
"Yes"	Atom	Character	
True	Atom	Boolean	

The final phase of this step is to analyze the synonym relationship between these attributes of the existing two systems. Table 7.4 shows the synonym of the attributes for this case.

There are two kinds of synonym degrees: i.e., Same and Semantic. "Same" means that the two attributes represent the same object with the same semantic. "Semantic" means that the two attributes use different semantics to represent the same object. In this case, the developer must solve the semantic conflict problem between these two attributes. For example, the Availability of HRM indicates whether an employee is available for the new vacancy job or not. The values for this attribute are "yes" or "no." Current-Status of the personnel database represents the job title for an employee. If the employee does not have any duty, its value will be "Vacancy." In order to make the synonym relationship between these two attributes, the following rule must be created.

```
IF Current-Status = "Vacancy"
THEN Availability = "yes"
ELSE Availability ="no"
```

The same problem will happen in the attributes of Average-Grade and Average-Mark for this case study. The following shows another semantic rule for this problem.

Table 7.4 The Synonym Table for the IHRMS

Attribute	System-Type	System-Name	Synonym-Degree	Attribute	System-Type	System-Name
Person-id	ES	HRM	Same	ID	DB	Personnel
Name	ES	HRM	Same	Name	DB	Personnel
Person-directorate	ES	HRM	Same	Directorate	DB	Personnel
Staff-type	ES	HRM	Same	Staff-type	DB	Personnel
Age	ES	HRM	Same	Age	DB	Personnel
Availability	ES	HRM	Semantic	Current-status	DB	Personnel
Average-grade	ES	HRM	Semantic	Average-mark	DB	Personnel
Person-Skill-1	ES	HRM	Same	Skill-1	DB	Personnel
Person-Skill-2	ES	HRM	Same	Skill-2	DB	Personnel

```
IF Average-Mark >= 80
hTHEN Average-Grade = "high"
ELSE IF average-mark >= 50
THEN Average-Grade = "middle"
ELSE Average-Grade = "low"
```

Step 2. Create Coupling Classes The frame model metadata will create two coupling classes for the IHRMS. Figure 7.11 shows the HRM ES coupling class and Fig. 7.12 shows the Personnel DB coupling class. The attributes of the ES coupling class will come from the attributes of HRM. The Variable style of HRM attributes will become to output part attributes of the ES coupling class (see Table 7.3). The system developer must define an input part attribute that will store the result of the HRM ES. In this case, the system developer defines an attribute, called find-employee. The attached method of this attribute will execute the external ES. The attribute of the DB coupling class is a mirror of the personnel database schema (see Table 7.4). Each attribute within the coupling class will contain a method.

The standard frame for the method will depend on the attribute that is an output part attribute or input part attribute. Figure 7.13 shows the standard algorithm of these two type of methods.

There are four generic functions for the frame model metadata to enable the process of the coupling class.

- **Request**: The function is to get a value from the other class's attribute of the system.
- **Write**: The function will write a value to the standard IO stream of the existing external system or a special defined IO stream.
- **Receive**: The function will read a value from the standard IO stream of the existing external system or a special defined IO stream.

```
Class Name: HRM
Attributes:
 Person-id : Method(person-id)                          /*output part*/
Name : Method(name)                                     /*output part*/
 Location : Method(location)                            /*output part*/
 Preferred-Working-Area : Method(preferred-working-area)
                                                        /*output part*/
Project-Directorate : Method(project-directorate)
                                                        /*output part*/
Person-Directorate : Method(person-directorate)
                                                        /*output part*/
Staff-Type : Method(staff-type)                         /*output part*/
Age: Method(age)                                        /*output part*/
Job-Required-Age : Method(job-required-age)/*output part*/
Availability : Method(availability)                     /*output part*/
Average-Grade : Method(average-grade)                   /*output part*/
Job-Required-Skill-1 : Method(job-required-skill-1)
                                                        /*output part*/
Person-Skill-1 : Method(person-skill-1)                 /*output part*/
Job-Required-Skill-2 : Method(job-required-skill-2)
                                                        /*output part*/
Person-Skill-2 : Method(person-skill-2)                 /*output part*/
Find-Employee: Method(find-employees)                   /* input part */
Methods:
   person-id() : text;{…………}
   name() : text; {…………}
   location() : text; {…………}
   preferred-working-area() : text; {…………}
   project-directorate() : text; {…………}
   person-directorate() : text; {…………}
   staff-type() : text; {…………}
   age():number; {…………}
   job-required-age() : number; {…………}
   availability ():text; {…………}
   average-grade ():text; {…………}
   job-required-skill-1() : text; {…………}
   person-skill-1 ():text; {…………}
   job-required-skill-2 ():text; {…………}
   person-skill-2():text; {……}
   find-employee():text; {…….}
```

Fig. 7.11 HRM ES coupling class

```
Class Name: Personnel
Attributes:
 ID: Method(id)                                      /*input part*/
 Name: Method(name)                                  /*input part*/
 Age: Method(age)                                    /*input part*/
 Staff-Type: Method(staff-type)                      /*input part*/
 Directorate: Method(directorate)                    /*input part*/
 Current-Status :Method(current-status)              /* input part*/
 Average-Mark: Method(average-mark)                  /*input part*/
 Skill-1: Method(skill-1)                            /*input part*/
 Skill-2: Method(skill-2)                            /*input part*/
Methods:
 id():text; {...........}
 name():text; {...........}
 age():number; {...........}
 staff-type():text; {...........}
 directorate():text; {...........}
 current-status():text; {...........}
 average-mark():number; {...........}
 skill-1():text; {...........}
 skill-2():text; {...........}
```

Fig. 7.12 Personnel DB coupling class

```
Standard-Output-Part-Attribute(); <result-data-type>;
{       Request the data from the system (i.e. Request)
        Send the data to the external existin system (i.e. Write)}

Standard-Input-Part-Of-Attribute();<result-data-type>;
{       Receive the data from the existing external system
                                        (i.e. Receive)
        Save the data to the system     (i.e. Save)}
```

Fig. 7.13 The standard algorithm of the method for the coupling class

- **Save**: The function will save a value to the other class's attribute of the system.

For example, the method for the "Name" attribute of HRM coupling class will be like:

```
HRM.name(): Text;
{
/* output part attribute variable */
Request (HRM.name);
Write(HRM.name, standard-IO-stream)
}
```

The same process will happen in the DB coupling class. For example, the method for the "Name" attribute of Personnel coupling class will be like:

```
Personnel.name(): Text;
{
/* input part attribute variable */
/* temp = temporary memory. */
Receive (temp, standard-IO-stream);
Save(temp, Personnel.name);
}
```

The real process of the four generic functions will depend on the coupling situation. They will represent the different processes for the different integrating requirements. For example, the Receive function may involve a SQL statement to request data from the external relational database or it processes an RPC (Remote Procedure Call) to execute an external existing ES. The process of these four generic functions will be decided in step 3.

Step 3. Integrate Database System and Expert System To integrate these two coupling classes, the developer must insert the synonym information (see Table 7.4) into the information resource dictionary system (IRDS) as an integrated class. IRDS is a repository for the integrated classes. The integrated class is to integrate and resolve naming conflicts among the coupling classes. The resultant synonym table (Table 7.4) in the form of an integrated class is to synchronize and integrate the coupling classes. The solution is to create two active classes for the two semantic rules described in step 1. Figure 7.14 shows the two active classes.

After this, the developer can insert the synonym data into the IRDS. Table 7.5 shows the synonym part information of the IRDS for the IHRMS.

The processing flow for the coupling class method is:

```
IF the attribute is an output part of attribute
THEN IF the attribute has a synonym
   THEN send message to the synonym object to retrieve
        the data
   ELSE ask users to input the data
ELSE execute the coupling module functions
```

The coupling module functions are a group of low-level communication procedures, e.g., RPC. Different systems will have different procedures.

The EDS is created as a result of the previous step and it consists of the integrated classes (static or active), coupling classes, source ES, and source DBS. When the current EDS needs any information from the external existing systems, the frame model metadata will execute an RPC function to trigger an interface program via the network. The interface program will accept the instructions from the output-channel and pass these onto the external system. The frame model metadata then receives the results from the external system and passes these back to the system via

```
Class Name:          Availability
Attributes:
        Person-id:                  text
        Current-Status:             Method(current-status)
        Availability:               Method(availability)
Methods:
        Current-status(): text
        { Request(Personnel.Current-Status) }

        availability(): text;
        ( IF Current-Status = "Vacancy"
          THEN Availability = "yes"
          ELSE Availability = "no"   }

Class Name:          Average-Grade
Attributes:
        Person-id:                  text
        Average-Mark:               Method(average-mark)
        Average-Grade               Method(average-grade)
Methods:
        Average-mark(): number
        { Request(Personnel.average-mark)   }

        Average-grade(): text;
        ( IF Average-Mark >= 80
          THEN Average-Grade = "high"
           ELSE IF Average-mark >= 50
           THEN Average-Grade ="middle"
           ELSE Average-Grade = "low" }
```

Fig. 7.14 Availability and average-grade active classes

Table 7.5 Synonym Information for the IHRMS

HRM.Person-id = Personnel.ID
HRM.Name = Personnel.Name
HRM.Person-Directorate = Personnel.Directorate
HRM.Staff-Type = Personnel.Staff-Type
HRM.Age = Personnel.Age
HRM.Person-Skill-1 = Personnel.Skill-1
HRM.Person-Skill-2 = Personnel.Skill-2
HRM.Availability = Availability.Availability
HRM.Average-Grade = Average-Grade.Average-Grade

the input-channel. Each external system has an identified input-channel and output-channel. This input-channel and output-channel information is stored in the IRDS. Figure 7.15 shows the coupling module data flow diagram.

Figure 7.16 shows the data flow diagrams of the developed EDS, which acts as a knowledge-based system for the new application.

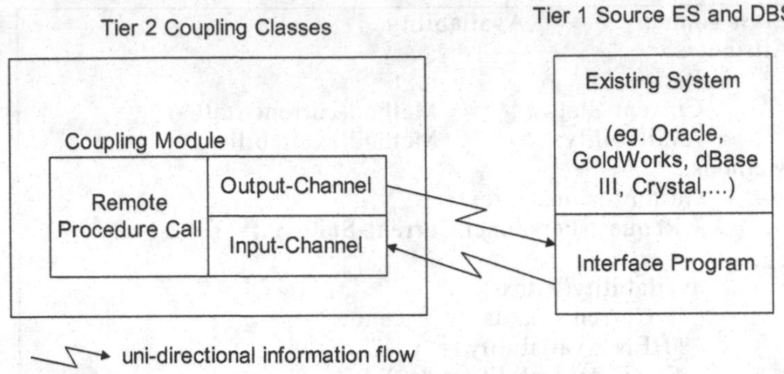

Fig. 7.15 The coupling module data flow diagram

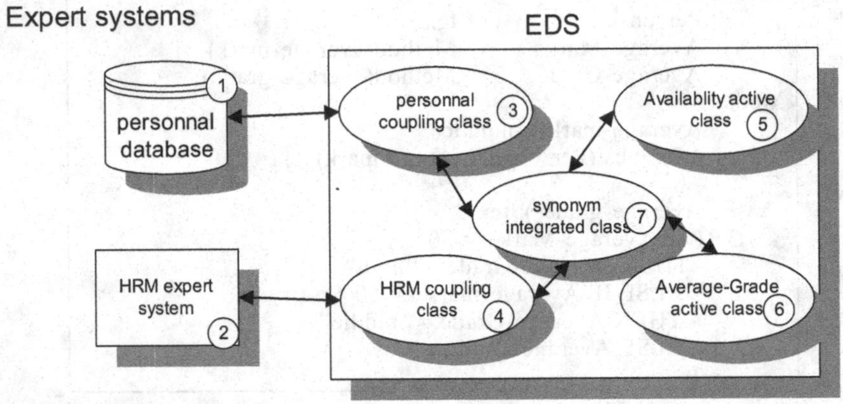

Fig. 7.16 Integrated environment of the IHRMS
Note: Each class (module) in the EDS has a number identifier to be used in Fig. 7.17.

Step 4. Application Development After integrating personnel DB and HRM ES, users can ask the IHRMS to give advice for a particular vacancy job. In this case, the EDS will ask users to key in the vacancy job information. Figure 7.17 shows the flow chart for the personnel information system using the developed EDS.

In this case of a human resource management (HRM) system, Person-Directorate must be derived. Messages will be passed to the HRM coupling object to execute the virtual attributes of Person-Directorate and Project-Directorate. The HRM Person-Directorate has a synonym Personnel Directorate. The system will generate a Personnel DB coupling object and pass a message to the object to derive the data of the Directorate. The Directorate is an input part attribute. The method will submit a SQL statement to retrieve the data from the external existing database. The data will pass back to the HRM ES. The reasoning continues. The second attribute Project-Directorate does not have a synonym. The system will generate a query to ask the end users to enter the data (see Fig. 7.18).

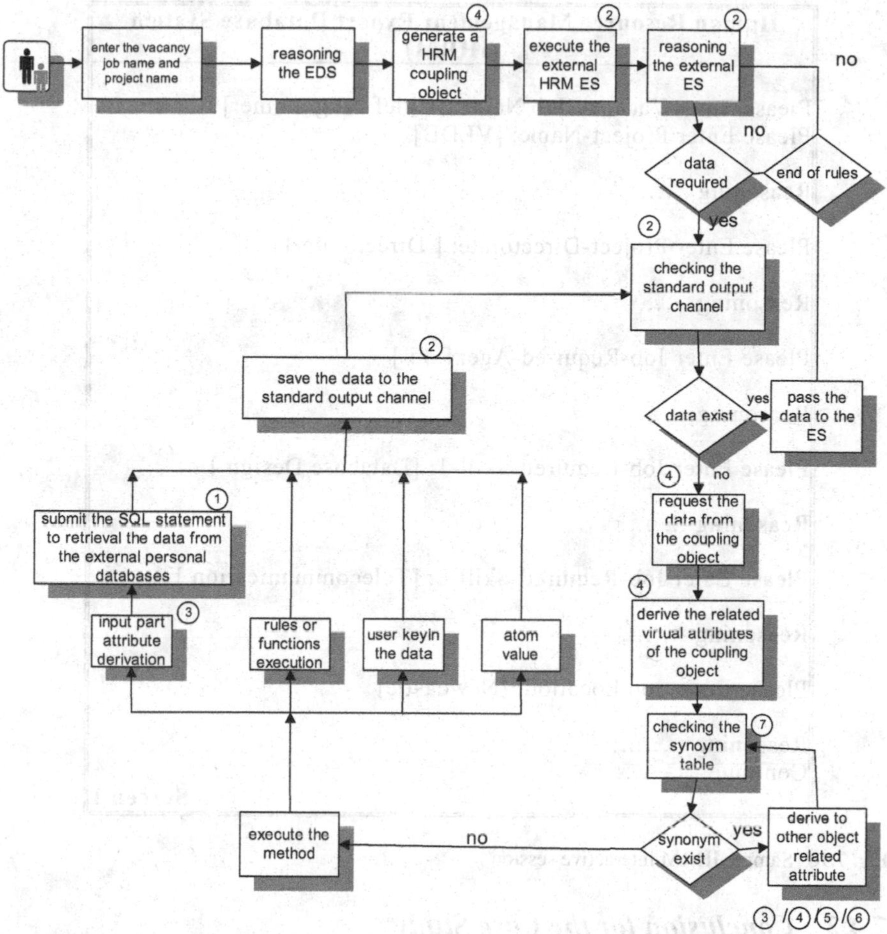

Fig. 7.17 The process flow of the IHRMS

The same process will happen in the other data-required variables, such as HRM. Person-id, HRM.Name, HRM.Staff-Type, and so on. Figure 7.17 shows the process flow mechanism of the IHRMS. There are seven different modules within the IHRMS integrated environment (see Fig. 7.16). Modules 1 to 7 represent the personnel database, HRM expert system, personnel coupling class, HRM coupling class, availability active class, average-grade active class, and synonym integrated class. Figure 7.17 identifies how these modules integrate with the process flow.

The basic mechanism to deal with virtual attributes, which applied a method one attribute at a time, will cause a heavy communication traffic problem. To minimize traffic, a cache or "batches up" communication mechanism is needed.

Figures 7.18, 7.19, and 7.20 show a prototype of the IHRMS. The source DBS provides personnel skill information. The source ES provides selection criteria. The integrated synonym table integrated class, availability class, and average-grade class provide connectivity among coupling classes.

Human Resource Management Expert Database System (IHRM)

Please Enter Vacancy Job Name: [Chief Programmer]
Please Enter Project-Name: [VLDB]

Reasoning ……

Please Enter Project-Directorate: [Directorate 1]

Reasoning ……

Please Enter Job-Required-Age: [35]

Reasoning ……

Please Enter Job-Required-Skill-1: [Database Design]

Reasoning …….

Please Enter Job-Required-Skill-2: [Telecommunication]

Reasoning ……..

Please Enter Job Location: [Newcastle]

Reasoning ……..
Continue ……….

Screen 1

Fig. 7.18 Sample IHRM interactive session

7.4.2 Conclusion for the Case Study

ESs and DBSs have previously been successfully applied to HRM domains (Byun and Suh 1994). This example is different from earlier systems because it couples both the technologies of ES and DB. It has the capability of embedding job-person match knowledge to allow reasoning on large amounts of employee personnel data.

An interface has been successfully established between the ES and DB components by using the frame model metadata so that the staff attributes stored in the personnel DB can be retrieved for reasoning and thus deducing optimal staff for vacancies.

Within its limitations, the HRM application is fully operational and has been evaluated both against the original objectives set for its construction and as a basis for full-scale development.

Human Resource Management Expert Database System (IHRM)

Please Enter 0001 Russell Parsons Preferred-Working-Area: [Newcastle]

Reasoning ....

Please Enter 0003 Paul Chris Preferred-Working-Area: [London]

Reasoning ....

Please Enter 0007 Joseph Fong Preferred-Working-Area: [Newcastle]

Reasoning ....

Please Enter 01001 Peter Smith Preferred-Working-Area: [Edinburgh]

Reasoning ....

Please Enter 0125 Jack Huang Preferred-Working-Area: [Newcastle]

Reasoning ....

Conclusion ....

Screen 2

Fig. 7.19 Sample IHRM interactive session

Human Resource Management Expert Database System (IHRM)

My Advice for the Vacancy Job (Chief Programmer in Project VLSI of Directorate 1) is:

Person ID: 0001
Name: Russell Parsons

Person ID: 0007
Name: Joseph Fong

Person ID: 0125
Name: Jack Huang

Total 3 persons are qualified for this job.

Press Any Key to Continue

Screen 3

Fig. 7.20 Sample IHRM conclusions

7.5 Summary

This chapter describes the need of reengineering ES (or DBS) for the purpose of updating ES (or DBS) information by integrating it with DBS (or ES) to form an EDS. The need for reengineering ES (or DBS) can come from the need to update an existing ES (or DBS). The approach is to develop a DBS (or ES) for the purpose of integrating the existing ES (or DBS) to form an EDS. The users can also reengineer an existing ES and DBS by integrating them into an EDS.

The technique to integrate an ES and a DBS is to form a common frame model metadata for both of them. This frame model metadata acts as an object-oriented-like database. It takes each Frame model metadata as a class that consists of the class name, static attribute, dynamic methods, and constraints. These frame model metadata form coupling classes that extract data from the source DBS, or rules from the source ES. To resolve the naming conflict between the source ES and the source DBS, an integrated class is formed to link them together by using a set of common names for their attributes (i.e., resolve naming conflict). With the integrated classes, the source ES, source DBS, and coupling class (in static or active class forms) can pass information via messages to each other. The resultant EDS thus becomes a knowledge base because it consists of both ES and DBS information and the application knowledge from the users after analysis. System developers can then use the EDS to develop new applications.

Questions Question 7.1

What are the benefits of a database system when compared with a standalone expert system and a standalone relational schema? What type of database is suitable to implement an expert database system?

Answer:

An expert system provides expert knowledge service to the users. A database system provides data to the users. Their functions are limited because the users need to apply them individually to meet their data requirements or to obtain expert system user rules service separately. On the other hand, an expert database system can meet both user data requirements as well as expert rules service because EDS consists of intelligent data such that data can react when user input their expert rules requirements. An object-oriented database is more suitable to implement EDS because it consists of both static and dynamic data which can be used to implement expert system rules inside a database.

Question 7.2

In Frame model metadata implementation, there are 2 class types: static and active, state their differences.

Answer:

In Frame model metadata, static class stores data only, and active class stores action of data because Frame model metadata is rule-based metadata such that it can be used to store expert system rules into a database. As a result, the Frame model can be used to implement expert system rules inside a database which results in an expert database system.

Question 7.3

Illustrate the difference between active generalization and heuristics by giving examples.

Answer:

Generalization is a concept in database design such that two subset groups of data can be generalized into one superset data. Overlap generalization means the data in the subset groups of data can exist in both groups. For example, class CS students is a subset group, and class BA students is another subset group. They can be combined with a superset group student which has all students' records. Since some students are double majors, CS and BA, they are in both subset group students, and therefore form an overlap generalization.

On the other hand, if subset groups data cannot co-exist in both of them, then we have a disjoint generalization. For example, subset group male students and subset group female students cannot co-exist, but they all exist in superset group students data, which is called disjoint generalization.

Heuristics are rules to follow in computerization such as disjoint generalization rules. We can use Frame model metadata to implement heuristics disjoint generalization rules as follows:

Frame Model Logical Schema Header class

Class Name	Primary key	Parents	Operation	Class Type
Students	SID	0		Static
Male students	SID	Students	Call Male_S	Static
Female students	SID	Students	Call Female_S	Static

Attribute class

Attribute Name	Class Name	Attribute type	Associate Attribute	Default Value	Method Name	Description
SID	Students	Integer			Create_S	Superclass primary key
S_Name	Students	Character			Create_S	Superclass non-key
SID	M_ Students	Integer			Create_MS	Subclass primary key
S_Name	M_ Students	Character			Create_MS	Subclass non-key
SID	F_ Students	Integer			Create_FS	Subclass primary key
S_Name	F_ Students	Character			Create_FS	Subclass non-key

Constraint class

Constraint_Name	Method_ Name	Class_ Name	Parameters	Ownership	Event	Sequence
Create male students	Create_MS	M_students	SID S_Name	Self	Create	Before
Create female students	Create_FS	F_students	SID S_Name	Self	Create	Before

Method class

Method_ Name	Class_ name	Parameter	Sequence	Method Type	Condition	Action
Create_ MS	M_ students	@ SID, @S_Name			If (select * from F_ students where SID = @SID) = null	Insert create (@ SID, @S_Name)
Create_FS	F_ students	@ SID, @S_Name			If (select * from M_ students where SID = @SID) = null	Insert create (@ SID, @S_Name)

Bibliography

Byun DH, Suh EH (1994) Human resource management expert system technology. Expert Syst 11(2):109–118

Gray PMD, Kulkarni KG, Paton NM (1992) Object-oriented databases: a semantic data model approach. Prentice Hall, Hoboken. ISBN 0-13-630203-3

Houtsma MAW, Apers PMG (1990) Data and knowledge model: a proposal, advances in database programming languages. ACM Press, New York. ISBN 0-201-50257-7

Huang SM (1994) An integrated expert database system, Phd Thesis, University of Sunderland, UK

Chapter 8
Data Normalization

Database normalization aims to remove irregularity (abnormality) of update. The unnormal database is difficult to maintain the correctness of the database after the update while the normalized database is more user-friendly for update. On the other hand, denormalization is the reverse of normalization. It transforms the normalized database design into an unnormal form. As a result, the denormalized database is difficult to update. Nevertheless, the denormalized database can perform faster than the normalized database because it requires less join operations for queries. Also, data normalization eliminates redundant data for better space utilization and user-friendliness in database update.

The XML data normalization requires an XML data modeling with minimum fragments among elements. The normalized XML database design shows how to eliminate data redundancy by replacing repeating data with pointers referring to their unique primary copy element under the root element. The minimum fragments XML design is more efficient and is derived from a minimum closure of data dependencies of representation of the data semantics among elements as a fragment under the root element.

8.1 Relational Data Normalization Without Update Irregularity

Relational data normalization is to eliminate data redundancy and update the irregularity of relational schema. Irregularity of database design needs to be normalized in order to ensure user-friendliness of updating the relational database.

There is an unnormal form, followed by first, second, third, Boyce-Codd, fourth, and fifth normal form. The higher normal form implies the lower normal form, but not vice versa. We need to analyze data dependency to determine the data's normal

J. S. P. Fong, K. Wong Ting Yan, *Information Systems Reengineering, Integration and Normalization*, https://doi.org/10.1007/978-3-030-79584-9_8

form. Data dependency relates data with each other in certain constraint rules. The unnormal form can be normalized up to fifth normal form as shown below (Fig. 8.1):

Data redundancy means that the elimination of redundant data is without loss of information. An unnormalized relation implies that too many data relationship dependencies in the same table, which is difficult to operate. A normalized database is easy to use for operations of insert, update, and delete.

Normalization starts with an unnormal form (UNF) with a universe of relations such that each table may have multiple values. For example, the following table is an unnormal form with its multiple valued attributes as shown below (Fig. 8.2):

where relation R (S#, S-Name, {Enrol}) is an UNF with { } as repeating group data

Functional dependency implies that a determinant can determine dependency fields. Inclusion dependency implies that a subclass data must be within its superclass data. Multivalued dependency implies that each determinant can determine a multiple value. Join dependency implies that the join of all of its attributes implies an n-ary relationship within the relation.

In general, a functional dependency describes the relationship between attributes such that a determinant (key field) determines dependent (non-key) fields as shown below:

Determines
FD: Determinant ➔ Dependent field

For example (Fig. 8.3),

A relation is in first normal form (1NF) if all attributes are atomic value, and there is a primary key attribute with a uniquely identifiable value which can determine non-key attributes.

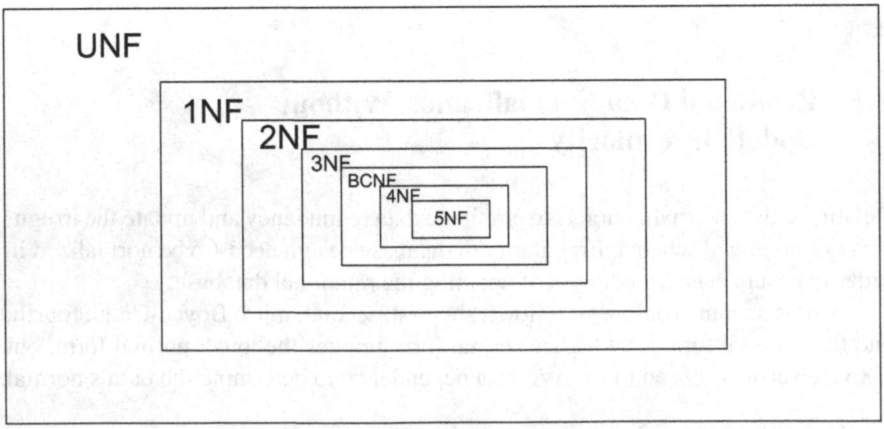

Fig. 8.1 Levels of relational data normal forms

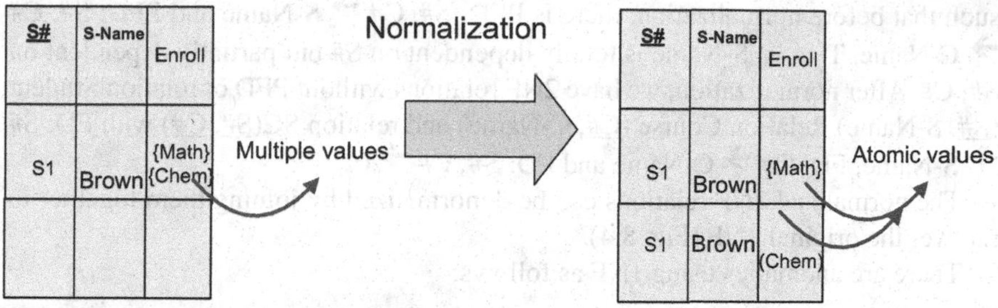

Fig. 8.2 Normalization of first norm form

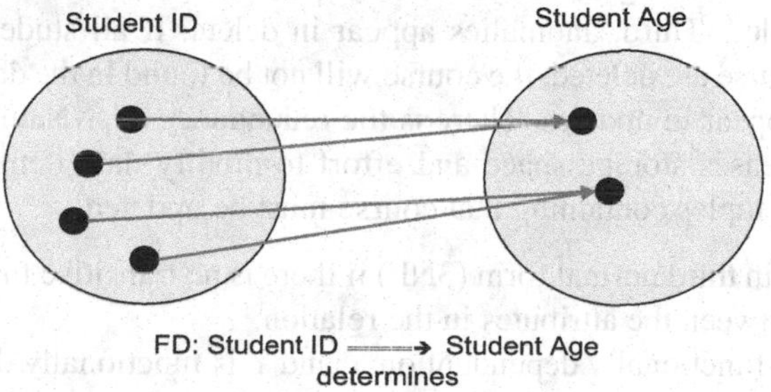

Fig. 8.3 Data determination of functional dependency

Normalized into

UNF ➔ 1NF

Eliminate multiple valued attributes

For example, after normalization by transforming multiple valued attributes into an atomic single value, the unnormal form becomes first normal form as follows:

Relation R (<u>S#</u>, S-Name, Enroll) is a 1NF where all attributes are atomic with S# as primary key.

A relation is in second normal form (2NF) if there is no partial data dependency (PFD) with the relation.

Normalized into

1NF ➔ 2NF

Eliminate partial functional dependency

For example, the following is a 1NF relation SCN (S#, S-Name, C#, C-Name) such that before normalization, there is PFD: S#, C# → S-Name and PFD: S#, C# → C-Name. That is, S-Name is totally dependent on S# but partially dependent on S#, C#. After normalization, we have 2NF relations without PFD of relation Student (S#, S-Name) Relation Course (C#, C-Name) and relation SC(S#, C#) with FD: S# → S-Name, FD: C# → C-Name and FD: S#, C# → 0.

The normalized 2NF relations can be denormalized by joining them together to recover the original 1NF (Fig. 8.4).

There are anomalies using 1NF as follows:

First, 1NF relations require a less complicated application to operate as opposed to unnormalized relations. Second, anomalies appear in insert. Since the primary key (PK) is composed of C# and S#, both details of student and course must be known before inserting an entry. For example, to add a course, at least one student is enrolled. Third, anomalies appear in delete. If all students attending a particular course are deleted, the course will not be found in the database. Fourth, anomalies appear in updates. There is the redundancy of S-Name and C-Name. Also, it increases storage space and effort to modify data item. If a course is modified, all tuples containing that course must be updated.

A relation is in third normal form (3NF) if there is no transitive functional dependency (TFD) between the attributes in the relation.

TFD: If X is functionally dependent on Y and Y is functionally dependent on Z, then X is transitively dependent on Z.

Normalized into

2NF → 3NF

Eliminate transitive functional dependency

For example, the relation PME (P#, M#, E#) with FD: P# → M#, FD: M# → E#, and TFD: P# → E# can be normalized into 3NF as relation PM (P#, M#) and ME

1NF

S#	S-Name	C#	C-Name
S1	Brown	C1	Math
S1	Brown	C2	Chem
S1	Brown	C3	Phys
S2	Smith	C2	Chem
S2	Smith	C3	Phys
S2	Smith	C4	Math
S3	Brown	C2	Chem
S3	Brown	C3	Phys

Normalization →

← Denormalization

2NF

S#	S-Name
S1	Brown
S2	Smith
S3	Brown

⋈

C#	C-Name
C1	Math
C2	Chem
C3	Phys
C4	Math

⋈

S#	C#
S1	C1
S1	C2
S1	C3
S2	C2
S2	C3
S2	C4
S3	C2
S3	C3

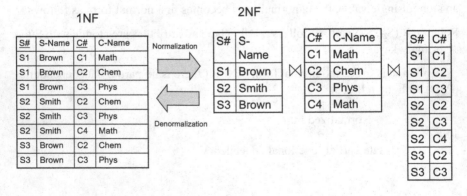

Fig. 8.4 Normalization of second normal form

(M#, E#) with FD: P# → M# and FD: M# → E#. The normalized relations can be denormalized by joining them together to recover the original 2NF relation (Fig. 8.5).

However, there are anomalies in 2NF. Suppose we have the relations PRODUCT, MACHINE, and EMPLOYEE as

Relation PME (P#, M#, E#) with FD: P# → M#, FD: P# → E#, FD: M# → E#.

The tuple (P1, M1, E1) means product P1 is manufactured on machine M1 which is operated by employee E1. There are anomalies in insert. It is not possible to store the fact that which machine is operated by which employee without knowing at least one product produced by this machine. There are anomalies in delete. If an employee is fired, the fact that which machine he operated and what product that machine produced is also lost. There are normalizes in update. If one employee is assigned to operate another machine, then several tuples have to be updated as well.

A relation is in Boyce-Codd normal form (BCNF) if all determinant is a candidate key.

Normalized into

3NF → BCNF

Case Study I:

Relation SCH (StudentID, CourseID, HKID) consists of FD: StudentID, CourseID → HKID and FD: HKID → StudentID. It is not in BCNF because HKID is a determinant but is not a candidate key. After normalization, Relation SC (StudentID, CourseID) with FD: StudentID, CourseID → 0 and Relation SH (HKID, StudentID) with FD: HKID → StudentID. Therefore, all determinants are candidate keys, and therefore they are in BCNF.

The normalized relations can be denormalized by joining them together to recover the original 3NF relation (Fig. 8.6).

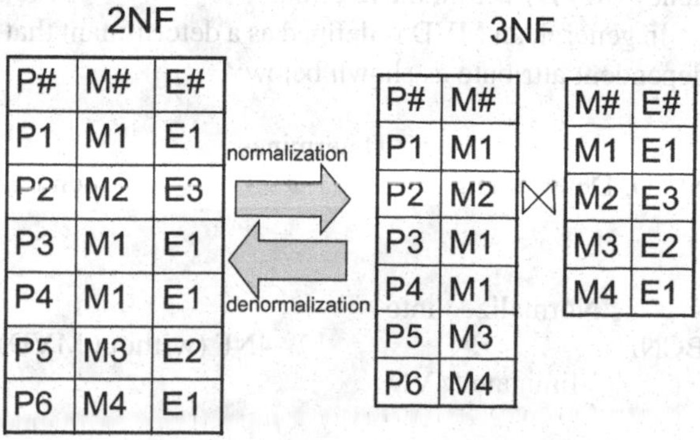

Fig. 8.5 Normalization of third normal form

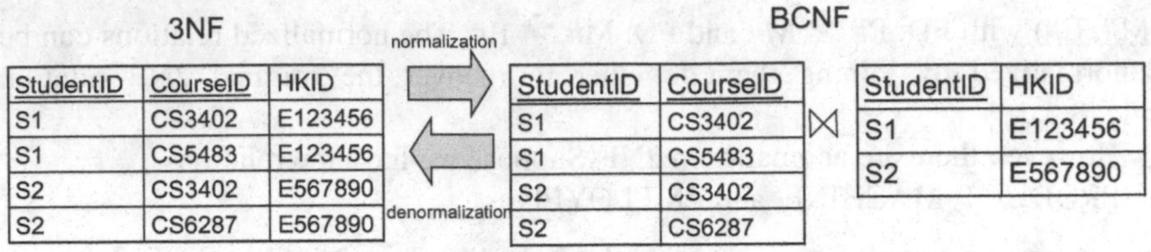

Fig. 8.6 Normalization and denormalization of BCNF

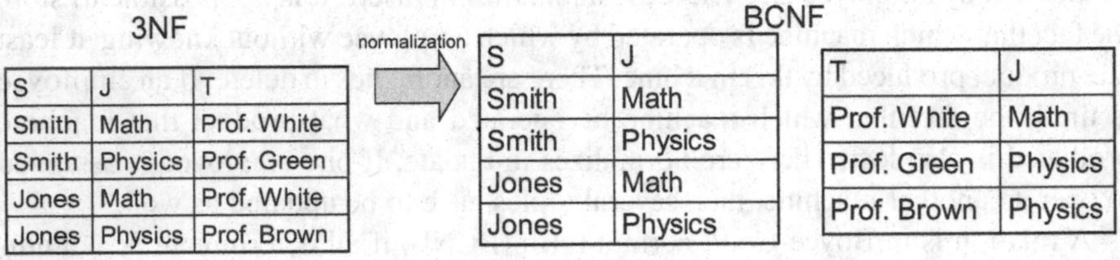

Fig. 8.7 Normalization only of BCNF

In 3NF, there are anomalies in update. If the fact that Student S1 takes more courses, then the HKID E123456 needs to repeat many times, which is a waste of computer time and space, which is similar for student S2. It is because H is a determinant but not a candidate key.

Case Study II:

Relation SJT (<u>S</u>, <u>J</u>, T) consists of FD: S, J ➔ T and FD: T ➔ J. It is not in BCNF because T is a determinant but is not a candidate key. After normalization, Relation SJ (<u>S</u>, <u>T</u>) with FD: S, T ➔ 0 and Relation TJ (<u>T</u>, J) with FD: T ➔ J. Therefore, all determinants are candidate keys, and therefore, they are in BCNF.

The normalized relations cannot be denormalized by joining them together because there is loss of information of who is the teacher of Smith taking physics in the joined relation (Fig. 8.7).

A relation is in fourth normal form (4NF) if there is no multivalued data dependency (MVD) within the relation.

In general, an MVD is defined as a determinant that determines a multiple valued dependent attribute as shown below:

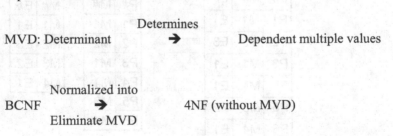

Determines

MVD: Determinant ➔ Dependent multiple values

Normalized into

BCNF ➔ 4NF (without MVD)

Eliminate MVD

For example, Relation CTT(<u>Course</u>, <u>Teacher</u>, <u>Text</u>) consists of MVD Course →→ Teacher, and MVD Course →→Text before normalization.

After normalization, Relation CT (<u>Course</u>, <u>Teacher</u>) with FD: Course, Teacher → 0, and Relation CX (<u>Course</u>, <u>Text</u>) with Course, Text → 0, and they are without MVD. Therefore, they are in 4NF. The normalized relations can be denormalized by joining them together to recover the original BCNF relation (Fig. 8.8).

There are anomalies of BNCF in insert. For example, to add the information that the physics course uses, a new text called Advanced Mechanism, it is necessary to create three new tuples, one for each of the three teachers.

Similarly, for two relations CT(Course, Teacher) and CX (Course, Text), they can be reconstructed into relation CTT (Course, Teacher, Text) with MVD Course →→ Teacher|Text in 2-decomposability.

A relation is in fifth normal form (5NF) if there is no join dependence (JD) within the relation as shown below:

JD: Project Attributes $\bowtie$ … $\bowtie$ Project Attributes → Relation (Attributes,… Attributes)

Relation with JD → (Normalized into / Eliminate JD) 5NF Relations(without JD)

A join dependency means that if binary relationships occur in three attributes a, b, and c, then there is a join dependency in these three attributes.

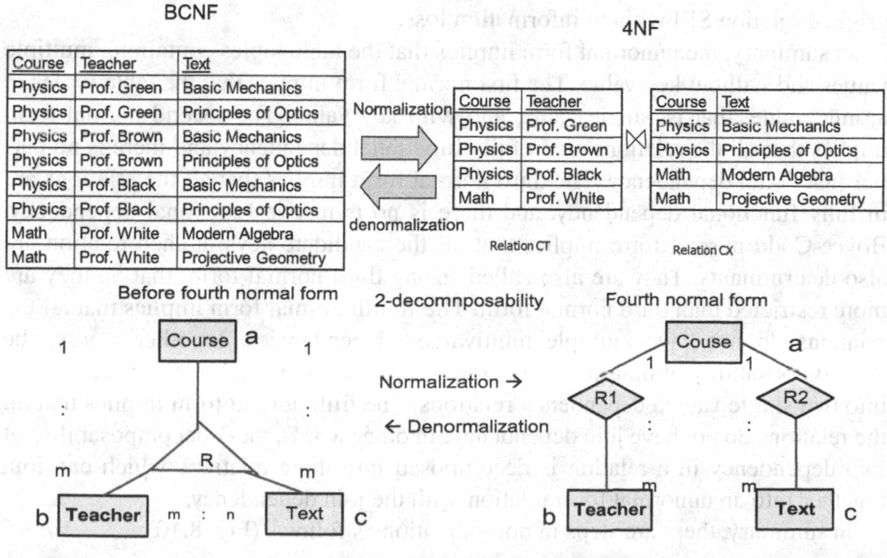

Fig. 8.8 Normalization of fourth normal form

For example, before normalization, Relation SPJ (S#, P#, J#) consists of JD such that

JD(join dependency):

If (s1, p1), (p1, j1), (s1, j1) occur, then (s1, p1, j1) occurs:

JD: SPJ(S#, P#, J#) = {S#, P#} $\bowtie$ {P#, J#} $\bowtie$ {S#, J#} where $\bowtie$ is a natural join.

Therefore, relation SPJ is not in 5NF.

After normalization, Relation SP (S#, P#) with FD: S#, P# ➔ 0, Relation PJ (P#, J#) with FD: P#, J# ➔ 0 and Relation SJ (S#, J#) with FD: S#, J# ➔ 0. Since they do not have JD, therefore, they are in 5NF. The normalized relations can be denormalized by joining them together to recover the original 4NF relation (Fig. 8.9).

Given a relation SPJ in 4NF, there are abnormalities in insert. If insert (S1, P1, J2), (S1, P2, J1), and (S2, P1, J1), then (S1, P1, J1) must also be inserted. On the other hand, if one of (S1, P1, J2), (S1, P2, J1), and (S2, P1, J1) is deleted, then (S1, P1, J1) must also be deleted.

For an n-ary relationship, a ternary relationship of three decomposability in this example is a relation with all three attributes as keys. The three decomposability of the relation into three binary relationships may or may not exist. If a relation can be decomposed into three relations, it implies that there is join dependency in the relation as shown in the above example of relation SPJ. Otherwise, the relation cannot be decomposed into three relations because there is no join dependency in the relation.

The normalized 5NF is relation JS (J#, S#), relation PJ (P#, J#), and relation SP (S#, p#). Therefore, for the three relations as a result of three decomposability as shown in relation SPJ with JD, these three relations can be joined together into original relation SPJ without information loss.

In summary, the unnormal form implies that the table tuples containing multiple values and without key value. The first normal form implies that the table tuples in atomic value, that is, single value, and with key value. The second normal form implies that all the relations are in fully functional dependency and there is no partial functional dependency. The third normal form implies that all the relations are in fully functional dependency, and there is no transitive functional dependency. Boyce-Codd normal form implies that all the candidate keys in each relation are also determinants. They are also called strong third normal form, that is, they are more restricted than third normal form. The fourth normal form implies that all the relations do not have multiple multivalued dependencies. In other words, the 2-decomposability of multiple multivalued dependency in a relation is decomposed into two single valued dependency relations. The fifth normal form implies that all the relations do not have join dependency. In other words, the 3-decomposability of join dependency in a relation is decomposed into three relations which can join together into an unnormal form relation with the join dependency.

In summary, there are steps in normalization as follows (Fig. 8.10):

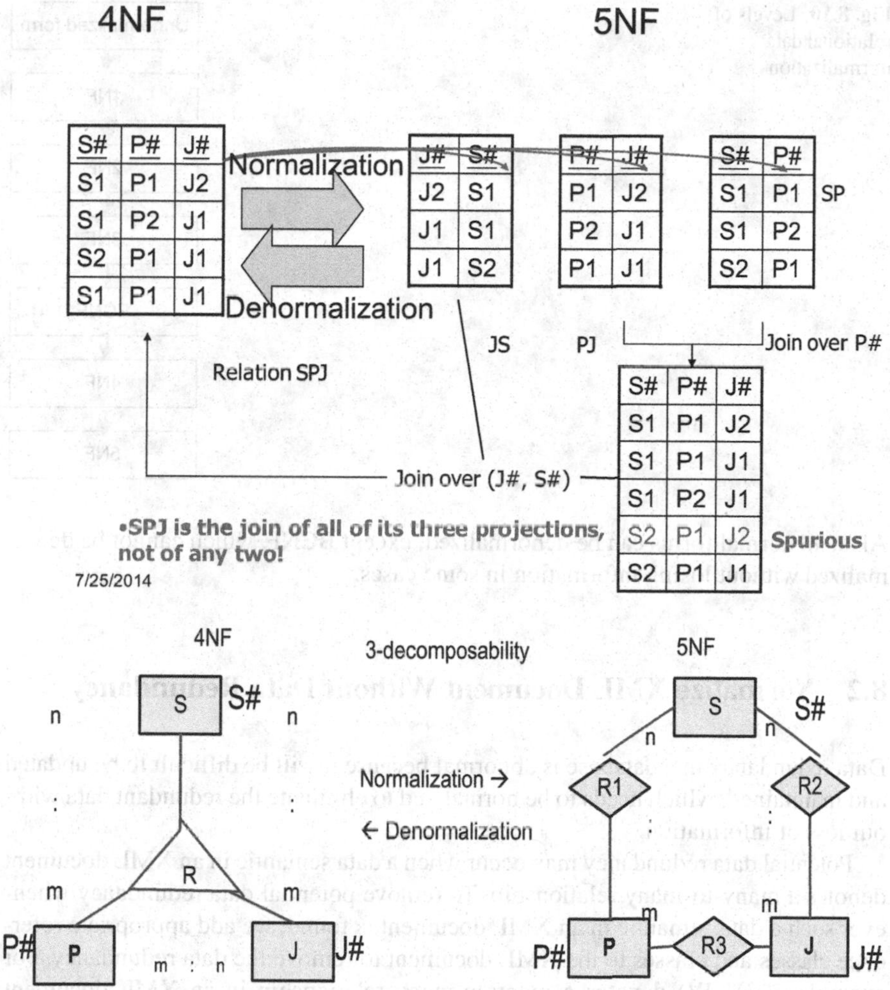

Fig. 8.9 Normalization of fifth normal form

(i) Decompose all data structures that are not 2D into 2D relations of segments.
(ii) Eliminate any partial dependency.
(iii) Eliminate any transitive dependency.
(iv) Eliminate any remaining FD in which determinant is not a candidate key.
(v) Eliminate any MVD.
(vi) Eliminate any JD that are implied by candidate keys.

In general, relations in a higher normal form implies the relations are already in a lower normal form. Data dependency are data constraints rules among data fields. Transitive functional dependency (TFD) is redundant information in the relations.

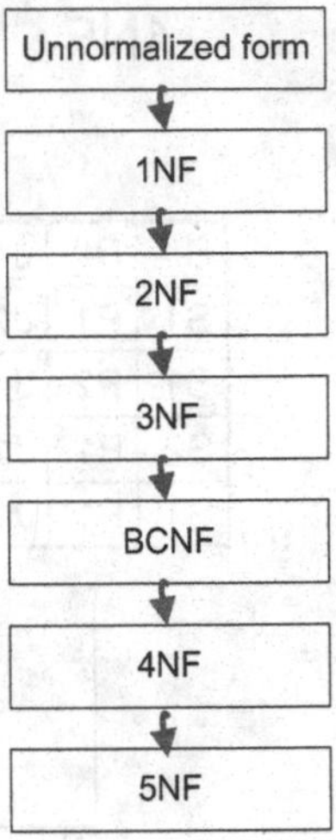

Fig. 8.10 Levels of relational data normalization

Also, all normal forms can be denormalized, except BCNF, which cannot be denormalized without losing information in some cases.

8.2 Normalize XML Document Without Data Redundancy

Data redundancy in a database is abnormal because it will be difficult to be updated and maintained, which needs to be normalized to eliminate the redundant data without loss of information.

Potential data redundancy may occur when a data semantic in an XML document denotes a many-to-many relationship. To remove potential data redundancy whenever such a data semantic in an XML document is found, we add appropriate reference classes and classes to the XML document to remove the data redundancy. For example, if (V, W) denotes a many-to-many relationship in an XML document where V is the parent node and W is the child node, then we add a new class W to the XML document and replace W in (V, W) by (V, W^) where W^ is a reference class to W. In other words, W^ denotes the IDs, or keys, of W. In this way, potential data redundancy is removed.

Of all the data semantics, only four data semantics may cause data redundancy. They are overlap generalization, partial participation, m-to-n cardinality, and n-ary relationships. The arguments for the other data semantics of this paper that do not cause data redundancy are as follows:

Specialization: Specialization does not cause data redundancy because each instance of specialization is also an instance of generalization. Hence, it does not have a many-to-many relationship from the parent node to the child node. Therefore, it does not cause data redundancy.

Disjoint generalization: This case is similar to the case of specialization except there is more than one specialization. Additionally, the specializations are all pairwise disjoint. Thus, there is no data redundancy.

Categorization: In this case, there is only one specialization, but there are multiple generalizations. However, an instance of specialization is an instance of only one generalization by definition. As such, there is no data redundancy.

Total participation: This data semantic is that there is a 1-to-1 or 1-to-many relationship from the parent node to the child node and that each instance in the child node participates totally in the relationship. Thus, it does not denote a many-to-many relationship, and therefore, it has no redundancy.

1-to-1 Cardinality: This data semantic is that there is a 1-to-1 relationship from the parent node to the child node and that each instance in the child node participates at most once in the relationship. Thus, it does not denote a many-to-many relationship, and therefore, it has no redundancy.

1-to-many Cardinality: This data semantic is that there is a 1-to-many relationship from the parent node to the child node and that each instance in the child node participates more than once in the relationship. Thus, it does not denote a many-to-many relationship, and therefore, it has no redundancy.

Algorithm:

```
For each data semantic in the input XML schema, do:
Begin
Case data semantic of
Overlap generalization:
Begin   Let (V, W) be an edge of the overlap generalization;
        Add each specialization W as a new child node to XML;
        Replace W by W^ in (V, W) to obtain (V, W^);
End;
Partial participation:
Begin   Let (V, W) be the partial participation;
        Add both V and W as new child nodes to XML;
        Replace V by V^, W by W^ in (V,W) to obtain (V^,W^);
End;
Many-to-many Cardinality:
Begin   Let (V, W, Z) be the m-to-n relationship;
        Add V, W, Z as new child nodes to XML;
        Replace V by V^, W by W^, Z by Z^ in (V, W, Z) to
        obtain (V^, W^, Z^);
end;
N-ary relationship:
Begin   Let (V, W1, W2, …, Wn) be the n-ary relationship;
        Add V, W1, W2, …, Wn as new child nodes to XML;
        Replace V by V^, W1 by W1^, W2 by W2^, …, Wn by
        Wn^ in (V, W1, W2, …, Wn) to obtain (V^, W1^,
        W2^, …, Wn^)
End
Case end
End
```

Graphically, the above transformations are depicted as follows:

Our strategy to prove that our normalization process preserves the information content of the input XML document by induction on the number *n* of normalization operations applied to the XML document. We use the notation D*i* to denote the input XML document that has *i* normalization operations performed on it. Particularly, D0 is the original input XML document.

Basis: When $n = 0$, no normalization operation has yet been applied. Thus, the information content remains the same and is obviously preserved.

Induction: Assume the information content of the input XML document is preserved after applying $k \geq 0$ normalization operations for some fixed integer *k*. That is, D0, D1, D2, …, D*k* all have the same information content. We now consider applying the $(k + 1)$th normalization operation, and we need to show that the information content of D*k* and D*k*+1 are the same. Our argument focuses on each of the data semantics that require normalization operations.

- Overlap generalization: In this case, two generalization XML elements Y and Z have the same content. Our normalization operation adds a new XML element E with the same content as e under the root element. As shown in Fig. 9.10. Since E has the same content as Y and Z and Y' and Z' are XML reference elements that point to E, the information content of D*k* is preserved. In other words, D*k* and D*k*+1 have the same information content.
- m-to-n Cardinality: In this case, some XML elements have the same information content, and they have many-to-many relationships among them. Again, for the XML elements that have the same information content, we create a new XML element E with the same information content under the root element. In other words, the instance of elements d type and e type are in many-to-many cardinality. We create new XML elements d_ref type and e_ref type with the same information content under the root element as shown in Fig. 9.11. Then, we make all other XML elements with the same information content as XML reference elements that point to E. As such, we preserve the m-to-n relationship between them.

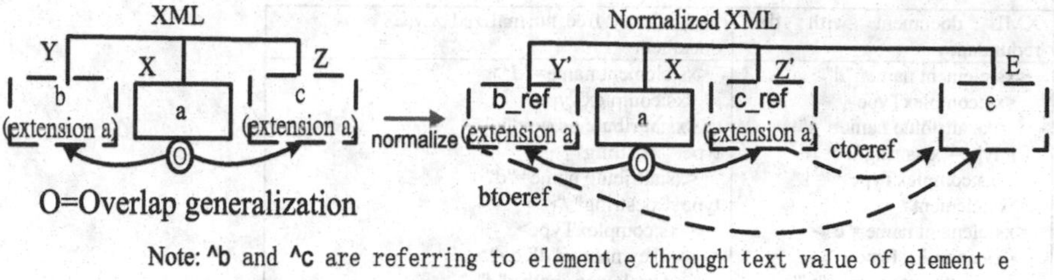

Fig. 8.11 Normalized XML document in overlap generalization

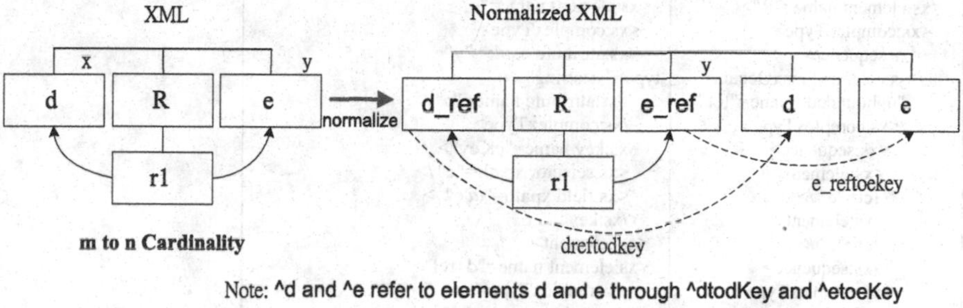

Fig. 8.12 Normalized XML document in many-to-many cardinality

By the induction hypothesis, D0, D1, D2, …, D*k* all have the same information content. We have also proved that D*k* and D*k*+1 have the same information content. Thus, D0 and D*k*+1 have the same information content and the proof is complete.

Example: Normalize XML document of Overlap Generalization (Fig. 8.11)

Notice that b_ref and c_ref refer the specific attributes and/or sub-elements of their own. The overlap parts (inherited from element "a" is normalized to be an instance of element e.

Example: Normalized XML document of m-to-n Cardinality (Fig. 8.12)

XML document of many-to-many cardinality

XML document with data redundancy	Redundancy free normalized XML document
<xs:element name="d"> <xs:complexType> <xs:attribute name="x" type="xs:string" /> </xs:complexType> </xs:element> <xs:element name="e"> <xs:complexType> <xs:attribute name="y" type="xs:string" /> </xs:complexType> </xs:element> <xs:element name="R"> <xs:complexType> <xs:sequence> <xs:element maxOccurs= "unbounded" name="R1"> <xs:complexType> <xs:sequence> <xs:element ref="d" /> <xs:element ref="e" /> </xs:sequence> </xs:complexType> </xs:element> </xs:sequence> </xs:complexType> </xs:element>	<xs:element name="d"> <xs:complexType> <xs:attribute name="x" type="xs:string" /> <xs:attribute name="d" type="xs:string" /> </xs:complexType> <xs:key name="dKey"> <xs:selector xpath="d" /> <xs:field xpath="@d" /> </xs:key> </xs:element> <xs:element name="e"> <xs:complexType> <xs:attribute name="y" type="xs:string" /> <xs:attribute name="e" /> </xs:complexType> <xs:key name="eKey"> <xs:selector xpath="e" /> <xs:field xpath="@e" /> </xs:key> </xs:element> <xs:element name="d_ref"> <xs:complexType> <xs:attribute name="d" type="xs:string" /> </xs:complexType> <xs:keyref name="d_refTodKey" refer="dKey"> <xs:selector xpath="d_ref" /> <xs:field xpath="@d" /> </xs:keyref> </xs:element> <xs:element name="e_ref"> <xs:complexType> <xs:attribute name="e" type="xs:string" /> </xs:complexType> <xs:keyref name="e_refToeKey" refer="eKey"> <xs:selector xpath="e_ref" /> <xs:field xpath="@e" /> </xs:keyref> </xs:element> <xs:element name="R"> <xs:complexType> <xs:sequence> <xs:element maxOccurs="unbounded" name="R1"> <xs:complexType> <xs:sequence> <xs:element ref="d_ref" /> <xs:element ref="e_ref" /> </xs:sequence> </xs:complexType> </xs:element> </xs:sequence> </xs:complexType> </xs:element>

The XML document before and after normalization

XML before normalization	XML document after normalization
<r1> <d>d1</d> <e>e1</e> </r1> <r1> <d>d1</d> <e>e2></e> </r1> <r1> <d>d2</d> <e>e1</e> </r1>	<d d–"123">d1</d> <e e="456">e1</e> <e e="789">e2</e> <r1> <d_ref d="123"/> <e_ref e="456"/> </r1> <r1> <d_ref d="123"/> <e_ref e="789"/> </r1> <r1> <d_ref d="000"/> <e_ref e="456"/> </r1>

Case Study
Given an XML schema on computer facility inventory, data redundancy with the same models appears twice as shown below (Fig. 8.13):

The following is the XML document before normalization with repeating data as data redundancy:

<?xml version="1.0"?>

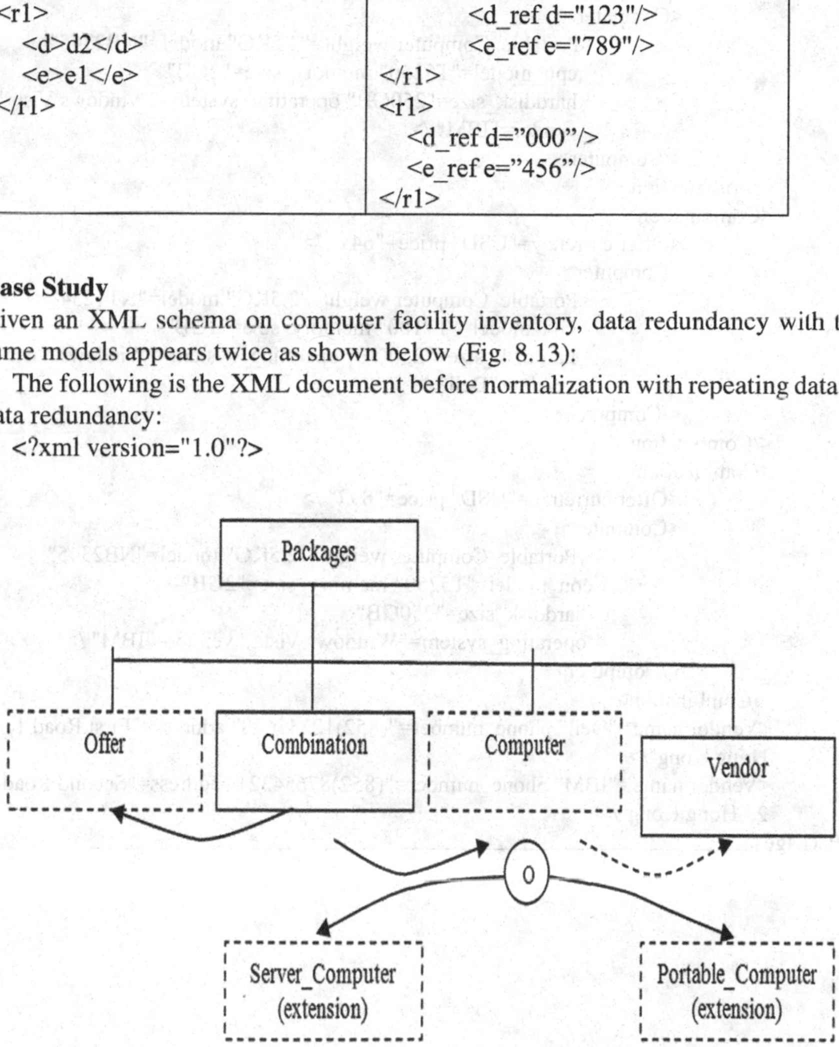

Fig. 8.13 XML schema before normalization

```xml
<Packages>
        <Combination>
                <Offer currency="HKD" price="5000" />
                <Computer>
                        <Portable_Computer weight="2.5KG" model="NT1234"
                         cpu_model="T7100" memory_size="1GB"
                         harddisk_size="250GB"
                         operating_system="Windows Vista" vendor="Dell" />
                </Computer>
        </Combination>
        <Combination>
                <Offer currency="HKD" price="7000" />
                <Computer>
                        <Portable_Computer weight="2.5KG" model="NB2345"
                         cpu_model="T5250" memory_size="2GB"
                         harddisk_size="250GB" operating_system="Windows Vista"
                         vendor="IBM" />
                </Computer>
        </Combination>
        <Combination>
                <Offer currency="USD" price="641" />
                <Computer>
                        <Portable_Computer weight="2.5KG" model="NT1234"
                         cpu_model="T7100" memory_size="1GB"
                         harddisk_size="250GB" operating_system="Windows Vista"
                         vendor="Dell" />
                </Computer>
        </Combination>
        <Combination>
                <Offer currency="USD" price="897" />
                <Computer>
                        <Portable_Computer weight="2.5KG" model="NB2345"
                        cpu_model="T5250" memory_size="2GB"
                         harddisk_size="250GB"
                         operating_system="Windows Vista" vendor="IBM" />
                </Computer>
        </Combination>
        <Vendor name="Dell" phone_number="(852)12345678" address="First Road 1,
        Hong Kong"/>
        <Vendor name="IBM" phone_number="(852)87654321" address="Second Road
        2, Hong Kong"/>
</Packages>
```

We normalize the data redundancy of the many-to-many cardinality between element Server-Computer and element Portable-Computer by replacing them with Server-Computer-Ptr and element Portable-Computer -Ptr. The two pointers refer to element Server-Computer and element Portable-Computer as shown below (Fig. 8.14):

The duplicated elements in the XML document are replaced with reference key, and the following is the normalized XML document with redundant elements removed.

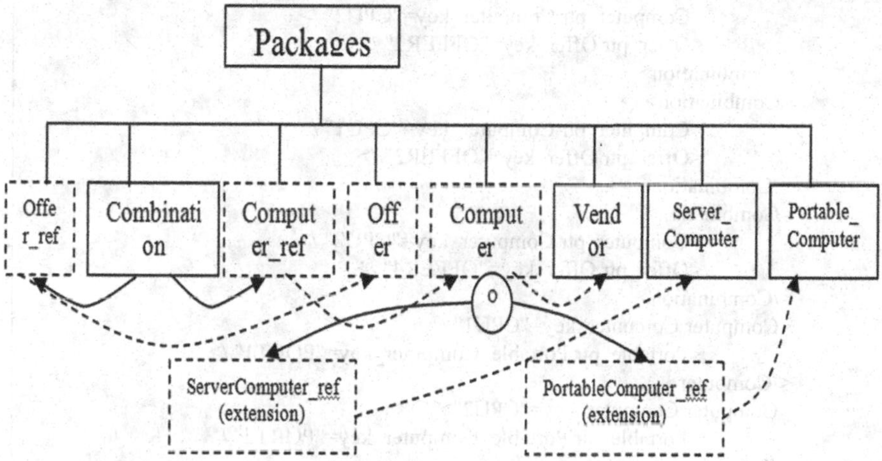

Fig. 8.14 The XML schema after normalization

```
<?xml version="1.0"?>
<Packages>
        <Offer currency="HKD" price="5000" Offer_key="OFFER1" />
        <Offer currency="HKD" price="7000" Offer_key="OFFER2" />
        <Offer currency="USD" price="641" Offer_key="OFFER3" />
        <Offer currency="USD" price="897" Offer_key="OFFER4" />
        <Combination>
                <Computer_ptr Computer_key="CPU1" />
                <Offer_ptr Offer_key="OFFER1" />
        </Combination>
        <Combination>
                <Computer_ptr Computer_key="CPU2" />
                <Offer_ptr Offer_key="OFFER2" />
        </Combination>
        <Combination>
                <Computer_ptr Computer_key="CPU1" />
                <Offer_ptr Offer_key="OFFER3" />
        </Combination>
        <Combination>
                <Computer_ptr Computer_key="CPU2" />
                <Offer_ptr Offer_key="OFFER4" />
        </Combination>
        <Computer Computer_key="CPU1">
                <Portable_ptr Portable_Computer_key="PORT1" />
        </Computer>
        <Computer Computer_key="CPU2">
                <Portable_ptr Portable_Computer_key="PORT2" />
        </Computer>
        <Vendor name="Dell" phone_number="(852)12345678" address="First Road 1,
    Hong Kong" />
        <Vendor name="IBM" phone_number="(852)87654321" address="Second Road
         2, Hong Kong" />
        <Portable_Computer Portable_Computer_key="PORT1" weight="2.5KG"
        model="NT1234" cpu_model="T7100" memory_size="1GB"
        harddisk_size="250GB" operating_system="Windows Vista" vendor="Dell" />
        <Portable_Computer Portable_Computer_key="PORT2" weight="2.5KG"
         model="NB2345" cpu_model="T5250" memory_size="2GB"
         harddisk_size="250GB" operating_system="Windows Vista" vendor="IBM" />

</Packages>
```

8.3 Normalize XML Schema with Minimum Fragments

This section aims to design an XML schema with minimum reference pointers and redundancy freed for better performance.

In XML data modeling, there are two aspects of considerations: the normal one-parent many-child element tree structure and pointer-referenced element structure. The former is more efficient than the latter. However, in order to implement certain data semantics such as many-to-many cardinality and partial participation, pointers must be used among elements for their connectivity (data navigation) to each other. Therefore, if we consider each branch of elements under the root element as a fragment, then the minimum fragmented element XML design is more efficient than fragmented element XML design.

The benefit of such design is illustrated in Fig. 8.15 which shows the difference for an XML schema with or without minimum fragments. The XML schema with minimum fragments can perform better than the XML schema without minimum fragments. Figure 8.15a shows a DTD graph without reference pointers. Figure 8.15b shows a DTD graph with a reference pointer such that an idref referring to an id. The effectiveness of deleting element A is the same on both sides because element B will be dangling with integrity error, that is, an idref without an id is an integrity constraint error.

Following this conceptual model tradition, we seek for algorithms to derive good XML schemas when the intended usage is for data storage in native XML databases with their child elements stored in minimum fragments. A fragment is defined as an element and its child elements immediately under the root element. Fragmented

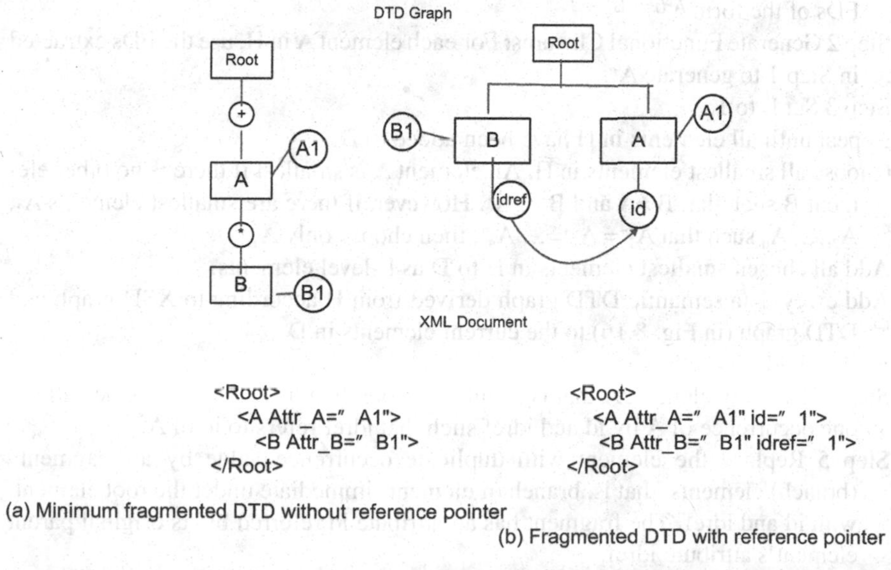

Fig. 8.15 XML database with and without minimum fragments

elements can be linked together through reference pointers. Storing element data in minimum fragments reduces query processing time. Preventing data redundancy reduces storage and allows for simple constraint-satisfying update checks, thus reducing both space and time. As a result, we propose a methodology to generate a minimum fragmented and redundancy-freed XML conceptual schema and map it into XML schema.

In order to avoid reference-pointer fragmentation, we need to locate the smallest closure elements and put them under a root element. Then according to the functional dependencies in the requested data semantics, we locate the dependent elements under these smallest closure elements as their child elements. For example, for FD: $A \rightarrow B$, we have child element A under parent element B. Similarly, for ID: $A \sqsubseteq B$, we have subclass element A under superclass element B. If there are replicate elements, we replace them with an element artifact to eliminate data redundancy.

Furthermore, if we allow the same child element under more than one parent element, then we will get data redundancy because its attribute values may have to be replicated. In other words, if an object O relating to multiple objects forces the corresponding element of O to appear multiple times, the attribute values of O will have to be replicated as well. Therefore, data redundancy may appear in both cases.

We can implement the above concepts in the following algorithm such that Step 1–4 designs a minimum fragmented XML schema and Step 5 eliminates data redundancy in the design.

Algorithm of a good XML design (FD=functional dependency)
Input: Data dependency in Metadata Data Model H.
Output: A DTD graph D.

Step 1 Extract FDs from H according to the data semantics in Fig. 9.16. Discard FDs of the form $A \ominus\!\!\rightarrow B$.

Step 2 Generate Functional Closures: For each element A in H, use the FDs extracted in Step 1 to generate A^+.

Step 3 Set L to 1.

Repeat until all elements in H have been added to D.

Choose all smallest elements in H. An element A is smallest if there is no other element B such that $B \neq A$ and $B^+ \sqsubset A^+$. However, if there are smallest elements A_1, $A_2, \ldots, A_n$ such that $A_1^+ = A_2^+ = \ldots A_n^+$, then choose only A_1.

Add all chosen smallest elements in H to D as L-level elements.

Add every data semantic DTD graph derived from H according to XSD graph and DTD graph (in Fig. 8.16) to the current elements in D.

Set L = L+1.

Step 4 For every element A that is a child of more than one element, replace all but one occurrence of A by id and idref such that idref refers to id of A.

Step 5 Replace the element with duplicate occurrence value by a "fragment" (branch) elements, that is, branch of elements immediate under the root element, with id and idref. The fragment has an attribute id referred by its original parent element's attribute idref.

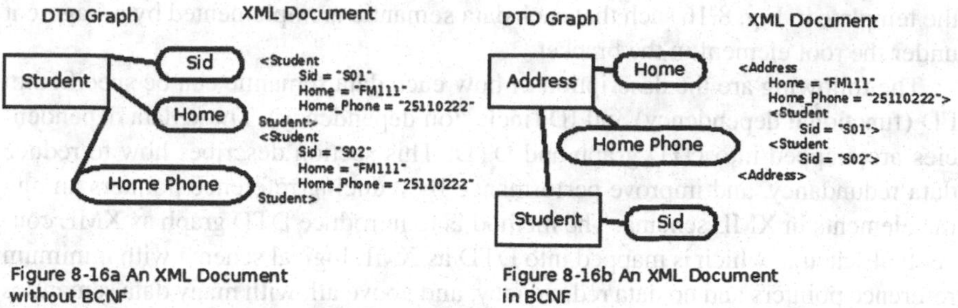

Fig. 8.16 An XML document (**a**) without BCNF, (**b**) in BCNF

For example, Fig. 8.16a shows the resultant non-BCNF element definition transformed from a non-BCNF object type. Because the original object type is not in BCNF, an XML document may suffer from redundancy caused by non-key FDs. In this case, it is the FD Home → HomePhone that causes the redundancy. Decomposing the object type results in two BCNF object types, and their corresponding element definitions are shown in Fig. 8.16. Note that the redundancy has been removed.

Case Study:
The following shows data requirements and their data semantics in brackets:

(a) Employee can be a spouse of another employee (unary relationship).
(b) A department has only one department head (one-to-one relationship).
(c) An instructor may be under a department (partial participation).
(d) An instructor can be either full-time or part-time (disjoint generalization).
(e) A full-time instructor has a retirement plan (one-to-one relationship).
(f) A part-time instructor has an hourly wage (one-to-one relationship).
(g) A course consists of lectures and laboratories (aggregation).
(h) Many courses are taught by many instructors (many-to-many cardinality).
(i) A tutor is tutoring students for a course (ternary relationship).
(j) A tutor can either be a lecturer or a professor (disjoint generalization).
(k) An employee can both be an instructor and a department head (overlap generalization).

Fig. 8.16 provides sample data occurrences with data redundancy illustrated where T=Tutor, PR=Professor, L=Lecturer, S=Student, C=Course, EV=Evaluation, RP=Retirement Plan, F=Full-time instructor, P=Part-time instructor, I=Instructor, D=Department, H=Head, LT=Lecture, and LB=Lab. In this example, we have redundant repeating data values 65 in the attribute Age of element Retirement Plan.

When we design an XML schema in a tree structure, we must start at the root element. Under the root element, we can implement data semantic of user requirements in a vertical fragment connected to the root element. Each one of the data requirements can be implemented by a fragment under the root element. These fragments use reference pointers to implement the required data semantics according to the template in Fig. 8.16 such that each data semantic is implemented by a fragment under the root element in the bracket.

The following are the description of how each data semantic can be specified in FD (functional dependency) and ID (inclusion dependency). These data dependencies are mapped into DTD graph and DTD. This section describes how to reduce data redundancy, and improve performance by reducing reference pointers among the elements in XML schema. The method is to introduce DTD graph as XML conceptual schema, which is mapped into DTD as XML logical schema with minimum reference pointers and no data redundancy, and above all, with many data semantics such as cardinality, participation, isa, generalization, categorization, aggregation, n-ary relationships and u-ary relationship as shown in Fig. 8.17.

Step 1: The initial semantic template and its data for each semantic are shown in Fig. 8.17 as follows:

The correspondent XML document with of Fig. 9.17 with redundant data of Age 65 is as follows:

```
<Teaching>
    <Employee id0="E1">
        <Artifact1 idref1="I1"/>
            <Artifact2 idref2="H1"/>
    </Employee>
    <Employee id0="E2">
        <Artifact1 idref1="I2"/>
    </Employee>
    <Employee id0="E3" idref0="E2">
        <Artifact1 idref1="I3"/>
    </Employee>
    <Employee id0="E4">
        <Artifact1 idref1="I4"/>
    </Employee>
    <Employee id0="E5">
        <Artifact2 idref2="H2"/>
    </Employee>
    <Department id0="D1">
        <Head id2="H1"/>
    </Department>
    <Department id0="D2">
        <Head id2="H2"/>
    </Department>
    <Instructor id1="I1" idref0="D1">
        <Artifact idref5="C1" Evaluation="EV1"/>
        <Artifact3 idref3="F1"/>
    </Instructor>
    <Instructor id1="I2" idref0="D1">
        <Artifact idref5="C1" Evaluation="EV2"/>
        <Artifact idref5="C2" Evaluation="EV3"/>
        <Artifact3 idref3="F2"/>
    </Instructor>
    <Instructor id1="I3" idref0="D2">
```

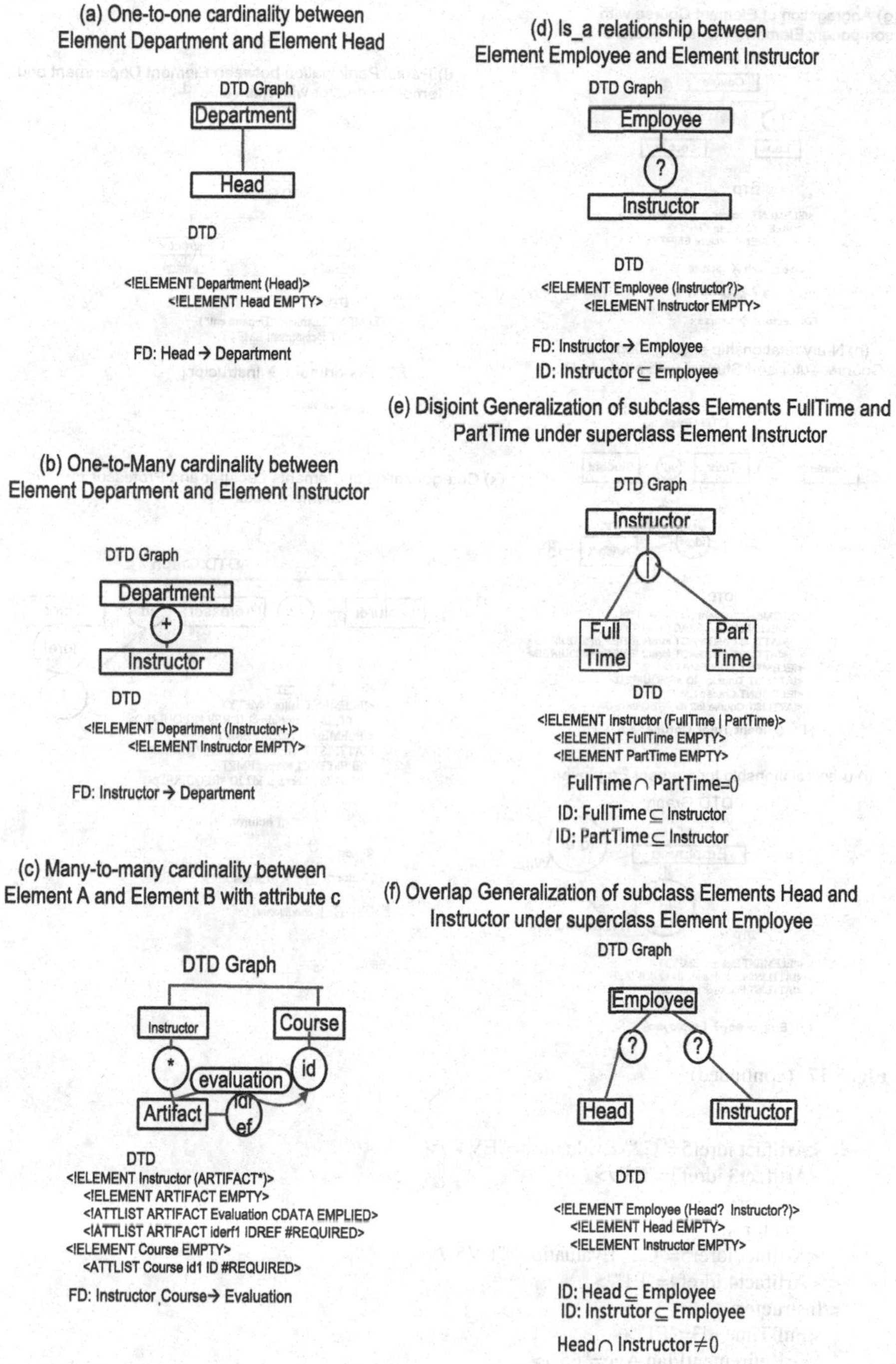
(a) One-to-one cardinality between Element Department and Element Head
DTD Graph
Department
Head
DTD
<!ELEMENT Department (Head)>
<!ELEMENT Head EMPTY>
FD: Head → Department
(b) One-to-Many cardinality between Element Department and Element Instructor
DTD Graph
Department
+
Instructor
DTD
<!ELEMENT Department (Instructor+)>
<!ELEMENT Instructor EMPTY>
FD: Instructor → Department
(c) Many-to-many cardinality between Element A and Element B with attribute c
DTD Graph
Instructor
Course
*
evaluation
id
Artifact
idr ef
DTD
<!ELEMENT Instructor (ARTIFACT*)>
<!ELEMENT ARTIFACT EMPTY>
<!ATTLIST ARTIFACT Evaluation CDATA EMPLIED>
<!ATTLIST ARTIFACT iderf1 IDREF #REQUIRED>
<!ELEMENT Course EMPTY>
<ATTLIST Course id1 ID #REQUIRED>
FD: Instructor, Course→ Evaluation
(d) Is_a relationship between Element Employee and Element Instructor
DTD Graph
Employee
?
Instructor
DTD
<!ELEMENT Employee (Instructor?)>
<!ELEMENT Instructor EMPTY>
FD: Instructor → Employee
ID: Instructor ⊆ Employee
(e) Disjoint Generalization of subclass Elements FullTime and PartTime under superclass Element Instructor
DTD Graph
Instructor
|
Full Time
Part Time
DTD
<!ELEMENT Instructor (FullTime | PartTime)>
<!ELEMENT FullTime EMPTY>
<!ELEMENT PartTime EMPTY>
FullTime ∩ PartTime=0
ID: FullTime ⊆ Instructor
ID: PartTime ⊆ Instructor
(f) Overlap Generalization of subclass Elements Head and Instructor under superclass Element Employee
DTD Graph
Employee
?
?
Head
Instructor
DTD
<!ELEMENT Employee (Head? Instructor?)>
<!ELEMENT Head EMPTY>
<!ELEMENT Instructor EMPTY>
ID: Head ⊆ Employee
ID: Instrutor ⊆ Employee
Head ∩ Instructor ≠ 0

Fig. 8.17 Data dependency of data semantics in DTD graph

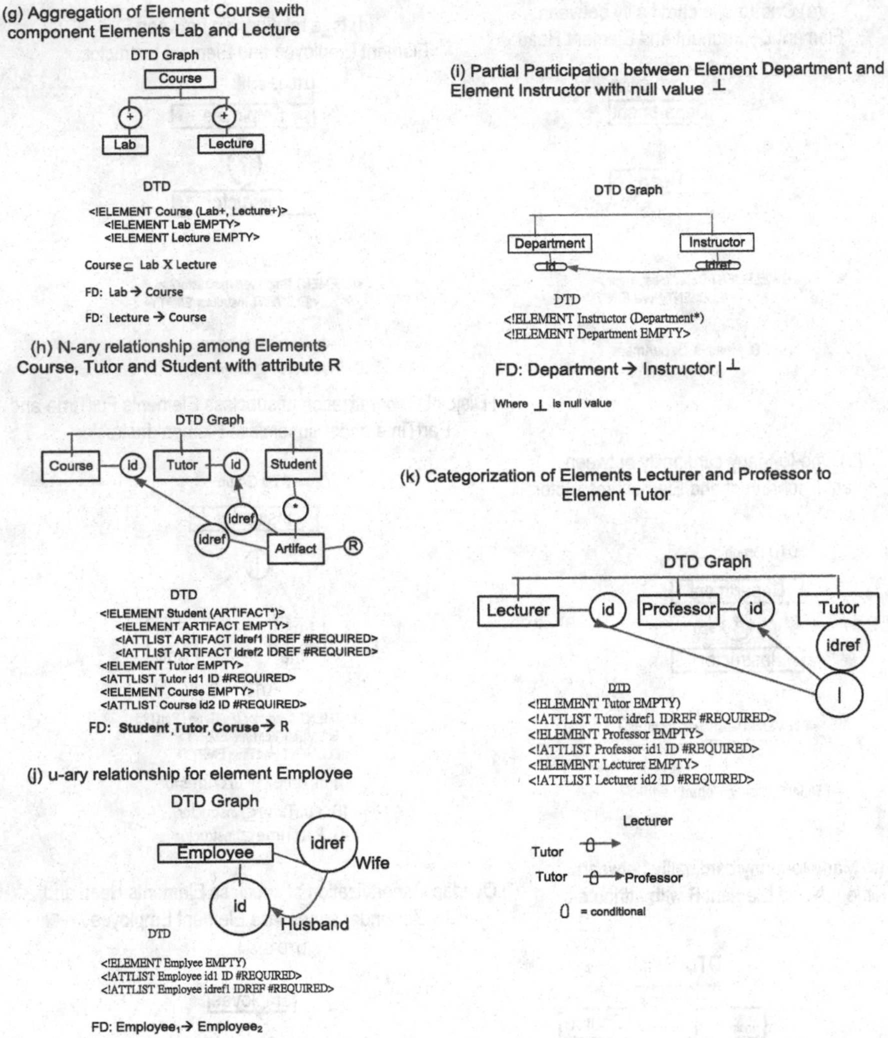
(g) Aggregation of Element Course with component Elements Lab and Lecture
DTD Graph
Course
+
+
Lab
Lecture
DTD
<!ELEMENT Course (Lab+, Lecture+)>
<!ELEMENT Lab EMPTY>
<!ELEMENT Lecture EMPTY>
Course ⊆ Lab X Lecture
FD: Lab → Course
FD: Lecture → Course
(h) N-ary relationship among Elements Course, Tutor and Student with attribute R
DTD Graph
Course
id
Tutor
id
Student
*
idref
idref
Artifact
R
DTD
<!ELEMENT Student (ARTIFACT*)>
<!ELEMENT ARTIFACT EMPTY>
<!ATTLIST ARTIFACT idref1 IDREF #REQUIRED>
<!ATTLIST ARTIFACT idref2 IDREF #REQUIRED>
<!ELEMENT Tutor EMPTY>
<!ATTLIST Tutor id1 ID #REQUIRED>
<!ELEMENT Course EMPTY>
<!ATTLIST Course id2 ID #REQUIRED>
FD: Student, Tutor, Coruse → R
(j) u-ary relationship for element Employee
DTD Graph
Employee
idref
Wife
id
Husband
DTD
<!ELEMENT Emplyee EMPTY)
<!ATTLIST Employee id1 ID #REQUIRED>
<!ATTLIST Employee idref1 IDREF #REQUIRED>
FD: Employee1 → Employee2
(i) Partial Participation between Element Department and Element Instructor with null value ⊥
DTD Graph
Department
Instructor
id
idref
DTD
<!ELEMENT Instructor (Department*)
<!ELEMENT Department EMPTY>
FD: Department → Instructor | ⊥
Where ⊥ is null value
(k) Categorization of Elements Lecturer and Professor to Element Tutor
DTD Graph
Lecturer
id
Professor
id
Tutor
idref
I
DTD
<!ELEMENT Tutor EMPTY)
<!ATTLIST Tutor idref1 IDREF #REQUIRED>
<!ELEMENT Professor EMPTY>
<!ATTLIST Professor id1 ID #REQUIRED>
<!ELEMENT Lecturer EMPTY>
<!ATTLIST Lecturer id2 ID #REQUIRED>
Lecturer
Tutor
Tutor
Professor
= conditional

Fig. 8.17 (continued)

```
    <Artifact idref5="C2" Evaluation="EV4"/>
    <Artifact3 idref3="F3"/>
  </Instructor>
  <Instructor id1="I4">
    <Artifact idref5="C2" Evaluation="EV5"/>
    <Artifact4 idref4="P1"/>
  </Instructor>
    <FullTime id3="F1">
      <RetirementPlan Age="65"/>
    </FullTime>
    <FullTime id3="F2">
      <RetirementPlan Age="65"/>
    </FullTime>
```

```
      <FullTime id3="F3">
        <RetirementPlan Age="60"/>
      </FullTime>
      <PartTime id4="P1">
        <HourlyRate HW="HW1"/>
      </PartTime>
      <Course id5="C1">
        <Lab lbname="LB1"/>
        <Lecture ltname="LT1"/>
        <Lecture ltname="LT2"/>
      </Course>
      <Course id5="C2">
        <Lab lbname="LB1"/>
        <Lecture ltname="LT3"/>
      </Course>
      <Student sname="S1">
        <Artifact5 idref5="C2" idref8="T1"/>
        <Artifact5 idref5="C1" idref8="T2"/>
      </Student>
      <Student sname="S2">
        <Artifact5 idref5="C1" idref8="T1"/>
      </Student>
      <Tutor id8="T1" idref910="L1"/>
      <Tutor id8="T2" idref910="PRO1"/>
      <Lecturer id9="L1"/>
      <Professor id10="PRO1"/>
</Teaching>
```

We can apply the XML schema design algorithm to derive the smallest closure functional dependency fragments and map them into a DTD graph for implementation as follows:

After the first pass of repeat loop in Step 3, we have the following closure of each element according to each given data semantic:

$Student^+$	= Student
$Tutor^+$	= Tutor
$Lecturer^+$	= Lecturer
$Professor^+$	= Professor
$RetirementPlan^+$	= RetirementPlan, FullTime
$HourlyRate^+$	= HourlyRate, PartTime
$Course^+$	= Course
$Instructor^+$	= Instructor, Employee
$Employee^+$	= Employee
$Head^+$	= Head, Employee, Department
$Department^+$	= Department, Employee, Head
$FullTime^+$	= FullTime, $Instructor^+$
$PartTime^+$	= PartTime, $Instructor^+$
Lab^+	= Lab, Course
$Lecture^+$	= Lecture, Course

We can group related closures into the same fragment by combining closures with the same element into a fragment as follows:

Fragment 1:	Student$^+$	= Student
Fragment 2:	Tutor$^+$	= Tutor
Fragmen 3:	Lecturer$^+$	= Lecturer
Fragment 4:	Professor$^+$	= Professor
Fragment 5:	Course$^+$	= Course
	Lab$^+$	= Lab, Course
	Lecture$^+$	= Lecture, Course
Fragment 6:	Employee$^+$	= Employee
	Instructor$^+$	= Instructor, Employee
	Head$^+$	= Head, Employee, Department
	Department$^+$	= Department, Employee, Head
	FullTime $^+$	= FullTime, Instructor$^+$
	PartTime $^+$	= PartTime, Instructor$^+$
	RetirementPlan$^+$	= RetirementPlan, FullTime
	HourlyRate$^+$	= HourlyRate, PartTime

The XML document of Fig. 8.19 has 6 fragments (branches) under the root element Teaching which is fewer than the 10 fragments in the initial XML schema design in the case study.

Nevertheless, the element RetirementPlan contains repeating data of Age 65 which causes data redundancy in the element Retirement Plan with same age 65 in two occurrences.

Step 5 – Since more than one full-time instructor may have the same retirement plan, the attribute values of a retirement plan may have to appear more than once. Both cases may lead to data redundancy. We need to replace the data redundant element RetirementPlan with a non-replicate element RetirementPlan such that it links with its original parent element FullTime with id and idref.

Similarly, part-time instructors may have the same hourly rate. As a result, we also replace the data redundant element Part-Time with a non-replicate fragment which links it with its original parent element Part-Time with id and idref to

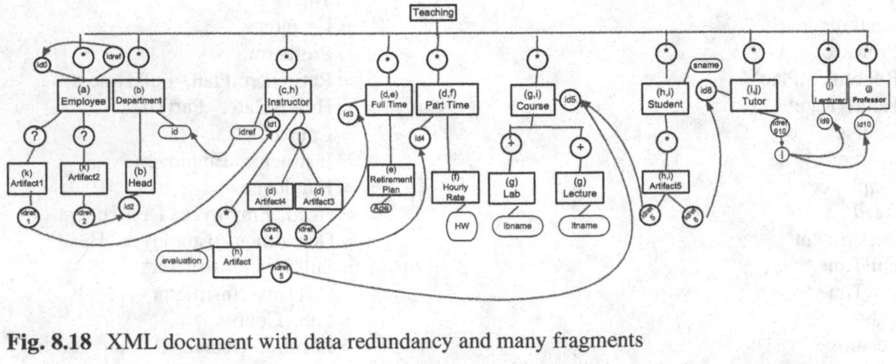

Fig. 8.18 XML document with data redundancy and many fragments

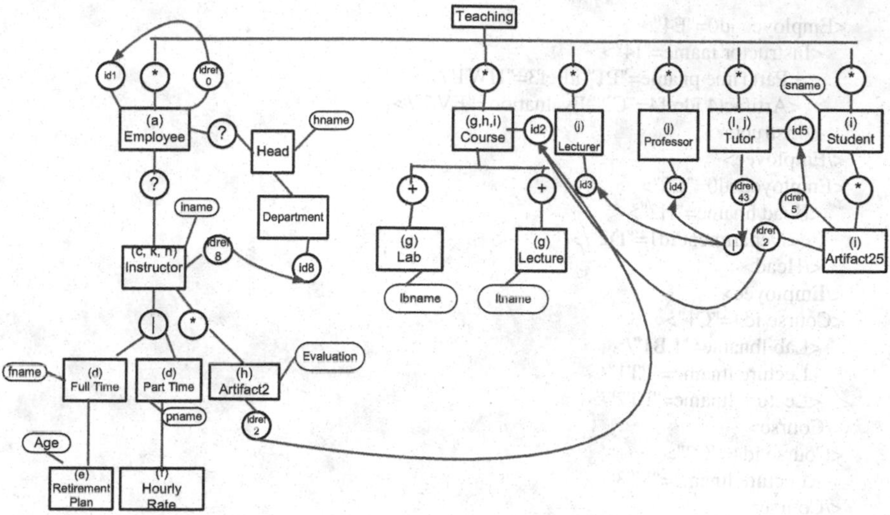

Fig. 8.19 A minimum fragmented XML schema with data redundancy

eliminate data redundancy. The revised XML schema stores the data semantics of the derived efficient XML schema design in Fig. 8.20 is as follows:

The data redundancy-freed XML document of Fig. 8.18 has 8 fragments under the root element Teaching which is fewer than the 10 fragments in the initial XML schema design in case study as follows:

```
<Teaching>
  <Employee id0="E1">
    <Head hname="H1">
      <Department id1="D1"/>
    </Head>
    <Instructor iname="I1" idref1="D1">
      <FullTime fname="F1" idref2="RP1"/>
      <Artifact4 idref4="C1" Evaluation="EV1"/>
    </Instructor>
  </Employee>
  <Employee id0="E2">
    <Instructor iname="I2" idref1="D1">
      <FullTime fname="F2" idref2="RP1"/>
      <Artifact4 idref4="C1" Evaluation="EV2"/>
      <Artifact4 idref4="C2" Evaluation="EV3"/>
    </Instructor>
  </Employee>
  <Employee id0="E3">
    <Instructor iname="I3" idref1="D2">
      <FullTime fname="F3" idref2="RP2"/>
      <Artifact4 idref4="C2" Evaluation="EV4"/>
    </Instructor>
  </Employee>
```

```
    <Employee id0="E4">
      <Instructor iname="I4">
        <PartTime pname="P1" idref3="HW1"/>
        <Artifact4 idref4="C2" Evaluation="EV5"/>
      </Instructor>
    </Employee>
    <Employee id0="E5">
      <Head hname="H2">
        <Department id1="D2"/>
      </Head>
    </Employee>
    <Course id4="C1">
      <Lab lbname="LB1"/>
      <Lecture ltname="LT1"/>
      <Lecture ltname="LT2"/>
    </Course>
    <Course id4="C2">
      <Lecture ltname="LT3"/>
    </Course>
    <Lecturer id7="L1"/>
    <Professor id6="PR1"/>
    <Tutor id8="T1" idref67="L1"/>
    <Tutor id8="T2" idref67="PR1"/>
    <Student sname="S1">
      <Artifact8 idref4="C2" idref8="T1"/>
      <Artifact8 idref4="C1" idref8="T2"/>
    </Student>
    <Student sname="S2">
      <Artifact8 idref4="C1" idref8="T1"/>
    </Student>
    <RetirementPlan id2="RP1" Age="65"/>
    <RetirementPlan id2="RP2" Age="60"/>
    <HourlyRate id3="HW1"/>
</Teaching>
```

8.4 Summary

In summary, data normalization involves schema restructure and data reorganization in a database. The former includes a redesign of the data definition language (DDL) of the database such that the new design is more user-friendly in update and management. The latter includes the download and upload of the data in the database. Therefore, data normalization is an important factor for users to consider in designing a database as a preprocess. On the other hand, data reorganization is only recommended when it is necessary to perform database reengineering for the benefit of information systems reengineering—in other words, when the benefit of information systems reengineering is more than the cost of database reengineering.

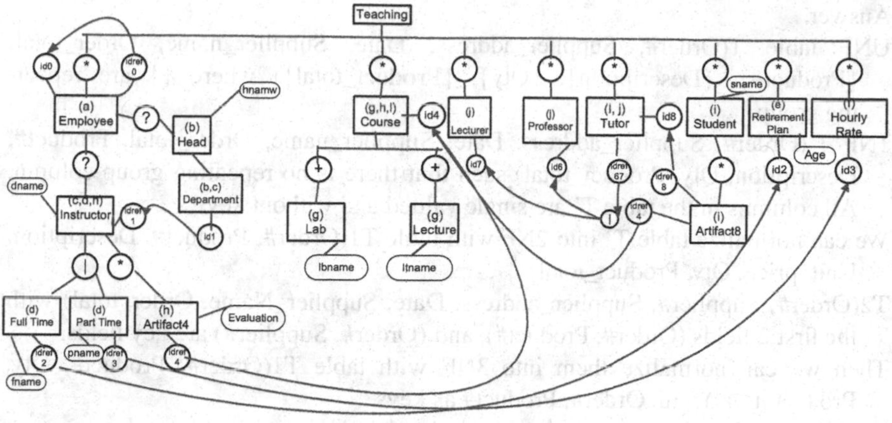

Fig. 8.20 A minimum fragmented and data redundancy-freed XML schema

The former is on the application aspect, and the latter is on the implementation aspect.

Similarly, data normalization and data denormalization are two aspects of meeting users' data requirements. If the users ask for user-friendliness in database manipulation, then data normalization is recommended. However, if the users ask for better performance in information retrieval such as data warehousing, then data denormalization is recommended. Very often, the normalized relations can be denormalized by performing natural join operations together to recover the original relation before data normalization in the relational database.

Questions

Question 8.1

What are the preconditions to perform normalization for the 4NF and the 5NF in terms of n-ary relationships?

Answer

The precondition for 4NF in n-ary relationship is MVD. For example, in table T(A1, A2, A3) with MVD: A1->A2

and A1->A3, then we can normalize Table T into 4NF with two tables T1(A1, A2) and T2(A1, A3)

The precondition for 5NF in n-ary relationship is JD. For example, in table T(A1, A2, A3) with JD, if (A1, A2), (A2, A3), and (A3, A1) exist, then we have (A1, A2, A3) exist in a table and can normalize table T into 5F with three tables T1(A1, A2), T2 (A2, A3), and T3 (A3, A1)

Question 8.2

Derive the 1NF, 2NF, and 3NF for the following UNF. Identify their FD.

Answer

UNF table T(Order#, Supplier_address, Date, Supplier_name, Order_total, {Product#}, {Description}, {Qty}, {Product_total}) where {} are repeating group

1NF T'(Order#, Supplier_address, Date, Supplier_name, Order_total, Product#, Description, Qty, Product_total) such that there is no repeating group column. All columns in the table T' are single valued and without key.

We can normalize table T' into 2NF with table T1(Order#, Product#, Description, Unit_price, Qty, Product_total)

T2(Order#, Supplier#, Supplier_address, Date, Supplier_Name, Order_total) with the first 2 fields (Order#, Product#), and (Order#, Supplier#) are key fields.

Then we can normalize them into 3NF with table T1(Order#, Product#, Qty, Product_total) with Order#, Product# as keys

T2(Product#, Description, Price) with Product# as key

T3(Order#, Supplier#, Date, Order_total) with Order#, Supplier# as key

T4(Supplier#, Supplier_address, Supplier_name) with Supplier# as key

In each table, there is a functional dependency such that key field value determines non-key field value.

<table>
<tr><td colspan="3">ORDER#</td><td colspan="2">DATE</td></tr>
<tr><td colspan="3">SUPPLIER#</td><td colspan="2">SUPPLIER_NAME</td></tr>
<tr><td colspan="3">SUPPLIER_ADDRESS</td><td colspan="2">ORDER_TOTAL</td></tr>
<tr><td>PRODUCT#</td><td>DESCRIPTION</td><td>UNIT PRICE</td><td>QTY</td><td>PRODUCT TOTAL</td></tr>
<tr><td></td><td></td><td></td><td></td><td></td></tr>
</table>

Bibliography

Elmasri R, Navathe SB (2011) Chapter 14 Database design theory: introduction to normalization using functional and multivalued dependencies. In: Database systems: models, languages, design, and application programming, 6th edn. Pearson

Fong J, Kwok LF, Cheung SKS (2011) Data modeling technique made easy with hybrid learning computer aided instruction. Lecture Notes in Computer Science, LNCS 6837:345–356

Shiu H, Fong J (2008) Reverse engineering from an XML document into an extended DTD graph. J Database Manage 19(4):62–80

Mok WY, Fong J, Embley DW (2014) Generating the fewest redundancy-free scheme trees from acyclic conceptual-model hypergraphs in polynomial time. Inf Syst 41:20–44

Chapter 9
Heterogeneous Database Connectivity

9.1 Architecture of Heterogeneous Database Connectivity

Because of their historical importance and the existing user database for these DBMSs, these models and systems are now referred to as legacy database systems (Ramez and Shamkant 2011, P. 56). There are many types of legacy databases since the 1960s. We focus on four data models only.

(1) Network database

Data structure: It is in flea structure which allows two owner records pointing to the same member, and each record can connect to any other record in a network "graph" structure. Johnson & Johnson is still using NDB (Raima users 2014).

(2) Relational database

Data structure: It is in table structure. Every relation is a table that must have a primary key with a foreign key referring to a primary key of another table in values matching. NCR is still using RDB (Relational database users 2014).

(3) Object-oriented database

Data structure: It is in a class structure such that a class associating with another class by an object's stored OID (Object Identity) referring another class object OID. Also, a sub-class object can inherit data and method of a superclass object with the same OID which is system generated. Objectivity and Gemstone are OODBMS (Object-Oriented 2014).

(4) XML

Data structure: It is in a tree structure, with one root element. Elements are under root elements. Each element links with multiple sub-elements. Elements can also be linked by using the IDREF attribute referring to another element attribute ID in the XML scheme DTD (Data Type Definition). Tomcat is still using XML. (XML users 2014)

J. S. P. Fong, K. Wong Ting Yan, *Information Systems Reengineering, Integration and Normalization*, https://doi.org/10.1007/978-3-030-79584-9_9

In fact, both XML and hierarchical data models are in the tree structure.

A legacy system is any corporate computer system' that isn't *Internet-dependent*.

Because of their *historical importance* and *the existing user databases* for these DBMSs, these models and systems are now referred to as legacy database systems. (Reference: Ramez and Shamkant (2011), "Database Systems, Models, Languages, Design, and Application programming", Pearson, 6th edition, P. 56)

The following table shows that RDB, OODB, XML, and NDB are still being used in the industry. Therefore, we consider these four data models as "legacy" systems.

DBMS	Customers still using in the industry today	Reference for evidence
RDB	NCR, Phoebe Putney Memorial Hospital, John Wayne Airport	https://www.oracle.com/search/customers/
NDB	Johnson & Johnson	http://raima.com/customers/
	IBM mainframe	www.ibm.com
OODB	Objectivity, Gemstone	http://www.objectivity.com/ http://www.gemstone.com/
	Orient Overseas Container Line (OOCL)	www.oocl.com
XML	Tomcat	https://tomcat.apache.org/tomcat-3.3-doc/serverxml.html

Because IBM is still using Hierarchical DBMS, so, there should be five current legacy databases.

The evolution of database technologies intends to meet different users requirements. For example, the complex Hierarchical and Network (Codasyl) databases (NDB) are good for business computing on large mainframe computers. The user-friendly relational databases (RDB) are good for end user computing on personal computers. The object-oriented databases (OODB) are good for multimedia computing on minicomputers. The XML databases (XML DB) are good for Internet computing on mobile devices. Table 9.1 shows the evolution of databases on various platforms. These are first-generation Hierarchical and Network databases,

Table 9.1 Platforms of legacy database technologies

	Network database	Relational database	Object-Oriented database	XML database
Computer Language	3GL Cobol / C	4GL, SQL/Visual Basic	4GL, OQL	XQuery, Web service
Operations	Batch Job	Triggers/ Stored procedures	Object-Oriented features	XQuery functions
User Interface	Text mode	Windows	Windows	Web pages
Machine	Mainframe	PC /Workstations	Web services/ Browsers	Web, Virtual machine

second-generation relational databases, and third-generation post-relational such as object-oriented and XML databases.

Flattened XML documents

Flattened XML documents are generic representations of any legacy database instance in any legacy database data model. It is because flattened XML structure combines tree structure and table structure data model, with relational database and object-oriented database as a table structure data model and Hierarchical database, network database, and XML database as a tree structure data model. Therefore, Flattened XML can represent them as a data model.

Flattened XML can represent most data semantics just like other legacy database systems, relational databases, object-oriented databases, hierarchical databases, network databases, and XML databases. The model can represent the static data of five legacy data models only. It is not a total representation of all legacy database data models.

Data semantic include ISA, cardinality, generalization:

ISA is a relationship between a superclass and a subclass. It is defined as a subclass relation that has the same primary key as its superclass relation and refers to it as a foreign key in the relational schema in the ISA relationship. It can also be implemented by a subclass inheriting its superclass's OID and attributes in an object-oriented schema. It can also be implemented by an owner record that has the same key as its member record in network schema via SET linkage. It can also be implemented by an element that links one-to-one occurrence with its sub-element in the XML schema.

Cardinality is one-to-one, one-to-many, and many-to-many relationships set between two classes. 1:n is constructed by foreign key on "many" side referring to primary key on "one" side in the relational schema. It can also be implemented by the association attribute of a class object on "one" side pointing to objects on the "many" side in another class in object-oriented schema. It can also be implemented by owner record occurrence on "one" side and member record occurrences on "many" side in network schema. It can also be implemented by element occurrence with IDREF on the "many" side linking with element occurrence with ID on the "one" side in XML schema.

As to m:n cardinality, it can be implemented by two 1:n cardinalities with two "one" side classes link with the same "many" side class.

Generalization is the relationship between one superclass and multiple subclasses.

They are in multiple ISA relationships. For example, A is a special kind of B, and C is also a special kind of B, then A and C subclasses can be generalized as B superclass. In a relational schema, both superclass relation and subclass relations contain the same key, with subclass relations' keys referring to the superclass key as a foreign key in generalization. In the object-oriented schema, multiple subclasses objects contain the same OID as their superclass object in generalization. In the network schema, one owner record links with multiple member records through a SET in generalization. In XML, multiple subclass elements and their superclass element are in 1:1 linkage with the same key attribute in generalization. Generalization can be implemented by multiple ISA relationships such that multiple subclasses are generalized into one superclass.

Firstly, the legacy database can be transformed into flattened XML documents which can be further transformed into another legacy database of Relational, Object-oriented, Network, and XML data models. A flattened XML document is a valid XML document that contains a collection of elements of various types and each element defines its own set of properties. The internal structure of the flattened XML document data file is a relational table structure. It has XML document tree structure syntax with internal elements in relational table structure. It replaces primary key with ID, and foreign key with sibling IDREF as follows:

```
<?xml version="1.0">
<root>
 <table1 ID="…" IDREF1="…" IDREF2="…" … IDREFN="…">
  <attribute1>…</attribute1>
  …
  <attributeN>…</attributeN>
 </table1>
 …
 <tableN ID="…" IDREF1="…" IDREF2="…" … IDREFN="…">
  <attribute1>…</attribute1>
  …
  <attributeN>…</attributeN>
 </tableN>
</root>
```

For each table, the name of the table determines its type name and the name of the property (attribute) determines its property name. Each table defines an ID type attribute that can uniquely identify itself and there are optional multiple IDREF type attributes that can refer to this ID in other tables in their sibling elements. Each property XML element encloses a property value in a proper textual representation format. In order to ensure a flattened XML document instance to be valid, there must be either an internal or an external DTD document that defines the XML structures and attributes types, in particular for those ID and IDREF type attributes.

A heterogeneous database gateway (HDBC) is a database middleware that provides more flexibility for the users to access legacy databases in their own chosen data model. In other words, users can apply HDBC to transform legacy databases into flattened XML documents, and then further transform them into the user's own familiar legacy database for access. Since XML is the data standard on the Internet, it becomes an information highway for the user to access data.

The reason we choose flattened XML document is due to its openness for DBMS independence. All other data models are DBMS dependent. For example, an Oracle database can only be accessed by Oracle DBMS, and an MS SQL Server database can only be accessed by MS SQL Server DBMS. Nevertheless, users can access flattened XML documents on the Internet by Internet Explorer without programming. Furthermore, an Oracle user can access an MS SQL Server database after transforming the MS SQL Server database into a flattened XML document, and then to the Oracle database by HDBC.

Similarly, the reason we choose relational table structure for elements in the flattened XML document is that relational table structure has a strong mathematical foundation of relational algebra to implement the constraints of major data semantics such as cardinality, ISA, generalization, and aggregation to meet users' data requirements.

In fact, Vincent Lum (Lum, V.Y, 1976) attempted to propose a similar method by using sequential files as the medium for data conversion between legacy databases in a logical level approach. But in his model, the source and target systems are limited to Hierarchical databases, network databases, and relational databases.

The HDBC can transform legacy databases into flattened XML documents, and then further transform the flattened XML document into another target legacy database of relational, object-oriented, XML, or network. The result is that HDBC allows users to transform a source legacy database into another target legacy database that is accessible in the user's computer.

Flattened XML documents are offered as a universal database medium for the interoperability of all legacy databases that can be accessed by the users using their own familiar legacy database language via HDBC. We consider the hierarchical data model the same as the XML data model because they are all in a tree structure. The five proprietary legacy data models can be interchangeable into flattened XML documents as the universal database as shown in Fig. 9.1.

HDBC has 2 phases:

Phase I: Transform the user's legacy database into flattened XML documents.
Phase II: Transform the flattened XML document into a target's legacy database.

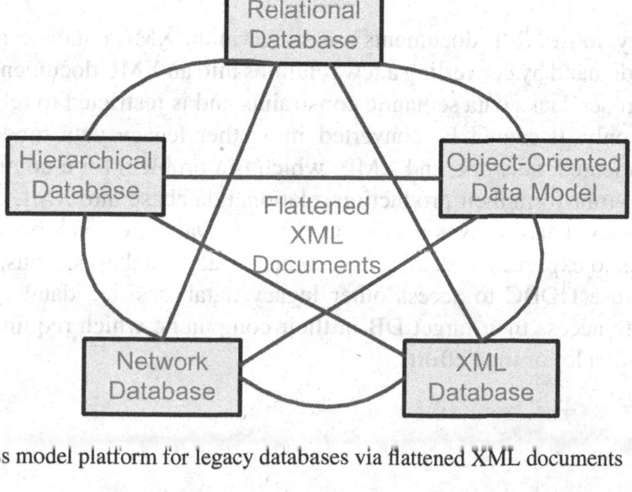

Fig. 9.1 Cross model platform for legacy databases via flattened XML documents

Each phase has 2 steps:

Step 1: Schema translation from source DB to target DB.
Step 2: Data conversion from source DB into target DB according to the translated target DB schema.

There is a benefit to the design. Through Flattened XML in the HDBC, all legacy database systems can be converted into each other. So users can use any legacy database language to access other legacy databases.

Because of HDBC, legacy DB of RDB, XML DB, NDB, OODB, HDB, and flattened XML can be interchangeable with each other. As a result, a company can convert all of its heterogeneous DB into a particular legacy DB or flattened XML, as homogeneous DB, which uses a combined DB model of users' choice.

"The five proprietary legacy data models can be interchangeable into flattened XML document as universal database as shown in Fig. 9.1."

Because through XML, all legacy databases can be interchangeable, we can view them as one legacy database system. The legacy database can be converted to another through Flattened XML. Therefore, multiple legacy databases can be converted into one legacy database.

For example, RDB can be converted into XML through Flattened XML. So, the user can view the DB as XML. Similarly, NDB and OODB can be converted into XML through Flattened XML. So, the user can view the DB as XML.

For example, XML can be converted into RDB through Flattened XML. So, the user can view the DB as RDB. Similarly, NDB and OODB can be converted into RDB through Flattened XML. So, the user can view the DB as RDB.

For example, OODB can be converted into NDB through Flattened XML. So, the user can view the DB as NDB. Similarly, RDB and XML can be converted into XML through Flattened XML. So, the user can view the DB as XML.

For example, NDB can be converted into OODB through Flattened XML. So, the user can view the DB as OODB.

Problems:

(1) Currently, most XML documents are stored in an XML database and are created on-demand by converting a few relations into an XML document. However, this approach lacks data semantic constraints and is restricted to relational data models only. It cannot be converted into other legacy data models such as object-oriented, network, and XML, which is a problem for e-commerce companies to transform their production relational database into XML documents.
(2) Most legacy database systems are proprietary. Database vendors do not facilitate tools to export their databases to other legacy databases. Thus, companies need to use ODBC to access other legacy databases, ie., databases with no DBMS to access their target DB in their computers, which requires programming with a lot of time effort.

(3) Most users cannot access all legacy databases because they do not know all legacy database languages. They rely on ODBC, which is not easy to learn.
(4) It is difficult to convert legacy databases into different data models because the data conversion of a legacy database involves data models transformation.

Solution:
In computing, ODBC (Open Database Connectivity) is a standard programming language middleware API for accessing database management systems (DBMS). OUDG has a similar function of accessing a different legacy database using Flattened XML as a middleware. (Reference http://en.wikipedia.org/wiki/Open_Database_Connectivity)

Both ODBC and HDBC allow users to access a legacy DB of his/her choice through different methods.

ODBC requires users to use an API programming solution to access a proprietary DB.

HDBC allows users to use the DB conversion method to convert a legacy DB into another legacy DB model of his/her choice for the users to access.

As a result, HDBC is an alternative solution of ODBC for the user to access a legacy DB without programming effort. Instead, the user needs to use a software tool to transform the DB conversion, such as a DB middleware as shown below.

The Internet provides an economical way for people to communicate around the world. It is obvious that businesses make use of this low-cost communication method to communicate and exchange information with their business partners. The XML document can be used in a myriad of ways across different platforms and different applications.

A methodology is offered to transform legacy databases into an equivalent and maintainable flattened XML document to achieve interoperability among all legacy databases because flattened XML document is user-friendly and open for most computer systems on the Internet.

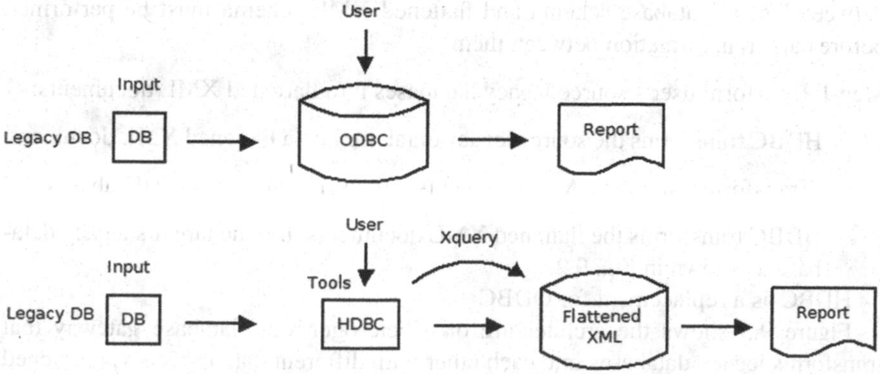

Fig. 9.2 Data flow diagram of HDBC and ODBC

Through HDBC, users can use the same database language to access other legacy databases including relational, object-oriented, network, and XML. The operation is more reliable and speedy because the same data can be concurrently processed by legacy database and their replicated flattened XML document on the web at the same time.

Academic merit:

It is feasible to supplement ODBC by HDBC transforming legacy database into the flattened XML document for database access. ODBC needs programming, but HDBC can be developed as an end user software tool.

Industrial merit:

The application of flattened XML documents is for information highway on the Internet for data warehouse, decision support systems (Fong et al. 2003), e-commerce, and cloud computing. The benefits are information sharing among users for database interoperability.

Application:

(1) HDBC can replace ODBC to access any legacy database by transforming them into a universal database of a flattened XML document for accessing the same data.

Long-term Impact:

At present, most database systems are proprietary. Each DBMS vendor has software tools that convert other legacy databases into their databases, but not vice versa for converting their own databases into other legacy databases (Hsiao and Kamel 1989). The result makes legacy databases not open to each other. On the other hand, by using HDBC, any legacy database can be transformed into any other legacy database via flattened XML documents. The benefit is that data sharing and data conversion among legacy databases becomes possible.

Processing:

Preprocess: We can reverse engineer legacy database schema into legacy database conceptual schema to recover data semantics. Moreover, schema translation between legacy database schema and flattened XML schema must be performed before data transformation between them.

Step 1 Transform user's source legacy databases into flattened XML documents:

HDBC transforms the source legacy database into a flattened XML document.

Step 2 Transform flattened XML documents into user's target legacy databases:

HDBC transforms the flattened XML documents into the target's legacy database as shown in Fig. 9.2.

HDBC as a replacement for ODBC

Figure 9.3 shows the architecture of a heterogeneous database gateway that transforms legacy databases into each other with different data models via flattened XML document as a supplement for open database connectivity.

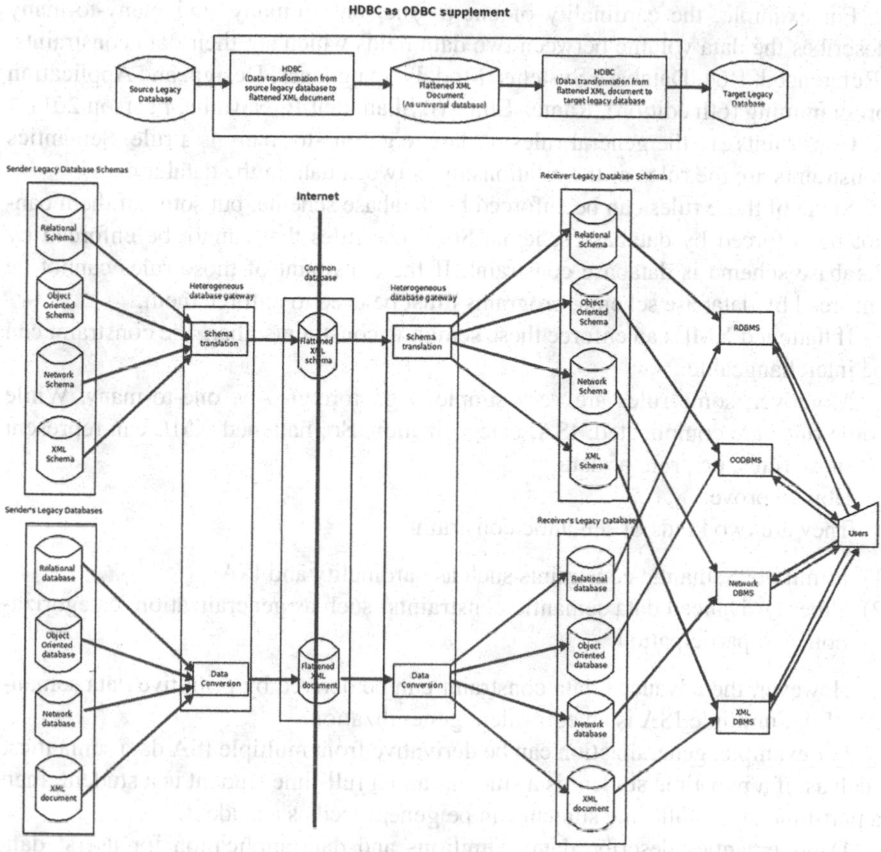

Fig. 9.3 A heterogeneous database gateway as a supplement for open database connectivity

Data flow of Fig. 9.3:

(1) The data semantics of an end user's first legacy database schemas are captured into metadata or conceptual schema.
(2) Legacy database schemas are mapped into a flattened XML document schema.
(3) The data of the source legacy database are transformed into a flattened XML document.
(4) The flattened XML schemas are mapped into target legacy database schemas.
(5) The flattened XML document is transformed into the target legacy database according to the mapped target legacy database schema.

Data Semantics Preservation in Legacy Databases

Semantic constraints are defined as constraints that cannot be directly expressed in the schemas of the data model, and hence, must be expressed and enforced by the application programs. We call these application-based, semantic constraints, or business rules.

For example, the cardinality of one-to-one, one-to-many, and many-to-many describes the data volume between two data fields which are their data constraints. (Referenced, P.64, Database Systems, Models, Languages, Design, and Application programming (6th edition), Ramez Elmasri, Shamkant B. Navathe, Pearson 2011)

Constraints are the general rules of data, e.g., one-to-many is a rule. Semantics constraints are the rules of the relationship between data in the database.

Some of these rules can be enforced by database schema, but some of them cannot be enforced by database schema. So, those rules that cannot be enforced by database schema is database constraint. If the constraint of those rules cannot be enforced by database schema, programs must be used to enforce them.

If flattened XML can enforce these semantic constraints, then, the constraint can be interchangeable.

Moreover, some rules are very simple, e.g., foreign key, one-to-many. While some rules are complicated: ISA, categorization. So, flattened XML can represent all those rules, i.e., rule of data.

How to prove:

They are two kinds of semantic constraints

1) Primitive: Semantic constraints such as cardinality and ISA.
2) Other (Advanced data semantic constraints) such as generalization, categorization, and participation.

However, the advanced data constraint can be derived by primitive data semantics. E.g., multiple ISA is an equivalent generalization.

For example, generalization can be derivative from multiple ISA data semantics, such as, if a part-time student is a student, and a full-time student is a student, then a part-time and a full-time student can be generalized as a student.

Data semantics describe data definitions and data application for users' data requirements, which can be captured in the database conceptual schemas. The following are the data semantics that can be preserved among the legacy conceptual schemas and their equivalent flattened XML schema:

(1) Cardinality: One-to-one, one-to-many, and many-to-many relationships set between two classes.

A one-to-one relationship between set A and set B is defined as the following: For all a in A, there exists at most one b in B such that a and b are related, and vice versa. The implementation of a one-to-one relationship is similar to a one-to-many relationship.

A one-to-many relationship from set A to set B is defined as the following: for all a in A, there exists one or more b in B such that a and b are related. For all b in B, there exists at most one a in A such that a and b are related.

A many-to-many relationship between set A and set B is defined as: For all a in A, there exists one or more b in B such that a and b are related. Similarly, for all b in B, there exists one or more a in A such that a and b are related.

1:n is constructed by foreign key on "many" side referring to primary key on "one" side in the relational schema. It can also be implemented by the association attribute of a class object on "one" side points to another class objects on the "many" side in another class in object-oriented schema. It can also be implemented by owner record occurrence on "one" side and member record occurrences on "many" side in network schema. It can also be implemented by element occurrence with IDREF on "many" side links with element occurrence with ID on "one" side in XML schema.

As to m:n cardinality, it can be implemented by two 1:n cardinalities with 2 "one" side classes link with the same "many" side class.

(2) ISA relationship between a superclass and a subclass.

The relationship A isa B is defined as: A is a special kind of B.

A subclass relation has the same primary key as its superclass relation and refers to it as a foreign key in a relational schema in an ISA relationship. It can also be implemented by a subclass inheriting its superclass's OID and attributes in the object-oriented schema. It can also be implemented by an owner record that has the same key as its member record in network schema via SET linkage. It can also be implemented by an element that links one-to-one occurrence with its sub-element in the XML schema.

(3) Generalization describes the relationship between one superclass and multiple subclasses.

They are in multiple ISA relationships. For example, A is a special kind of B, and C is also a special kind of B, then A and C subclasses can be generalized as B superclass. In a relational schema, both superclass relation and subclass relation contain the same key, with subclass relations' keys referring to superclass key as the foreign key in generalization. In the object-oriented schema, multiple subclasses objects contain the same OID as their superclass object in generalization. In a network schema, one owner record links with multiple member records through a SET in generalization. In XML, multiple subclass elements and their superclass element are in 1:1 linkage with the same key attribute in generalization. Generalization can be implemented by multiple ISA relationships with multiple subclasses generalized into one superclass.

9.2 Heterogeneous Database Connectivity Schema Translation

Before data transformation, HDBC performs mapping of major data semantics of cardinality, ISA, generalization, and aggregation among legacy data models as shown in Table 9.2:

Functional Dependencies

The preservation of data semantics among legacy databases can be verified by the preservation of their data dependencies as follows:

Definition of FD (Functional Dependency)

Table 9.2 Data semantics implementation in legacy data models and Flattened XML document

Data model\ Data Semantic	Relational	Object-Oriented	Network	XML (in DTD)	Flattened XML(in DTD)
1:n cardinality	Many child relations' foreign key referring to the same parent relation's primary key	A class's association attribute refers to another class's objects' OID(s) as a Stored OID	An owner record points to many member records via SET linkage	An element contains many sub-elements	The IDREF(s) of a sibling element refer to an ID of another sibling element
m:n cardinality	A relationship relation's composite key refers to 2 other relations' primary keys	2 class's association attributes refer to the same third-class OID	Two owner records point to the same member record via 2 SETs linkages	A sub-element of 1 element links another element by IDREF referring to ID	A sibling element's 2 IDREF(s) refer to the ID of 2 other sibling elements under the root element
Isa	Subclass relation's primary key is also a foreign key referring to its superclass relation's same primary key	A subclass inherits OID(s) and attributes of its superclass as its own attributes	An owner record links to a member record in 1:1 occurrence with the same key	An element occurrence links its sub-element occurrence in 1:1 linkage	The IDREF of a subclass sibling element data refers to the ID of its superclass sibling element with the same key
Generalization	2 subclass relations' primary keys are also foreign keys referring to the same superclass relation's primary keys	Two subclasses inherit OID(s) and attributes of same superclass as their own additional attributes	An owner record data points to two member records data with the same key under 2 SET linkages	An element occurrence links with two sub-elements in 1:1 occurrence linkages	The IDREF(s) of 2 subclass sibling elements refer to the ID of a superclass sibling element with the same key

Given a relation R, attribute Y of R is functionally dependent on attribute X of R, i.e., FD: R.X □ R.Y, if each X-value in R has associated with it precisely one Y value in R. attribute X and Y may be composite.

Definition of ID (inclusion dependency)

ID: Y $\subseteq$ Z states that the set of values appearing in attribute Y must be a subset of the set of values appearing in attribute Z.

Definition of MVD (multi-valued dependency)

Let R be a relation variable, and let A, B, and C be the attributes of R. Then B is multi-dependent on A if, and only if, in every legal value of R, the set of B values matching a given AC pair value depends on the A value, and is independent of the C value.

In general, the presentation of the data semantics of cardinality, ISA, generalization, and aggregation among legacy databases schemas can be shown in Fig. 9.3. The above data semantics can be preserved in flattened XML documents with sibling elements only, linking with each other via IDREF and ID as shown in Fig. 9.4.

We use data dependencies FD, MVD, and ID as a formal method to represent semantic constraints of different data models.

Our approach is to prove that the data dependencies are preserved before and after data transformation through HDBC.

For example, in proving one-to-many cardinality, we can use FD: any "many" side data determine one and only one "one" side data such as each that ID can determine the student's department (one department many students).

Similarly, in proving the ISA relationship, we can use ID (Inclusion dependency) such that each part-time student's is a subset of all students' ID because a part-time student must be also a student. Similarly, in proving many-to-many cardinality we can use MVD (Multi-valued dependency) such as a student can take many courses, and a class can be taken by many students:

```
MVD: student ->> class
MVD: class ->> students
```

FD means functional dependence, i.e., a determinant that can determine the value of dependant fields. E.g., a student ID is a determinant that can determine the student's age as a dependant field.

We use FD to specify the data constraints before and after data conversion (transformation).

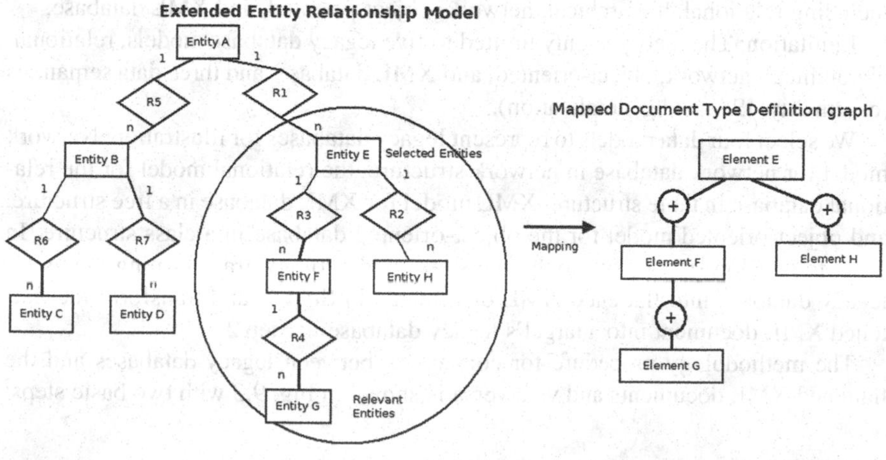

Fig. 9.4 Selected "Root element" and Relevant Entities are mapped into a DTD graph

If the FD is preserved, before, and after database conversion, then we claim that the data semantics are preserved before and after database conversion.

Refer to Chapter 3 for schema translations between hierarchical, network, relational, object-oriented, and XML databases.

9.3 Heterogeneous Database Connectivity Data Transformation

HDBC is a database middleware to access legacy databases via flattened XML documents as follows:

Source Legacy databases → Flattened XML documents → Target Legacy databases

Hypothesis: Since HDBC is feasible, legacy DB and flattened XML are interchangeable, and since flattened XML can be accessed on the Internet, therefore, any legacy DB can be accessed as flattened XML representation on the Internet. Therefore, HDBC can become an end user computing tool to connect most legacy DB, such as the Internet can connect most computers.

Our contribution is, based on our theory, HDBC could act as a database middleware to access five legacy databases via flattened XML documents at the same time. The five legacy databases are relational, hierarchical, network, object-oriented, and XML database. While research from the others only allowed two legacy databases transformation, e.g., relational-to-XML, relational-to-hierarchical, etc., there is no such contribution among five legacy databases interchangeable to each other in the same paper.

Our theory: There are different legacy databases with different data models. They need to be interchangeable without loss of information. Our method is using flattened XML as the middleware to interchange among five legacy databases, including relational, hierarchical, network, object-oriented, and XML database.

Limitation: The theory is only limited to five legacy database models, relational, hierarchical, network, object-oriented, and XML database, and three data semantics (cardinality, ISA, and generalization).

We select four data models to represent legacy databases for illustration: Network model for network database in network structure, the relational model for the relational database in table structure, XML model for XML database in a tree structure, and object-oriented model for the object-oriented database in a class structure. In order to develop HDBC, we apply two steps methodology, transforming the user's legacy database into flattened XML documents in Step 1, and transform the flattened XML document into a target's legacy database in Step 2.

The methodology procedure for conversion between legacy databases and the flattened XML documents and vice versa is shown in Fig. 9.3 with two basic steps:

```
Main algorithm:
Begin
      If legacy database conceptual schema does not exist
Then Reverse engineering legacy logical schema into legacy
database conceptual schema; /* pre-process */
      Transform source's legacy database into flattened XML
document; /* step 1*/
      Transform flattened XML document into a target legacy
database; /* step 2 */
End;
```

Preprocess: Reverse engineer legacy database logical schemas into their conceptual schemas

As shown in Table 9.2, for the structural constraints of each legacy database, we can recover their data semantics accordingly.

For example, to reverse relational schema into an Extended Entity-Relationship model, a classification table can be used to define the relationship between keys and attributes in all relations, and data semantics can be recovered accordingly. A 1:n cardinality in the relational schema can be recovered from a foreign key(FKA) between two relations in the classification table, with foreign key relation on the "many" side and referred primary key relation on "one" side (Fong 1992).

Similarly, we can reverse engineer object-oriented schema into UML by recovering 1:n association between two associated objects with a Stored OID on the "many" side in a class referring to an OID on the "one" side in another associated class in OODB. We can also reverse Network schema into Network database conceptual schema Network Graph by recovering owner record on "one" side and member records on "many" side. Similarly, we can reverse engineer XML schema DTD into XML conceptual schema DTD Graph because their logical and conceptual schemas are identical except the latter is in graph format.

Define a Root element.

We recover the legacy database conceptual schema in a diagram. The selection of the root element of flattened XML schema represents the view of users' data requirements on each legacy database. To select a root element, its relevant information must be put into a flattened XML schema. Relevance is concerned with entities that are related to an entity selected by the user for processing. The relevant classes include the selected entity and all its related entities that are navigable. Navigability specifies whether traversal from an entity to its related entity is possible.

For example, given an entity-relationship model as shown in Fig. 9.8. We can select entity E as the root element for flattened XML schema. As a result, the mapped flattened XML schema is extracted from the EER model as shown in Fig. 9.8. On the other hand, we can also select an artifact root element that includes all entities in the ER model for data transformation as shown in the case study.

Step 1: Transform user's source legacy databases into flattened XML documents

Firstly, in preprocess, we capture the data semantics of a legacy database into its conceptual schema, for example, EER model for a relational database, UML for object-oriented database, Network graph for network database, and DTD graph for XML database. These data semantics can be mapped into the flattened XML document schema by storing each data semantic in the XML DTD (data type definition) schema. The data semantics include one-to-one, one-to-many, many-to-many cardinalities, and relationships, generalizations, and which can be mapped among the flattened XML document and the legacy databases.

Secondly, we perform data transformation from the legacy database into a flattened XML document using a logical level approach (Shoshani 1975, Lum 1976, Fong 2006).

Case 1: Transform relational databases into flattened XML documents

Firstly, we perform the preprocess of mapping relational schema into flattened XML schema. Secondly, we perform their correspondent data transformation. The Input is a relational database and the output is a flattened XML document. The system will read the relational table according to the legacy relational schema. In one-to-many data semantic, it will post parent and child relations into flattened sibling XML elements linked with id and idref. In many-to-many data semantic, it will post two relations and their relationship relation into flattened XML sibling elements linked with idref(s) and id(s). In ISA data semantic, it will post superclass and subclass relations into table structured XML sibling elements linked with id and idref with the same key. In generalization data semantic, it will post superclass relation and subclasses relations into XML sibling elements linked with id(s) and idref(s) with the same key in sibling elements.

Preprocess algorithm: Map relational schema into flattened XML schema:

```
Begin
  Select a root element for flattened XML schema;
     If relation B foreign key refers to relation A primary key
     Then begin
  /*Map relations A and B of 1:n cardinality into sibling ele-
   ments A and B
  of 1:n cardinality; where A is one and B is many */
 Map relation A into sibling element A with ID;
    Map relation B into sibling element B with IDREF refer to
    the above
ID;
          end;
 If relation B has a primary key which is also a foreign key
  refers to
  relation A primary key
    Then begin
```

```
/*Map relation A isa relation B into sibling element A isa sib-
ling element B;
where A is subclass and B is superclass */
  Map relation A into sibling element A with ID value of
  relation key
value;
        Map relation B into sibling element B with IDREF value
        of the same
     relation key value;
          end;
   If (relation A and relation B is in 1:n cardinality) And
(relation C and relation B is in 1:n)
  Then relation A and relation C are in m:n cardinality;
       If (relation A isa relation B) and (relation C isa
relation B)
       Then relation A and relation C are generalized into
relation B;
 /* A and C are subclasses, and B is their superclass */
      End;
```

Process algorithm: Transform relational database to a flattened XML document

Input: Relational database
Output: Flattened XML document

```
begin
 Create a raw XML document with an arbitrary root element r
 For each table do
 begin
    For each record rec do
          begin
          Create an XML element e named as its table name
       If table of the record defines a primary key pk
       then begin
          Create an ID attribute id named table-name.column-name
with value table-name.primary-key-value;
                        Add the above id as attribute of e;
                  end;
                  For each foreign key fk of the table do
                  begin
                 Create an IDREF attribute idref named primary-
table-name.foreign-key-column-name with value primary-table-name.
foreign-key-value;
                        Add the above idref as attribute of e;
                  end
```

```
            end
            Add e as child element of r;
      end
```

Case 2: Transform XML databases into flattened XML documents

Firstly, we perform the preprocess of mapping XML schema into flattened XML schema. Secondly, we perform their correspondent data transformation. The Input is an XML document and the output is a flattened XML document. The system will read XML documents according to the XML schema. In one-to-many data semantic, it will post element and sub-element into flattened XML document sibling elements linked with id and idref. In many-to-many data semantic, it will post three elements linked with id(s) and idref(s) into flattened XML document sibling elements linked with id(s) and idref(s). In ISA data semantic, it will post superclass and subclass elements into flattened XML document sibling elements linked with id and idref with the same key. In generalization data semantic, it will post element and sub-elements into flattened XML document sibling elements linked with id(s) and idref(s) with the same key in DTD "," separator in the flattened XML schema.

Preprocess algorithm: Map XML schema into flattened XML schema:

```
    Begin
  If element A and its sub-element B have same key attribute a1 in XML schema
    Then begin
     Map element A isa element B into sibling elements A isa B;
            /*A is subclass and B is superclass */
     Map element A with attributes into sibling element A with same attributes and an ID value into flattened XML schema;
     Map element B with attributes into sibling element B with same attributes and IDREF referring above ID value into XML schema;
            end;
If (sub-element B under element A) or (element B has an IDREF referring to
           element A ID value)
    Then begin
         Map sibling elements A and B in 1:n cardinality into elements A and B in 1:n cardinality;/*A is subclass & B is superclass */
         Map element A into sibling element A wth an ID value in flattened XML schema;
         Map element B into sibling element B with an IDREF referring to the above ID value in flattened XML schema;
           End;
     If (element A and element B is in 1:n cardinality) And (element C and element B
     is in 1:n)
```

```
    Then element A and element C are in m:n cardinality in
XML schema;
  If (element A isa element B) and (element C isa element B)
  Then element A and element C are generalized into element B;
    /* A,C are subclasses to superclass B */
    End;
```

Process algorithm: Transform an XML document to a flattened XML document

Input: an XML document
Output: a flattened XML document

```
   Begin
 Read XML document elements instances by using depth first search;
     While not at end of instances do
     begin
          For each element obtained
          Add a sibling element with an ID attribute id
          with value
          "entity:sequence_number";
          For each sub-element obtained
          Add a sibling element with an IDREF attribute idref
with value "parent_element_name:seqeuence number of its element;
      end;
  end;
```

Case 3: Transform object-Oriented database into flattened XML document
Firstly, we perform the preprocess of mapping object-oriented schema into flattened XML schema. Secondly, we perform their correspondent data conversion. The Input is an OODB and the output is a flattened XML document. The system will read OODB according to OODB schema. In one-to-many data semantic, it will post object and set of associated objects into XML sibling elements linked with id and idref. In many-to-many data semantic, it will post two sets of associated objects with a common object into XML sibling elements linked with id(s) and idref(s). In ISA data semantic, it will post superclass and subclass objects with the same OID into XML sibling elements linked with id and idref with the same key. In generalization data semantic, it will post superclass and multiple subclasses objects into sibling elements linked with id(s) and idref(s) with the same key in DTD "," separator in the flattened XML document schema.

Preprocess algorithm: Map object-oriented schema into flattened XML schema:

```
Begin
 If B is a subclass of class A
 Then begin
```

```
/* Map classes A and class B into sibling element A and B
        where B is subclass and A is superclass */
        Map class A with OID into sibling element A with ID
value the same as OID;
    Map class B with the same OID as above into sibling element
    B with IDREF referring to the above ID value;
        end;
  If class A has association attribute referring to class B's
multiple objects
Then begin
    /*Map Classes A and B in 1:n cardinality into sibling ele-
ments B and C in 1:n cardinality where A is one and B is many */
Map class A with OID into sibling element A with ID value the
same as OID;
    Map class B with stored OID into sibling element B with IDREF
referring to the above ID value;
        End;
If (sibling element A and sibling element B are in 1:n cardinal-
ity) And (sibling element C and sibling element B is in 1:n)
    Then sibling element A and sibling element C are in m:n
cardinality;
    If (sibling element A isa sibling element B) and
    (sibling element C isa sibling element B)
    Then sibling element A and sibling element C are general-
ized into sibling element B; /*A,C are subclasses to superclass B*/
    End;
```

Process algorithm of transforming OODB to flattened XML documents

Input: An OODB instance

Output: A flattened XML document

```
Begin
 Create a flattened XML document with a root element
 For each class c in OODB do
 Begin
  For each object obj in class c do
  Begin
        Derive an OID for class c for object obj;
        Create a sibling XML element for object obj as a sib-
ling element of flattened XML document with OID as ID type attribute;
        End
 For each association attribute of obj do
     Begin
     For each referred obj with stored OID do
```

```
        Begin
                Locate the corresponding sibling XML element e
in flattened XML document:
            Create an IDREF attribute for element e:
            End
        End
    For each association attribute of obj do
        Begin
        Map the superclass object into sibling element with an
ID and OID as key value;
          Map the subclass object with another sibling element
with an IDREF referring to the above ID and OID as key value
        End
     End
   End
```

Case 4: Transform Network databases into flattened XML documents
Firstly, we perform the preprocess of mapping network schema into flattened XML schema. Secondly, we perform their correspondent data conversion. The Input is a Network database(NDB) and the output is a table structured flattened XML document. The system will read NDB according to the NDB schema. In one-to-many data semantic, it will post owner and member records into XML sibling elements linked with id and idref. In many-to-many data semantic, it will post two owners and one common member record into XML sibling elements linked with id(s) and idref(s). In ISA data semantic, it will post an owner and member records into XML sibling elements linked with id and idref with the same key. In generalization data semantic, it will post owner and member records into table structured XML sibling elements linked with id(s) and idref(s), with the same key in the flattened XML document schema DTD "," separator.

Preprocess algorithm: Map Network schema into flattened XML schema:

```
Begin
 If (owner record A has a key value attribute a1) and (member
 record B
 under owner record A has same key value a1)
 Then begin
     /* Map Record B isa record A into sibling element A isa
     sibling element B
     where A is subclass and B is superclass */
     Map record A into sibling element A with key attribute a1
and with ID value into flattened XML schema;
     Map record B into sibling element B with the same key attri-
     bute a1 and an
 IDREF referring to above ID value into flattened XML schema;
```

```
        End;
If member record B under owner record A
Then begin
   /*Map Records A and B in 1:n cardinality into sibling elements
A and B in
  1:n cardinality where A is one and B is many */
     Map record A into sibling element A with ID value into flat-
tened XML schema;
 Map record B into sibling element B with IDREF referring to the
above ID
   value into flattened XML schema;
 End;
 If (sibling element A and sibling element B is in 1:n cardinal-
ity) And (sibling
   element C and sibling element B is in 1:n)
 Then sibling element A and sibling element C are in m:n
cardinality;
    If (sibling element A isa sibling element B) and (sibling
element C isa sibling
   element B)
 Then sibling element A and sibling element C are generalized
into sibling
   element B;
 /* A,C are subclasses to superclass B*/
 End;
```

Process algorithm: Transform an NDB to a flattened XML document

Input: A NDB instance

Output: a flattened XML document

```
Begin
  Read NDB record occurrences by using depth first search;
       While not at end of occurrences do
  begin
                For each owner record occurrence obtained
                Add a sibling element with an ID attribute id
                 with value
                "entity:sequence_number";
                For each member record occurrence obtained
                Add a sibling element with an IDREF attribute idref
with value
             "parent_element_name:seqeuence number"of its element;
    end;
     end;
```

Step 2: Transform Flattened XML Documents into Target's Legacy Databases[17]

In Step 2, we can translate the flattened XML schema into another legacy database schema, followed by the data transformation of the flattened XML documents into a legacy database according to the translated legacy database schema. In this way, each source database data type can be read by the legacy database schema. Therefore, there is no need for physical data type conversion in this approach as shown in Fig. 9.3. Therefore, we can post the flattened relational structured XML document into a legacy database of relational, object-oriented, network, or XML.

Case 1: Transform flattened XML documents into relational databases

Firstly, we perform the preprocess of mapping flattened XML schema into a relational database schema. Secondly, we perform their correspondent data conversion. The Input is a flattened XML document and the output is a relational database. The system will read flattened XML documents according to flattened XML document schema. In one-to-many data semantic, it will post XML sibling elements into parent and child relations. In many-to-many data semantic, it will post XML sibling elements linked with id(s) and idref(s) into two parents and one child relations. In ISA data semantic, it will post XML sibling elements into superclass relation and sub-class relation. In generalization data semantic, it will post XML sibling elements into a superclass relation and two subclass relations.

Preprocess algorithm: Map flattened XML schema into relational schema:

```
Begin
 If (sibling element A with ID value of relation key value) and
(sibling element B with IDREF value of the same relation key value)
 Then begin
     /* Map Siblings elements A and B into relations A and B where
B is a subclass to A */
     Map sibling element A into relation A with primary key =
ID value;
Map sibling element B into relation B with primary key = foreign
key with
     same value;
          End;
    If (sibling element A with ID value) and (sibling element B
with IDREF value of the same value)
 Then begin
 /* Map Sibling elements A and B in 1:n cardinality into relations
A and B in
        1:n cardinality where A is one and B is many*/
      Map sibling element A into relation A with primary key =
ID value;
```

```
      Map sibling element B into relation B with foreign key
referring to
      primary key ID value;
      End;
   If  (sibling element A and sibling element B is in 1:n
cardinality)
   And (sibling element C and sibling element B is in 1:n)
        Then sibling element A and sibling element C are in
m:n cardinality;
      If (sibling element A isa sibling element B) and (sibling
element C isa
         sibling element B)
   Then sibling A and sibling element C are generalized into sib-
ling element B;
  /* A,C are subclasses, and B is their superclass */
   End;
```

Process algorithm: Create RDB SQL statements from flattened XML document

Input: flattened XML document
Output: A sequence of SQL statements

```
Begin
Let s be an empty statement sequence;
   For each sibling XML element with entity prefix e do
    begin
  Derive table name t from sibling element name of e without
entity prefix;
       For each sibling element c of e do
     /* extract attributes from the sibling-elements in flattened
XML document */
   Begin
             Derive col from name of c without property prefix;
     Derive val from child text node contents of c;
             If c is the first sibling element
            Then begin
                Let cols = "col";
                Let vals = "'val'";
            End;
            Else begin
             Append ",col" to cols;
                Append ",'val'" to vals;
            End;
            End
            Let i = "INSERT INTO t (cols) VALUES (vals)";
```

```
            Add i to s;
        End
        Return s
    End
```

Case 2: Transform flattened XML documents into object-oriented databases

Firstly, we perform the preprocess of mapping flattened XML schema into an object-oriented schema. Secondly, we perform their correspondent data conversion. The Input is a flattened XML document and the output is an object-oriented database. The system will read flattened XML documents according to flattened XML document schema. In one-to-many data semantic, it will post XML sibling elements into a pair of associated objects with OID and Stored OID. In many-to-many data semantic, it will post XML sibling elements linked with id(s) and idref(s) into a pair of associated objects. In ISA data semantic, it will post XML sibling elements into a superclass and its sub-class object. In generalization data semantic, it will post flattened structured XML sibling elements with the same key into objects and their subclass objects with the same OID.

Preprocess algorithm: Map flattened XML schema into object-oriented schema:

```
1 Begin
2  If (sibling element A with key attribute a1 and an ID value) And
(sibling element
 B with the same key attribute a1 and an IDREF value the same as
the above ID value)
3  Then begin
   /* Map sibling element B isa sibling element A into class B isa
class A;
    where subclass B refer to superclass A*/
4        Map sibling element A into class A with attribute a1 into
object-oriented
         schema;
5        Map sibling element B into subclass B of class A in object-
oriented schema;
6     end;
7  If (sibling element A with an ID value)
  And (sibling element B with an IDREF value referring to the above
ID value)
8  Then begin
    /* Map sibling elements A and B in 1:n cardinality into classes
A and B in 1:n
      cardinality where A is one and B is many */
9  Map sibling element A into class A with association attribute
A2B referring
  to class B's multiple objects in OODB schema;
```

```
10  Map sibling element B into class B with association attribute
B2A referring
   to class A's object in OODB schema;
11          end;
12  If      (sibling element A and sibling element B is in 1:n
cardinality)
 And     (sibling element C and sibling element B is in 1:n)
13  Then sibling element A and sibling element C are in m:n
cardinality;
14  If (sibling element A isa sibling element B) and (sibling ele-
ment C isa sibling
 element B)
15   Then sibling A and sibling element C are generalized into
sibling element B;
   /* A,C are subclass, and B is their superclass */
16  end;
```

Process algorithm: Create OODB statements from flattened XML documents

Input: flattened XML document

Output: A sequence of OODB OQL statements

```
1 Begin
2 Given sibling element A1 is with idref=id as "one" side only;
3 For i = 1 to m do
   /* for each sibling element Ai with data occurrence A1….Am */
4 For j = 1 to n do
    /* for each sibling element Aj data occurrence A1…An such
that i≠j*/
5 Begin
6  If (sibling element Ai ID name = sibling element Ai IDREF name)
          and (sibling element Aj ID name = sibling element Ai
IDREF name)
7         Then sibling element Ai isa sibling element Aj;
          /* subclass element Ai and superclass element Aj */
8              If sibling element Ai ID name = sibling element Aj
IDREF name
9         Then sibling element Ai and sibling element Aj are in 1:n
cardinality;
      /* element Ai links many element Aj */
10             If sibling element Ai IDREF name = sibling element
Aj ID name
11       Then sibling element Ai and sibling element Aj are in n:1
cardinality;
   /* many element Ai links element Aj */
```

```
      Case sibling element Ai and sibling element Aj are in
  1:n begin
     Output insert statement with Ai data + association attri-
bute value "{}";
      Output insert statement with Aj data;
      End;

   n:1 begin
      Output insert statement with Ai data;
     Output insert statement with Aj data + association attri-
bute null value;
      End;
  Isa: begin
      Output insert statement with Ai data + to-be-inherited
superclass attributes
     null value;
      Output insert statement with Aj data;
      End;
  Case end;
  End;
For i = 1 to m do
  /* for each sibling element Ai with data occurrence A1….Am */
For j = 1 to n do
  /* for each sibling element Aj data occurrence A1…An such
that i≠j*/
Begin
    Case sibling element Ai and sibling element Aj are in
  1:n: Output update statement of Aj to replace "{}" value
by selected
  OID(s);
  n:1: Output update statement of Aj to replace null value
by selected
  OID;
   isa: Output update statement of Ai to replace null value
with inherited Aj
        data by select statement;
   case end;
   end;
  end
```

Case 3: Transform flattened XML documents into network databases

Firstly, we perform the preprocess of mapping flattened XML schema into network schema. Secondly, we perform their correspondent data conversion. The Network database model is the earliest database model among the four legacy databases being concerned. There are no standard data definition language (DDL) and data manipulation language (DML). Database in a network database model is accessed by making function invocations of the application-programming interface (API) that comes with the database products. Database manipulation operations are written in third-generation languages (3GL's) such as COBOL and C.

The Raima database is used as the reference network database implement. In order to import data to the NDB, Raima provides a utility that can read the sequence data files. Therefore, the algorithm provided below is to translate the flattened XML document file into plain text sequential file.

For example, the Raima database defines its own data definition language. To define an entity type with properties, use a record definition:

```
record investor {
double money_mkt;
char name;
unique key short invID;}
```

To define the linkages among the entities, use the set definition:

```
set inv_trans {
order last;
owner investor;
member asset;}
```

Once the database definition is properly defined with a DDL file, Raima provides a utility application and API for creating the database.

The Input is a flattened XML document and the output is a network database. The system will read flattened XML documents according to flattened XML document schema. In one-to-many data semantic, it will post XML sibling elements into a pair of owner and member records. In many-to-many data semantic, it will post XML sibling elements linked with id(s) and idref(s) into two owners link with one member record with the same key. In ISA data semantic, it will post XML sibling elements into one owner and one member record with the same key. In generalization data semantic, it will post XML sibling elements linked with id(s) and idref(s) into one owner and two member records with the same key.

Preprocess algorithm: Map flattened XML schema into network schema:

```
1 Begin
2 If (sibling element A with an attribute a1 and an ID value) And
(sibling
  element B with the same attribute a1 and an IDREF value the same
as the above ID value)
3 Then begin
 /*Map sibling element B isa sibling element A into record B isa
record A where
  B is subclass, and A is superclass */
```

```
4 Map sibling element A with key attribute a1 into owner record A
with key
     attribute a1 into network schema;
5      Map sibling element B with key attribute a1 into member
record B under
  record A with the same key attribute a1 into network schema;
6  end;
7 If    (sibling element A with an ID value)
    And (sibling element B with an IDREF value referring to the
above ID value)
8 Then begin
  /* Map sibling elements A and B in 1:n cardinality into records
A and B in 16 1:n cardinality where A is one and B is many */
9    Map sibling element A with attribute ID value a1 into owner
record A with 18 key attribute a1 into network schema;
10    Map sibling element B into member record B under record A
into network
 schema;
11      end;
12 If     (sibling element A and sibling element B is in 1:n
cardinality)
   And     (sibling element C and sibling element B is in 1:n)
13 Then  sibling  element  A  and  sibling  element  C  are  in  m:n
cardinality;
14 If (sibling element A isa sibling element B) and (sibling ele-
ment C isa sibling
 element B)
15  Then sibling A and sibling element C are generalized into sib-
ling element B;
  /* A,C are subclasses, and B is their superclass */
16 end;
```

Process algorithm Step 1: Create CSV file from flattened XML document

```
1 Read flattened XML document
2    For each XML element e do
3    Begin
4         Derive the internal table name t from element name of e;
5         Use t as the CSV file name;
6         For each sibling element c of e do;
7         Begin
8             Derive val from attribute contents of c;
9             If c is the first sibling element
10             Then begin
11                      Let valo ='val';
```

```
            End;
        Else begin
                Let vals =',';
                Append "val" to vals;
            End;
        Add vals to the CSV file;
    End;
    Export the CSV file;
End
```

```
//Step 2: Macro-call program
```

Macro-call: We need to use a utility provided by NDB DBMS (Raima) to import the data from the CSV file to the database. The utility is named "dbimp." The "dbimp" is in command format and only executable in the command prompt. Before we use the "dbimp", we must write a text-based import file. The import file first defined which database we want to import data. Then, for each record, we need to specify the CSV file to import data. This is achieved by the "foreach" command and followed by the CSV file name. After this, we used "{" and "}" to include the record name and attribute name. We used the keyword "field" in front of each attribute. For example,

```
Database !network database name
foreach "!data file name.csv" {
 record ! ="record name"
field !field name = 1;
…
Field !field name = n"
}
```

```
        //Step 3: Upload data and query the NDB instance (in
Raima) by computer automation
        Import data to the NDB instance by use of utility "dbimp."
        If the data import successfully, all data will be query
and output simultaneously.
        End
```

Case 4: Transform flattened XML documents into XML databases

Firstly, we perform the preprocess of mapping flattened XML schema into XML schema. Secondly, we perform their correspondent data conversion. The flattened XML documents format is in XML format with three nested levels, which are root, entity element, and column element, and each column element instance encloses a text node for the column value. On the other hand, the usual XML document can be in any nested structure and the number of nested levels is unlimited. Therefore, in order to convert arbitrary XML documents into the corresponding flattened relational structured XML document format structure, the following process is used:

The Input is a flattened XML document and the output is an XML document. The system will read flattened XML documents according to flattened XML documents schema. In one-to-many data semantic, it will post XML sibling elements into a pair of XML elements and sub-elements. In many-to-many data semantic, it will post XML sibling elements linked with id(s) and idref(s) into XML elements and sub-element. In ISA data semantic, it will post XML sibling elements with the same key into XML element and sub-elements with the same key. In generalization data semantic, it will post XML sibling elements into XML elements and sub-elements with the same key.

Preprocess algorithm: Map flattened XML schema into XML schema

```
1 Begin
2 If (sibling element A with an attribute a1 and an ID value) And
(sibling
 element B with the same attribute a1 and an IDREF value the same
as the above ID value)
3 Then begin
  /*Map sibling element B isa sibling element A into element B isa
element A
  where B is subclass and A is superclass */
4        Map sibling element A into element A with attribute a1 in
XML schema;
5     Map sibling element B into element B with attribute a1 and
IDREF value
 the same as the above ID value in XML schema;
6     end;
7 If (sibling element A with an ID value)
  And (sibling element B with an IDREF value referring to the above
ID value)
8 Then begin
  /*Map sibling elements A and B in 1:n cardinality into elements
A and B in 1:n
 cardinality where A is one and B is many */
9         Map sibling element A into element A in XML schema;
10        Map sibling element B into element B under element A in
XML schema;
11 end;
12  If  (sibling  element  A  and  sibling  element  B  is  in  1:n
cardinality)
 And    (sibling element C and sibling element B is in 1:n)
13 Then  sibling  element  A  and  sibling  element  C  are  in  m:n
cardinality;
14 If (sibling element A isa sibling element B) and (sibling ele-
ment C isa sibling
 element B)
```

```
Then sibling A and sibling element C are generalized into sib-
ling element B;
  /* A,C are subclasses, and B is their superclass */
end;
```

Process algorithm: Post flattened XML document into an XML document

Input: A flattened XML document
Output: An XML document

```
Begin
Let xml = replicate of flattened XML document;
Call Restructure XML with xml;
Return xml
End
Function: Restructure XML
Begin
 For each sibling XML element e with one IDREF attribute idref do
 begin
   Locate sibling element e' with ID referred by idref;
   Move e as child element of e';
   Remove attribute idref from element e;
  End
 End
```

9.4 Heterogeneous Database Connectivity Case Study

In general, a DB (database) can be converted without any loss of information if p maps a state of a legacy database into another legacy DB, and p' maps a state of a legacy DB into another legacy DB, then it can be shown that p(p'(N)) = N where N is the legacy DB before conversion.

A logistic system records the customer shipment information including which orders are being packed and what the packing information is. Based on the relational schema below, there are three intermediate independent entities: PL_INFORMAION recording the general information of the shipment, PL_LINE_INFORMATION storing the packing information — particularly information about the BOXES — and ORDER_INFORMATION storing the information of orders such as the product information. A many-to-many relationship between ORDER_INFORMATION and PL_LINE_DETAIL must be resolved early in the modeling process to eliminate repeating information when representing PL_INFORMATION or ORDER_INFORMATION. The strategy for resolving a many-to-many relationship is to replace the relationship with two one-to-many cardinalities. As a result, these two one-to-many relationships are between PL_LINE_INFORMATION and PL_LINE_DETAIL, and between ORDER_INFORMATION and PL_LINE_DETAIL. Similarly, the superclass ORDER_INFOR MATION can be divided into two subclasses BulkOrder and CustomerOrder in generalization as shown in Fig. 9.9. (Table 9.3)

Step 1: Transform from Relational Database into Flattened XML Document:

Example 1: Transform from a relational database into a flattened XML document

The input relational conceptual schema in the Extended Entity-Relationship model (Fig. 9.5)

There are six tables. Each table has its primary key in italic, and foreign key prefixed with "*." Their data dependencies (DD) are such that each foreign key determines its referred primary key in FD, and subclass foreign key is a subset of its superclass primary key in ID as follows:

FD_1: *PL_Line_information.* PL_INFORMATION_SEQNO → *PL_information.*PL_INFORMATION_SEQNO

FD_1 represent PL_INFORMAION and PL_Line_information are in one-to-many cardinality.

ID_1: *Bulk_Order.* BulkOrder.ORDER_NUMBER $\sqsubseteq$ *Order_information . Order_NUMBER*

ID_1 represent subclass BulkOrder and superclass ORDER_INFORMATION are in ISA relationship.

ID_2: *TailorMadeOrder.*TailorMadeOrder.ORDER_NUMBER $\sqsubseteq$ *Order_information . Order_NUMBER*

ID_2 represent subclass TailorMadeOrder and superclass ORDER_INFORMATION ae in ISA relationship.

MVD_1: *PL_Line_information.* PL_INFORMATION_SEQNO →→ *Order_information . Order_NUMBER*

MVD_2: *Order_information . Order_NUMBER* →→ *PL_Line_information.* PL_INFORMATION_SEQNOTherefore: MVD_1 and MVD_2 represent that PL_Line_information and ORDER_INFORMATION are in many-to-many cardinality. (Note: two one-to-many cardinalities are equivalent to many-to-many cardinality)

Table 9.3 Source relational database

Table PL_IFORMATION

PL_ IFORMATION SEQNQ	ISSUE DATE	DATA_LAST MODIFIED	LAST_MODIFIED_BY	PL_ STATUS	PL_ HEADER+REMAKERS	SHPMENT_TYPE	SHPMENT_ DATA	EXPERCED_ ARRIVAL_DATE
EFG123DS	2004-07-31	2004-08-02	JOEY	S	SOME GOODS ARE BREAKBLE	RAIN	2004-08-03	2004-08-03

Table PL_LINE_IFORMATION

*PL_ IFORMATION SEQNQ	PL_LINE_ IFORMATIONSEQNQ_	PACKAGE_ TYPE	LENGTH_UNIT_OF_ MEASURE	WIDTH_UNIT_OF_MEASURE	HEIGT_UNIT_OF_ MEASURE	WEIGHT_UNIT_ OF_MEASURE
EFG123DS	ABCV234F	BOX	20	20	20	40
EFG123DS	ABCN43WS	BAG	7	13	10	13

Table PL_LINE_DETAIL

*PL_ IFORMATION SEQNQ	PL_LINE_ IFORMATIONSEQNQ_	ORDER_ NUMBER	ITEM_ NUMBER	TOTAL_PACKED_QTY	TOTAL_ GROSS_ WEIGHT	TOTAL_ VOLUME_ LENGTH	TOTAL_VILUME_ WIDTH	TOTAL_ VOLUME_ HIGHT
EFG123DS	ABCV234F	135792468	1	4	12	5	2	6
EFG123DS	ABCV234F	135792468	2	1	28	8	4	6
EFG123DS	ABCN43WS	135792468	1	4	12	5	2	6

Table ORDER_IFORMATION

ORDER_ NUMBER	BRAND	DIVISION	CUSTOMER_ ORDER_ NUMBER	CUSTOMER_ NUMBER	ORDER_ TYPE	MODEL_NUMBER	MODEL_ DESCRIPION	ORDER_ DATE	ORDER_ QTY	PRICE_ UNIT	DISCOUNT
135792468	ABC	CLOTHING	135792468	MA23456	MAIL	AS1234	ADULTT_ SHIRT SIZE M	2004-07-27	8	10.5	
123469999	DONY	TOYS	123469999	MA23456	PHONE	PS2	PLASAION	2004-07-2	1	1399	10

Table Bulk Order

*ORDER NUMBER	CUSTOMER_NAME	SIZE_INDEX	ORDER_QTY	UNIT_PRICE
135792468	AMAZON	S	2000	12.1

Table TallorMade Order

*ORDER NUMBER	CUSTOMER_NAME	SIZE_INDEX	ORDER_QTY	UNIT_PRICE
123469999	PETER CHAN	L	3000	12.3

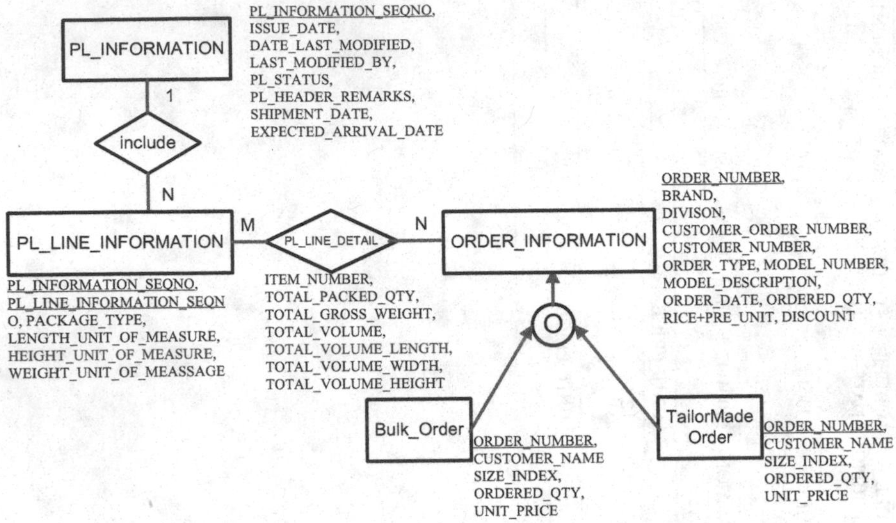

Fig. 9.5 Input relational database in Extended Entity-Relationship model

Example: The layout of the input relational database can be shown in Fig. 9.6. We map input relational schema into a flattened XML HDBC schema with relational structure in two levels tree only as shown in Fig. 9.13. Notice that the second level sibling elements (under root elements) are linked together using idref referring to id, which is similar to foreign key referring to the primary key in a relational database. (Fig. 9.7)

There are seven elements. The second level elements has id(s) and/or idref(s). Their data dependencies are such that each idref determines its referred id FD as follows:

FD_1: t-pl_line_information. t-pl_information.1→ t-pl_information. t-pl_information.1

FD_1 represent PL_INFORMAION and PL_Line_information are in one-to-many cardinality. FD_1 in flattened XML is the same as FD_1 in RDB source. Therefore, one-to-many cardinality between PL_INFORMAION and PL_Line_information is preserved.

ID_1: t-bulk_order. *t-order_information.1* $\subseteq$ t-order_information. *t-order_information.1*

ID_1 represent BulkOrder and ORDER_INFORMATION are in ISA relationship. ID_1 in flattened XML is the same as ID_1 in RDB source. Therefore, ISA relationship between BulkOrder and ORDER_INFORMATION is preserved.

mysql> select * from pl_information;

SHIPMENT_DATE	ISSUE_DATE	DATE_LAST_MODIFIED	PL_INFORMATION_SEQNO	PL_STATUS	SHIPMENT_TYPE	PL_HEADER_REMARKS	EXPECTED_ARRIVAL_DATE	LAST_MODIFIED_BY
2004-08-03	2004-07-31	2004-08-02	EFG123DS	S	TRAIN	SOME GOODS	2004-08-03	JOEY

1 row in set (0.00 sec)

mysql> select * from pl_line_information;

PL_INFORMATION_SEQNO	PL_LINE_INFORMATION_SEQNO	WIDTH_UNIT_OF_MEASURE	HEIGHT_UNIT_OF_MEASURE	PACKAGE_TYPE	WEIGHT_UNIT_OF_MESSAGE	LENGTH_UNIT_OF_MEASURE
EFG123DS	ABCH439WS	13	10	BAG	13	7
EFG123DS	ABCV234F	20	20	BOX	40	20

2 rows in set (0.00 sec)

mysql> select * from pl_line_detail;

TOTAL_VOLUME_LENGTH	PL_INFORMATION_SEQNO	TOTAL_GROSS_WEIGHT	TOTAL_VOLUME_WIDTH	TOTAL_VOLUMEN_HEIGHT	ORDER_NUMBER	TOTAL_PACKED_QTY	PL_LINE_INFORMATION_SEQNO	ITEM_NUMBER
5	EFG123DS	12	2	6	135792468	4	ABCH439WS	1
8	EFG123DS	28	4	6	123469999	1	ABCV234F	2
5	EFG123DS	12	2	6	135792468	4	ABCV234F	1

3 rows in set (0.00 sec)

mysql> select * from order_information;

CUSTOMER_ORDER_NUMBER	DISCOUNT	CUSTOMER_NUMBER	ORDER_TPYE	BRAND	MODEL_DESCRIPTION	MODEL_NUMBER	ORDER_NUMBER	ORDERD_QTY	DIVISION	ORDER_DATE	PRICE_PER_UNIT
123456999	10	MA23456	PHONE	DONY	PLAYSTATIO	PS2	123469999	1	TOYS	2004-07-29	1399.0
135792468	5	MA23456	MAIL	ABC	ADULT T-SH	AS1234	135792468	8	CLOTHING	2004-07-27	10.5

2 rows in set (0.00 sec)

mysql> select * from bulk_order;

CUSTOMER_NAME	UNIT_PRICE	ORDER_NUMBER	SIZE_INDEX
AMAZON	12.1	135792468	S

1 row in set (0.00 sec)

mysql> select * from tailor_made_order;

CUSTOMER_NAME	UNIT_PRICE	ORDER_NUMBER	SIZE_INDEX
PETER CHAN	12.3	135792468	L

1 row in set (0.00 sec)

Fig. 9.6 Source Relational database in the case study

ID_2: t-tailor_made_order. t-pl_information.2 $\sqsubseteq$ t-order_information. t-pl_information.2

ID_2 represent TailorMadeOrder and ORDER_INFORMATION are in ISA relationship. ID_2 in flattened XML is the same as ID_2 in RDB source. Therefore, ISA relationship between TailorMadeOrder and ORDER_ INFORMATION is preserved.

MVD_1: $id_2 \rightarrow\rightarrow id_3$

MVD_2: $id_3 \rightarrow\rightarrow id_2$

Therefore: MVD_1 and MVD_2 represent PL_Line_information and ORDER_INFORMATION are in many-to-many cardinalities. MVD_1 and MVD_2 in flattened XML is the same as MVD_1 and MVD_2 in the RDB source. Therefore, many-to-many cardinality between TailorMadeOrder and ORDER_INFORMATION is preserved.

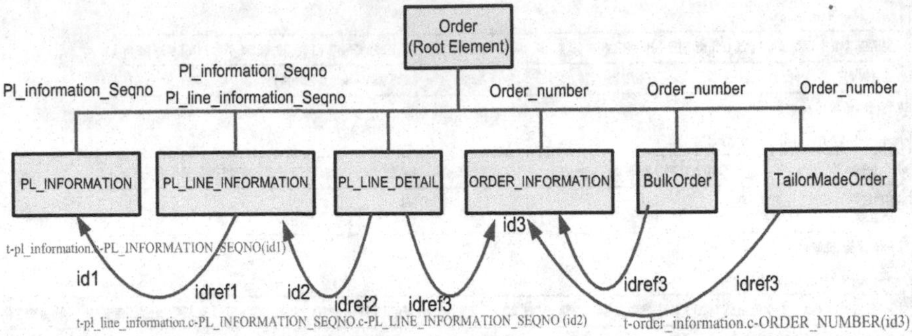

Fig. 9.7 Transformed flattened XML document conceptual schema in DTD Graph

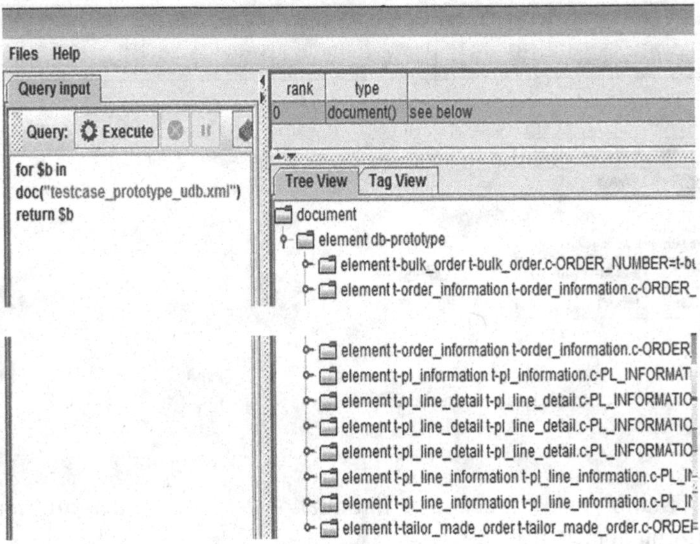

Fig. 9.8 Part of transformed flattened XML Schema

The flattened XML document is shown in Fig. 9.8.

Step 2: Transform from Flattened XML Document into Legacy Databases

We can then map the open universal database schema into legacy databases as follows:

1) Data transformation from flattened XML document into XML document.

We can map the open universal database schema into XML database schema as shown in Fig. 9.9 which shows that elements Pl_information and Pl_line_information are in element and sub-element 1:n association. Elements Pl_line_information, Pl_line_detail, and Order_information are in m:n association linked by pairs of idref referring to id. Elements Order_information and Bulk_Order are in an ISA relationship. Elements Order_information and TailorMadeOrder are also in an ISA

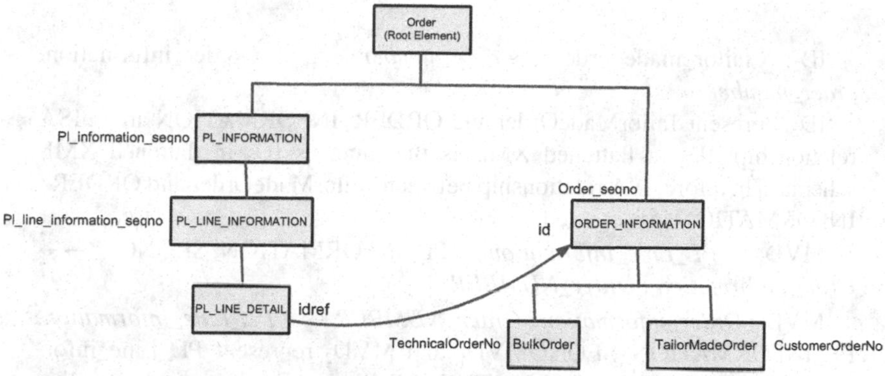

Fig. 9.9 Translated XML document schema in DTD Graph

relationship. This XML structure has multiple levels of elements that are different from the two levels of elements in a flattened XML document.

Example 2: Transform from a flattened XML document into legacy databases

For example, Fig. 9.9 shows the mapping from flattened XML schema into an object-oriented database schema in UML. The class PL_Information and class Pl_line_information are in 1:n association. Classes Pl_line_information and Order_information are in m:n association with class Pl_line_detail as association class in between subclasses BulkOrder and TailorMadeOrder which are in disjoint generalization under their superclass Order_information such that the two subclasses data are mutually exclusive.

There are seven elements. The sub-element key determines its element key in FD. The idref can determine its referred id in FD. The subclass element key is a subset of its superclass key in ID as follows:

FD_1: pl_line_information. pl_information.seqno 1_line_information. pl_information.se pl_information. pl_information seqno

FD_1 represent PL_INFORMAION and PL_Line_information are in one-to-many cardinality. FD_1 in XML is the same as FD_1 in flattened XML schema. Therefore, one-to-many cardinality between PL_INFORMAION and PL_Line_information is preserved.

ID_1: bulk_order. *order_number* $\sqsubseteq$ order_information. *order_number*

ID_1 represent BulkOrder and ORDER_INFORMATION are in ISA relationship. ID_1 in XML is the same as ID_1 in flattened XML schema. Therefore, ISA relationship between BulkOrder and ORDER_INFORMATION is preserved.

ID_2: tailor_made_order. *order_number* $\sqsubseteq$ order_information. *order_number*

ID_2 represent TailorMadeOrder and ORDER_INFORMATION are in ISA relationship. ID_2 in flattened XML is the same as ID_2 in flattened XML schema. Therefore, ISA relationship between TailorMadeOrder and ORDER_INFORMATION is preserved.

MVD_1: *PL_Line_information.* PL_INFORMATION_SEQNO $\to\to$ *Order_information . Order_NUMBER*

MVD_2: *Order_information . Order_NUMBER* $\to\to$ *PL_Line_information.* PL_INFORMATION_SEQNOMVD$_1$ and MVD_2 represent PL_Line_information and ORDER_INFORMATION are in many-to-many cardinality. MVD_1 and MVD_2 in XML is the same as MVD_1 and MVD_2 in flattened XML schema. Therefore, many-to-many cardinality between TailorMadeOrder and ORDER_INFORMATION is preserved.

The transformed XML database document is (Fig. 9.10):

2) Transform flattened XML documents into Object-Oriented databases

Example 3: Transform flattened XML documents into Object-oriented databases.

In Fig. 9.11, record Pl_informations and Order_information are under object-oriented DBMS as first records for database navigation access path. The path can go from class Pl_information to class Pl_line_information in 1:n relationship. Classes Pl_line_information, Order_information and Pl_line_detail are in m:n relationship. Classes Order_information and BulkOrder are in an ISA relationship. Similarly, records Order_information and TailorMadeOrder are in an ISA relationship.

There are six classes. Each class has its OID and Stored OID. Their data dependencies are such that each Stored OID key determines its referred OID in FD, and each subclass OID is a subset of its superclass OID in ID as follows:

FD_1: pl_line_information. Stored_OID $\to$ pl_information. OID

FD_1 represent PL_INFORMAION and PL_Line_information are in one-to-many cardinality. FD_1 in OODB is the same as FD_1 in object-oriented schema source. Therefore, one-to-many cardinality between PL_INFORMAION and PL_Line_information is preserved.

ID_1: bulk_order. OID $\sqsubseteq$ order_information. *OID*

ID_1 represent BulkOrder and ORDER_INFORMATION are in ISA relationship. ID_1 in OODB is the same as ID_1 in object-oriented schema source. Therefore, ISA relationship between BulkOrder and ORDER_INFORMATION is preserved.

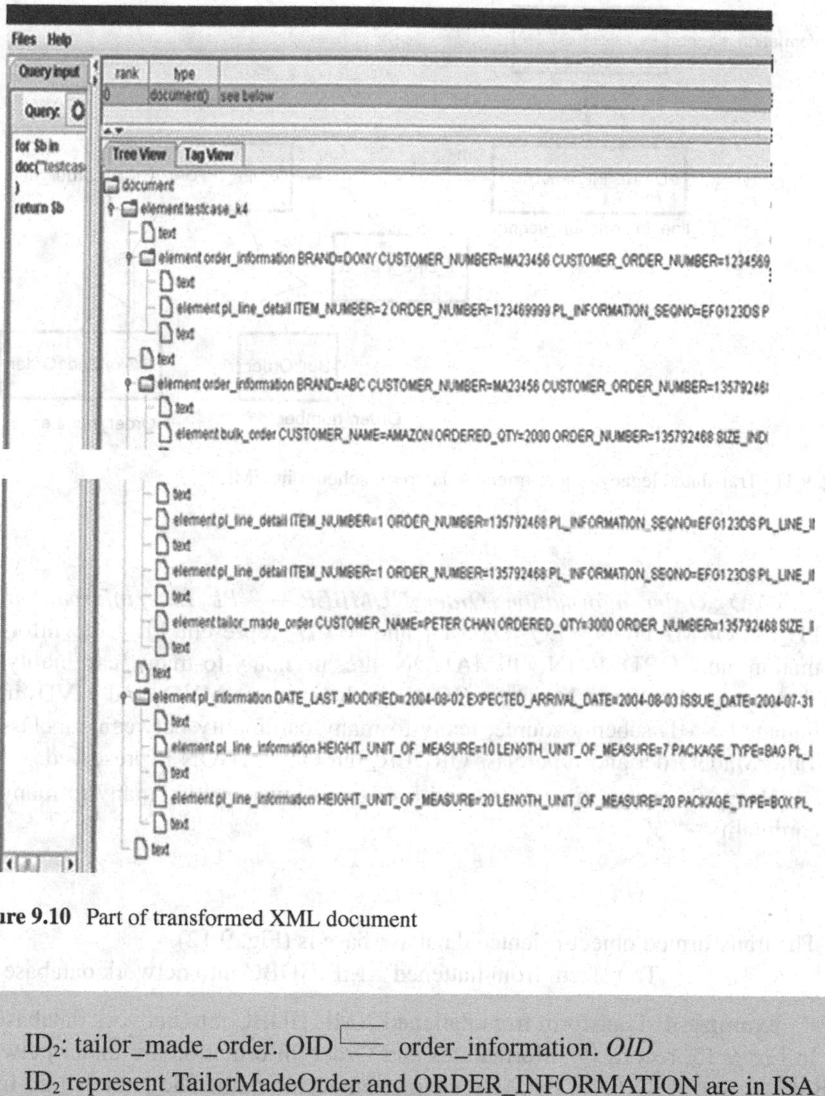

Figure 9.10 Part of transformed XML document

ID_2: tailor_made_order. OID $\sqsubseteq$ order_information. *OID*

ID_2 represent TailorMadeOrder and ORDER_INFORMATION are in ISA relationship. ID_2 in OODB is the same as ID_2 in object-oriented schema source .Therefore, ISA relationship between TailorMadeOrder and ORDER_INFORMATION is preserved.

MVD_1: *PL_Line_information.* PL_INFORMATION SEQNO $\rightarrow\rightarrow$ *Order_information . Order_NUMBER*

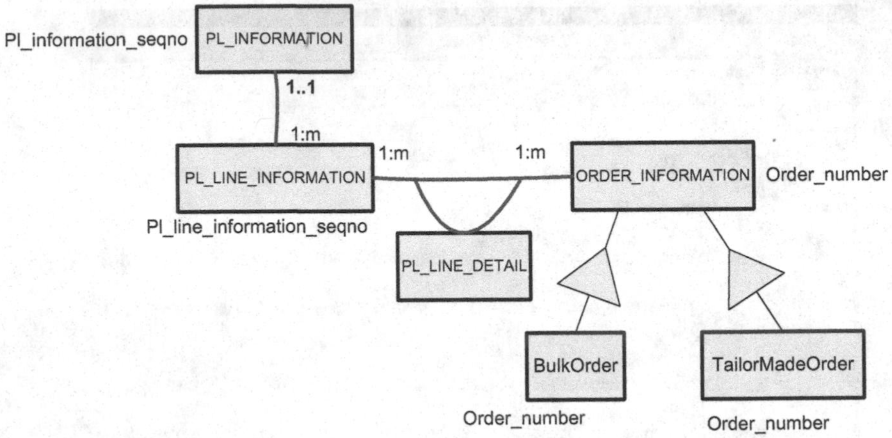

Fig. 9.11 Translated legacy object-oriented database schema in UML

MVD$_2$: *Order_information . Order_NUMBER →→ PL_Line_information.* PL_INFORMATION_SEQNOMVD$_1$ and MVD$_2$ represent PL_Line_information and ORDER_INFORMATION are in many-to-many cardinality. Therefore, MVD$_1$ and MVD$_2$ in OODB is the same as MVD$_1$ and MVD$_2$ in flattened XML schema source, many-to-many cardinality between subclass TailorMadeOrder and superclass ORDER_INFORMATION is preserved.

(Note: 2 one-to-many cardinalities are equivalent to many-to-many cardinality)

The transformed object-oriented database base is (Fig. 9.12):

3) Transform from flattened XML HDBC into network database

Example 4: Transform from flattened XML HDBC into network database.

In Fig. 9.13, record Pl_informations and Order_information are under network DBMS as first records for database navigation access path. The path can go from record Pl_information to record Pl_line_information in owner and member record in 1:n relationship. Records Pl_line_information (owner), Order_information(owner) and Pl_line_detail (member) are in flex structure such that records Pl_line_information and Order_information they are in m:n relationship. Records Order_information and BulkOrder are in 1:1 relationship. Similarly, records Order_information and TailorMadeOrder are in 1:1 relationship. The set records are pointers only.

There are six records. Each recorded class has the key. The member record key determines its owner record key in FD, and the subclass record key is a subset of its superclass record key as follows:

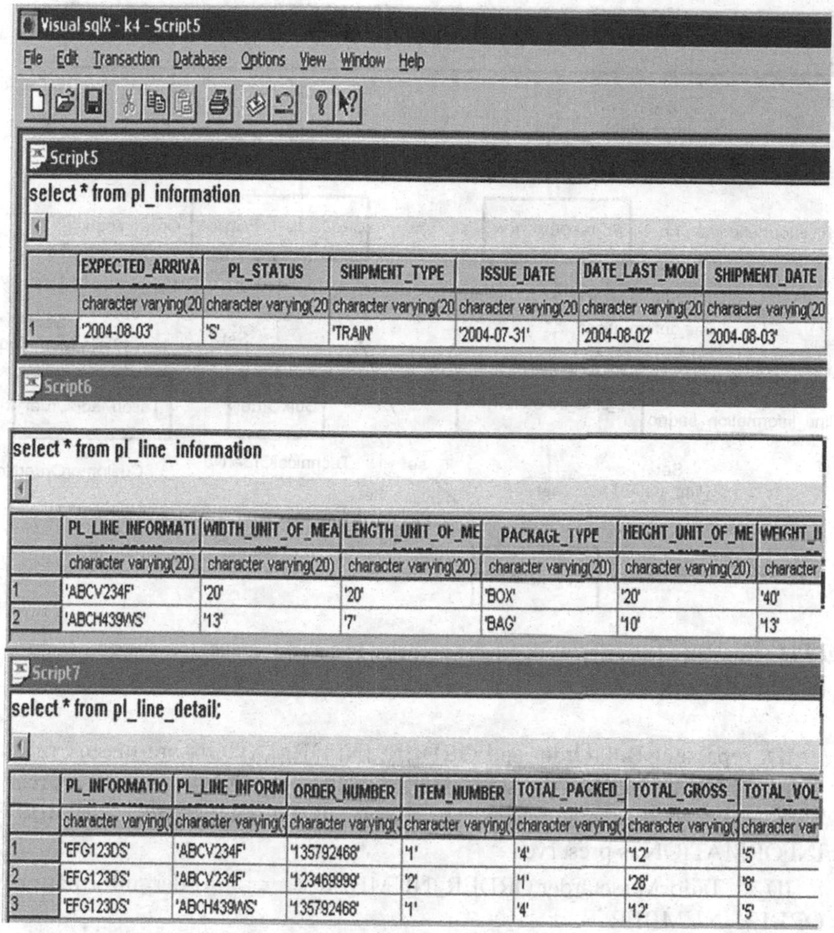

	EXPECTED_ARRIVA	PL_STATUS	SHIPMENT_TYPE	ISSUE_DATE	DATE_LAST_MODI	SHIPMENT_DATE
	character varying(20	character varying(20	character varying(20	character varying(20	character varying(20	character varying(20
1	'2004-08-03'	'S'	'TRAIN'	'2004-07-31'	'2004-08-02'	'2004-08-03'

	PL_LINE_INFORMATI	WIDTH_UNIT_OF_MEA	LENGTH_UNIT_OF_ME	PACKAGE_TYPE	HEIGHT_UNIT_OF_ME	WEIGHT_U
	character varying(20)	character varying(20)	character varying(20)	character varying(20)	character varying(20)	character
1	'ABCV234F'	'20'	'20'	'BOX'	'20'	'40'
2	'ABCH439WS'	'13'	'7'	'BAG'	'10'	'13'

	PL_INFORMATIO	PL_LINE_INFORM	ORDER_NUMBER	ITEM_NUMBER	TOTAL_PACKED_	TOTAL_GROSS_	TOTAL_VOL
	character varying(	character varying(	character varying(	character varying(	character varying(	character varying(	character var
1	'EFG123DS'	'ABCV234F'	'135792468'	'1'	'4'	'12'	'5'
2	'EFG123DS'	'ABCV234F'	'123469999'	'2'	'1'	'28'	'8'
3	'EFG123DS'	'ABCH439WS'	'135792468'	'1'	'4'	'12'	'5'

Fig. 9.12 Part of transformed object-oriented database

FD_1: pl_line_informtion. PL_INFORMATION_SEQNO → pl_information. PL_INFORMATION_SEQNO

FD_1 represent PL_INFORMAION and PL_Line_information are in one-to-many cardinality. FD_1 in NDB is the same as FD_1 in flattened XML schema sourcc. Therefore, one-to-many cardinality between PL_INFORMAION and PL_Line_information is preserved.

ID_1: BulkOrder.ORDER_NUMBER $\sqsubseteq$ order_information. ORDER_NUMBER

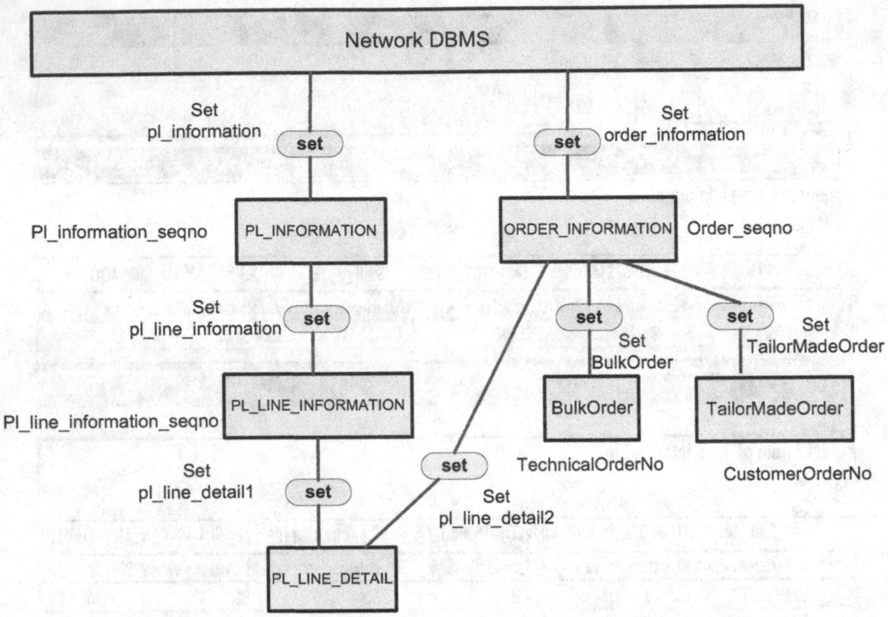

Fig. 9.13 Translated legacy network database schema in network graph

ID_1 represent BulkOrder and ORDER_INFORMATION are in ISA relationship. ID_1 in NDB is the same as ID_1 in flattened XML schema source. Therefore, ISA relationship between BulkOrder and ORDER_INFORMATION is preserved.

ID_2: TailorMadeOrder.ORDER_NUMBER $\sqsubseteq$ order_information.ORDER_NUMBER

ID_2 represent TailorMadeOrder and ORDER_INFORMATION are in ISA relationship. ID_2 in NDB is the same as ID_2 in flattened XML schema source. Therefore, ISA relationship between TailorMadeOrder and ORDER_INFORMATION is preserved. MVD_1: *PL_Line_information.* PL_INFORMATION_SEQNO →→ *Order_information . Order_NUMBER*

MVD_2: *Order_information . Order_NUMBER →→ PL_Line_information.* PL_INFORMATION_SEQNOTherefore: MVD_1 and MVD_2 represent PL_Line_information and ORDER_INFORMATION are in many-to-many cardinality. Therefore, MVD_1 and MVD_2 in NDB is the same as MVD_1 and MVD_2 in flattened XML schema source, many-to-many cardinality between TailorMadeOrder and ORDER_INFORMATION is preserved.

(Note: 2 one-to-many cardinalities are equivalent to many-to-many cardinality)

```
C:\Raima\RDM\11.0\win32\bin>initdb NDB1

Database Initialization Utility


Document Root: C:\Raima\RDM\11.0\win32\bin\
Initialization of database: NDB1

WARNING: this will destroy contents of the following files:

   NDB1.000
   NDB1.001
   NDB1.002
   NDB1.003
   NDB1.004
   NDB1.005
   NDB1.006
   NDB1.k01
   NDB1.k02
   NDB1.k03
   NDB1.k04
   NDB1.k05
   NDB1.k06

continue? (y/n) y

NDB1 initialized


C:\Raima\RDM\11.0\win32\bin>dbinp NDB1.inp

Database Inport Utility


Document Root: C:\Raima\RDM\11.0\win32\bin\
Compilation conplete:

Starting data import
[pl_information.csv:000001] '2004-08-03','8','TRAIN','2004-07-31','2004-08-02','2004-08-03','JOEY','SOME GOODS ARE BREAK
ABLE','EFG123DS'
[pl_line_information.csv:000001] 'ABCH439WS','13','7','BAG','10','13','EFG123DS'
[pl_line_information.csv:000002] 'ABCV234F','20','20','BOX','20','40','EFG123DS'
[pl_line_detail.csv:000001] '2','ABCH439VS','6','4','5','1','135792468','12','EFG123DS'
[pl_line_detail.csv:000002] '4','ABCV234F','6','1','8','2','123469999','28','EFG123DS'
[pl_line_detail.csv:000003] '2','ABCV234F','6','4','5','1','135792468','12','EFG123DS'
[order_information.csv:000001] '1399.0','TOYS','2004-07-29','123456999','PHONE','PS2','PLAYSTATION','MA23456','DONY','10
','123469999','1'
[order_information.csv:000002] '10.5','CLOTHING','2004-07-27','135792468','MAIL','AS1234','ADULT T-SHIRT SIZE M','MA2345
6','ABC','10','135792468','8'
[bulkorder.csv:000001] '10.5','2004-07-27','AMAZON','12.1','13592468','MAIL','123456789','S','8','CLOTHING','AS1234','AD
ULT T-SHIRT SIZE M','ABC','MA23456','5','2000'
[tailormadeorder.csv:000001] '1399','2004-07-29','Peter Chan','12.3','123456999','PHONE','123469999','L','1','TOYS','PS2
','PLAYSTATION','DONY','MA23456','10','3000'
Successful import
```

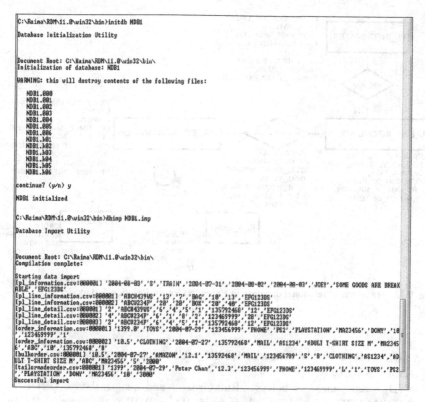

Fig. 9.14 Transformed network database

The transformed network database records are (Fig. 9.14):

4) Transform from flattened XML documents to a relational database.

Example 5: Transform from flattened XML documents to relational database

The transformed relational conceptual schema in the Extended Entity-Relationship model (Fig. 9.15).

There are six tables. Each table has its primary key in italic, and foreign key prefixed with "*." Their data dependencies (DD) are such that each foreign key determines its referred primary key in FD, and subclass foreign key is a subset of its superclass primary key in ID as follows:

FD_1: *PL_Line_information*. PL_INFORMATION_SEQNO → *PL_information*.PL_INFORMATION_SEQNO

FD_1 represents PL_INFORMAION and PL_Line_information are in one-to-many cardinality. FD_1 in RDB is the same as FD_1 in flattened XML schema source. Therefore, one-to-many cardinality between PL_INFORMAION and PL_Line_information is preserved.

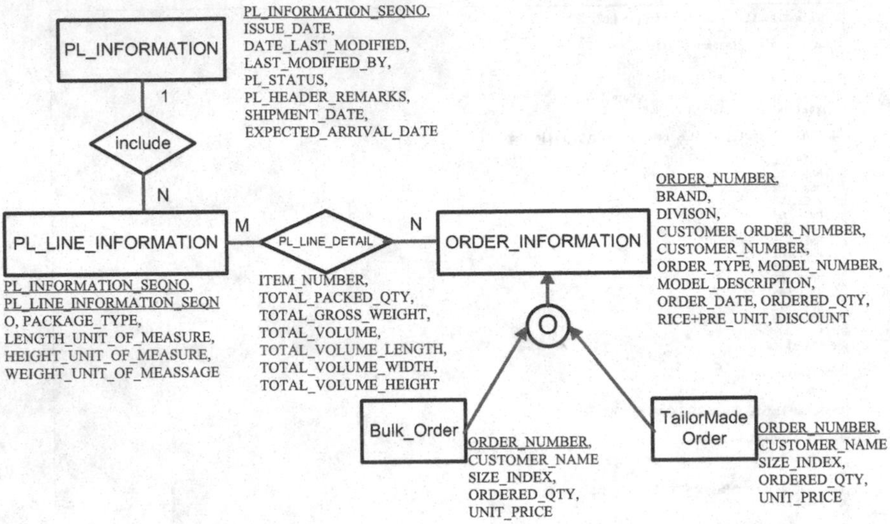

Fig. 9.15 Transformed relational database in Extended Entity-Relationship model

ID_1: *Bulk_Order*. BulkOrder.ORDER_NUMBER $\sqsubseteq$ *Order_information . Order_NUMBER*

ID_1 represents subclass BulkOrder and superclass ORDER_INFORMATION are in ISA relationship. ID_1 in RDB is the same as ID_1 in flattened XML schema source. Therefore, the ISA relationship between BulkOrder and ORDER_INFORMATION is preserved.

ID_2: *TailorMadeOrder*.TailorMadeOrder.ORDER_NUMBER $\sqsubseteq$ *Order_information . Order_NUMBER*

ID_2 represents subclass TailorMadeOrder and superclass ORDER_INFORMATION ae in ISA relationship. ID_2 in RDB is the same as ID_2 in flattened XML schema source. Therefore, the ISA relationship between TailorMadeOrder and ORDER_INFORMATION is preserved.

MVD_1: *PL_Line_information.* PL_INFORMATION_SEQNO $\rightarrow\rightarrow$ *Order_information . Order_NUMBER*

MVD_2: *Order_information.Order_NUMBER* $\rightarrow\rightarrow$ *PL_Line_information.* PL_INFORMATION_SEQNOTherefore: MVD_1 and MVD_2 represent PL_Line_information and ORDER_INFORMATION are in many-to-many cardinalities. Therefore, MVD_1 and MVD_2 in RDB are the same as MVD_1 and MVD_2 in flattened XML schema source, many-to-many cardinality between TailorMadeOrder and ORDER_INFORMATION is preserved. (Note: Two one-to-many cardinalities are equivalent to many-to-many cardinality) (Fig. 9.16).

Performance Analysis

1) Performance System Platform

To access the relative performance of the database legacy, we performed the OODB experiment in a VM installed on an IBM server (xSeries 335 / 8676) with Intel(R) Xeon(R) CPU X5650 with a clock rate of 2.67 GHz, 2GB of main memory. The other experiments are performed on an IBM blade server with Intel(R) Xeon(R) CPU X5660 with a clock rate of 2.80 GHz, 2GB of main memory. The operating system and DMBS using for the experiment are recorded in Table 9.4. The UDB software is written in Java 2.

2) DBMS for database

3) Result in Diagram

```
mysql> select * from pl_information;
+---------------+------------+--------------------+---------------------+-----------+---------------+-------------------+-----------------------+------------------+
| SHIPMENT_DATE | ISSUE_DATE | DATE_LAST_MODIFIED | PL_INFORMATION_SEQNO | PL_STATUS | SHIPMENT_TYPE | PL_HEADER_REMARKS | EXPECTED_ARRIVAL_DATE | LAST_MODIFIED_BY |
+---------------+------------+--------------------+---------------------+-----------+---------------+-------------------+-----------------------+------------------+
| 2004-08-03    | 2004-07-31 | 2004-08-02         | EFG123DS            | S         | TRAIN         | SOME GOODS        | 2004-08-03            | JOEY             |
+---------------+------------+--------------------+---------------------+-----------+---------------+-------------------+-----------------------+------------------+
1 row in set (0.00 sec)

mysql> select * from pl_line_information;
+----------------------+---------------------------+-----------------------+------------------------+--------------+------------------------+------------------------+
| PL_INFORMATION_SEQNO | PL_LINE_INFORMATION_SEQNO | WIDTH_UNIT_OF_MEASURE | HEIGHT_UNIT_OF_MEASURE | PACKAGE_TYPE | WEIGHT_UNIT_OF_MESSAGE | LENGTH_UNIT_OF_MEASURE |
+----------------------+---------------------------+-----------------------+------------------------+--------------+------------------------+------------------------+
| EFG123DS             | ABCH439WS                 | 13                    | 10                     | BAG          | 13                     | 7                      |
| EFG123DS             | ABCV234F                  | 20                    | 20                     | BOX          | 40                     | 20                     |
+----------------------+---------------------------+-----------------------+------------------------+--------------+------------------------+------------------------+
2 rows in set (0.00 sec)

mysql> select * from pl_line_detail;
+---------------------+----------------------+--------------------+--------------------+----------------------+--------------+------------------+---------------------------+-------------+
| TOTAL_VOLUME_LENGTH | PL_INFORMATION_SEQNO | TOTAL_GROSS_WEIGHT | TOTAL_VOLUME_WIDTH | TOTAL_VOLUMEN_HEIGHT | ORDER_NUMBER | TOTAL_PACKED_QTY | PL_LINE_INFORMATION_SEQNO | ITEM_NUMBER |
+---------------------+----------------------+--------------------+--------------------+----------------------+--------------+------------------+---------------------------+-------------+
| 5                   | EFG123DS             | 12                 | 2                  | 6                    | 135792468    | 4                | ABCH439W3                 | 1           |
| 8                   | FFG123DS             | 28                 | 4                  | 6                    | 123469999    | 1                | ABCV234F                  | 2           |
| 5                   | EFG123DS             | 12                 | 2                  | 6                    | 135792468    | 4                | ABCV234F                  | 1           |
+---------------------+----------------------+--------------------+--------------------+----------------------+--------------+------------------+---------------------------+-------------+
3 rows in set (0.00 sec)

mysql> select * from order_information;
+-----------------------+----------+-----------------+------------+-------+-------------------+--------------+--------------+------------+----------+------------+----------------+
| CUSTOMER_ORDER_NUMBER | DISCOUNT | CUSTOMER_NUMBER | ORDER_TPYE | BRAND | MODEL_DESCRIPTION | MODEL_NUMBER | ORDER_NUMBER | ORDERD_QTY | DIVISION | ORDER_DATE | PRICE_PER_UNIT |
+-----------------------+----------+-----------------+------------+-------+-------------------+--------------+--------------+------------+----------+------------+----------------+
| 123456999             | 10       | MA23456         | PHONE      | DONY  | PLAYSTATIO        | PS2          | 123469999    | 1          | TOYS     | 2004-07-29 | 1399.0         |
| 135792468             | 10       | MA23456         | MAIL       | ABC   | ADULT T-SH        | AS1234       | 135792468    | 8          | CLOTHING | 2004-07-27 | 10.5           |
+-----------------------+----------+-----------------+------------+-------+-------------------+--------------+--------------+------------+----------+------------+----------------+
2 rows in set (0.00 sec)

mysql> select * from bulk_order;
+---------------+------------+--------------+-------------+------------+
| CUSTOMER_NAME | UNIT_PRICE | ORDER_NUMBER | ORDERED_QTY | SIZE_INDEX |
+---------------+------------+--------------+-------------+------------+
| AMAZON        | 12.1       | 135792468    | 2000        | S          |
+---------------+------------+--------------+-------------+------------+
1 row in set (0.00 sec)

mysql> select * from tailor_made_order;
+---------------+------------+--------------+-------------+------------+
| CUSTOMER_NAME | UNIT_PRICE | ORDER_NUMBER | ORDERED_QTY | SIZE_INDEX |
+---------------+------------+--------------+-------------+------------+
| PETER CHAN    | 12.3       | 135792468    | 3000        | L          |
+---------------+------------+--------------+-------------+------------+
1 row in set (0.00 sec)
```

Fig. 9.16 Transformed relational database

Table 9.4 DBMS table

	RDB source	Flattened XML	RDB	XML	OODB	NDB
Server OS	Window 7	Window 7	Window 7	Window 7	Window 2000	Window 7
DBMS	MySQL	eXist	Oracle	eXist	UniSQL	Raima

First, we bulk load 400 records of the Relational database source of the prototype HDBC. Then we measure the time for these four output database legacy for this bulk load in Table 9.5.

Second, we query the data from one table from each database legacy. We measure the time and recorded it in Table 9.6.

Figure 9.17 compared the bulk load and selection performance analysis in four transformed legacy databases. The X-axis represents the record time (second) while

Table 9.5 Bulk load

Dataset	RDB source	Flattened XML	RDB (Oracle)	XML	OODB	NDB
x400	27 sec	0.51 sec	2 sec	0.51 sec	0.5 sec	0.53 sec
x4000	180 sec	3 sec	3 sec	3 sec	5 sec	7 sec

Table 9.6 Selection (based on a condition, eg, Select bulk_order table)

Dataset	RDB source	Flattened XML	RDB (Oracle)	XML	OODB	NDB
x400	4 sec	0.006 sec	1 sec	0.006 sec	0.5 sec	0.14 sec
x4000	30 sec	0.007 sec	0.7 sec	0.014 sec	5 sec	1 sec

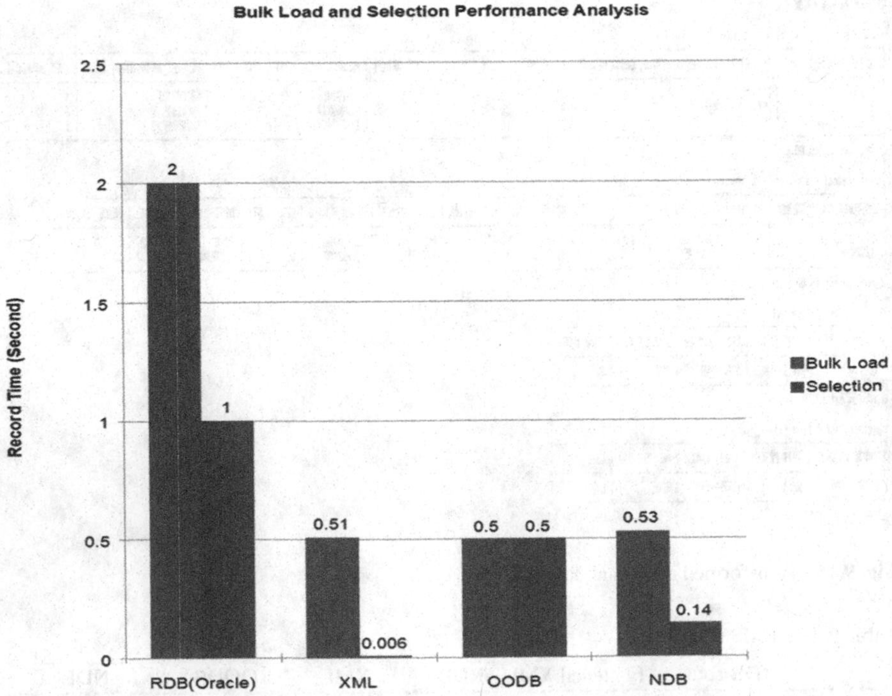

Fig. 9.17 Performance analysis among legacy databases (x400)

the Y-axis represents four transformed legacy databases from OUDB. From the figure above, RDB is the poorest in performance in both bulk load and selection while XML is the best for selection.

Result

In bulk load, the performance of OODB, NDB, XML are better than RDB, in the sequence of selection performance is XML > NDB > OODB> RDB. It is because XML is in Dom Tree structure which is the best for selection. RDB requires values matching, therefore its performance is the poorest. NDB is a pointer structure. Therefore it is better than OODB which requires table format and pointer structure.

As a result, we showed that it is valuable for the user to transform the Relational database to other legacy databases by HDBC if the user wants to have a higher performance of their databases.

Since the relational database is the most user-friendly legacy database, and XML database is the most portable database for information highway on the Internet. We offer a Flattened XML database as a universal database such that it can be a user-friendly database middleware for all legacy databases.

In this chapter, we cover:

(1) The data models of legacy databases are compatible with each other for the preservation of their data semantic such as cardinality, ISA, and generalization.
(2) The legacy databases can be reengineered into each other through flattened XML documents such that a source legacy database can be transformed into a flattened XML document which can be further transformed into another target legacy database.
(3) The performance of HDBC (Heterogeneous Database Connectivity) is acceptable through a prototype performance analysis.
(4) Use cloud computing: All of the legacy databases and the HDBC are developed in the cloud platform.

The applications of this chapter are:

(1) **Openness of a Heterogeneous Database Connectivity**: The reason we choose flattened XML document is its openness, and DBMS independence. All other data models are DBMS dependent. Nevertheless, users can use HDBC to access any legacy database via flattened XML documents on the Internet through Internet Explorer without programming. Furthermore, an Oracle user can access an MS SQL Server database after transforming the Oracle database into a flattened XML document, and then to the MS SQL Server database by HDBC.
(2) **Recovery of the legacy database**: Since flattened XML document is an information equivalent legacy database such that it can be used to recover any legacy database whenever the production legacy database is down. As a result, an equivalent XML document can be parallel processing with legacy database in nonstop computing as their backup copy.
(3) **Heterogeneous databases integration for data warehousing:** By transforming all in-house legacy databases into a common legacy database, companies

can use HDBC to transform its heterogeneous databases into homogeneous databases, and integrate them into a logical view for data warehousing applications.

(4) **Portability of Flattened XML document as Universal database**: The HDBC solution is not limited to using a particular DBMS, but also allows users to access any legacy database through HDBC, which is similar to ODBC.

9.5 Summary

In summary, the HDBC unites all legacy database data models into one data model of flattened XML schema. The portability of the proposed flattened XML document can be transferred to any open platform. The methodology of this HDBC is to download the raw data of source legacy database into flattened XML document according to source legacy database schema and upload it into target database using translated target legacy database schema, which is a logical level approach to avoid physical data type conversion. Therefore, the methodology can transform any legacy database into any other legacy database. The reason for using a flattened XML document as a medium is to reduce the number of data conversion programs. Without OUDB, we need 4 * 4 = 16 programs. With HDBC, we need 4 + 4 = 8 programs for data conversion.

Above all, all legacy databases can be transformed into each other via flattened XML documents for data access in the same way as computers connect to each other via the Internet for information retrieval.

9.6 Questions

Question 9.1

How can we compare Open Database Connectivity with Heterogeneous Database Connectivity with respect to functionality, user-friendliness, and performance?

Answer:

ODBC is used to connect the relational database and flat files. HDBC can be used to connect to Hierarchical, Network, Relational, Object-oriented, and XML document databases, Therefore HDBC can be connected to a more heterogeneous database than ODBC. On the other hand, ODBC has an Application Program Interface to meet user requirements directly in one step approach whereas HDBC is a database gateway that needs to process data conversion inside its gateway to meet user requirements. Therefore, ODBC is more user-friendly than HDBC. About the performance, ODBC should be faster than HDBC, because ODBC is handled by windows, but HDBC performance is affected by windows and Java, which is more complicated.

Question 9.2

What are heterogeneous databases? What is a universal database? What is heterogeneous database connectivity? How are they related functionally?

Answer

Heterogeneous databases are databases with different data models, different vendors, and files. A universal database is a common database that can be converted to different other databases. Heterogeneous database connectivity is a database gateway that can be connected to different other databases. Inside the HDBC gateway, there are two phases of operations. Phase 1: heterogeneous databases can be converted into a common universal database. Phase 2: common database can be converted to a target database to meet users' requirements. Therefore, in this book, HDBC can connect all heterogeneous databases by phase 1 collection - Collect input heterogeneous databases by converting them into common universal XML documents. Phase 2 distributes the common universal database to the users by converting them into the target database to meet users' requirements.

References

Fong J (1992) Methodology for Schema Translation from Hierarchical or Network into Relational. Inf & Software Technol 34(3):159–174

Fong J (2006) Information Systems Reengineering and Integration, Springer Verlag, ISBN 1-84628-382-5, 370 pages

Fong J, Li Q, Huang SM (2003) Universal Data Warehousing Based on a Meta-Data Modeling Approach. Int J Cooperative Inf Syst 12(3):325–363

Hsiao DK, Kamel MN (1989) Heterogeneous Databases: Proliferations, Issues, and Solutions. IEEE Trans Knowl Data Eng 1(1):45–62

Lum VY, Shu NC, Housel BC (1976) A General Methodology for Data Conversion and Restructuring. IBM J Res & Develop 20(5):483–497

Object-Oriented Database Users (2014). http://www.objectivity.com/; http://www.gemstone.com/

Raima Users (2014) http://raima.com/customers/

Ramez E, Shamkant B (2011) Database Systems, Models, Languages, Design , and Application programming, Pearson, 6th edition, p. 56

Relational Database Users (2014) https://www.oracle.com/search/customers/

Shoshani A (1975) A Logical-Level Approach to Data Base Conversion. ACM SGMOD International Conference on Management of Data, pp. 112–122

XML Users (2014) https://tomcat.apache.org/tomcat-3.3-doc/serverxml.html

Chapter 10
Conclusion

As computer technologies evolve, it becomes a necessity for companies to upgrade their information systems. The objective of reengineering is to protect their huge investments and to maintain their competitive edge. However, information systems reengineering is a complicated task that requires much expertise and knowledge. It needs users' input to recover lost semantics inside the existing database system and/or the existing expert system. It also requires technical expertise to replace obsolete information systems with newer systems. Very often, because of the lack of methodologies and expertise, companies choose to redevelop rather than reengineer when upgrading their information systems. The purpose of this book is to convince these companies that reengineering is a more cost-effective and feasible solution.

An information system consists of almost all the computer application systems in a company. The major components of such systems are databases for production operation and expert systems for managerial decision-making. The methodologies discussed in this book aim to protect the investment that companies have already put into these systems. The aim is to find methods of reusing these systems with new technologies and/or to meet new applications. The proposed methodology for reengineering information systems is twofold: database conversion and/or database and expert system integration as follows:

Database Conversion

Our objective is to replace (convert) traditional record-based, hierarchical, or network database systems with table-based relational databases and then replace the relational database with an object-oriented database and XML database. The justification is that a relational database is more user-friendly than a hierarchical database or network database. Similarly, an object-oriented database is more productive than a relational database. Our technique in converting the database systems is to

J. S. P. Fong, K. Wong Ting Yan, *Information Systems Reengineering, Integration and Normalization*, https://doi.org/10.1007/978-3-030-79584-9_10

develop a common data structure for the hierarchical database, network database, relational database, object-oriented database, and XML database. The goal is to eliminate the database navigation steps needed in accessing hierarchical or network databases. This can be accomplished by imposing secondary indices on each record type of network database (besides the system-owned record types) and the non-root segments of the hierarchical database. The result is that these record types or segment types of the existing nonrelational database can be accessed like a table.

To convert a relational database to an object-oriented database, we must map the static data from the relational database to the object-oriented database in schema translation and data conversion. We then capture the dynamic behavior of each mapped class by translating each database I/O statement into the operations (methods) of each class. We have described the schema translation and data conversion in our methodology. The translation of database programs between the relational databases and the object-oriented databases is difficult to automate. To convert a relational database into an XML database, we extract an XML view of an EER model and load the relational data into an XML document according to the translated XML schema.

Database System and Expert System Integration
System reengineer, broadly defined as the use of engineering knowledge or artifacts from existing systems to build new ones, is a technology for improving system quality and productivity. Much traditional work is focused on the reuse of existing software systems, (i.e., software programs, files, and databases). Since the use of the knowledge-based system is emerging in information systems, many of these systems have been built or will be built. In order for knowledge-based systems such as expert systems to make further contributions to our society, it will be necessary to reuse their knowledge for other expert systems. The idea of reusing knowledge between expert systems and database systems is an attractive one for much the same reasons as the reuse of software. For example, knowledge from an application for process monitoring may be useful in an application for training the operators. Furthermore, knowledge must be shared among different applications.

A reengineering methodology for these systems must capture the information and the knowledge of the existing systems. Information can be represented by programming. Knowledge can be represented by rules. In our methodologies, we have developed ways to derive and store the knowledge. The rationale behind such a decision is that a class encapsulates both the static data structure and its feasible operations, (i.e., its dynamic behavior,) in its methods. Our reengineering technique is to map the data structure of the database system into the static data of each class and to map the operations of each rule of the expert system into the method of a corresponding class (i.e., a class with the same name).

10.1 Application of Database Conversion Methodologies

The methodologies described in this book provide an alternative approach for schema translation in which user input contributes to the process. Direct schema translation from hierarchical or network into relational cannot guarantee to capture all of the original conceptual schema semantics. With user input, we can provide a relational schema that is closer to the user expectation and preserves the existing schema constraints such as record key, records relationships, and attributes.

For data conversion, the methodology provides algorithms to unload a hierarchical or network database into sequential files directly and effectively, with minimum user involvement. These files can then be uploaded onto the target system with little additional effort.

In program translation, the methodology provides an "open" data structure by adding secondary indices to the existing hierarchical or network database. This eliminates the navigation access path required to retrieve a target record from a system record. Instead, each target record type can be accessed directly without database navigation. The database access time is thus reduced and the program conversion effort simplified. The methodology also provides algorithms to translate SQL statements into hierarchical or network DML statements. These are sound solutions to the program conversion problem.

Basically, the methodology is similar to the relational interface approach in that both provide a relational interface to make the hierarchical or network DBMS a relational-like DBMS. The methodology can help the users in the following ways:

1. Apply the methodology to convert a hierarchical or network database system into a relational database system.

   The methodology is an integrated approach to solve the conversion problem. The user has a solution for the whole task.
2. Apply part of the methodology to reduce conversion problems.

   The methodology includes schema translation, data conversion, and program translation. Each process can be applied independently as required.
3. Apply schema translation to construct a distributed database system.

   In a distributed database system, many local schemas act independently for their own local applications. To implement a major application or a global application, we must integrate these schemas into a global schema. Our methodology is used to obtain a common EER model for a number of local hierarchical or network schema.
4. Apply the technique of adding secondary indices to provide an "open" structure database gateway.

   Currently, many vendors provide database gateways to allow other vendors' database programs to access their databases. The addition of secondary indices is an alternative approach.
5. Apply the methodology for a more user-friendly interface to end users.

   The methodology is used to provide a relational interface to a nonrelational system. It allows a company to continue using a network or hierarchy whilst, at the same time, users can use the friendly interface supported by a relational database.

6. Apply the methodology as a guideline for conversion to a next-generation database.

   As database technology continues to evolve, people will discover the limitations of relational databases and will look for the next-generation databases on the market. To convert from a relational database system to the next-generation database system is not an easy task. However, we can make use of the techniques in this book as a guideline.

In conclusion, this book provides an alternative approach for a conversion methodology that is practical enough to be applied. Even though many problems have been resolved in database conversion, difficulty arises in the translation of semantics. Not only do we not know whether there is a 1:1 or a 1:n relationship between the parent (owner) and the child (member) segments (records) in the hierarchical or network schema, but also we cannot obtain a unique key transformation. The assumption is that they are all either partially internally identified if the record key exists, or internally unidentified if the record key does not exist. This assumption is based on the data structure inherent in the hierarchical or network database where database navigation is needed to retrieve a target record (segment). This implicit constraint is a result of the default assumption of partially internally identified or internally unidentified types that do not apply to relational databases. Therefore, the semantics of the translated relational database may not be correct. There is a possibility that the existing record (segment) key itself is unique and therefore a fully internally identified record (segment).

The complication in semantic analysis appears not only in the DDL of the schema but also in the database programs. The major weakness of this methodology is that it cannot translate directly a low-level hierarchical or network database program DML to a high-level relational database program DML by decompilation. The automation of the direct translation from procedural (with database navigation) nonrelational DML statement to non-procedural (without database navigation) relational DML statement (e.g., SQL) is still a classical problem in computer science. Application programmers wrote programs based on the conditions and assumptions that they had about the nonrelational database. These conditions and assumptions may not be well documented. If we decompile them to a higher level non-procedural language such as SQL, the outcome will be variable and it will be difficult to prove its correctness.

10.2 Application of the Integration of Database and Expert Systems

The integration of database systems and expert systems forms an expert database system that combines several different technologies and perspectives. Our methodology for developing such systems by reengineering existing database systems and expert systems uses a higher-level synthesis model in a frame model metadata. The reengineering capability and the frame model metadata combine together to produce a very powerful and sophisticated expert database system development methodology. The output of the methodology is an expert database system that reuses existing database and expert systems technology.

A traditional problem with expert systems is the difficulty in representing knowledge in an appropriate and effective structure. Our methodology supports a fixed frame structure of rule-based knowledge representation. This addresses the representation problem and provides better storage and retrieval facilities. For example, in our frame model, data and rules are represented in the same way; hence, it is easier to manage knowledge.

The applications of the methodology are as follows:

1. Reuse existing database and expert system

   Produce an (integrated) expert database system as a result of the methodology.
2. Produce a higher-level synthesis model

   Provide an object-oriented conceptual model in a frame model metadata for the integrated expert database system.
3. Knowledge integrity

   Our methodology supports an integrity constraint mechanism. This allows knowledge to be applied with event-condition-action or demon rules. The implementation of knowledge integrity constraints then becomes very easy.
4. Deductive functionality

   The data model in our methodology, our frame model metadata, was embedded with a deductive mechanism, allowing the system to deduce many additional facts from the existing data.

10.3 Data Normalization for Information Systems

An information system without data normalization is not user-friendly due to the data redundancy and abnormality in database update. An un-normalized database design will utilize more data storage than necessary. Furthermore, it will affect the performance of data access in certain databases such as XML documents.

Every production application system needs to be evaluated for its level of data normalization, for example, relational database system. The higher level of data normalization, the more user-friendliness in data manipulation in the database. On the other hand, if the user prefers application system performance rather than user-friendliness in application system operations, then data de-normalization is more suitable for the company, for example, data warehousing uses data de-normalized data cube for information retrieval only.

Similarly, when we design a database such as XML schema, we have to minimize branch elements under the root element. It is because the more fragments of branch elements, there will be more pointer references among elements to implement certain user's data requirements such as many-to-many cardinality among elements. Therefore, fragments minimization is a data normalization for XML database design.

10.4 Future Trends for NoSQL

The main idea for information system reengineering is to reuse the existing knowledge as opposed to simply the reuse of data. The techniques for knowledge reuse are extremely important not only because they aid in building an information system, but also because they help to improve the reliability of the information system.

This book has provided a systematic approach to reuse existing information systems. Since the existing system may not be perfect and may be partially nonproductive, it may be necessary to reuse only certain parts of the existing system, but not all.

To reuse knowledge, we must know its structure. The current knowledge representation structure has multiple frames. Data modeling from database research and knowledge representation from artificial intelligence both still have difficulty representing the knowledge completely. A distortion exists between the real world and the information system. It is extremely difficult to recapture the original knowledge from the existing information systems. To solve this problem, a heuristic approach has been taken by computer scientists. This approach is to use an expert system to assist the system developer to recapture the missing knowledge or semantics.

Another approach for knowledge reuse is to define a standard specification for the information systems. In spite of the economical success of reengineering applications, some problems have been detected in using this technology, the largest problem being the lack of agreed standards for information systems. For example, there is no standard for object-oriented technology. Providing standards for information systems is a way of supporting reengineering, partly because it can provide portability and transparent communications. Some work on high-level standards, sometimes referred to as the knowledge level, has been carried out. One example of knowledge level representation is the language developed in the KADS (Tansley and Hayball 1993) methodology for analyzing domain knowledge. KADS allows developers to build libraries of inference models for specific domains (for example, diagnosis). Computer scientists are now looking at providing a similar approach for sorting the content of knowledge bases in a reusable way; these reusable knowledge bases are called Entologies'.

The object-oriented paradigm has been seen as the most common technique for conventional software and knowledge base reuse. Object-oriented technology is still growing.

Data is a collection of "facts." Information is the meaning of data. Knowledge is the application of information. Knowledge is also a necessity of reengineering.

Unless a method for the complete representation of knowledge in a computer system is found, the reengineering process will never be finished.

What Is NoSQL Database
NoSQL Database is used to refer to a non-SQL or nonrelational database.

It provides a mechanism for storage and retrieval of data other than the tabular relations model used in relational databases. In general, NoSQL database doesn't use tables for storing data. It is generally used to store big data and real-time web applications.

However, there are some cases NoSQL systems are called "Not only SQL." We emphasize, in these cases, NoSQL also supports SQL-like query language and table format.

How NoSQL Benefit to Our Project
Because NoSQL will be spread to use, it is valuable to research how our HDBC includes NoSQL.

MongoDB(NoSQL)	RDBMS
Database	Database
Collection	Table
Document	Tuple/Row
Field	Column

The above table shows the equivalent terms between RDBMS and MongoDB(NoSQL).

In NoSQL, e.g., MongoDB, the database has a schema and a document in the same collection. Even though, the schema in NoSQL is much more flexible compare to the RDBMS schema.

Therefore, in case if there is a NoSQL database, which is a table format, data stored in the document and the NoSQL schema contains fields, we believe, conceptually, it can act as the source database of our HDBC, and transform into flattened XML, just like RDBMS.

On the other hand, if the NoSQL database is not in a table format, in fact, refer to the below example, it is a tree structure. Therefore, similar to the Network database and hierarchical database, it can act as the source database of our HDBC, and transform into flattened XML.

An example of MongoDB(NoSQL) inserted three documents in it using the insert() method and retrieves all the documents in the collection, as shown below (Figs. 10.1 and 10.2):

Therefore, the continuation of this book, NoSQL will be our future development of the research of this area.

```
MongoDB Enterprise > db.k2.insert([
... {
... title: "Kenneth try MongoDB",
... description: "Kenneth try no SQL database",
... tags: ["mongodb", "database", "NoSQL"],
... likes: 1000
... },
... {
... title: "NoSQL Database",
... description: "Write a book about NoSQL",
... tags: ["mongodb", "database", "NoSQL"],
... likes: 500,
... comments: [
... {
... user:"user1",
... message: "My first comment",
... dateCreated: new Date(2021,11,10,2,35),
... like: 100
... }
... ]
... }
... ])
BulkWriteResult({
        "writeErrors" : [ ],
        "writeConcernErrors" : [ ],
        "nInserted" : 2,
        "nUpserted" : 0,
        "nMatched" : 0,
        "nModified" : 0,
        "nRemoved" : 0,
        "upserted" : [ ]
})
```

Fig. 10.1 Example of insert data in NoSQL database

```
MongoDB Enterprise > db.k2.find()
{ "_id" : ObjectId("60bad750afd88eb3ac5b064d"), "title" : "Kenneth tr
y MongoDB","description" : "Kenneth try no SQL database", "tags" : [
 "mongodb", "database", "NoSQL" ], "likes" : 1000 }
{ "_id" : ObjectId("60bad750afd88eb3ac5b064e"), "title" : "NoSQL Data
base", "description" : "Write a book about NoSQL", "tags" : [ "mongod
b", "database", "NoSQL" ], "likes" : 500, "comments" : [ { "user" : "
user1", "message" : "My first comment", "dateCreated" : ISODate("2021
-12-09T18:35:00Z"), "like" : 100 } ] }
MongoDB Enterprise >
```

Fig. 10.2 Example of retrieves all the documents in the collection of NoSQL database

10.5 Epilogue

Application knowledge is required for information systems reengineering, integration, and normalization.

Questions

Question 10.1.

What are the basic justification (rationales) for database reengineering and integration in terms of data semantics? How can you compare them?

Answer:

Data semantics represent the relationships between data. They are the actual data requirements to meet user's needs. As a result, both database re-engineering and database integration need to preserve data semantics to meet user's requirements. The only difference between database reengineering and database integration in preserving data semantics is that when we integrate two databases together, we have to define the data relationships between them; otherwise, the integration is an artifact, that is, technically feasible, but applicational difficult.

Question 10.2.

What is the significance of Heterogeneous Database Connectivity?

Answer:

In computer science, database and data communication are the two most important foundation areas for computerization. The success of the Internet is the most significant breakthrough for data communication because it can connect all computer networks together as one computer network for all users. Similarly, the success of HDBC aims to connect all databases as one database for all users. The difference between the Internet and HDBC is that the Internet is very user-friendly for end users. People just key in a URL link to access the Internet by Wi-Fi. Whereas HDBC is a database gateway which needs technical support to operate. The significance of HDBC is its architecture, which is almost the same as Interface, an Internet database gateway.

Bibliography

Fong J (1995) Mapping extended entity relationship model to object modeling technique. ACM SIGMOD Rec 24(3):18–22

Fong J (1996) Adding a relational interface to a nonrelational database. IEEE Software, pp 89–97

Huang SM, Smith P, Tait JI, Pollitt S (1993) A survey of approaches to commercial expert database system development tools, Occasional paper 93–4. University of Sunderland

Rumbaugh J et al (1991) Object-oriented modelling and design. Prentice Hall Inc, pp 183–185

Smith P, Bloor C, Huang SM, Gillies A (1995) The need for re-engineerung when integrating expert system and database technology. In: The proceeding of the 6th international Hong Kong Computer Society database workshop, database re-engineering and interoperability, pp 14–23

Tansley DSW, Hayball CC (1993) PRENTICE HALL, knowledge based systems analysis and design A KADS developer's handbook

Epilogue

Question

Answer

Question

Answer

Bibliography

Index

J. S. P. Fong, K. Wong Ting Yan, *Information Systems Reengineering, Integration and Normalization*, https://doi.org/10.1007/978-3-030-79584-9

Printed in the United States
by Baker & Taylor Publisher Services

Printed in the United States
by Baker & Taylor Publisher Services